PERSUASION, RHETORIC AND ROMAN POETRY

IRENE PEIRANO GARRISON
Yale University

CAMBRIDGE
UNIVERSITY PRESS

University Printing House, Cambridge CB2 8BS, United Kingdom

One Liberty Plaza, 20th Floor, New York, NY 10006, USA

477 Williamstown Road, Port Melbourne, VIC 3207, Australia

314–321, 3rd Floor, Plot 3, Splendor Forum, Jasola District Centre,
New Delhi – 110025, India

79 Anson Road, #06–04/06, Singapore 079906

Cambridge University Press is part of the University of Cambridge.

It furthers the University's mission by disseminating knowledge in the pursuit of
education, learning, and research at the highest international levels of excellence.

www.cambridge.org
Information on this title: www.cambridge.org/9781107104242
DOI: 10.1017/9781316219355

© Irene Peirano Garrison 2019

This publication is in copyright. Subject to statutory exception
and to the provisions of relevant collective licensing agreements,
no reproduction of any part may take place without the written
permission of Cambridge University Press.

First published 2019

Printed in the United Kingdom by TJ International Ltd, Padstow Cornwall

A catalogue record for this publication is available from the British Library.

Library of Congress Cataloging-in-Publication Data
NAMES: Peirano, Irene, 1979– author.
TITLE: Persuasion, rhetoric and Roman poetry / Irene Peirano Garrison.
DESCRIPTION: Cambridge : Cambridge University Press, 2019. | Includes bibliographical
references and index.
IDENTIFIERS: LCCN 2019007844 | ISBN 9781107104242
SUBJECTS: LCSH: Latin poetry – History and criticism. | Rhetoric, Ancient.
CLASSIFICATION: LCC PA6047 .P37 2019 | DDC 871/.0109–dc23
LC record available at https://lccn.loc.gov/2019007844

ISBN 978-1-107-10424-2 Hardback

Cambridge University Press has no responsibility for the persistence or accuracy of
URLs for external or third-party internet websites referred to in this publication
and does not guarantee that any content on such websites is, or will remain,
accurate or appropriate.

To Aaron

Contents

Acknowledgments	*page* viii
Introduction	1

PART I POETRY IN RHETORIC

1 Poetry *and* Rhetoric and Poetry *in* Rhetoric	9
2 Poetry and the Poetic in Seneca the Elder's *Controuersiae* and *Suasoriae*	46
3 The Orator and the Poet in Quintilian's *Institutio Oratoria*	88

PART II ORATORY IN EPIC

4 The Orator in the Storm	135
5 Epic Demagoguery	174

PART III "RHETORICIZING" POETRY

6 *Non minus orator quam poeta*: Virgil the Orator in Late Antiquity	219

References	244
Index Locorum	263
General Index	282

vii

Acknowledgments

This book could not have been written without the unstinting support of so many colleagues, members of staff and students in the Classics department at Yale and a year of leave funded by the university. The unrelenting generosity of Egbert Bakker, Victor Bers, Emily Greenwood, Pauline LeVen and Joseph Solodow inspired and sustained me in profound ways throughout the writing of this book. I am especially grateful to Milette Gaifman for intellectual exchange and friendship. With his unique grace, his scholarly acumen and deep thoughtfulness, Kirk Freudenburg has improved literally every page of this book. None of this would have been remotely possible without the support and encouragement of Chris Kraus, whose comments have improved, and at times literally shaped, much of this book.

At Yale, I have also been able to share work in progress on this project with many of our brilliant students. I am especially grateful to Jennifer Weintritt, and to Niek Janssen and Kyle Conrau-Lewis, who participated in a seminar on rhetoric and poetry I taught when I was first starting to develop the project. For feedback on the final manuscript, I am grateful to my colleague Michal Beth Dinkler, who also agreed to co-teach a class on rhetoric, and to the students who participated.

Audiences at the City University of New York (CUNY), the Freie Universität Berlin, Chicago, Harvard, Princeton, Penn, Oxford and Yale, as well as International Society for the History of Rhetoric (ISHR) provided me with generous feedback on many of the arguments advanced in this book. I am grateful to Curtis Dozier and to the other participants of the one-day colloquium on Quintilian book 12 held at Yale, especially to Chris van den Berg, who also indulged me with many thought-provoking conversations on Quintilian and rhetoric over the last few years. The arguments of Chapter 5 were first presented at a seminar on *Aeneid* 11 held at the Fondation Hardt in 2013. I am extremely grateful to Damien Nelis for the invitation, and to all participants, and especially to Alessandro

Acknowledgments ix

Barchiesi, for substantive feedback at this early stage of the project. Conversations and/or email exchanges with the following greatly helped me clarify my ideas: Yelena Baraz, Rita Copeland, Joseph Farrell, Nancy Felson, Tom Geue, Emily Gowers, Bart Huelsenbeck, Doreen Innes, Robert Kaster, James Ker, Michèle Lowrie, Scott McGill, Luigi Pirovano, James Porter, Tobias Reinhardt, Gianpiero Rosati, Richard Tarrant, Richard Thomas, Leah Whittington, Christopher Whitton, Michael Winterbottom and Nancy Worman. My heartfelt gratitude goes to Lowell Edmunds, whose comments greatly improved Chapters 3 and 4, to Jaś Elsner who, among many other things, first inspired me to think about Macrobius, and to Hindy Najman for life-sustaining intellectual partnership and for her friendship.

I wish to thank Michael Sharp of Cambridge University Press for supporting this project from the start and Sophie Taylor for help with countless questions. The two anonymous readers for the Press offered generous criticism, improved the manuscript in countless ways and saved me from many errors and omissions. My thanks also go to Samuel Turner and Lucy Western, my research assistants in the final stages, to Rona Johnston Gordon for her invaluable help in preparing the manuscript for publication, and to Marta Steele for help with the index.

Last but not least, I am grateful to my wonderful friend Emilia Wilton-Godberfforde and to my parents for their support, especially to my mothers Grazia, Giovanna and Kathy. This book is dedicated to my husband Aaron with thanks for leading the way: his vision, love and example have guided and inspired me through it all.

Introduction

This book explores the relationship between rhetorical theory and the production and reception of Imperial Roman poetry. While scholarship has typically constructed the history of Roman poetry as one of progressive hybridization by rhetoric, I examine instead, and ultimately question, the very notion of rhetorical influence on which this paradigm is built.[1] My work differs in this way from previous studies of the issue, which have generally taken the form of lists enumerating technical elements of style and arrangement that any given poet is said to have "borrowed" from rhetorical critics.[2] Instead, this study fundamentally shifts the approach to the ancient evidence: rather than taking rhetoric as a self-contained discourse whose norms infiltrate literary culture, I argue that it is more fruitful to focus on the cultural *relevance* of this intellectual divide and its articulation in Roman culture. Part I looks at the role of poetry and the poetic in rhetorical theory.[3] Chapter 1 traces key thematic moments in the rhetorical tradition, in the context of which the problematic relationship of difference and similarity between rhetorical and poetic discourse is evoked and discussed. I argue that starting from the first attested rhetorical text, Gorgias' *Encomium of Helen*, definitions of the nature and scope of rhetoric have always hinged on variously argued points of similarity to and difference from poetry. Tracing the history of this debate from Gorgias' definition of poetry as speech with meter (*Hel.* 9) to Isocrates and Aristotle's

---

[1] On the rhetoric of rhetorical influence in Classics, see Farrell (1997), calling for a shift away from the traditional system of framing the interaction of rhetoric and poetry as the study of "rhetoric *in* epic," i.e. of "elements of an alien discursive system that have somehow made their way into the epic genre" and Fox (2007) 377–80.

[2] E.g. Decker (1913); Billmayer (1932); Bonner (1966); Highet (1972); Dominik (1994); Helzle (1996). This approach has also been influential outside Classics: e.g. Joseph (1947) or Vickers (1968).

[3] My use of the term "poetry" is intentionally loose. Because of its pivotal role in the hierarchy of genres and in rhetorical education, epic has naturally the lion's share in the case studies of this book. Yet, in addition to the fact that rhetorical sources use poetry as an encompassing term, in Part I, Virgil and Ovid are engaged with as poets who transcend the boundaries of one genre.

2   Introduction

insistence on mimesis, not meter, as the defining characteristic of poetry (*Poet.* 1451b11), to Cicero and Quintilian's recognition of the kinship of orator and poet, I approach the competing claims of affinity and difference between poetic and rhetorical discourse as different aspects of rhetoric's complex strategy of self-definition.

Chapters 2 and 3 explore the role of the poetic in two key Roman rhetorical texts from the early Empire: the *Controuersiae* and *Suasoriae* of Seneca the Elder and Quintilian's *Institutio Oratoria*. These writers ostensibly disavow the improper use of ornate and poetic devices, in the case of Seneca the Elder constructing deviant rhetorical discourse of declamation as a dangerous approximation to poetry. At the same time, Quintilian's textual presentation of the orator and of rhetorical practice is thoroughly informed by poetic, especially epic, models. Quintilian's adoption of epic models and intricate deployment of poetic metaphors in constructing both his would-be orator and his own authorial persona betray a complex desire to compete with and strive for the social and cultural authority of poets at a time of decreased public standing for orators and their teachers. A close reading of these sources reveals that rhetorical discourse is constructed by these writers as a hybrid ambiguously related to poetry, which it both mines as a source of examples and disavows as foreign.

While Part I aims to complicate our view of what counts as "rhetorical" in antiquity and to explicate the role of poetry in definitions of the art of rhetoric, Part II moves on to poetic texts. Moving away from the traditional focus on stylistic elements deemed "rhetorical" in poetic texts, I look instead for the poets' own perspective on the role of the rhetorical medium.[4] My focus here is figures of orators in Roman epic. I argue that, through these embedded scenes of rhetorical performance, Roman poets commented on and even challenged cultural narratives found in rhetorical texts. This form of self-conscious generic commentary is already evident in Virgil whose placement of the figure of the orator in the very first simile of the *Aeneid* puts rhetoric's difference from and similarity to poetry center stage. From Virgil's orator in the storm to Cicero's and Caesar's public speaking in Lucan, I read the orators of Roman epic as ironic figures who can be seen to disappoint and contradict models of behavior for the *bonus orator* found in rhetorical texts:[5] instead of arousing an emotional storm, the orator quells one, or, worse, is depicted as falling victim to the

---

[4] See Rebhorn's approach to Renaissance literature as a form of dramatization of contemporary rhetorical ideas in Rebhorn (1995).
[5] Along these lines, see Tarrant (1995).

Introduction 3

elements unleashed by the poet's art. My analysis, however, further insists that definitions of what counts as poetic or rhetorical were deeply provisional and contested. Thus, while in clinging to words as opposed to deeds, demagogues such as Thersites, Drances and Cicero breach the epic code, qua verbal performers they are repeatedly associated with the authorial voice.[6] As hybrid figures, these "poetic rhetors" show that, not unlike rhetorical writers, poets were interested in distancing their art from the rhetorical medium while simultaneously staking a claim to it. In my reading, far from being the victims of influence, Roman poets were aware of and reacted to the cultural narratives found in rhetorical sources.

Part III concludes the book by focusing on one of the best attested and yet utterly vilified and understudied ancient traditions of rhetorical analysis of poetry: starting from the second century CE, whether Virgil was to be considered an orator or a poet was one of the key issues in the reception of his work, as is attested by discussions in Florus and Macrobius but also in Servius and Tiberius Cl. Donatus. Rather than belittling this approach as reductive, I look at the work of these ancient critics as evidence of a mode of engagement with the Virgilian epic that is both micro-rhetorical, mining the Virgilian text for examples of rhetorical principles, and macro-rhetorical, treating both text and the critical interpretation thereof as epideictic performances. This analysis of *Vergilius orator* undermines the predictable charge of anachronistic "rhetoricizing" that is typically leveled at these sources, not only by pointing to the continuity between these and prior rhetorical reading practices but also by showing how these defensive rhetorical readings help to shape a new relevance for the Virgilian classic.

Ultimately, this book argues that the standard narrative of rhetorical influence should be replaced with one of self-conscious struggle for cultural supremacy fought between poets and rhetorical theorists. In my reading, rhetorical theory has always used poetry as a (largely negative) foil against which to define its own authoritative use of language, at the same time as it has tapped into the cultural and metaphorical resources of poetry to characterize its emotional and stylistic power. In turn, far from being passive recipients of inherited rhetorical taxonomies, the poetic texts that I explore in the book react to the cultural narratives found in rhetorical works and respond with new narratives that question and undercut rhetorical theorists' take on the genealogy of their art. The resulting picture is one of dynamic confrontation between rhetoric and poetry, of competing

---

[6] See Hardie (2012) 126–49.

4   Introduction

claims and counterclaims about authoritative speech, cultural status and priority.

My approach is necessarily selective in coverage, as no one single study could reasonably claim to examine every aspect or instance of "communication" between Roman poets and the rhetorical tradition. Rather, I have preferred to focus on select case studies in the hope of suggesting how we could replace the narrative of rhetorical influence with one that would do more justice not just to the complex traffic between rhetoric and poetry but also to the critical awareness of ancient readers. Furthermore, this study is selective in its goals as well as in its focus. My central concern is the discourse of rhetorical influence as it pertains to Roman *poetry*. My discussion of the ancient critics – Seneca the Elder, Quintilian, Macrobius and Servius – focuses on the role of poetry in the construction of rhetorical theory and on poetry as rhetorically constructed discourse. My discussion of poetic texts is centered on the poets' response to this discourse. By necessity, my analysis does focus on how rhetorical texts construct their own (nonpoetic) speech versus poetry. Mine, however, is not a study of poetry or poeticisms in prose texts; nor does it address the question of rhetoric's "influence" on prose, although I hope that my conclusions will be of use to those working on these related questions.[7] In my reading, rhetoric and prose are not synonymous. Certainly, rhetorical theory is written in prose and it is without question that rhetorical texts and rhetorical education shaped writers of the various genres of Roman prose. Yet the focus of my work in so far as it pertains to Roman prose is firmly on rhetorical sources, their construction of poetry and the poets' response to rhetorical readings.

In this way, this is fundamentally a study of ancient reading and reception practices, not of style.[8] Thus I define "rhetoric" *narrowly* as "rhetorical theory" – the set of stylistic and compositional prescriptions for persuasive discourse found in Greco-Roman rhetorical texts – and "rhetorical influence" as the (allegedly one-way) traffic between rhetorical texts and Roman poetry. For the purpose of this study, the term "rhetoric" refers to the historically specific cultural production of the Greco-Roman rhetorical tradition. This definition is undoubtedly more limited than some. For example, as we have just seen, it excludes rhetoric understood as the elements of style and register that belong to prose (e.g. Cicero) and

---

[7] Leaving aside issues of practicality and feasibility, the presence of rhetorical elements in prose texts, particularly historiography, has been well studied by Wiseman (1979) and Woodman (1988).

[8] For example, this work does not claim to fill the gap in our knowledge of the difference between the style of formal speeches and that of narrative in Roman epic: Horsfall (1995) 232.

Introduction 5

less frequently to poetry. In addition, this study neither departs from nor accepts at face value ancient definitions of rhetoric as persuasive discourse – rather, it interrogates them. Mine, that is, is not a "rhetorical reading" of Roman poetry as I make no attempt to describe and evaluate poetic texts according to the categories of Roman rhetorical theory, as a Quintilian or Servius would have done in an effort to underline and catalogue elements in poetry geared toward persuasion (i.e. rhetoric).

To the contrary, my interests revolve around ancient attempts to define rhetoric and poetry and contestations to these definitions. To pursue the issue further: if we allow ourselves to be guided by Aristotle's famous definition of rhetoric as "the art of discovering in any given situation the available means of persuasion" (*Rhet.* 1.1.1355b10–11), we may very well be justified in labeling any poetry or elements thereof that are geared toward persuasion as "rhetorical."[9] In so doing, we would be following in the steps of the ancient rhetorical theorists who clearly considered such elements of interest to their art. The drawback of this approach is that we pay attention only to the perspective of rhetorical theorists and overlook the responses and rebuttals coming from the poetic tradition. To give one example, taking the persuasion/goal-oriented genre of, for example, the *paraklausithyron* as "rhetorical" assumes the priority of definitions offered by rhetoricians. Yet, as we will see, from Horace's definition of the goal of poetry as a mixture of pleasure and utility in the *Ars Poetica* to Renaissance definitions of poetry as a superior form of rhetoric, poetry has repeatedly been defended as the primitive and original form of persuasion.[10] Thus, at different times throughout history, poetry has been defined as instructive or civilizing discourse and speech designed to inspire action and poets thought of as "from the beginning the best perswaders and their eloquence the first Rethoricke of the world" (George Puttenham, *Arte of English Poesie*, 1589). Similarly, as we will see, to assume that declamatory motifs in poetry are "rhetorical features" ignores not only that those motifs are more often than not grounded in and illustrated from poetry but also that declamation was labeled as "poetic" to begin with (see Chapter 1, "Poetry as Epideictic: *Voluptas* and *Ostentatio*").

My project is not unique (nor does it claim to be) in observing the traffic between poetry and rhetorical texts. The question that preoccupies my

---

[9] See the illuminating analysis of Propertian elegy as "rhetorical" persuasion in Reinhardt (2006) and esp. 200, where he states as his goal to "suggest ways of looking at Propertius through the eyes of a student of rhetoric." On the productive gap between rhetoric as persuasion and rhetoric as self-conscious markers of oratorical forms, see the remarks in Carey (2013).

[10] See Chapter 1.

work is how such "communication" was framed, represented and envisaged by ancient audiences. By delving deep into the Roman usage of these categories, I suggest that the standard approach of isolating certain elements in poetry as "rhetorical" is ultimately anachronistic: whereas for the modern reader certain elements are firmly "rhetorical" by virtue of their role in the history of Western rhetoric, Roman readers contested these definitions and the extent to which, for example, ornaments of style could be considered a poetic or rhetorical phenomenon, and persuasion the prerogative of rhetoric or poetry. In my reading, rhetorical theory is interesting not as a system of classification that poets follow or depart from but rather as a powerful cultural lens through which poetry is viewed, read and sometimes disowned as a rhetorically constructed genre. In revisiting the standard narrative of rhetorical influence, my aim is to bring the conflicted and layered perspectives of ancient readers on these questions to our understanding of Roman literary culture.

PART I

Poetry in Rhetoric

CHAPTER I

Poetry and *Rhetoric and Poetry* in *Rhetoric*

"Influence"

This book focuses on a widely acknowledged and yet much under-theorized aspect of Roman literary history. The pervasive influence of rhetoric on poetic practice may well be said to be one of the most recurrent and persistent motifs in literary histories of the post-Augustan period.[1] According to this narrative, "the age of rhetoric," as the Imperial period is often called, gave rise to a literary culture whose defining characteristic was a tendency to disturb and destabilize established generic boundaries between poetry and rhetoric. A pivotal role in this literary history is assigned to Ovid, whose poetry is most often characterized as "rhetorical," and who is seen therefore as marking what has been traditionally perceived as a deplorable shift away from the restrained use of formal techniques of persuasion in Republican authors toward the excesses of Imperial writers.[2] A corresponding tendency has been to try to portray pre-Ovidian poetry as pre- or hypo-rhetorical – for example, such is the tone of Gilbert Highet's book on speeches in the *Aeneid*, a study that promotes the picture of a poet aware of but fundamentally independent of the experience of rhetorical training.[3] The pervasive scholarly view is encapsulated in Eduard Norden's pronouncement in his influential account of ancient prose style, that,

---

[1] E.g. Curtius (1953) 145–66; Leeman (1963) 311–14; Kennedy (1972) 384–7; Kenney and Clausen (1982) 1: "the first century of the Christian era has often been termed 'the age of rhetoric'"; and Fantham (1996) 93: "gradually the barriers between the decorum of prose and poetry were being forced by the jaded taste of participants and audience."

[2] See Fränkel (1945) 168–9; Higham (1958); and Williams (1980) 231–2, who constructs pre-Ovidian poetry as "a poetry of meditation" in opposition to the "rhetorical poetry" of the Empire; Vickers (1988a) 418–50 is a powerful critique of Williams's anti-rhetorical stance.

[3] Highet (1972). In some ways, Highet followed the lead of Richard Heinze's reductionist account of Virgilian rhetoric. See Heinze (1993) 330–2, esp. 331: "Virgil remained well aware of the boundaries between poetry and prose; he was not like Ovid, who did not hesitate, in fact was proud, to show at every opportunity that he was a poet who had been trained in rhetoric." In turn, Heinze was reacting to Norden's appreciation for the rhetorical background of Virgilian epic: see esp. Norden (1957) 334–7, *ad Aen.* 6.847–53, and 380–5.

Poetry *and* Rhetoric and Poetry *in* Rhetoric

following Ovid, "all the rest of Latin poetry of the Imperial age, with the exception of some Christian genres, is notoriously dominated by rhetoric."[4]

This narrative, which constructs the history of Roman poetry as the steady, gradual triumph of rhetoric over poetry, is partially shaped by the long-standing negative association of rhetoric with partisanship and mendacity. Thus critics have tended to associate rhetoric with inauthenticity and artifice, while viewing so-called rhetorical elements in poetry as arising from "corruption," "adulteration" and "contamination." In essence, the development of Latin literature has been framed as a story of influence and decline, with rhetoric playing the role of catalyst. More to the point, in maintaining that poetry and rhetoric are two distinct fields that have been inappropriately conflated in the Imperial period, whether consciously or unconsciously classicists have been essentially under the sway of lingering Romantic views of poetry as a form of self-expression.[5] It is a commonplace that the standing of Classical rhetoric was fundamentally eroded for the first time during Romanticism.[6] One need only quote Immanuel Kant's exaltation of poetry as the supreme art and his condemnation of rhetoric as abuse of poetry's stylistic tools in the *Critique of Judgment* (1790), a text that was to be influential for Romantic theories of art:

> Poetry (which owes its origin almost entirely to genius and is least willing to be led by precepts or example) holds the first rank among all the arts ... Rhetoric, so far as this is taken to mean the art of persuasion, i.e. the art of deluding by means of a fair semblance (as *ars oratoria*), and not merely excellence of speech (eloquence and style), is a dialectic, which borrows from poetry only so much as is necessary to win over men's minds to the side of the speaker before they have weighed the matter, and to rob their verdict of its freedom. (Kant, *Critique of Judgment*, book 2.53, Trans. J. Creed Meredith, Oxford)

Thus Romantic critics such as John Stuart Mill repeatedly insisted that poetry is not communication but expression of emotions to be distinguished from eloquence, whose object is persuasion addressed to an audience.[7] Thus, Mill argued, "poetry and eloquence are both alike the

---

[4] Norden (1898) vol. 2, 893.

[5] For the influence of Romanticism on the study of Greco-Roman rhetoric, see Russell (1967).

[6] On the anti-rhetorical tendency in Romanticism, see Curtius (1953) 62–3, 269–72; and Genette (1982) 103–26. While Curtius argued that Romanticism broke away from rhetoric altogether, recent critics such as de Man (1984) and Wellbery (2000) have tended to reevaluate this relationship as one of transformation rather than radical abandonment.

[7] Such a distinction is echoed in several key texts of poetics between the mid-nineteenth and early twentieth century: e.g. Thomas De Quincey's distinction between the literature of knowledge

expression or utterance of feeling: but ... eloquence is *heard*; poetry is *over*heard. Eloquence supposes an audience. The peculiarity of poetry appears to us to lie in the poet's utter unconsciousness of a listener" (Mill, "Thoughts on poetry and its varieties," 348 cited in *Collected Works of John Stuart Mill*, vol. 1, ed. J. Robson). Furthermore, "when the act of an utterance is not itself the end ... but a means to an end ... then it ceases to be poetry, and becomes eloquence" ("Thoughts on poetry and its varieties," 349). In this reading, poetry is defined by the lack of an essential quality of rhetorically constructed discourse, namely intentionality, and the privileged mode of poetic expression is considered to be natural/artless language.

In the early twentieth century, New Criticism paradoxically solidified this belief that poetry and rhetoric are essentially different uses of language and, in so doing, added fuel to the narrative of rhetorical influence that already dominated accounts of Roman literary history. Countering the tendency to subsume the meaning of a poem in a generalized message to be abstracted from it, a tendency that critic Cleanth Brooks defined as the "heresy of paraphrase," New Critics preached the interconnectedness of poetic form and content.[8] Once again, they constructed the "disinterested use of words" by poets in opposition to rhetorical models of communication in which language is put to use for a motive.[9] Thus Northrop Frye argues poetry is different from "descriptive or assertive writing which derives from the active will and conscious mind and which is primarily concerned to 'say something'."[10] Similarly, according to I. A. Richards, "statements which appear in the poetry are there for the sake of their effects upon feeling, not for their own sake."[11] These views are echoed in an influential essay on the relation of rhetoric to poetry by the scholar of orality Walter Ong, according to whom poetry is geared "to the making of a thing for contemplation," while rhetoric "to the production of action in another" and "poetic and rhetoric are confused when,

---

(rhetorically aimed at imparting information) and the literature of power (poetry that works through the emotions) in "The Literature of Knowledge and the Literature of Power" (first published in the *North British Review*, August 1848) all the way to W. B. Yeats; "We make out of the quarrel with others, rhetoric, but of the quarrel with ourselves, poetry. Unlike the rhetoricians, who get a confident voice from remembering the crowd they have won or may win, we sing amid our uncertainty": Yeats (1918) chap. 5.

[8] Brooks (1947) 192. See Eagleton (1983) 46–53 on the New Critics' construction of poetry as a "self-contained object."

[9] Frye (2000) 4: "poetry is a disinterested use of words."   [10] Frye (2000) 5.

[11] I. A. Richards (2004) 180.

in an attempt to strengthen its logic, poetic is made to proceed by means of the rhetorical enthymeme and example."[12]

In the field of Classics, this tendentiously constructed opposition between practical eloquence and contemplative poetry inherited from Romanticism inevitably led to a rejection of what was perceived in Roman poetry of the Imperial period as an inappropriate pastiche of rhetorical and poetic elements. Meanwhile, the Romantic ideals that informed this critical opposition between rhetoric and poetry – poetry as disinterested expression of emotions, the privileging of nature over art, the narrowing of rhetoric from a theory of communication to one of tropes and figures – were attacked from multiple critical and disciplinary angles in the twentieth century. Focusing on issues of authorial voice and narrative presentation, it was reader-response critics such as Wayne Booth who first insisted that all forms of literature, including poetry, are ultimately an act of persuasion, that is, forms of discourse constructed in order to achieve certain effects on the reader.[13] Although Booth was primarily interested in the novel, his work is an important reaction to the Romantic construct of poetry as a "pure" object. Booth argued that literature is a communication by an author to a reader and that all elements of the text's presentation are subordinated to the author's rhetorical strategy. Therefore, the choice to rhetoricize or not to rhetoricize is essentially a false one: "an author cannot choose whether to use rhetorical heightenings. His only choice is of the kind of rhetoric he will use."[14] Put differently, texts are to be investigated both as objects endowed with formal devices and as "forms of activity inseparable from the wider social relations between writers and readers . . . and so as largely unintelligible outside the social purposes and conditions in which they were embedded."[15]

With their loss of faith in the possibility of neutral discourse, poststructuralist critics have taken this insight even further, arguing that the rhetorical is not an attribute of certain speakers or texts but the very condition of language. To cite Bender and Wellbery, in this reading "rhetoric is no longer the title of a doctrine and a practice, nor a form of cultural memory; it becomes instead something like the condition of our existence."[16] A key text in this reevaluation of rhetoric is Jacques Derrida's essay "White

---

[12] Ong (1942) 27, 25.
[13] See Walker (2000) esp. 139–273 for a study of Greek lyric as "rhetorical poetics."
[14] Booth (1983) 116.
[15] Eagleton (1983) 206 and see passim 194–217. This position has been forcefully articulated by Kenneth Burke most famously in *A Rhetoric of Motives* (1950), on which see J. Richards (2008) 161–79.
[16] Bender and Wellbery (1990) 25.

"*Influence*" 13

Mythology."[17] Derrida's starting point is Aristotle's definition of metaphor as a swerve from ordinary usage, which, when used appropriately in philosophical discourse, is employed not as an ornament but to elucidate philosophical ideas. The problem, argues Derrida, is that we cannot escape metaphor in discourse so that any account of metaphor is always expressed through metaphors such as those of light ("elucidate") and physical movement ("swerve"): "[the] entire philosophical delimitation of metaphor already lends itself to being constructed and worked by metaphors."[18] Derrida's argument focuses on the role of metaphors in philosophy but has important implications for poetry, whose discourse is traditionally characterized from Aristotle onward as figurative and ornamental (see "Poetry as Epideictic: *Voluptas* and *Ostentatio*" below): if it is language that is essentially figurative and unstable, and if philosophy is no less "figurative" than poetry, then any discourse cannot escape the realm of the poetic. Indeed, according to Jonathan Culler, deconstructive readings "in arguing for the revelatory importance of poetic or contingent elements in philosophical [i.e. non poetic] texts, [adumbrate] the possibility of treating philosophy *as a specific form of a generalized poetic discourse*" (emphasis my own).[19]

In Classics, these productive insights have mostly translated into an increasing appreciation for and study of Greco-Roman rhetorical theory as "text," as performance of gender, social and political identities.[20] The problem of how to capture the traffic between Roman poetry and rhetorical theory, however, remains an open question and the cautionary words of Donald Russell in his seminal 1967 article "Rhetoric and Criticism" still ring true:

> the words "rhetoric" and "rhetorical influence" come readily enough to the tongue when people talk of Greek and Latin literature but all too often a great vagueness hangs about them; one is seldom sure whether they are being used historically with reference to certain facts of ancient education or as terms of abuse for some "insincerity" or "artificiality" which the speaker invites us to deplore. (Russell [1967] 130)

For example, more recent responses to the narrative of rhetorical influence and decline in Classics have tended to defend as normative what is

---

[17] Derrida (1982) 207–71.   [18] Derrida (1982) 252.

[19] Culler (1982) 147. Cf. de Man (1979) 115: "literature turns out to be the main topic of philosophy and the model for the kind of truth to which it aspires." This form of rhetorical criticism is famously developed by Paul de Man: see esp. de Man (1979) 3–19, 103–18; and Norris (1988) 65–71.

[20] E.g. Gleason (1995); Gunderson (2000), (2009); Dugan (2005); and Connolly (2007a).

Poetry *and* Rhetoric and Poetry *in* Rhetoric

constructed as the poets' recourse to rhetorical models, while not necessarily questioning the entrenched terms of analysis. Critics might, for example, defend a poet's use of rhetoric in the service of his overall poetic goal.[21] In presupposing the existence of a pure poetic purpose to which "rhetorical elements" are seemingly subservient, however, this approach does not, in essence, question the Romantic paradigm of rhetorical influence based as that is on the notion of an irreconcilable alterity between rhetoric and poetry.

Most often, rhetoric's role in education is made to explain, or one might even say excuse, a poet's play with "rhetorical tools."[22] In this reading, poets tend to be constructed as victims of a relentless cultural process that is centered in the schools of the Empire where rhetorical analysis of poetry and rhetorical exercises inevitably shaped their approach to their material. It is true that this way of framing rhetorical influence on poetry as a result of the "intellectual metabolism" of Greco-Roman writers can at times resonate with old-fashioned apologetic undertones.[23] However, in so far as it reframes the question of rhetorical influence into one about readerships and reading contexts, this approach is part of a welcome wave of historicist reevaluation of the rhetorical tradition.[24] These critics insist that Greco-Roman rhetorical criticism must be taken seriously as an "emic" mode of reading that is foundational not just to ancient reception but also to literary practice.[25] In this perspective, the Romantic value judgment on rhetoric is nothing but an anachronistic stance that precludes our full appreciation of the ancient sources. Brian Vickers's assessment of the isolation of the terms "rhetoric" and "poetics" in relation to the field of Renaissance literature could very well be straightforwardly applied to address the diffuse complaints about rhetorical influence by Classicists:

> Their isolation [i.e. the isolation of rhetoric and poetics] as critical terms is a product of post-Romantic literary theory, deriving from a period in which traditional rhetoric had been banished from education. To approach a rhetorical culture like the Renaissance with post- or even anti-rhetorical

---

[21] See, for example, Narducci (2007) 395: "Lucan's poem can certainly be described as 'rhetorical epic', but only if we understand by this term a poem that makes substantial use of rhetoric in order to achieve aims that are eminently poetic."

[22] See, for example, Jacobson (1974) esp. 322–9 on the approach to Ovid's *Heroides* as school *suasoriae*; and Schiesaro (2002) 70–4 for an explanation of the damning implications of this reading.

[23] The phrase "intellectual metabolism" is borrowed from Vickers (1988b) 741. For a distinctively unapologetic and rich examination of the complex relationship between rhetorical instruction and literary texts in a different context, see Enterline (2012); and Lyne (2011).

[24] Plett (2004) 1–10; and Vickers (1988a), (1982).   [25] See Elsner and Meyer (2014).

"Influence"

expectations is obviously anachronistic, and can only produce complaints about the "confusion" of rhetoric with poetics.[26]

In Classics, Francis Cairns's 1972 *Generic Composition in Greek and Roman Poetry* is a most extreme example of the historicist approach exemplified by Vickers. For Cairns, the rhetorical tradition elucidates what Iser would call "the horizon of expectations" of ancient readers, that is, the set of conventions against which the Augustan poets self-consciously build their compositions. Thus Cairns used the third-century CE handbook on epideictic speeches of Menander Rhetor as a guide to reconstruct the original audience's understanding of Augustan poetry. In Cairns's reading, "rhetoric," "poetry" and "literature" cannot be easily isolated, at least not from the perspective of Roman readers who identified Homer as the inventor of what he defines as the rhetorical genres of antiquity.[27] Cairns's strictly historicist approach, however, drew criticism because it used the readings of ancient critics as a straitjacket placed on modern interpreters whose approaches were discounted as anachronistic, if they did not conform to what was assumed to be a normative ancient standard unchanged throughout time.[28] In so doing, it ignited an important debate about the validity of the historicist claim to recover the "original" intentions and the contribution of modern readers to the creation of meaning. While Cairns saw ancient rhetorical theory as the only valid lens through which to read ancient texts, others reacted vigorously to the idea that this body of cultural evidence is, in Donald Russell's words, "fundamentally . . . equal to the task of appraising classical literature."[29] In other words, the issue of rhetoric's role in the production and reception of Roman poetry was now rephrased as a question about the relation between the sophisticated "high culture" sphere of poetic production and "low literary culture," to which rhetorical manuals and the practice of education are thought to belong. Although it purports to capture an ancient phenomenon, this scheme often hides a deeper set of assumptions about scholarly readings, as modern interpreters have tended to cast themselves as the implied sophisticated readers constructed by Roman poets and therefore as superior to rhetorical critics of antiquity, less intellectually equipped and more prone to misunderstand the intentions of poets. In short, as Simon Goldhill reminds us, while everyone agrees that rhetoric

---

[26] Vickers (1988b) 715.
[27] Hence the idea that Homer invented the rhetorical genres is defined by Cairns (2007) 70 as "an ancient belief equally untrue from a historical point of view but equally useful in practice."
[28] Feeney (1995).   [29] Russell (1981) 6.

16 Poetry *and* Rhetoric and Poetry *in* Rhetoric

and the study thereof were essential elements of Greco-Roman literary culture, Classicists have been unsure "how this undoubted *influence* is to be comprehended, and what the role of the rhetoric manuals is in relation to the practice of texts" (emphasis my own).[30]

The Poet Writes (to) the Orator

The narrative of "rhetorical influence," which we have been tracing, is predicated on the existence of a definable direction of intellectual traffic, with rhetoric being cast as the invader and poetry as the victim.[31] The underlining assumption is that rhetoric is a cultural force to which poets must necessarily either surrender or which they must overcome. This picture, however, is immediately complicated, if not outright contradicted, not only by the overlapping terminology that describes the domains of rhetoric and poetry but also by the fact that poets reacted to the claims of rhetorical writers with counterclaims endowing their own art with the properties of rhetorical speech.

This idea that poetry and rhetoric are essentially two branches of the same art is repeatedly found in Roman culture, and words such as *eloquentia* (in verse *eloquium* is the word used instead) and *facundia* are used with reference to the ability to use pointed language understood as a shared domain of poets and orators. In Tacitus' *Dialogus*, Maternus' choice to pursue poetry (*carmina*) instead of a public career as an orator is framed by his opponent, Aper, as a choice between two related aspects of *eloquentia*:[32]

> Ego uero omnem eloquentiam omnisque eius partis sacras et uenerabilis puto, nec solum cothurnum uestrum aut heroici carminis sonum, sed lyricorum quoque iucunditatem et elegorum lasciuias et iamborum amaritudinem [et] epigrammatum lusus et quamcumque aliam speciem eloquentia habeat, anteponendam ceteris aliarum artium studiis credo.

> It is my belief that the whole field of *eloquentia* in all its different departments is sacred and venerable: I am of the opinion that it is not only your tragic

---

[30] Goldhill (2009) thus invites the field of Classics to "think hard about what it means by the 'role of rhetoric' in elite texts."

[31] On the connection between rhetoric and empire, see Barthes (1988) 14–15: "rhetoric, a veritable empire, greater and more tenacious than any political empire in its dimensions and its duration, flouts the very concepts of science and historical reflection."

[32] Mayer (2001) 118 ad loc. defines it as "the artistic use of language," "language as an artifact," not specifically "oratory." See also Gudeman (1914) 206 *ad* Tacitus, *Dial.* 4.4; and van den Berg (2014) 146–8, 172–8.

The Poet Writes (to) the Orator

buskin or the sound of epic that we must prefer above the pursuits of all the other arts but also the charm of the lyric poets, the licentiousness of elegy, the bitterness of iambic poetry, the playfulness of epigram and whatever other forms *eloquentia* may take. (Tacitus, *Dial.* 10.4–5)

Poetry, including here tragedy, epic, lyric poetry, iambic and epigram, and oratory are both forms of *eloquentia* that differ in the degree of social recognition and influence.[33]

Facundia is also frequently employed with reference to the art or the work of the poet as well as that of the orator.[34] In *Silv.* 1.4, a poem dedicated to the wealthy Rutilius Gallicus, Statius declares that he will draw poetic inspiration not from the usual sources such as Apollo, Mercury or Bacchus but from Rutilius' *facundia,* whose powers are manifested both in prose and in verse:

> ipse ueni uiresque nouas animumque ministra,
> qui caneris; docto nec enim sine numine nactus
> Ausoniae decora ampla togae centumque dedisti
> iudicium mentemque uiris. licet enthea uatis   25
> excludat Piplea sitim nec conscia detur
> Pirene: largos potius mihi gurges in haustus
> qui rapitur de fonte tuo, seu plana solutis
> quom struis orsa modis seu quom tibi dulcis in artem
> frangitur et nostras curat facundia leges   30
> quare age, si Cereri sua dona merumque Lyaeo
> reddimus, et diues praedae tamen accipit omni
> exuuias Diana tholo captiuaque tela
> Bellipotens; nec tu (quando tibi, Gallice, maius
> eloquium fandique opibus sublimis abundas)   35
> sperne coli tenuiore lyra. uaga cingitur astris
> luna, et in Oceanum riui cecidere minores.

---

[33] *Eloquentia* is used first in this broader sense that encompasses poetry in Valerius Maximus 1.6.ext.3 (*Musarum Heliconios colles omni genere doctrinae uirentis dearum instinctu depastae maximo ingenio dulcissima summae eloquentiae instillasse uidentur alimenta*) but it is also used specifically of, for example, historiography (Tacitus, *Ann.* 4.34 *Titus Liuius eloquentiae ac fidei praeclarus in primis*) and medical writing (Cicero, *De or.* 1.62–3). *Eloquium* with reference to oratory or abundant speech: see *TLL* 5.2.412.44–9 and Propertius 3.22.41 *hic tibi ad eloquium ciues*; Virgil, *Aen.* 11.383 *tona eloquio* (of Drances); Ovid, *Tr.* 4.10.17–18 *frater ad eloquium uiridi tendebat ab aeuo* | *fortia uerbosi natus ad arma fori*; Lucan 7.62–3 *Romani maximus auctor* | *Tullius eloquii* (of Cicero); Silius 8.410–11 *nec deinde relinquet* | *par decus eloquio cuiquam sperare nepotum* (of Cicero). Yet *eloquium* also refers to the persuasion of the elegiac lover: Ovid, *Am.* 1.8.20 *nec tamen eloquio lingua nocente caret; Ars am.* 1.461–2 *quam populus iudexque grauis lectusque senatus,* | *tam dabit eloquio uicta puella manus.* See also *Tr.* 1.9.45–6 *siue per ingenuas aliquis caput extulit artes,* | *quaelibet eloquio fit bona causa tuo* where we do not know who the addressee is and what *artes* (poetry or oratory) he is pursuing.

[34] See *TLL* 6.1.158.74–159.42 and especially Horace, *Ars. P.* 41 with Brink (1971) 126; Valerius Maximus 9.12.ext.7; Columella 1.*Praef.*30; Gellius 1.21.5.

> Come in person and grant me new strength and spirit, you that are my theme. For not without divine power of eloquence did you attain the ample distinctions of Ausonia's gown and give judgment and wisdom to the Hundred. Though inspired Pimplea shut out the poet's thirst and Pirene's partnership be denied, better for my deep draughts is the flood snatched from your fountain, whether you compose plain prose in measures unconstrained or your sweet flow of words be broken into rule and respects our laws. So to work! If we return her own gifts to Ceres and wine to Lyaeus, if spoil-rich Diana accepts trophies in every dome and the Lord of War our captured weapons: Gallicus, do not scorn the tribute of a humbler lyre because your voice is mightier and you abound sublimely in wealth of speech. The wandering moon is girt with stars and lesser streams descend to Ocean. (Statius, *Silv.* 1.4.22–37, trans. Shackleton Bailey)

On a first reading, Statius may seem to be presenting Rutilius' *facundia* as a kind of versatile linguistic artistry: his work as an orator is the highest, richest and most sublime manifestation of his *facundia* and Statius' slender lyre is its subordinate. This hierarchy, however, is easily deconstructable once we pay attention to the language of Statius' panegyric: for, while he ostensibly extols as exemplary Rutilius' *facundia* as an orator in the centumviral court (see vv. 24–5 *centumque . . . iudicium*) as well as a poet (vv. 29–30 *seu quom tibi . . . leges*), Statius casts Rutilius as spring (v. 28 *fonte tuo*), Ocean and river (v. 37), all imagery that is typically applied to Homer.[35] Furthermore, as John Henderson has noted, Statius bridges the gap between the two sides of Rutilius' *facundia* (as an orator and as a poet) by suggesting that poetic activity is not so dissimilar from work in the forum in that poetry too has its own laws (v. 30 *leges*) and requires skill and experience (v. 29 *in artem*).[36] Statius, therefore, seemingly pays homage to the distinguished career of Rutilius but his claim to be drawing his inspiration from the orator is facetious since Rutilius qua orator is praised as the supreme *poet* (i.e. Homer).[37]

As well as casting light on the overlapping vocabulary of rhetoric and poetics, this brief glance at the terminology of eloquence undermines another aspect of the standard narrative of rhetorical influence (or resistance thereto), namely the notion that poets "absorbed" rhetorical precepts passively. On the contrary, ancient sources bear witness to poets

---

[35] E.g. Quintilian 10.1.46 *igitur, ut Aratus ab Ioue incipiendum putat, ita nos rite coepturi ab Homero uidemur. hic enim, quem ad modum ex Oceano dicit ipse amnium fontiumque cursus initium capere, omnibus eloquentiae partibus exemplum et ortum dedit.*

[36] Henderson (1998b) 54.

[37] Thus the Homeric figure of Rutilius suffers from the faults of epic *abundantia* (v. 27 *largos . . . haustos*; v. 35 *abundas*) in contrast to Statius' Callimachean voice (v. 36 *tenuiore lyra*).

The Poet Writes (to) the Orator

participating in an intense debate on the nature of rhetoric, rhetorical instruction and persuasion. For example, in the *Orator*, Cicero prefaces his discussion of what constitutes a man of eloquence with a long digression aiming at proving that the *eloquentia* of his ideal orator is a unique entity and has to be distinguished from that of the philosopher, sophist, historian and poet. As he begins the discussion of poetic *eloquentia*, he makes a tantalizing statement:

> ab his non multo secus quam a poetis haec eloquentia quam quaerimus seuocanda est. nam etiam poetae quaestionem attulerunt, quidnam esset illud quo ipsi differrent ab oratoribus: numero maxume uidebantur antea et uersu, nunc apud oratores iam ipse numerus increbruit.

> The eloquence we seek must be separated from those [of the historians] no less than from the poets. For indeed it was the poets who have given rise to the enquiry as to how they differ from orators: it once used to be thought of as an issue of rhythm and verse but now among the orators the use of rhythm has been growing steadily. (Cicero, *Orat.* 66)

Cicero here states that the *poets* "gave rise to the question" (*quaestionem attulerunt*) of how their art differs from that of orators. It is not clear whether Cicero is describing the process whereby the *lectio* of poetic texts by grammarians gave rise to the scholarly *quaestio* of poetry's difference from oratory or whether he is indeed referring to one or more specific poetic sources that raised the question.[38] Be that as it may, Cicero clearly perceives that the question of the difference and similarity between rhetoric and poetry is one that belonged not just to rhetorical manuals but also to poetic texts.

One of the very few pronouncements on the relationship of poetry and rhetoric in the Imperial period by a poet occurs in a passage from the second book of Ovid's *Ex Ponto*. In *Pont.* 2.5, Ovid is writing to Cassius Salanus, who is addressed both because of his appreciation for Ovid's poetry (vv. 7–40) and for his role as Germanicus' rhetoric teacher (41–end).[39] Salanus is thus an intermediary for Germanicus who is the dedicatee of this book of the *Ex Ponto* and in celebration of whose triumph (v. 27 *ut huc magni peruenit fama triumphi*) Ovid has written some lines

---

[38] Sandys (1979) 74–5 ad loc. takes it as a reference to grammatical *quaestiones* but *quaestionem afferre* (e.g. Pliny, *Ep.* 4.30.1 *attuli tibi ex patria mea pro munusculo quaestionem altissima ista eruditione dignissimam*) implies an active role on the part of poets in raising the question. In addition, as Sandys (1979) 75 ad loc. notes, Cicero may be echoing Aristotle, *Rh.* 3.1.8 (ἤρξαντο μὲν οὖν κινῆσαι τὸ πρῶτον, ὥσπερ πέφυκεν, οἱ ποιηταί) in which Aristotle states that "it was the poets who first set in motion [artistic style]."

[39] Also mentioned in Pliny the Elder, *HN* 34.47 as Germanicus' *praeceptor*: see Syme (1978) 88.

Poetry *and* Rhetoric and Poetry *in* Rhetoric

(vv. 25–31), perhaps a reference to the first poem of the book (cf. *Pont.* 2.1.1 *huc quoque Caesarei peruenit fama triumphi*) in which the triumph is commemorated. In turn, Salanus' role as a bridge between rhetoric and poetry is mirrored in Germanicus, who is praised for his excellence in oratory and poetry in the revised proem of the *Fasti*.[40] Ovid here pursues a logical argument to prove an affinity between himself and the rhetor: although Salanus' job is to make Germanicus into a perfect orator (v. 51 *disertus*), nevertheless he has time for Ovid's poetry because the rhetor and the poet are naturally kindred spirits (v. 59 *ingeniis . . . iunctis*). The truth of this statement is then illustrated with an elaborately "rhetorical" priamel presenting a series of examples of "like goes with like" leading up to the direct comparison of poetry and rhetoric.

> scilicet ingeniis aliqua est concordia iunctis,
>   et seruat studii foedera quisque sui: 60
> rusticus agricolam, miles fera bella gerentem,
>   rectorem dubiae nauita puppis amat.
> tu quoque Pieridum studio, studiose, teneris
>   ingenioque faues, ingeniose, meo.
> distat opus nostrum, sed fontibus exit ab isdem   65
>   artis et ingenuae cultor uterque sumus.
> thyrsus abest a te gustata et laurea nobis,
>   sed tamen ambobus debet inesse calor,
> utque meis numeris tua dat facundia neruos,
>   sic uenit a nobis in tua uerba nitor.   70

Surely there is some agreement between kindred spirits and each keeps the compacts of his own pursuit. The country man loves the farmer, the warrior him who wages bitter wars, the sailor the captain of the wavering ship. Studious one, you too are preoccupied with devotion for the Pierians and because of your talented nature, you are well disposed towards my talent. Our work is different, but comes from the same sources and we are both devotees of the liberal art. The thyrsus and laurel tasted by me are foreign to you, but we both need ardor: as your eloquence gives vigor to my poetry so brilliance comes to your words from our work. (Ovid, *Pont.* 2.5.59–70)

Reusing Ciceronian phraseology from the *De oratore*, Ovid is presenting poetry and rhetoric as separate disciplines (v. 60 *studia*) belonging to the *artes ingenuae* ("liberal arts").[41] Viewed as essential components of the

---

[40] Ovid, *Fast.* 1.21–4: *quae sit enim culti facundia sensimus oris,* | *ciuica pro trepidis cum tulit arma reis.* | *scimus et, ad nostras cum se tulit impetus artes,* | *ingenii currant flumina quanta tui.*
[41] The expression *artes ingenuae* is Ciceronian (e.g. *De or.* 1.73; 3.21 and *TLL ingenuus* 1547.27ff.) and occurs eight times in Ovid: see Gaertner (2005) 358 *ad Pont.* 1.6.7 and see Gudeman (1914) 421 *ad* Tacitus, *Dial.* 30.8.

The Poet Writes (to) the Orator

education of the freeborn (*ingenuus*) Roman male, the *artes ingenuae* have a civilizing influence (e.g. *Pont.* 2.9.47–8 *adde quod ingenuas didicisse fideliter artes | emollit mores nec sinit esse feros* and cf. *Pont.* 1.6.7) and are formative to one's eloquence (*Tr.* 1.9.45 *siue per ingenuas aliquis caput extulit artes, quaelibet eloquio fit bona causa tuo*). While Ovid recuperates Ciceronian phraseology, his presentation of the affinity and difference between poetry and rhetoric is less conventional than critics have allowed.[42] Ovid claims that the work (*opus*), respectively of the orator and poet, is different (*distat*) but each derives from the same unspecified sources (v. 65 *fontibus ab isdem*). Crucially, Ovid does not specify what these "fountains" are but it is almost impossible not to think of Homer who, as we have just seen, is often presented as the Ocean and source (*fons*) of all arts. In addition to subtly portraying rhetoric as a derivative of Homeric poetry, the remainder of the comparison is also heavily skewed in favor of poetry. Thus, in a carefully arranged structure, Ovid lists one thing that both poets and orators need, namely passion (*calor*), followed by one thing that each needs from the other, that is, *nervi*, which poets take from the orator's *facundia*, and *nitor*, which comes to the orator's words from the poet's arsenal. This last point is conventional: brilliance (*nitor*) is frequently cited as a trait of good speech (rhetorical and poetic) and often connected with *ornatus*, whose main source, as we will see, is poetry.[43] The shared interest in emotion (*calor*) is also conventional but crucially associated with the manic inspiration of poets.[44] So Statius, in his proem to the *Thebaid*, speaks of the *calor* of the Muses (*Theb.* 1.3 *Pierius menti calor incidit*) and Seneca uses it in reference to the quasi poetic heat of declamatory performance (*Controv.* 7.*Praef.*1; *Controv.* 10.*Praef.*3). By contrast, the notion that the orator teaches the poet "vigor" (*nerui*) is quite unprecedented: typically, stylistic vigor (*nerui*) is associated with the grand style as opposed to the *genus tenue* but is in no way specific to either poetry or rhetoric.[45]

---

[42] See Higham (1958) 44; Galasso (1995) 280–1 ad loc.

[43] Ovid, *Pont.* 2.2.49 *eloquii nitor* of Messalla's eloquence which survives in his son Messalinus but cf. *Pont.* 2.29, where Ovid's lines on Germanicus lack *nitor* (*obruit audentem rerum grauitasque nitorque*). On *nitor* and *ornatus*, see Lausberg (1998) §540.2, who lists *nitor* as one of the main qualities of *ornatus*. See further Cicero, *De or.* 1.81; Tacitus, *Dial.* 20.4 *poetico cultu enituit*.

[44] *TLL calor* 3.181.40–84. The present passage looks back at Ovid, *Tr.* 4.1.43 where Ovid's own poetic inspiration is described in similar terms: *sic ubi mota calent uiridi mea pectora thyrso*. See further Cicero, *De or.* 2.194, in the course of a discussion of emotion cites Plato and Democritus on poetic *furor: saepe enim audiui poetam bonum neminem – id quod a Democrito et Platone in scriptis relictum esse dicunt – sine inflammatione animorum exsistere posse et sine quodam adflatu quasi furoris.*

[45] E.g. as a property of the *genus grande* in oratory: Cicero, *Orat.* 92 *hoc in genere neruorum uel minimum, suauitatis autem est uel plurimum; Brut.* 121; Quintilian 10.1.76. In poetry: Horace,

Poetry *and* Rhetoric and Poetry *in* Rhetoric

What appears initially as a conventional presentation of the overlapping but distinct domains of rhetoric and poetry turns out to be an indirect claim for the priority of poetry as a source for rhetorical ornament and emotional force. Furthermore, Ovid's theoretical pronouncement must be read in the broader context of his overall poetic project in the exilic work where his mounting of his self-defense could be labeled as quintessentially "rhetorical."[46] Thus the poem to Salanus is exactly the mid-point of *Pont.* 1–3 and its place of honor is explained not only by virtue of it being an indirect homage to Germanicus but also by the fact that the topic at hand – rhetoric – is thematically pivotal to Ovid's own project.[47] In particular, the address to Salanus belongs to a series of poems in the *Ex Ponto* addressed to influential orators such as Fabius Maximus and Cotta whose services Ovid is beseeching in an effort to obtain Augustus' pardon. In these poems, Ovid tries to elicit the orator's *facundia* in the service of his own cause as, for example, in the second epistle of book 1, where he begs Fabius Maximus to take up his case with Augustus:

> suscipe, Romanae facundia, Maxime, linguae
> difficilis causae mite patrocinium.

> Maximus, eloquence of the Roman tongue, take upon yourself the gentle advocacy of this difficult case. (Ovid, *Pont.* 1.2.67–8)

The poems addressed to the sons of Messalla – Cotta Maximus (*Pont.* 1.5, 9; 2.3 and 8; 3.2 and 5) and Messalinus (1.7 and 2.2) – repeatedly praise the *facundia* that they inherited from their eloquent and distinguished father and attempt to enlist it in the cause of pleading with (e.g. 2.2.53 *defendere*, v. 55 *excuses*, v. 62 *uerba fac*) and begging (v. 67 *precibus*) Augustus on behalf of the author:[48]

Sat. 2.1.2–3 *sine neruis . . . quidquid* | *composui*; Horace, *Ars P.* 26 *sectantem leuia nerui deficiunt*; Ovid, *Am.* 1.1.18 *attenuat neruos . . . proximus ille meos.* Could Ovid be making a punning allusion to *nerui* in the sense of "strings" and by extension lyric poetry (e.g. Propertius 3.3.4)? To solve the problem Higham (1958) 44 n. 2 suggested that *nerui* should be taken to mean "structure", for which he cites as parallels Cicero, *De or.* 3.106 *consequentur etiam illi loci, qui quamquam proprii causarum et inhaerentes in earum neruis esse debent*; Quintilian 8.*Praef.*18 *resistam iis qui omissa rerum, qui nerui sunt in causis, diligentia quodam inani circa uoces studio senescunt.* But the emphasis in these examples seems to be not on *dispositio* but on the "sinews" (*nerui*) as "that which gives strength or vitality to a thing" *OLD* 5.

[46] See Ingleheart (2010) 12–21 for a reading of the relationship between Ovid, *Tr.* 2 and forensic oratory, especially Cicero, *Pro Ligario*.

[47] On the arrangement of *Pont.* 1–3, see Gaertner (2005) 2–6 and Evans (1976).

[48] See further *Tr.* 4.4.1–10; *Pont.* 2.3; 3.5.15ff.; 4.9.49ff. (addressed to Graecinus).

The Poet Writes (to) the Orator   23

> nunc tibi et eloquii nitor ille domesticus adsit
>   quo poteras trepidis utilis esse reis.   50
> uiuit enim in uobis facundi lingua parentis
>   et res heredem repperit illa suum.
> hanc ego non ut me defendere temptet adoro:
>   non est confessi causa tuenda rei.
> num tamen excuses erroris origine factum   55
>   an nihil expediat tale mouere uide

Now let that brilliant eloquence of your house assist you with which you have been able to help the fearful accused! For in you lives the tongue of your eloquent father which has found in you its heir. This I beseech, not that I may try to defend myself: the case of a self-confessed criminal must not be defended. Nevertheless, consider whether you may excuse my deed through the source of my mistake or whether it would do any good at all to stir up such matter. (Ovid, *Pont.* 2.2.49–56)

Yet Ovid's request for the assistance of the orator's *facundia* is more disingenuous than it may at first seem, especially when we consider that the orator's eloquence in essence will mirror, if not replicate, Ovid's persuasive approach to his addressee. Ovid himself makes this point in a self-consciously rhetorical moment in *Pont.* 1.2:

> Caesaris haec animum poterant audita mouere,
>   Maxime, mouissent si tamen ante tuum.
> uox, precor, Augustas pro me tua molliat aures,   115
>   auxilio trepidis quae solet esse reis,
> adsuetaque tibi doctae dulcedine linguae
>   aequandi superis pectora flecte uiri.

These tales could move the soul of Caesar, if they had only moved yours first. Let your voice, I beg you, soften on my behalf the ears of Augustus which are accustomed to aid fearful defendants, and with the usual sweetness of your learned tongue move the heart of a man who must be considered equal to the gods. (Ovid, *Pont.* 1.2.113–18)

Ovid's prayer (v. 115 *precor*) to his addressee will be repeated in the persuasive words he elicits from Fabius (cf. v. 115 *molliat*, v. 118 *flecte*). Indeed, Ovid's words must move Fabius' soul first (v. 114 *mouissent . . . ante*), if they are to move Augustus' (v. 113 *Caesaris . . . animum mouere*). The idea that a speaker has to be moved himself first before he can command his audience's emotions is of course ubiquitous in ancient rhetorical theory.[49] But what is particularly striking here is that the orator's

---

[49] See Cicero, *De or.* 2.189–96; Horace, *Ars P.* 101–3; Quintilian 6.2.25–6.

Poetry *and* Rhetoric and Poetry *in* Rhetoric

eloquence, which is presented at first as a cure for the poet's error, is one among several persuasive performances addressed to the emperor that actually begin with the poem at hand.

It would be simplistic to read Ovid's insistence on the persuasive force of his poetry as a symptom of inappropriate levels of "rhetoricity." On the contrary, defenses of poetry's didactic and civilizing purposes often claim that poets were the first to practice persuasion.[50] In a key passage from the *Ars Poetica*, Horace argues that even before Homer and Tyrtaeus, the mythical poets Orpheus and Amphion were the first civilizers of humanity. Orpheus taught them to abstain from slaughter and with his music, Amphion persuaded even the rocks to come together to form the walls of Thebes:

> siluestris homines sacer interpresque deorum
> caedibus et uictu foedo deterruit Orpheus,
> dictus ob hoc lenire tigris rabidosque leones;
> dictus et Amphion, Thebanae conditor urbis
> saxa mouere sono testudinis et prece blanda   395
> ducere quo uellet. Fuit haec sapientia quondam,
> publica priuatis secernere, sacra profanis,
> concubitu prohibere uago, dare iura maritis,
> oppida moliri, leges incidere ligno.
> sic honor et nomen diuinis uatibus atque   400
> carminibus uenit.

> Orpheus, the priest and interpreter of the gods, deterred men living in woods from slaughters and a foul diet and was said because of that to tame tigers and blood thirsty lions. Amphion too, the founder of the Theban city, was said to cause the stones to move by the sound of his lyre and to lead them where he wanted with alluring prayer. Once upon a time wisdom was considered this: to distinguish the public from the private, the sacred from the profane, to refrain from promiscuous unions, to give laws to married people, to build cities, to engrave laws on wooden tablets. In this way, did honor and fame come to the divine poets and their poems. (Horace, *Ars P.* 391–401)

The notion that poets (*uates*) are responsible for the establishment of the law, family and social and political communities echoes a passage from Aristophanes, *Frogs* in which Aeschylus illustrates the usefulness of poetry by a reference to Orpheus', Musaeus', Hesiod's and Homer's teachings (1029–36).[51] Crucially, in his civilizing role, Horace's poets deploy the three

---

[50] See Ferguson (1983) on the Renaissance tradition of defenses of poetry.

[51] See esp. v. 392 *caedibus et uictu foedo <u>deterruit</u> Orpheus* - Aristophanes, *Ran.* 1032 Ὀρφεὺς μὲν γὰρ τελετάς θ' ἡμῖν κατέδειξε <u>φόνων</u> τ' <u>ἀπέχεσθαι</u> and see further Brink (1971) 384–5 and Brink (1963) 132–4. A similar point is made in Suetonius, *Poet. Praef.* (=Isidore, *Etym.* 8.7.1–2).

functions of rhetorical discourse: *docere* (v. 392 *deterruit* and v. 396 *sapientia*), *mouere* (v. 395 and v. 396 *ducere*) and *delectare* (v. 393 *lenire* and v. 395 *blanda*).[52] Horace's blend of rhetoric and poetry is famously problematic: Norden's first idea that the *Ars Poetica* is arranged according to the rubrics of *poiema* (verbal composition), *poiesis* (content) and *poietes* (*poet*) has been much debated and little consensus exists as to whether this alleged tripartite division in terms of style and content is an application of rhetorical principles to the study of poetry and to what extent, if any, it is indebted to Hellenistic poetic theory.[53]

Be that as it may, Horace's model for a poetry that combines utility with pleasure (v. 333 *prodesse ~ delectare*) was highly influential during the Renaissance when scholars combined Cicero, Aristotle and Horace's *Ars* to form a uniquely eclectic body of work synthetizing rhetoric and poetics.[54] In so doing, Renaissance readers frequently echo and rework Horace's claims over the persuasive force of poetic discourse. In his own work on poetics – *Poetices libri septem* (1561) – Scaliger cites Horace's line about mingling the useful with the pleasing to argue that poetry and oratory need one another to fulfill their twin functions of instruction and pleasure. Thus, according to Scaliger,

> the early orators had only one end in view, to persuade and move their hearers, and their language was correspondingly rude; the poets sought only to please, and they whiled away their pleasure simply with alluring songs. In due time, however, orator and poet secured from each other that which they lacked respectively. Isocrates is credited with having first given graceful movement to a hitherto rude diction ... As to poetry on the other hand, it was rendered more thoughtful by being transferred from the country to the town, where plots were added to furnish examples, and sentiments to furnish precepts. (Scaliger, *Poetices* 3.25, trans. Padelford)

Similarly, George Puttenham's *Arte of English Poesie* (1589) reuses Horace's foundation myth of the poets as civilizers to argue not only for poetry's didactic function but also for poetry being the original form of rhetoric:

---

[52] Cf. Horace, *Carm.* 1.12.5–12; 3.11.1–3; Quintilian 1.10.9.

[53] On the question, see Brink (1963) and Norden (1905). The division is attributed to Neoptolemus in Philodemus, *On Poems* 5 col. 14.5–11 Mangoni, on which see Asmis (1992), and Neoptolemus is in turn claimed as Horace's source by Porphyrio, *In Hor. Artem Poet.* 1. For a more nuanced appreciation of how Horace blends the sections on form and content, see Innes (1989) 259–60, and for a recent discussion of the *Ars Poetica* see Reinhardt (2013). Regardless of how far we believe in Horace's reliance on Neoptolemus, Cicero was also a key intermediary: Grant and Fiske (1924) and Barwick (1922).

[54] For an overview of these texts, see Herrick (1948), Tateo (1960), Weinberg (1961) 38–249, Howell (1975).

> For if it was first that Poesie was th'originall cause and occasion of their first assemblies; when before the people remained in the woods and mountains, vagarant and dipersed like the wild beasts; lawlesse and naked, or verie ill clad, and of all good and necessarie prouision for harbour or sustenance vtterly vnfurnished: so as they litle diffred for their maner of life, from the very brute beasts of the field. Whereupon it is fayned that *Amphion* and *Orpheus*, two Poets of the first ages, one of them, to wit *Amphion*, builded vp cities, and reared walles with the stones that came in heapes to the sound of his harpe, figuring thereby the mollifying of hard and stonie hearts by his sweete and eloquent perswasion. (Puttenham, *The Arte of English Poesie* 1.3)

This Renaissance image of the poet-orator is deeply rooted in the Classical tradition: to give just one further example, in Sidney's *Defence of Poesy* (1595), the classical figure of the orator Menenius Agrippa illustrates not only Sidney's theory of poetry as a rhetorical art but also his own project of producing a rhetorical defense of poetry.[55] According to Sidney, although Menenius was "an excellent orator," "came not among them upon trust either of figurative speeches or cunning insinuations" characteristic of rhetoric; rather, "but, forsooth, he behaves himself like a homely and familiar poet" (*Defence of Poesy* 96) telling the riotous plebs a tale that effected a total transformation and restored calm to the city. Sidney concludes thus:

> By these, therefore, examples and reasons, I think it may be manifest that the poet, with that same hand of delight, doth draw the mind more effectually than any other art doth. And so a conclusion not unfitly ensueth: that as virtue is the most excellent resting-place for all worldly learning to make his end of, so poetry, being the most familiar to teach it, and most princely to move towards it, in the most excellent work is the most excellent workman. (Sidney, An Apology for Poetry, 342 cited from *The Norton Anthology of Theory and Criticism*, 2001)

The argument about the civilizing influence of early poets can actually be traced to the sophists, whose theory of the origin of human societies was built on the premise that mankind transitioned from a primitive lawless state of nature to civilization thanks to *logos*. Thus, in the homonymous Platonic dialogue, Protagoras claims that the art of the sophists was responsible for the formation of ordered societies as witnessed by the work of Orpheus, Musaeus, Homer and other poets who were nothing but sophists in disguise:[56]

---

[55] See Ferguson (1983) and Javitch (1978) 100–4.
[56] See also Democritus B5.8.1 and Critias B25.1–4 Diels-Kranz with Kerferd (1981) 139–42.

The Poet Writes (to) the Orator 27

ἐγὼ δὲ τὴν σοφιστικὴν τέχνην φημὶ μὲν εἶναι παλαιάν, τοὺς δὲ μεταχειριζομένους αὐτὴν τῶν παλαιῶν ἀνδρῶν, φοβουμένους τὸ ἐπαχθὲς αὐτῆς, πρόσχημα ποιεῖσθαι καὶ προκαλύπτεσθαι, τοὺς μὲν ποίησιν, οἷον Ὅμηρόν τε καὶ Ἡσίοδον καὶ Σιμωνίδην, τοὺς δὲ αὖ τελετάς τε καὶ χρησμῳδίας, τοὺς ἀμφί τε Ὀρφέα καὶ Μουσαῖον

Now I say that sophistic art is ancient and those among the ancients who practiced it, fearing the hatred that may result from it, made up a disguise, using sometimes poetry, as in the case of Homer, Hesiod and Simonides, sometimes mystic rites and oracles as the followers of Orpheus or Musaeus. (Plato, *Prt.* 316d)

Although the poetry of Orpheus, Hesiod and others represents a primitive version of sophistic art, in later accounts the civilizing force is attributed specifically to rhetoric. In the preface to the *De Inuentione*, for example, Cicero recuperates the sophistic narrative to make the case for the importance of the study of *eloquentia*:[57]

> quo tempore quidam magnus uidelicet uir et sapiens cognouit, quae materia esset et quanta ad maximas res opportunitas in animis inesset hominum, si quis eam posset elicere et praecipiendo meliorem reddere; qui dispersos homines in agros et in tectis siluestribus abditos ratione quadam conpulit unum in locum et congregauit et eos in unam quamque rem inducens utilem atque honestam primo propter insolentiam reclamantes, deinde propter rationem atque orationem studiosius audientes ex feris et inmanibus mites reddidit et mansuetos.

> At this time then, a really great and a wise man perceived what kind of material and what great aptitude for the most important affairs there were in the minds of men, if only someone could get it out, and improve it by instruction. And this man by way of a rational system gathered into one place men who were scattered all over the fields and hidden in shelters in the woods, and brought them together, and introducing them to all things useful and honorable, though at first they were recalcitrant due to their lack of familiarity, as they started listening to him more eagerly on account of his wisdom and eloquence, from savage and monstrous he made them gentle and civilized. (Cicero, *Inv. rhet.* 1.2)

A wise man, a kind of primitive version of the Ciceronian *uir bonus dicendi peritus*, made use of his intellect and persuasive speech (*oratio*) to soothe savage men and teach them not only useful skills but also the very art of living in a community. Horace has tapped into this narrative of the origin of rhetoric but only to reassign the original civilizing influence not to

---

[57] See also Isocrates, *Nicocles* 12–14 (cited at *Antid.* 209–14); Xenophon, *Mem.* 4.3.11; Cicero, *De or.* 1.33.

28   Poetry *and* Rhetoric and Poetry *in* Rhetoric

rhetoric but to poetry.[58] In Horace's reading of Aristophanes, a sophistic *topos*, often employed in praise of rhetoric's role in civil society, is adapted to construct a defense of the utility of poetry. Thus Horace argues that poets are responsible not just for developing the artistic use of language but for putting persuasion to the service of civilization.

To conclude, the paradigm constructed by narratives of rhetorical influence not only casts rhetoric as the offending party and poetry as the victim but is also predicated on the assumption that a stable body of material deemed "rhetorical" was in some cases "imported" or "taken over" by poets. The issue with this picture is not that what we may choose to identify from rhetorical texts as "rhetorical norms" do not make their appearance in poetry or that rhetorical theory as a "tree of operations, a 'program' designed to produce discourse" is not a useful tool with which to read and interpret Roman poetry.[59] Rather, the issue is one of internal cultural self-definition: even as they acknowledge that the orator's art partially overlaps with their own, poets such as Ovid and Statius challenge the autonomy of rhetoric and invest poetry with the traditional attributes of rhetorically persuasive discourse.

Poetry as Epideictic: *Voluptas* and *Ostentatio*

As we have seen, the exploration of the relationship between rhetorical theorizing and Roman poetry requires a fundamental shift in our approach to the ancient evidence. Rather than taking rhetoric as a self-contained discourse whose norms infiltrate literary culture, we need to focus on the cultural *relevance* of this intellectual divide and its articulation in Roman literary culture. As the poems we have examined and their complex construction of rhetoric reveal, these Roman poets are not "rhetoricizing" or "adulterating" their art, as it is sometimes held, but rather defining it and redefining it as all-encompassing in response to the claims of rhetorical writers. In order to better situate the poets' response, it is time to switch our attention to rhetorical texts and the special role held by poetry therein.

The affinity between poetry and rhetoric, their respective natures and limits, are subjects much discussed and debated in rhetorical theory throughout antiquity. It is well known that rhetorical writers claimed that poets starting with Homer, preceded prose-writers in their use of artistic devices of style.[60] Thus Menander the Rhetor cites Homer as the

---

[58] A point developed by Solmsen (1932) 151–4.   [59] Barthes (1988) 16.
[60] E.g. Cicero, *Brut.* 40; Manilius 2.8 and see further Kennedy (1957).

Poetry as Epideictic: Voluptas and Ostentatio

inventor of several of the epideictic types discussed in his treatise (*syntakti-kon*: 430.12–28; *monody*: 434.11), while Quintilian states that he provided "an example and a starting point for all parts of eloquence" (10.1.46 *omnibus eloquentiae partibus exemplum et ortum dedit*).

In light of these narratives, it is no surprise that poetry held a prominent position in the training of ancient orators.[61] This is particularly true of Roman poetry, which was closely linked with education from its inception. Thus, as Suetonius reports in his historical survey of Roman rhetoric and grammar, *De grammaticis et rhetoribus*, the first grammarians – Livius Andronicus and Ennius – were also the first poets (*Gram. et rhet.* 1.1–2).[62] Both gave exemplary readings (*praelegere*) from their own work (1.2), and, starting from the second century BCE, the elementary stages of the Roman educational curriculum, which were geared toward the forma-tion of public speakers, were dominated by poetry. The *grammaticus* gave preliminary readings (*praelectiones*) of poems followed by expositions (*enarrationes*) outlining not only issues of pronunciation, meter, vocabu-lary and grammar but also the use of figures of speech, which were often illustrated with reference to poetic examples.[63]

Moreover, definitions of the nature and scope of rhetorical theorizing have always had to confront and compete with the authority of poets.[64] Gorgias' *Encomium of Helen*, arguably the first attested rhetorical text, shows off the author's power of argumentation by taking on the indefen-sible point that Helen is not only free from blame but even laudable in her conduct.[65] As scholars have recognized, the piece is deeply self-conscious: for while ostensibly the topic at hand is the defense of Helen, the *Encomium* can also be read as an extensive meditation on the power of persuasion, that is, on rhetoric. Crucial for unlocking this parallel argu-ment is the central section of the work in which Gorgias seeks to excuse Helen on the grounds that if it was a persuasive discourse that caused her to follow Paris to Troy, she ought to be absolved from blame since persuasion

---

[61] North (1952).

[62] On this passage and on the reliability of Suetonius' reconstruction of the work of the early grammarians, see Kaster (1995) 52–4 ad loc.

[63] See Quintilian 8.5.35 *reddam nunc quam proximam esse dixeram partem de tropis, quos motus clarissimi nostrorum auctores uocant. horum tradere praecepta et grammatici solent* with Bonner (1977) 212–49.

[64] For the idea that poetry is the quintessential form of authoritative discourse to which prose is in some ways secondary, see Nagy (1990) 46–7 and 215–49, Habinek (1998), Lowrie (2009) and Sciarrino (2011) esp. 1–37 on the prose/poetry dichotomy in early Roman literature.

[65] On the problematic issue of dating the beginnings of rhetoric, see Sansone (2012) 119–46; Schiappa (1999); and T. Cole (1991).

Poetry *and* Rhetoric and Poetry *in* Rhetoric

is a power that cannot be resisted (9–14).[66] The point is demonstrated by appeal to poetry:

> And if it was speech that persuaded her and deceived her soul, it is not difficult to make her defense and get the charge dismissed. Thus: speech is a great prince. With tiny body and strength unseen, he performs marvelous works. He can make fear cease, take away pain, instill joy, increase pity. I will explain how; the audience must feel convinced of this. I hold all poetry to be speech with meter, and that is how I use the word. Those who hear poetry feel the shudders of fear, the tears of pity, the longings of grief. (Gorgias, *Hel.* 8–9, trans. D. Russell in Russell and Winterbottom (1972))

The argument is constructed around an implied syllogism: since poetry acts as a powerful agent on the soul causing uncontrollable fear, pity and sorrow, and poetry is but "speech with meter" (λόγον ἔχοντα μέτρον), it follows that speech possesses the same ability to control the emotions of the audience.[67] It is easy to gauge how the argument over the power of *logos* is self-referential: for the *logos* under discussion is not just Paris' persuasive speech but also Gorgias' very *logos* that is therefore indirectly compared in its intended effects to poetic discourse. At stake in Gorgias' effort to present rhetoric and poetry as kindred forms of discourse is the credibility and authority of the new medium. When Gorgias writes in the fifth century, poetry is the unmarked form of authoritative discourse and the emerging new medium – rhetorical prose – asserts itself by claiming to both subsume and replace the poetic medium.[68]

Gorgias' pupil, Isocrates, continues to self-consciously present his medium as a rival to the expressive resources of poetry. Distinguishing writers of court-speeches from those who, like himself, compose *logoi politikoi*, he presents the latter as firmly poetic:

> For there are men who, albeit they are not strangers to the branches which I have mentioned, have chosen rather to write discourses, not for private disputes, but which deal with the world of Hellas, with affairs of state, and are appropriate to be delivered at the Pan-Hellenic assemblies – discourses which, as everyone will agree, are more akin to works composed in rhythm and set to music than to the speeches which are made in court. For they set forth facts in a style more poetic and more ornate (τῇ λέξει ποιητικωτέρᾳ καὶ ποικιλωτέρᾳ); they employ thoughts which are more lofty and more original, and, besides, they use throughout figures of speech in greater

---

[66] See Wardy (1996) 39–51.

[67] Hence some of the verbs associated with the effects of *logos* are those typically used of poetry – *thelgein, peithein*: Ford (2002) 175–82 and Romilly (1975) 3–22.

[68] Goldhill (2002) 5; Bers (1984) 1–4.

Poetry as Epideictic: Voluptas and Ostentatio

number and of more striking character. All men take as much pleasure (χαίρουσιν) in listening to this kind of prose as in listening to poetry, and many desire to take lessons in it (μαθηταί γίγνεσθαι), believing that those who excel in this field are wiser and better and of more use to the world than men who speak well in court. (Isocrates, *Antid.* 46–7, trans. adapted from Norlin)

The *logos politikos*, Isocrates argues, can employ the same ornate diction as poetry and both please and instruct in the manner of poets.[69] By contrast, in the *Evagoras*, Isocrates complains that prose writers do not have the expressive resources of poetry and for this reason no writer before him has ever attempted to eulogize in prose:

For to the poets is granted the use of many embellishments of language, since they can represent the gods as associating with men, conversing with and aiding in battle whomsoever they please, and they can treat of these subjects not only in conventional expressions, but in words now exotic, now newly coined, and now in figures of speech, neglecting none, but using every kind with which to embroider their poesy. Orators, on the contrary, are not permitted the use of such devices; they must use with precision only words in current use and only such ideas as bear upon the actual facts. Besides, the poets compose all their works with meter and rhythm, while the orators do not share in any of these advantages; and these lend such charm that even though the poets may be deficient in style and thoughts, yet by the very spell of their rhythm and harmony they bewitch their listeners. (Isocrates, *Evag.* 8–10, trans. Norlin)

The disavowal of the poetic in this passage should be read as an ironic statement: Isocrates' protestations over the inferiority of his chosen medium are better taken as a *recusatio* designed to amplify the orator's encomium of the Cypriot king Evagoras than as a symptom of a change of heart.[70]

Issues of similarity and dissimilarity between poetic and prosaic discourse are repeatedly raised in discussions of the authority of the rhetorical medium with ambiguous outcomes. On the one hand, like Gorgias and Isocrates, rhetorical writers may claim that their medium possesses expressive powers equal to poetry. On the other, Plato and other critics seize on this point of similarity to charge rhetoric with impinging on ornament, pleasure and display, all elements that are thought to pertain to poetry. Thus, given the fact that Gorgias himself presented rhetoric and poetry as kindred media, it is perhaps unsurprising that Plato's

---

[69] This point is also made by Isocrates in *Nicocles* 42–9 and *Panath.* 2.

[70] See Ford (2002) 236–7; Graff (2005) 319–22; Morton Braund (1998); Too (1995) 33–5.

32 Poetry *and* Rhetoric and Poetry *in* Rhetoric

critique of rhetoric in the *Gorgias* uses its similarity to poetry as one among several targets of criticism. Socrates argues that rhetoric is no different than music or poetry, all of which "pursue pleasure and care for nothing else" (*Grg.* 501e τὴν ἡδονὴν ἡμῶν μόνον διώκειν, ἄλλο δ᾽ οὐδὲν φροντίζειν). Repeating the definition of poetry as metrical logos from Gorgias' *Encomium of Helen*, he states that poetry is a form of "public oratory" (*Grg.* 502d δημηγορία) and "poets play the role of rhetoricians in the theatres" (*Grg.* 502d ῥητορεύειν δοκοῦσί σοι οἱ ποιηταὶ ἐν τοῖς θεάτροις):[71] just like tragedy wants only to entertain the audience, so the rhetoricians' only goal is not to speak for the betterment of the citizens but to entertain them (*Grg.* 502e πότερόν σοι δοκοῦσιν πρὸς τὸ βέλτιστον ἀεὶ λέγειν οἱ ῥήτορες, τούτου στοχαζόμενοι, ὅπως οἱ πολῖται ὡς βέλτιστοι ἔσονται διὰ τοὺς αὐτῶν λόγους, ἢ καὶ οὗτοι πρὸς τὸ χαρίζεσθαι τοῖς πολίταις ὡρμημένοι).

This polemical evocation by rhetorical sources of the boundaries between the poetic and the rhetorical is nowhere more evident than in the treatment of epideictic genre, the branch of oratory that deals with praise and blame.[72] We have already seen that, beginning with Gorgias in the *Helen* and Isocrates in the *Evagoras* (9–11), epideictic writers acknowledged the primacy of poetry and, from Pindar to the Hellenistic court encomia to the *Siluae* of Statius, poetry competed with epideictic prose as a vehicle for eulogy.[73] In addition, from the fourth century, during Panhellenic festivals and games, poets and orators shared the stage in performing encomia of different kinds.[74] It was therefore natural for later theorists to criticize the *genus demonstratiuum* on similar grounds as poetic language and vice versa to criticize poetry as ostentatious and display-driven. In the fourth century, Alcidamas can dismiss teachers of rhetoric who insisted too much on written speeches at the expense of extemporaneous performance as "poets rather than sophists" (*Soph.* 10–11 Avezzu' καὶ πολὺ δικαιότερον ἂν ποιητὰς ἢ σοφιστὰς προσαγορεύεσθαι νομίζων).[75] The same phrase recurs in Isocrates who, despite his self-proclaimed poetic aspirations in the *Antidosis*, is just as capable of rebuking a sophist as a "poet of speeches" (λόγων ποιητὴς) in *Antid.*

---

[71] For this critique of tragic poetry as *dēmēgoria*, see also Plato, *Leg.* 7.817c.

[72] Webb (1997) 359–66; Russell (1998) 23–4; Pernot (1993); Russell and Wilson (1981); Burgess (1902).

[73] See Hardie (1983). As we can see from Menander Rhetor, in the Imperial period, prose writers took up genres such as the epithalamium, which had been the domain of poets: see Russell and Wilson (1981) and Russell (1979).

[74] Hardie (1983) 20–1 and see Isocrates, *Panegyrikos* ("Great Festival"), from which the term panegyric, a synonym of epideictic, derives.

[75] On Alcidamas and his relation to Isocrates, see O'Sullivan (1992) 23–31.

Poetry as Epideictic: Voluptas *and* Ostentatio   33

192 and *C. soph.* 15.[76] Later writers routinely characterize the style of Gorgias and of the sophists as "poetic."[77] Finally, rhetorical sources criticize epideictic, whose aim is after all to amplify and embellish (Quintilian 3.7.6 *res amplificare et ornare*), as empty pleasure and unemotional entertainment more suited to the middle style rather than to the emotional heights of the genus *grande*.[78]

Above all, the two key negative concepts of pleasure (*uoluptas*) and display (*ostentatio*) link poetry and epideictic. While the deliberative and forensic genres are associated with persuasion, the aim of epideictic is simply to please and "the object of evaluation is not the juridical and legislative issue but the speech itself: the observer views the speech as an oratorical display (*epideixis*)."[79] Thus the term epideictic already implies a degree of condemnation, pointing as it does to the self-serving nature of the genre and its lack of practical purposes. As a result, the overlap between poetry and panegyric in discussions of the epideictic is often framed in negative terms. For example, Quintilian defines the epideictic genre as "the kind directed towards display [which] seeks only the pleasure of the audience" (8.3.11 *illud genus ostentationi compositum solam petit audientium uoluptatem*).[80] As we hear in a later passage, poetry too is "a genre designed for display" (10.1.28 *genus ostentationi comparatum*) and for pleasure (*audientum uoluptatem*).[81] We have already seen how in the *Orator* (67–9), Cicero discusses epideictic oratory together with poetry as foils against which to set up his ideal style of oratory. Elsewhere, Cicero connects epideictic with the same kind of *licentia* with unusual vocabulary and figurative language that he associates with poetry.[82] The otherness of

---

[76] On this apparent contradiction, see Graff (2005) 319–22; Ford (2002) 235–40.

[77] E.g. Cicero, *Orat.* 37–40 and 65; Dionysius of Halicarnassus, *Dem.* 5 rejecting Plato's poeticisms inspired by Gorgias: σχήμασί τε ποιητικοῖς ἐσχάτην προσβάλλουσιν ἀηδίαν καὶ μάλιστα τοῖς Γοργιείοις ἀκαίρως καὶ μειρακιωδῶς ἐναβρύνεται and see further Denniston (1952) 3–22.

[78] On *ornatus* and pleasure, see Quintilian 8.3.5 *sed ne causae quidem parum conferet idem hic orationis ornatus. nam qui libenter audiunt et magis attendunt et facilius credunt, plerumque ipsa delectatione capiuntur, nonnumquam admiratione auferuntur* with Lausberg (1998) §538–40. For a critique of epideictic, see Aristotle, *Rh.* 3.12; Cicero, *Orat.* 37–42 and 96; Quintilian 3.8.62–3; Dionysius of Halicarnassus, *Dem.* 20; Longinus, *Subl.* 9.3 and see Innes (2011).

[79] Lausberg (1998) §239, 103. For ancient definitions, see Aristotle, *Rh.* 1.3; Quintilian 3.4.12–14.

[80] Cf. Quintilian 3.4.6 and 2.10.11.

[81] Cf. Quintilian 1.8.11 *poeticis uoluptatibus*; 8.6.17 *quod ea quae poetis, qui et omnia ad uoluptatem referunt.*

[82] Cicero, *Orat.* 37–8; *Inv. rhet.* 2.177–8; *Part. or.* 72 *et quoniam in his causis omnis ratio fere ad uoluptatem auditoris et ad delectationem refertur, utendum erit eis in oratione singulorum uerborum insignibus quae habent plurimum suauitatis: id est ut factis uerbis aut uetustis aut translatis frequenter utamur, et in ipsa constructione uerborum ut paria paribus et similia similibus saepe referantur, ut contraria, ut geminata, ut circumscripta numerose, non ad similitudinem uersuum, sed ad explendum aurium sensum, apto quodam quasi uerborum modo; De or.* 2.43–7, 341–9. See also *Rhet. Her.* 3.10–15.

34 Poetry *and* Rhetoric and Poetry *in* Rhetoric

epideictic can also be expressed in terms of national and cultural origin. Thus Crassus characterizes panegyric as a Greek invention designed for the purposes of reading, entertainment or to honor a particular individual (*De or.* 2.341 *ipsi enim Graeci magis legendi et delectationis aut hominis alicuius ornandi quam utilitatis huius forensis causa laudationes scriptitauerunt*) and contrasts this type with the more naturally Roman genres of deliberative and forensic oratory. This approach to epideictic as poetic is clearly polemical: for as rhetorical writers displace the excessive and unabashed characteristics of poetry onto the epideictic genre, they implicitly construct a hierarchy in which deliberative and forensic oratory are presented as controlled and appropriate.

Nevertheless, the overlap between the epideictic and the poetic is most clearly articulated in later rhetorical theory when not only does epideictic become central but all literary production, including poetry, is interpreted through its lenses. In the second century, for example, the rhetor Hermogenes of Tarsus divides all styles in two categories, namely political rhetoric, which consists of deliberative and forensic oratory, and panegyric, which embraces both panegyrics in prose (the chief model being Plato) and all poetry: "all poetry is panegyric and is, in fact, the most panegyric of all literary styles" (*Id.* 2.10.231–3, trans. Wooten).[83] The reasons for this startling statement are not so much stylistic but thematic: poetry, like panegyric, deals with "mythical stories," "marvels about men and animals" and in general "poetry indulges in the marvelous stories that are impossible and unbelievable" (2.10.297–9).[84] In addition, Hermogenes' reading is part of a broader tendency to approach all forms of discourse, including poetry, as either praise or blame. Already Aristotle traces the origins of poetry to the two basic types of panegyric and invective.[85] This epideictic approach emphasizes the ethical function of poetry, since encomia of virtuous men are thought to have a protreptic function, stimulating the listeners to virtuous deeds.[86] Hermogenes' statement (2.10.253–5), according to

---

[83] Rutherford (1998) esp. 43–53 and Wooten (1987).

[84] Cf. Hermogenes, *Id.* 2.10.266–72 "Homer is the best at using every kind of style. Indeed he is the man who more than any other poet has created passages of Grandeur and those that produce pleasure and those that exhibit a carefully wrought style and Force"; *Id.* 2.10.330–2 "there are no figures that are particularly characteristic of poetry but it uses the same ones that are typical of panegyric oratory."

[85] Aristotle, *Poet.* 1448b24–7 "poetry, arising from their improvisations, split up according to the authors' divergent characters: the more dignified represented noble actions and those of noble men, the less serious those of low-class people; the one group produced at first invectives, the others song praising gods and men" (trans. Hubbard in Russell and Winterbottom (1972)). See Woodman (1988) 41–4.

[86] See Plato, *Resp.* 10.607 banishes all poetry except for "hymns to gods and encomia to good men," *Prt.* 325; *Leg.* 7.801ff; Isocrates, *Evag.* 5; Aristotle, *Rh.* 1.9.1367b35–1368a7.

Ornatus: Poetry as Adornment

which Homer is the best panegyrist because he "imitates both orators delivering speeches and singers singing panegyrics, such as Phemius and Demodocus," already implies that the embedded performance of epic bards was read as praise. As we will see in Chapter 6, Hermogenes' assessment of Homer has a counterpart in Servius, for whom Virgil's aim in writing the *Aeneid* was to imitate Homer and praise Augustus from his ancestors (Servius, *Praef. intentio Vergilii haec est, Homerum imitari et Augustum laudare a parentibus*). Similarly, Tiberius Cl. Donatus reads the *Aeneid* as a long oration in support and praise of Aeneas, and the tradition of reading the poem as an extended encomium of its hero and his descendants has a long history that stretches well into the modern period, as eloquently analyzed by Craig Kallendorf.[87]

Ornatus: Poetry as Adornment

It is in light of this critique of the epideictic genre that we must approach Aristotle's presentation of poetry in the *Rhetoric*.[88] There, while introducing the subject of style (*lexis*), Aristotle presents a teleological account in which poetry gave way to poetic prose, as exemplified by Gorgias, which in turn made space for simple prose and prosaic poetry:

> Now the first originators [of style] were naturally the poets ... Since the poets, because what they said was naïve, were held to have earned their repute by the way they said it, [prose] style was at first poetical, for instance, that of Gorgias; and even today, the majority of the uneducated think such speakers the best. This is wrong, the style of oratory being different from that of poetry. (Aristotle, *Rh.* 3.1.1404a24–34, trans. Hubbard in Russell and Winterbottom (1972))

Aristotle stresses that rhetoricians first aimed at poetic language to win the fame that poets possessed. But, as poetry, or at least tragedy, progressively became more prosaic, so prose ought to guard against the ridicule that ensues from adopting poetic language.

It is clear that in Aristotle's presentation, while rhetorical speech may be considered a different kind of discourse from poetry, nevertheless its effectiveness is felt to be inextricably connected with the presence of an appropriate degree of poetic language. In another passage of the third book of the *Rhetoric*, Aristotle asserts that the ideal style is one free from both meanness and undue elevation, that is, a style that is neither too close to

---

[87] Kallendorf (1989) and Starr (1992) and see further Vickers (1983).
[88] Schiappa (1999) 98–105; Sansone (2012) 144–5.

36 Poetry *and* Rhetoric and Poetry *in* Rhetoric

common speech nor too ornate.[89] Elevated or ornate language is represented by poetry from which the ideal style will borrow selectively and appropriately:

> Now let us define the excellence of prose style (λέξεως ἀρετή) as being clear ... and neither mean nor too elevated for its purpose, but appropriate (καὶ μήτε ταπεινὴν μήτε ὑπὲρ τὸ ἀξίωμα, ἀλλὰ πρέπουσαν); for a poetic style is perhaps not mean, but it is not appropriate to prose (ἡ γὰρ ποιητικὴ ἴσως οὐ ταπεινή, ἀλλ᾽ οὐ πρέπουσα λόγῳ). Now among nouns and verbs those that produce clarity are the standard ones, whereas the others discussed in the *Poetics* [chapters 21–2] make the style decorated rather than flat [μὴ ταπεινὴν δὲ ἀλλὰ κεκοσμημένην]. Departure from the ordinary makes it look more dignified. (Aristotle, *Rh.* 3.1.1404b2–10, trans. Hubbard in Russell and Winterbottom (1972))

In this passage, Aristotle establishes a clear connection between ornate (*kekosmene lexis*) and poetic language: both prose and poetry need to adorn (*kosmein*) their style by departing from everyday language but the difference between the two resides in the degree to which poets are allowed to deviate from the norm. Thus Aristotle distinguishes between prevailing or proper (*kyrios*) meaning, which is highly suitable to prose, and improper meaning, which deviates from prevailing usage, and which he associates with the ornamental style of poetry discussed in the *Poetics*, to which he refers.[90] If good style must deviate from the usage of everyday speech, and poetry represents the medium most associated with unfamiliar language, it follows that good *lexis* will contain some (restrained) use of poetic style.

Aristotle uses a political metaphor to characterize further the difference between the poetic and the prosaic:

> ὥσπερ γὰρ πρὸς τοὺς ξένους οἱ ἄνθρωποι καὶ πρὸς τοὺς πολίτας τὸ αὐτὸ πάσχουσι καὶ πρὸς τὴν λέξιν· διὸ δεῖ ποιεῖν ξένην τὴν διάλεκτον· θαυμασταὶ γὰρ τῶν ἀπόντων εἰσίν, ἡδὺ δὲ τὸ θαυμαστόν ἐστιν.

> Men have the same reaction to style as they do when comparing strangers with fellow citizens. That's why, one should make one's style out of the ordinary; men feel wonder at what is not at hand, and what rouses wonder gives pleasure. (Aristotle, *Rh.* 3.1404b, trans. Hubbard in Russell and Winterbottom (1972))

---

[89] See Graff (2005).
[90] In the subsequent discussion, Aristotle refers several other times to the treatment of poetic *lexis* in the *Poetics*, especially with reference to metaphor, glosses and coinages (3.2.6–15).

Ornatus: Poetry as Adornment 37

While poetry is associated with foreignness, prose discourse is associated with the language of the *polis*.[91] The foreignness of poetry does not rest simply on its ability to summon unusual words (e.g. archaisms or neologisms not acceptable in prose) but also extends to its use of ornamental devices. Thus, in a famous passage of the *Poetics*, Aristotle defines the metaphorical (*to metaphorikon*) as "the most important gift in poetry" (*Poet.* 22, 1459a5–8). Here it is crucial to note that Aristotle's *metaphora* includes not just metaphor (which is itself one of the tropes) but also other figurative uses of language on which the theory of tropes and figures is built.[92] Thus he defines *metaphora* as "the application of a name belonging to something else either from the genus to the species, or from species to genus or from species to species or by analogy" (*Poet.* 1457b1–13). Among these four classes, the second kind is represented by hyperbole – "many tens of thousands of fine deeds Odysseus accomplished" (*Il.* 2.272) – and the fourth kind based on analogy – "the evening of life" – comes closer to what we understand as metaphor, and both of these will later be treated as tropes. With the ideologically loaded political metaphor, Aristotle creates an implicit hierarchy in which prose as civic discourse dominates over the poetic, implicitly constructing the latter as an alluring and yet temporary guest in the *polis* of prose.

In subsequent rhetorical theory, the main components of *kosmos/ornatus* are thought to be tropes and figures, which are commonly illustrated by way of poetic exempla.[93] The theory of tropes and figures, which was probably developed by Aristotle's pupil Theophrastus in the Hellenistic period, presupposes Aristotle's theory about the existence of "proper" or "ordinary" meanings of words from which poetic language is seen to diverge.[94] Some theorists make this connection explicit, often referring to tropes as "poetic" both because of their widespread use in poetry and because they were taught by grammarians by way of poetic exempla.[95] Thus, Tryphon writes:[96]

---

[91] Aristotle may be alluding here to Isocrates' use of the same metaphor in the context of a discussion of the difference between prose and poetry in *Evag.* 9–10 (see p. 32), where poets are said to use foreign words (*xenois*), while writers of prose use words of the polis (*politikois*).

[92] Silk (2003) 116–17.

[93] On the doctrine of tropes and figures, see Rowe (1997) 124–9; Calboli (1998); Torzi (2000); Schenkeveld (1991); Innes (1988).

[94] See Calboli (1998) 56–65.

[95] Ps. Plut. *Life and Poetry of Homer* 15–71; Dionysius Thrax 1.1.5 defines the explanation according to poetic tropes (ἐξήγησις κατὰ τοὺς ἐνυπάρχοντας ποιητικοὺς τρόπους) as one of the parts of grammar and see Silk (1974) 211, appendix iii.1.

[96] On this text, see West (1965).

Poetry *and* Rhetoric and Poetry *in* Rhetoric

τούτους δὲ ποιητικοὺς καλοῦσιν, ἐπεὶ κατά γε τὸ πλεῖστον ἡ τούτων χρῆσις παρὰ ποιηταῖς, καὶ ὅτι τούτοις οἱ γραμματικοὶ χρῶνται ἐξηγούμενοι τὰ κυρίως ἢ τροπικῶς τοῖς ποιηταῖς εἰρημένα

These are called poetic [tropes] since for the most part their use is found in the poets or because the grammarians use them when they explain that which is said appropriately or in a tropic manner by the poets. (Tryphon, *De Tropis* 191.18–22 Spengel)

While ancient critics explain the label "poetic" mechanically as resulting from the fact that tropes are found in poets or discussed by readers of poetry, there is in fact a deeper underlying connection between poetry and these elements of style based on their very definition, rooted as that is in the notion that tropes and figures are essentially alterations to the "natural" structure of the language. *Ad Herennium* defines tropes as "having this in common, that the language departs from the ordinary meaning of the words and is with a certain grace applied in another sense."[97] Although Cicero lists both figures and tropes in the *Orator* (135–9) and *De oratore* (3.166–70; 3.202–7), he avoids definitions and gives limited examples in line with his general tendency to avoid technical categorizations.[98] However, when he does give a complete definition of *ornatus* in the *Brutus* (69), he stresses that "the Greeks consider that language is embellished (*ornari orationem*) if they use changes in the use of words (*uerborum immutationibus*) which they called tropes, and figures of thought and speech which they called *schemata*." The fifth-century compilation *De figuris* attributed to Phoebammon cites several theorists of figurative language, the earliest of whom is the Augustan Caecilius of Calacte, who defines a schema as a "change to the unnatural in thought and diction" (*De figuris* 1.30.1 σχῆμά ἐστι τροπὴ εἰς τὸ μὴ κατὰ φύσιν τὸ τῆς διανοίας καὶ λέξεως). Thus, since tropes and figures are understood as purposeful deviations from everyday language at the level of the individual word and sentence respectively, it is easy to understand why *ornatus* understood as figurative and artistic use of language might be especially linked with poetic discourse.

---

[97] *Rhet. Her.* 4.42 *nam earum omnium hoc proprium est, ut ab usitata uerborum potestate recedatur atque in aliam rationem cum quadam uenustate oratio conferatur.* The author calls these "*exornationes uerborum*" rather than tropes. Quintilian's discussion of tropes and figures is the most extensive to have survived. Cf. Demetrius, *Eloc.* 59–67 and 78–90; Lesbonax in Montanari, Blank and Dyck (1988); Longinus, *Subl.* 16–29.

[98] On the discussion in the *De oratore*, see Innes (1988); Fantham (1972) 176–80; May and Wisse (2001) appendix B, 301–6.

Ornatus: *Poetry as Adornment* 39

The metaphors through which the theory of tropes is constructed help to understand its underlining principles. Thus, according to Quintilian, "a trope is a shift of a word or phrase from its proper meaning to another in a way that has positive value" (8.6.1 *tropos est uerbi uel sermonis a propria significatione in aliam cum uirtute mutatio*). Among the devices typically considered tropes are synecdoche, in which, for example, a blade stands in for a sword (8.6.19), and metaphor and hyperbole, so that, for example, Camilla's flying over the untouched crop (*Aen.* 7.808) is an exaggeration of the truth through metaphor (8.6.69). By contrast, *figurae* involve the same notional distancing from natural language but this time through an unnatural arrangement of words in a sentence (9.1.4 *figura sicut nomine ipso patet conformatio quaedam orationis remota a communi et primum se offerente ratione*) and are further subdivided into figures of thought (9.2) such as rhetorical questions, aposiopesis and apostrophe, which "form a departure from a simple way of making a statement" (9.2.1), and figures of speech such as antithesis, anaphora and chiasmus to name a few, which involve different arrangement of words (9.3). This ideological construct whereby style is thought of as a modification of regular, everyday language is supported in Quintilian through a process of pseudo-etymology. Thus, in 9.1.1, he argues that the noun *tropos* is derived from Gr. *trepein*, implying a turn or deviation in function and translated in Latin as *motus* (8.5.35), though he is aware of the more obvious translation of *tropos lexeos* as "manner of speech."[99] Quintilian's discussion of figures in book 9 likewise establishes by appeal to etymology the need for language to deviate from standard usage. Thus Quintilian argues that rhetorical *figurae* – as opposed to grammatical ones that comprise the necessary inflections of nouns and verbs[100] – are like the postures of the body: they deviate from the default settings of language just as sitting, bending or looking back are departures from the straight pose.

> altero, quo proprie schema dicitur, in sensu uel sermone aliqua a uulgari et simplici specie cum ratione mutatio, sicut nos sedemus, incumbimus, respicimus.

> In the second sense, which is the proper meaning of schema, it means a purposeful deviation in sense or language from the ordinary, simple

---

[99] Cf. Tryphon 191.12 Spengel τρόπος δέ ἐυ τι λόγω, κὺ τὰ παρατροπὴν τοῦ κυρίου λεγόμενος κατά τινα δήλωσιν κοσμιωτέραν ἢ κατὰ τὸ ἀναγκαῖον.

[100] On this distinction between the grammatical and the rhetorical use of *figurae* in 9.1 and its role in the history of rhetoric, see Granatelli (1994). See further Ps. Dionysius, *Ars Rhet.* 9 with Russell (2001a) and Heath (2003). Text and translation of Quintilian are from Russell's Loeb edition.

40   Poetry *and* Rhetoric and Poetry *in* Rhetoric

> form. The analogy is now with sitting, bending forwards, or looking back. (Quintilian 9.1.11)

In a passage of pivotal importance in book 2, the need for style to change "posture" to achieve beauty (*ut deceat*) in style is illustrated with reference to art (2.13.8–12). Figures of thought and diction bring charm and delight in that they "make changes in the set traditional order" (*mutare ex illo constituto traditoque ordine*), just as "the upright body has very little grace" (*nam recti quidem corporis uel minima gratia est*) and the contorted pose (*distortum et elaboratum*) of Myron's *Discobulus* wins praise for not being straight (*parum rectum*). Just as in sculpture figures are pleasing in so far as their pose is varied and displays a variety of movements (*motus*), so too in style we ought to aim at variety and deviation from the norm through tropes (*motus*) and *figurae*.

As Quintilian himself acknowledges (9.1) and as scholars have amply demonstrated, these distinctions between tropes and figures and between figures of thought and diction are tenuous at best and endlessly problematic.[101] What concerns us, however, is not the validity of the categories but rather their intellectual function in rhetorical discourse. For in so far as it presents ornaments of style as departures from the norm and therefore as "poetic," according to rhetorical theory, "every trope constitutes an impropriety because a trope by definition causes a deviation from the proper meaning of the word."[102] This pointed connection between rhetorical adornment and poetry is brought out most clearly in Strabo's defense of his own use of Homer as a source of geography against the Hellenistic geographer Eratosthenes' assertion that poetry is mere entertainment and has no educational value. Strabo argues that Homer is as good a source for many things, including knowledge of the art of rhetoric, as demonstrated by the character of Odysseus (1.2.4–5). Moreover, given Homer's preeminence as a poet it would be absurd to deny him knowledge of rhetoric:

> τὸ δὲ δὴ καὶ τὴν ῥητορικὴν ἀφαιρεῖσθαι τὸν ποιητὴν τελέως ἀφειδοῦντος ἡμῶν ἐστι. τί γὰρ οὕτω ῥητορικὸν ὡς φράσις; τί δ' οὕτω ποιητικόν; τίς δ' ἀμείνων Ὁμήρου φράσαι; νὴ Δία, ἀλλ' ἑτέρα φράσις ἡ ποιητική. τῷ γε εἴδει, ὡς καὶ ἐν αὐτῇ τῇ ποιητικῇ ἡ τραγικὴ καὶ ἡ κωμική, καὶ ἐν τῇ πεζῇ ἡ ἱστορικὴ καὶ ἡ δικανική. ἆρα γὰρ οὐδ' ὁ λόγος ἐστὶ γενικός, οὗ εἴδη ὁ

---

[101] Williams (1980) ix–xii, 23–31; Lanham (1991) 102 summarizes the problem: "the issues involved seem complex enough to preclude an adequate distinction." For an effort to rehabilitate the classical theory of tropes and figures, see Vickers (1988a) 294–339.

[102] Rowe (1997) 125.

Ornatus: Poetry as Adornment 41

ἔμμετρος καὶ ὁ πεζός; ἢ λόγος μέν, ῥητορικὸς δὲ λόγος οὐκ ἔστι γενικὸς καὶ φράσις καὶ ἀρετὴ λόγου; ὡς δ᾽ εἰπεῖν, ὁ πεζὸς λόγος, ὅ γε κατεσκευασμένος, μίμημα τοῦ ποιητικοῦ ἐστι. πρώτιστα γὰρ ἡ ποιητικὴ κατασκευὴ παρῆλθεν εἰς τὸ μέσον καὶ εὐδοκίμησεν· εἶτα ἐκείνην μιμούμενοι, λύσαντες τὸ μέτρον, τἆλλα δὲ φυλάξαντες τὰ ποιητικά, συνέγραψαν οἱ περὶ Κάδμον καὶ Φερεκύδη καὶ Ἑκαταῖον

So, then, to deny the art of rhetoric to Homer is to disregard my position entirely. For what is so much a part of rhetoric as style? And what is so much a part of poetry? And who has surpassed Homer in style? "Assuredly," you answer "but the style of poetry is different from that of rhetoric." In species, yes; just as in poetry itself the style of tragedy differs from that of comedy, and in prose the style of history differs from that of forensic speech. Well then, would you assert that discourse is not a generic term, either, whose species are metrical discourse and prose discourse? Or, rather, is discourse, in its broadest sense, generic, while rhetorical discourse is not generic, and style and excellence of discourse are not? – But prose and discourse – I mean artistic prose – is, I may say, an imitation of poetic discourse; for poetry, as an art, first came upon the scene and was first to win approval. Then came Cadmus, Pherecydes, Hecataeus, and their followers, with prose writings in which they imitated the poetic art, abandoning the use of metre but in other respects preserving the qualities of poetry. (Strabo 1.2.6, trans. Jones)

For Strabo, poetry is the spring and source of ornate (κατεσκευασμένη) style (φράσις), and, because Homer preceded prose writers, prose style as a form of ornate discourse can be nothing but an imitation of poetic discourse (μίμημα τοῦ ποιητικοῦ) or at best poetry and prose are different species of the same discourse (ἆρα γὰρ οὐδ᾽ ὁ λόγος ἐστὶ γενικός, οὗ εἴδη ὁ ἔμμετρος καὶ ὁ πεζός;).

Moreover, poetic *ornatus*, especially in epic, is also associated with an essential function of discourse, namely emotional arousal (*mouere*). In Quintilian's account, the acclamation of the public in response to Cicero's defense of Gaius Cornelius is compared to the ecstasy associated with poetry ever since Plato (8.3.4 *sed uelut mente captos et quo essent in loco ignaros erupisse in hunc uoluptatis adfectum*). Thus certain prose writers such as Plato and Demosthenes can be praised as "poetic" for their capacity to stir the emotions with the grand style.[103] It will be no surprise then that

---

[103] E.g. Demetrius, *Eloc.* 181; Cicero, *Orat.* 67 *itaque uideo uisum esse non nullis Platonis et Democriti locutionem, etsi absit a uersu, tamen quod incitatius feratur et clarissimis uerborum luminibus utatur, potius poema putandum quam comicorum poetarum*; Philodemus, *On poems* 1, 200 Janko; Dionysius of Halicarnassus on Demosthenes' style: *Comp.* 25.8–10 φέρε δὴ τίς οὐκ ἂν ὁμολογήσειεν τοῖς κρατίστοις ἐοικέναι ποιήμασί τε καὶ μέλεσι τοὺς Δημοσθένους λόγους; Quintilian 10.1.81 *quis dubitet Platonem esse praecipuum siue acumine disserendi siue eloquendi facultate diuina quadam et Homerica?*; Tacitus, *Dial.* 31; Longinus, *Subl.* 13.3–4 on Plato καὶ οὐδ᾽ ἂν ἐπακμάσαι μοι δοκεῖ

42   Poetry *and* Rhetoric and Poetry *in* Rhetoric

theorists of the grand style, in which the emotions play a pivotal role, recommend the use of figures often illustrated from poetry specifically to arouse the emotions. In Demetrius, *De elocutione*, for example, figures of speech are discussed in conjunction with the grand style (*megaloprepes*) and its need for emotional arousal, and pride of place is given to metaphors that "make the greatest contribution of charm and grandeur" (*Eloc.* 78). In discussing the use of figures, Longinus argues that whereas poets aim at *ekplexis*, orators use metaphors for the purpose of *enargeia*:

> ὡς δ' ἕτερόν τι ἡ ῥητορικὴ φαντασία βούλεται καὶ ἕτερον ἡ παρὰ ποιηταῖς οὐκ ἂν λάθοι σε, οὐδ' ὅτι τῆς μὲν ἐν ποιήσει τέλος ἐστὶν ἔκπληξις, τῆς δ' ἐν λόγοις ἐνάργεια, ἀμφότεραι δ' ὅμως τό τε <παθητικὸν> ἐπιζητοῦσι καὶ τὸ συγκεκινημένον

> It will not escape you that rhetorical visualization has a different intention from that of the poets: in poetry the aim is astonishment, in oratory it is clarity. Both, however, seek emotion and excitement. (Longinus, *Subl.* 15.2, trans. Russell in Russell and Winterbottom (1972))

In practice, however, the only example from prose that Longinus discusses – Demosthenes' oath on the fallen at Marathon – is singled out for its emotional use of a figure of speech. Although the grand style does not exactly map onto poetry, there are several points of contact, not least among them the appeal to the emotions achieved through the pointed recourse to rhetorical figures.

As we have seen, poetry can be said to fulfill a paradoxical role as both a source for *ornatus* and a (largely negative) foil against which rhetorical theorists can define their own judicious and appropriate departure from "natural language."[104] As Joy Connolly has noted in her study of rhetoric and masculinity, "rhetoric and eloquence ... are constituted in and made possible by things that the Romans ... defined as not manly."[105] This tension is what Todorov referred to as the "splendor and misery of rhetoric": "in the face of this contradictory requirement – that rhetoric be concerned exclusively with the beauty of discourse but at the same time that it must not valorize this beauty – there remains only one possible attitude: that of bad conscience ... Rhetoric goes about its business reluctantly."[106]

τηλικαῦτά τινα τοῖς τῆς φιλοσοφίας δόγμασι καὶ εἰς ποιητικὰς ὕλας πολλαχοῦ συνεμβῆναι καὶ φράσεις, on which see Innes (2002). These references may expand on Plato's description of his own style at *Phdr.* 257A.

[104] On the artificiality of this construction of prose as closer to nature, see Godzich and Kittay (1987) xi–xiii.

[105] Connolly (2007b) 84.   [106] Todorov (1982) 79.

Ornatus: *Poetry as Adornment*

This paradox should lead us to approach the competing claims of affinity and difference between poetic and rhetorical discourse as different aspects of rhetoric's complex strategy of self-definition. Already in the *Rhetoric*, we can begin to gauge how the ancient debate over the relationship of poetry and rhetoric is structured around an endlessly repeated set of dichotomies that implicitly assert the superiority of the rhetorical medium.[107] Thus rhetorical writers construct the distinction between rhetoric and poetry by recourse to binary oppositions such as male/female, free/slave, rationality/passion, nature/artifice, Roman/unRoman, citizen/foreign, in relation to which poetry receives a largely negative definition.

This strategy is clearly visible in an often-cited passage from the *De oratore* dealing with the distinction between poet and orator. There, Cicero states that the poet is a "kin" to the orator (1.70: *finitimus oratori poeta*), a partner (*socius*) and almost a peer (*par*), though differing from him in the liberty (*licentia*) with which he can employ such devices and in his use of meter:[108]

> etenim si constat inter doctos, hominem ignarum astrologiae ornatissimis atque optimis versibus Aratum de caelo stellisque dixisse; si de rebus rusticis hominem ab agro remotissimum Nicandrum Colophonium poetica quadam facultate, non rustica, scripsisse praeclare, quid est cur non orator de rebus eis eloquentissime dicat, quas ad certam causam tempusque cognorit? est enim finitimus oratori poeta, numeris astrictior paulo, verborum autem licentia liberior, multis uero ornandi generibus socius ac paene par; in hoc quidem certe prope idem, nullis ut terminis circumscribat aut definiat ius suum, quo minus ei liceat eadem illa facultate et copia uagari qua uelit.

> Indeed, if scholars agree that a man who knew no astronomy, Aratus, spoke about the heavens and the stars in very fine and distinguished verses, or that Nicander of Colophon, a complete stranger to country life, wrote splendid lines on farming by virtue of the skill of a poet, not that of a farmer, I don't see why an orator couldn't speak eloquently about what he has learned from a particular case or occasion. The poet, after all, closely resembles the orator. While the former is slightly more restricted as to rhythm, and enjoys greater license in his choice of words, they have an almost equal share in many of the devices of style. And however that may be, the poet is almost identical to the orator in this respect: he does not restrict or confine his right of possession

---

[107] Todorov (1982) 72–9 is particularly illuminating on this discourse.

[108] For this meaning of *finitimus* as "kindred," as opposed to "neighbor," see *OLD* 4. For the Romans, the boundary line (*confinium*) was "a strip of land constituting a border between two adjoining plots" (Berger [2002] 406) and see *Digest* 10.1. Therefore, the image of the poet and orator as neighbors suggests that they share an unmarked boundary line that belongs to both.

44   Poetry *and* Rhetoric and Poetry *in* Rhetoric

> by any boundaries that will prevent him from wandering – employing this
> same ability to express himself copiously – wherever he wishes to go.
> (Cicero, *De or.* 1.69–70, trans. May and Wisse)

The orator's ability to speak competently and eloquently about any topic is
illustrated with the example of poetry. Just as Aratus and Nicander wrote
most elaborately (*ornatissime*) and with great distinction (*praeclare*) about
two subject matters – astrology and farming – far removed from their
experiences, the orator can be expected to speak most eloquently (*eloquen-
tissime*) on any topic of which he is informed. For the orator shares with the
poet a capacity for ornamentation though he is in other ways both more
constricted (e.g. in the freedom with which he can deploy *ornatus*) but also
more free (e.g. not being constrained by meter). It is impossible not to note
that the key terms selected by Cicero to distinguish orator and poet in the
passage from *De oratore* (1.70) are heavily moralizing. By referring to the poet
as "possessing more freedom with regards to his license" (*licentia liberior*),
Cicero is hinting at the proverbial expression *licentia poetarum* – the allowance granted to poets to deviate from natural language.[109] The English
phrase "poetic license" is in many respects a misleading translation of *licentia
poetarum*: while the former refers to the "freedom allowed [to] the poet to
depart from the norms of prose discourse," the Latin word *licentia* carries an
overwhelmingly negative connotation, signifying "wantonness," "lack of
restraint" (*OLD* 1).[110] Put differently, *licentia* can be described as "an exercise
of freedom of which the speaker does not approve."[111] Characterized as
licentia, the "liberty" afforded to poets is not a permission but rather a tool
of criticism of the poetic medium whose need to exceed constantly the
boundaries of everyday language is contrasted to the orator's purposeful,
controlled and manly deviation from the norm.[112] Thus the poet's unrest-
ricted freedom (*licentia*) can also paradoxically be envisaged as a form of
slavery to the requirements of meter.[113] In addition, Cicero's polemical intent
emerges from his suggestive usage of metaphorical language drawn from the
law: the poet is described as an unruly neighbor who is unwilling to have his
freedom to wander around (*uagari*) restricted. The orator, on the other

---

[109] On *licentia poetarum*, see Lausberg (1998) §983; *TLL* 7.2.1356.17; Brink (1963) 91–100 *ad* Horace, *Ars
P.* 9–10; Nünlist (2009) 174–84 and Meijering (1987) 62–7.

[110] Brogan and Burris (1993) 928.   [111] Morton Braund (2004) 409.

[112] Brogan and Burris (1993) call this polemical aspect of poetic license "an indictment of the
competence of the poet, who on this account is not a master of the meter for his or her own
purposes but is mastered by it."

[113] See Cicero, *Orat.* 68 *ego autem, etiam si quorundam grandis et ornata uox est poetarum, tamen in ea
cum licentiam statuo maiorem esse quam in nobis faciendorum iungendorumque uerborum, tum etiam
non nulli eorum uoluntati uocibus magis quam rebus inseruiunt* with Kroll (1964) 70–1 ad loc.

Ornatus: *Poetry as Adornment* 45

hand, is cast in the guise of a responsible landowner who wishes to establish legally (*circumscribat aut definiat ius suum*) the proper boundaries of the land.

To sum up, the selective appeal to poetry as a precedent for rhetoric does not simply serve an obvious illustrative purpose by providing examples of particular techniques but also has an important ideological function, helping to construct the art of refined speech as a "natural" activity and as civic discourse. The polemical construction of poetic language as foreign and out of bounds is evident in a constellation of related points of difference – *ornatus, ostentatio, uoluptas* – between poetry and rhetoric through which rhetorical language emerges as appropriate, restrained and decorous at the expense of the excesses of poetry. Chief among them is the question of *ornatus*. Aristotle's categorization and its subsequent formulations throughout the history of Greco-Roman rhetoric are built around a structural tension that continues to influence the subsequent tradition: on the one hand, Aristotle is at pains to distinguish prosaic style as unique and different from the poetic; on the other, this differentiation is based not on intrinsically different characteristics but on a degree of deviation from the everyday, which prose and poetry both exhibit, albeit in different degrees. Since tropes and figures are understood as purposeful deviations from everyday language at the level of the individual word and sentence respectively, many of the devices of style that we consider nowadays "rhetorical" were both illustrated by poetry and considered as poetic in tone. As Northrop Frye reminds us, because poetry was first framed as adornment, "any attempt to give literary dignity [i.e. *ornatus*] to prose is likely to give it some of the characteristics of verse."[114] Modern critics have challenged the possibility of distinguishing firmly between poetry and prose and poetic and prosaic registers based on purely formal traits, arguing instead that we ought to speak not of poetry but of a "poetic function" of language capable of being deployed in any kind of discourse.[115] What matters for our purposes is the moralizing discourse that accompanies such definitions of proper rhetorical discourse and the role of poetry in these narratives: verbal ornament, with which poetry is associated, is both negatively framed as "poetic" and positively inflected as essential to the performance of rhetoric.

---

[114] Frye (2000) 263.

[115] Poetic function is a term coined by Jakobson (1960) 356: "any attempt to reduce the sphere of poetic function to poetry or to confine poetry to poetic function would be a delusive over-simplification"; and see further Lanham (1974) 65: "nothing but confusion has ever come from the effort to fix the prose-poetry boundary"; Fish (1980), esp. 97–111. On the problems involved in defining poetic register in Latin literature, see Coleman (1999) and Axelson (1945).

CHAPTER 2

Poetry and the Poetic in Seneca the Elder's Controuersiae *and* Suasoriae

Introduction

The fragmentary collection of excerpts of declamatory exercises known as *Controuersiae* and *Suasoriae* by Seneca the Elder is one of the most often-cited sources in scholarly reconstructions of rhetoric's growing influence over the poetry of the early Empire.[1] Seneca's work has been pivotal in constructing Ovid as the first Roman poet to have been fundamentally "influenced" by rhetorical education and therefore as a linchpin in any account of rhetorical influence over the poetry of the early Empire. As T. F. Higham writes in his account of Ovid's rhetorical background, Seneca the Elder's work is "the best evidence for Ovid's connection with rhetoric."[2] Most influential of all is perhaps Seneca's account of Ovid's training under the rhetor Arellius Fuscus in the second book of the *Controuersiae* (2.2.8–12), which also preserves a fragment from Ovid's treatment of the theme under examination. This passage is key evidence not only that Ovid received formal rhetorical training at the hands of Fuscus but also that in his poems he specifically alluded to *sententiae* of famous declaimers including Porcius Latro, whose style he admired and whose work he cited (*transtulerit*) in his poems. More importantly, Seneca's chastising of the promiscuity of rhetoric and poetry seems to anticipate modern accounts of the role of rhetorical influence: in the same passage from *Controv.* 2, Ovid's prose (*oratio*) is defined as "poetry without meter" (*solutum carmen*); in another passage, it is the turn of a professional orator, Votienus Montanus, to be labeled as "an Ovid among orators" (*Controv.* 9.5.17). Finally, Seneca paints a picture of

---

[1] The full title of this work is *Oratorum et Rhetorum Sententiae Diuisiones et Colores*. Unless otherwise noted, I have followed the text and translation of Michael Winterbottom's Loeb edition. On Seneca the Elder's collection, see Huelsenbeck (2018); Berti (2007); Connolly (2007a) 237–54; Bloomer (1997b) and Bloomer (1997a) 110–53; Fairweather (1981); Sussman (1978).

[2] Higham (1958) 33.

46

Introduction

a literary society in which poets and declaimers shared a common stage: Virgil was imitated and cited by declaimers such as Arellius Fuscus (*Suas.* 3.4–5 and 4.4–5) and Cestius (*Controv.* 7.1.27) at declamations attended by Messalla, Pollio, Maecenas and other notable literary figures of the late Republic and early Empire.

Poetry and the category of the poetic are deeply implicated in Seneca's often misunderstood cultural project. The *Controuersiae* and *Suasoriae* are typically read as the work of a disillusioned moralist embarking reluctantly on a history of declamation. Seneca's attitude toward his chosen topic is ambivalent from the very beginning: in the main preface, addressed to his sons, he agrees to their request to pass on the memory of declaimers who are no longer alive: "You tell me to give you my opinion of the declaimers who have been my contemporaries, and to put together such of their sayings as I haven't yet forgotten" (*Controv.* 1.*Praef.*1 *iubetis enim quid de his declamatoribus sentiam qui in aetatem meam inciderunt indicare et si qua memoriae meae nondum elapsa sunt ab illis dicta colligere*). Yet he denounces the moral and stylistic corruption of eloquence after Cicero, arguing that "some grudge on nature's part has sent eloquence into decline. Everything that Roman oratory has to set alongside or even above the haughty Greeks reached its peak in Cicero's day ... since, things have got daily worse" (*Controv.* 1.*Praef.*6–7 *nescio qua iniquitate naturae eloquentia se retro tulerit: quidquid Romana facundia habet, quod insolenti Graeciae aut opponat aut praeferat, circa Ciceronem effloruit ... in deterius deinde cotidie data res est*). The preface to the last book of the *Controuersiae* begins with a plea by Seneca to be allowed to leave the "studies of schoolmen" (*Controv.* 10.*Praef.*1 *scholasticorum studia*), of which he is now tired and ashamed (*Controv.* 10. *Praef.*1 *fatebor uobis, iam res taedio est ... deinde iam me pudet tamquam diu non seriam rem agam*). It is hard not to register a blatant contradiction at the heart of Seneca's project: in the words of Michael Winterbottom, "while holding that things have declined ever since Cicero, [Seneca] gives extracts from post-Ciceronian declaimers to provide models for his sons, and ... to prove that Roman declamation surpassed Greek."[3]

Missing from the standard account of Seneca's role in this narrative of decline, however, is an appreciation of the literary form in which his endlessly excerpted literary anecdotes are couched. In the *Controuersiae*

---

[3] Winterbottom (1979) 232.

48 Seneca the Elder's *Controuersiae* and *Suasoriae*

and *Suasoriae*, Seneca has assembled excerpts from the declamations of the most acclaimed practitioners of his generation arranged by theme and interspersed with his own judgments and observations addressed to his sons, for whose benefit and at whose request the work is written. As we will see, the author's pronouncements about poetry and declamation are embedded in a sophisticated narrative structure in which Seneca alternates between expressing his own opinions and reporting, sometimes in direct speech, the views of others. Seneca's recourse to poetic citations and criticism thereof must be understood in the context of this sophisticated and rhetorically pointed layering of voices.

An appreciation of the literary form of this deceptively accessible collection of excerpts must begin from an examination of Seneca's authorial strategy. As a native of Spain and member of its elite, Seneca was an outsider and new arrival onto Rome's literary scene.[4] His appropriation of the conventional Roman persona of the moralist in his criticism of the corruption of his contemporaries can be read as a strategy of self-promotion. On a more subtle level, however, his narrative elevates declamation by showcasing not just its stylistic possibilities but also its connection to eminent Augustan literary figures. Moreover, throughout the work, criticism of declamation is increasingly displaced into the mouth of career orators such as Cassius Seuerus and Votienus Montanus. Furthermore, an implicit contrast is developed between the prefatory sections, which frame the work and in which declamation is criticized, and the individual sections on *diuisiones* and *colores*, which are often constructed to respond to negative prefatory content.[5] Finally, a more positive picture of declamation is created by the juxtaposition of Latro, also a Spaniard and who functions in many ways as the author's mouthpiece, and other declaimers, among whom Arellius Fuscus is the most conspicuous. Seneca's representation of poetry and his depiction of Ovid's "rhetorical style" must be understood in the context of this overall strategy by a cultural outsider for elevating and promoting Latronian rhetoric as restrained, Roman and wholesome at the expense of the foreign, "poetic" and "feminine" style of the Hellenizing Fuscus.

---

[4] Griffin (1972) is an essential study of Seneca's cultural background.
[5] *Pace* Bonner (1949) 72–4, who notes Seneca's embedding of the views of Cassius Seuerus and Votienus Montanus in his work but argues that Seneca's reply "if he made one, is not extant." I will argue that while we may speculate as to whether Seneca replied to these critics in a lost preface, an implicit rebuttal to the various speakers emerges from close reading of the *diuisiones* and *colores* sections.

Disowning Declamation

excudent alii spirantia mollius aera
(credo equidem), uiuos ducent de marmore uultus,
orabunt causas melius, caelique meatus
describent radio et surgentia sidera dicent.

Without a doubt I believe, others will beat out breathing bronze in softer lines, will draw living expressions from marble, will plead causes more proficiently, will trace the movements of the heaven with a rod and tell of the rising stars. (Virgil, *Aen.* 6.847–50)

Anchises' presentation of oratory in book 6 of the *Aeneid* as an area in which the Greeks (*alii*) surpassed the Romans has puzzled generation of Virgilian readers: some critics have read the passage as an authorial sneer at the Republican Cicero whose self-proclaimed contribution is implicitly obscured by Virgil; others analyze the passage as a rhetorically constructed priamel designed to praise the achievements of the Romans, while others still prefer to read Anchises' disavowal of oratory as a sign of his limitations as an interpreter of future events.[6] Be that as it may, this disowning posture in relation to both rhetoric and rhetorical instruction is repeatedly found in Roman sources and Seneca the Elder is no exception:[7] already in the preface to book 1 of the *Controuersiae*, for example, Seneca makes a point of advertising the relative youth of Roman declamation. He stresses that he has heard all those who had a reputation for eloquence with the exception of Cicero, whom he could not frequent on account of the Civil Wars, which prevented travel to Rome. According to Seneca, however, the primitive kinds of declamation practiced by Cicero were different both from the modern-day legal *controuersiae* and from the Greek *progymnasmata* known as *theseis*. Seneca argues that *controuersiae* and *declamationes* are thoroughly new inventions and proceeds to paint an anthropomorphic picture of declamation as his coeval known to him from the cradle (*Controv.* 1.*Praef.*12 *ab incunabulis nosse rem post me natam*).

As scholars have argued, Seneca's account of the recent birth of declamation is demonstrably tendentious.[8] Roman sources of the Imperial

---

[6] Norden (1957) 335–7 discusses the lines in the context of the rhetorical tradition of encomia; see Hine (1987) and Highet (1972) 142 on this passage as a comment on Cicero's challenge to the Greeks in the field of oratory (e.g. Cicero, *Brut.* 254–5, Quintilian 10.1.105, Plutarch, *Cic.* 4). More recently, Horsfall (2013a) has argued for reading Anchises' lines in the context of third-century BCE history and literature (as opposed to first-century).

[7] Along these lines, see the important observations in Gunderson (2003) 104–10.

[8] See Fairweather (1981) 115–31; Kennedy (1972) 312–22; Bonner (1949) 18–20.

period insist in presenting declamation as a new form, yet rhetorical exercises of different kinds had been around in Rome since the early first century BCE. Legal and deliberative questions, very similar to what will later become known as *controuersiae* and *suasoriae* respectively, are mentioned already in the first-century BCE anonymous treatise known as the *Ad Herennium*.[9] The practice of developing rhetorically philosophical questions (Gr. *theseis*), which informed many of the themes found in Imperial declamations, is mentioned by Cicero in the *Orator*.[10] Suetonius' account of how modern-day *controuersiae* differ from these earlier themes taught by rhetoricians is confusing at best:[11] an earlier reliance on fables, encomia, translations and preliminary exercises, which are later taught in the school of the *grammaticus*, gave way to an emphasis on *controuersiae* (25.4). The older *controuersiae* were inspired by either historical themes (*ex historiis*) or real-life scenarios (*ex ueritate ac re*). Of the latter kind, Suetonius gives us two examples, which do not, however, differ substantially from the kinds recorded in Seneca the Elder. Thus, while the evidence from Seneca himself suggests that by the early Empire declamation was not just an established school exercise but a public performance genre that attracted orators such as Pollio (*Controv.* 4.*Praef.*2), Labienus (*Controv.* 10.*Praef.*4), Messalla and Maecenas, rhetorical exercises of different kinds had been around from at least the beginning of the first century BCE.

Nevertheless, it is clear that, in his work, Seneca has to confront an already engrained cultural paradigm according to which declamation is constructed (tendentiously so) as a Greek genre. The character of Crassus in Cicero's *De oratore* (set in 91 BCE but written around 55 BCE) explains that, in Rome, much of the distrust of rhetorical instruction was caused by

---

[9] The legal questions are discussed in *Rhet. Her.* 1.18–25 under the rubric of *constitutiones coniecturales, legitimae and iuridicales*. They include a legal case with questions based on Roman realities – the Law of the 12 Tables (1.23) and laws concerning augury (1.20) – as well as Greek topics – one about Ulysses (1.18) and an unspecified case involving a shipwreck (1.19). While they are given as examples of the types of cases and not explicitly referred to as scholastic exercises, scholars assume that they were practiced as such in the schools of rhetoric. For the deliberative questions, see *Rhet. Her.* 3.1: Should Carthage be destroyed? Should citizenship be granted to the Allies in the Social wars?

[10] Cicero, *Orat.* 46 *haec igitur quaestio a propriis personis et temporibus ad uniuersi generis rationem traducta appellatur thesis. in hac Aristoteles adulescentis non ad philosophorum morem tenuiter disserendi, sed ad copiam rhetorum in utramque partem, ut ornatius et uberius dici posset, exercuit.* And see also Cicero, *De or.* 3.109, where the basic types of causes are sketched out: *atque horum superius illud genus causam aut controuersiam appellant eamque tribus, lite aut deliberatione aut laudatione, definiunt; haec autem altera quaestio infinita et quasi proposita consultatio nominatur.*

[11] Kaster (1995) 283 calls it "one of Suetonius' less transparent remarks." On the alleged difference between the pre-Augustan and the Imperial *controuersiae*, see Kaster (1995) 283–6 ad loc.; Bonner (1949) 18–20.

Disowning Declamation

rhetoric being taught in Latin rather than Greek as was previously the custom:

> nam apud Graecos, cuicuimodi essent, uidebam tamen esse praeter hanc exercitationem linguae doctrinam aliquam et humanitate dignam scientiam, hos uero nouos magistros nihil intellegebam posse docere, nisi ut auderent; quod etiam cum bonis rebus coniunctum per se ipsum est magno opere fugiendum: hoc cum unum traderetur et cum impudentiae ludus esset, putaui esse censoris, ne longius id serperet, prouidere. quamquam non haec ita statuo atque decerno, ut desperem Latine ea, de quibus disputauimus, tradi ac perpoliri posse.

> I saw that with the Greeks, however inadequate they were, there was, apart from this exercise of the tongue, still some learning to be found and some knowledge worthy of humane culture. But these new teachers, I realized, were capable of teaching nothing but boldness, certainly something that must be avoided in itself, even when combined with good qualities. Since this was the only thing taught there, and since this was really a school of shamelessness, I thought it a censor's duty to take steps to prevent it from spreading further – though by this verdict and judgment I do not mean to imply that I despair of seeing the subjects we are discussing treated and refined in Latin. (Cicero, *De or.* 3.94–5, trans. May and Wisse)

Although the character of Crassus is hopeful about the possibility of providing rhetorical instruction in Latin, in the late Republic writers still believed that Greek had been the first and obvious choice for rhetorical exercises. Suetonius transmits a fragment of a letter by Cicero in which the statesman says that, as a boy, he would have liked to attend the school of the first Latin teacher of rhetoric, Lucius Plotius Gallus, but was prevented "on the advice of some very learned authorities who thought that native talents could be better nurtured by Greek training" (*Gram. et rhet.* 26 *continebar autem doctissimorum hominum auctoritate, qui existimabant Graecis exercitationibus ali melius ingenia posse*).[12] Still, in the *Brutus*, Cicero himself talks about his habit of "declaiming (as they call it nowadays) in Latin but much more often in Greek," this habit being explained by the fact that Greek was a more ornate language and that most of the teachers available to instruct him were Greek.[13] In a letter to Atticus dated

---

[12] On Plotius, see Kaster (1995) 291–4 ad loc.; on Plotius as the first teacher of rhetoric, see also Seneca, *Controv.* 2.*Praef.*5; Quintilian 2.4.42.

[13] Cicero, *Brut.* 310 *Commentabar declamitans – sic enim nunc loquuntur – saepe cum M. Pisone et cum Q. Pompeio aut cum aliquo cotidie, idque faciebam multum etiam Latine sed Graece saepius, uel quod Graeca oratio plura ornamenta suppeditans consuetudinem similiter Latine dicendi adferebat, uel quod a Graecis summis doctoribus, nisi Graece dicerem, neque corrigi possem neque doceri.* See also Cicero,

52 Seneca the Elder's *Controuersiae* and *Suasoriae*

to 49 BCE, Cicero anticipates the rhetorical elaboration of his death found in Seneca the Elder, providing Atticus with a snippet from a *susasoria* in Greek on the question of "whether one must remain in one's country if it turns into a tyranny" (*Att.* 9.4.2 Εἰ μενετέον ἐν τῇ πατρίδι τυραννουμένης αὐτῆς).

Conversely, there is evidence of considerable social bias directed against rhetors who taught in Latin starting with Plotius Gallus, who is cited as the first to have broken away from privileging Greek as the language of rhetorical instruction:[14] a fragment from Varro's *Menippean Satires* mentions an otherwise unknown character who had learned to "scream like an ox-driver" (*bubulcitrat*) in the school of Plotius.[15] Suetonius also cites Marcus Caelius Rufus' insult directed at Plotius, whom he called "barley-bread rhetorician" (26.2 *hordearium rhetorem*), a slur that focuses both on his cheapness and on his poor role as a substitute for real rhetorical instruction, presumably in Greek.[16] The bias against provincials who taught in Latin is well apparent in Messalla Corvinus' remark cited by Seneca in *Controv.* 2.4.8 Messalla, a fastidious connoisseur of Latin (*Latini utique sermonis obseruator diligentissimus*), dubbed the Spaniard Latro "eloquent in his own language" (*sua lingua disertus*).

In its gradual rise in rhetorical schools, declamation thus had to contend with a long tradition of negative assessment of rhetoric and in particular of rhetorical instruction in Rome. Writing in the early second century CE, Suetonius notes that rhetoric had a more difficult reception in Rome than had grammar and teachers of rhetoric were publicly denounced as immoral as late as 92 BCE, in an edict published by the censors Licinius Crassus and Domitius Ahenobarbus (*Gram. et rhet.* 25.1).[17] Interestingly, already in Cicero "declaiming" is linked with inaction, old age and retirement. Cicero presents the *Tusculan Disputations*, written around 45 BCE, as a philosophical extension of his long practice of declaiming, a kind of declamation for old age (*Tusc.* 1.7.13 *senilis declamatio*). Similarly, in July of

---

    QFr. 3.3.4 and *Fam.* 16.21.5 on Cicero's son training in declamation while in Athens, where he practiced in both Greek and Latin.

[14] Bloomer (1997a) 67–71.

[15] Varro, *Sat. Men.* 257 Bücheler *Automedo meus, quod apud Plotium rhetorem bubulcitarat, erili dolori non defuit.* And see also 379 punning on Plotius' *cognomen: ille ales gallus qui suscitabat Atticarum Musarum scriptores, an hic qui gregem rabularum?*

[16] For a similar example of sneer at rhetoricians, see *Controv.* 3.*Praef.* and *Suas.* 7.13 on Cestius Pius discussed below.

[17] They were banned from the city together with philosophers in 161 BCE, for which, see Suetonius, *Gram. et rhet.* 25.1 and Gellius 15.11.1–2. On the significance of the edict of 91 BCE in the context of the politics of the period, see Gruen (1990) 158–91.

Disowning Declamation 53

46 BCE, Cicero writes a letter to Paetus describing his present activities at Tusculum. In it, he draws a comparison between himself and Dionysius II, the Syracusan tyrant and former pupil of Plato, who after being kicked out of his city by Timoleon, went into exile in Corinth, where he opened a school to survive (*Fam.* 9.18.1).[18] According to Quintilian (8.6.52), the expression "Dionysius in Corinth" had become proverbial for a person who has fallen from previous glory. Here, Cicero explicitly sets up declamation as an activity that befits someone who, like him, has lost the ability to speak in the forum (*sublatis iudiciis amisso regno forensi*). While declamation is part of the expected training in Greek letters already in the time of Cicero and a suitable pastime for the practicing orator, in his later years Cicero increasingly pairs declamation with loss of political status, inaction and mourning over the death of the Republic.

Moreover, the figure of the *declamator* is repeatedly invoked by Cicero for polemical purposes as a foil for the proper orator: the orator who has not received a full education in all the neighboring arts of law, rhetoric and philosophy has merely "jostled about while training his voice in one of the common rhetorical workshops" (*De or.* 1.73 *tantum modo in hoc declamatorio sit opere iactatus*). In the *Orator*, Cicero contrasts the most learned and perfect orator, which is the subject of his work, with some declaimer from the school or a pettifogger from the forum (*Orat.* 47 *non enim declamatorem aliquem de ludo aut rabulam de foro, sed doctissimum et perfectissimum quaerimus*). A true orator like himself, Cicero says in the *Pro Plancio*, is a disciple of the forum and of hard work, not a declaimer (*Planc.* 83 *non uobis uidetur cum aliquo declamatore, non cum laboris et fori discipulo disputare?*). No one can forget Cicero's jibes at Antony for having hired the rhetorician Sextus Clodius, with whom he spent seventeen days declaiming in preparation for his retort to Cicero's *First Philippic* in the Senate (*Phil.* 2.42 *Haec ut colligeres, homo amentissime, tot dies in aliena uilla declamasti? Quamquam tu quidem, ut tui familiarissimi dictitant, uini exhalandi, non ingenii acuendi causa declamas*). Antony's dependence on this shadowy figure is certainly meant to contrast with Cicero's self-presentation as a mature politician. The use of declamation as a topic of abuse is particularly striking in the context of the *Second Philippic*: itself a fictional retort to Antony's practiced speech, the invective was never delivered and therefore itself closely resembles a declamatory piece.

---

[18] On the reversal of fortune that befell Dionysius, see also Plutarch, *Tim.* 13, where he is seen drinking in taverns and pretending to instruct the female singers in the theatre, and Cicero, *Tusc.* 3.27.

54   Seneca the Elder's *Controuersiae* and *Suasoriae*

One anecdote mentioned by Imperial sources encapsulates the connection, already implicit in Cicero's work, between declamation and the death of the Republic. In the wake of Caesar's assassination and in the hope of exerting his influence on the developing political situation in Rome, Cicero cultivated an ulterior friendship with the consuls designate Aulus Hirtius and Gaius Vibius Pansa, who visited with him at Puteoli in April of 44.[19] In one of the letters to Atticus from that period, Cicero jokingly refers to the fact that he was made to declaim by them (*Att.* 9.14.12.2 Shackleton Bailey 366 *haud amo uel hos designatos, qui etiam declamare me coegerunt*) and repeatedly refers to Hirtius as his political disciple (14.20.4 *quod Hirtium per me meliorem fieri uolunt, do equidem operam et ille optime loquitur,* and 14.22.1 *meus ... discipulus*).[20] The story is brought up by Suetonius, according to whom "Cicero declaimed in Greek all the way through his praetorship, whereas in Latin he declaimed when already elderly, and was even accompanied in this by the consul Hirtius and Pansa, whom he called his 'students' and 'grown-up schoolboys'" (*Gram. et rhet.* 25.3 *Cicero ad praeturam usque etiam Graece declamitauit, Latine uero senior quoque et quidem cum consulibus Hirtio et Pansa, quos discipulos et grandis praetextatos uocabat*).[21] Seneca the Elder mentions the same event when he says that, had he been in Rome at the time of the Civil Wars, he "could have been present in that little hall where he [i.e. Cicero] says two grown-up boys declaimed with him" (*Controv.* 1.*Praef.*11 *alioqui in illo atriolo in quo duos grandes praetextatos ait secum declamasse pouti adesse*).[22] None of Cicero's extant letters call Hirtius and Pansa *grandes praetextati*, but regardless of its origin and historicity, the anecdote as recounted by the Imperial writers is a double-edged narrative sword. On the one hand, it legitimizes the genre of declamation, constructing a genealogy that stretches all the way back to Cicero's last valiant attempt to influence the Republic. On the other, the epithet "grown-up schoolboys" is clearly an endearing oxymoron: it highlights declamation's uncertain footing as an activity for adult men (*grandes*), whose political credibility is, however, undermined by their "school-boy" (*praetextatus*) status.

---

[19] On Cicero's relation to Hirtius, see White (2010) 125; Shackleton Bailey (1965) 225 on *Att.* 14.12.9 (SB 366).

[20] Hirtius is already listed as a *dicendi discipulus* in Cicero, *Fam.* 9.16.7, written in 46 BCE (*Hirtium ego et Dolabellam dicendi discipulos habeo, cenandi magistros*).

[21] On the source for *grandes praetextati* in Seneca and Suetonius, see Kaster (1995) 275–6 *ad* Suetonius, *Gram. et rhet.* 25.3.

[22] See also the remark in Quintilian 12.11.6 *sic Pansam, Hirtium, Dolabellam ad morem praeceptoris exercuit cotidie dicens audiensque*.

Disowning Declamation   55

Quintilian offers a different and yet comparable etiology for declamation. While Seneca and Suetonius locate the beginning of declamation in the last days of the Republic, Quintilian discusses its origins in Greece:

> nam fictas ad imitationem fori consiliorumque materias apud Graecos dicere circa Demetrium Phalerea institutum fere constat. an ab ipso id genus exercitationis sit inuentum, ut alio quoque libro sum confessus, parum comperi: sed ne ii quidem qui hoc fortissime adfirmant ullo satis idoneo auctore nituntur. Latinos uero dicendi praeceptores extremis L. Crassi temporibus coepisse Cicero auctor est: quorum insignis maxime Plotius fuit.

> Speaking on imaginary themes, constructed to imitate judicial or deliberative cases, is said to have begun with the Greeks around the time of Demetrius of Phalerum. Whether he himself invented this type of exercise, I have been unable to discover, as I have admitted in another work. Even those who affirm it most strongly have no sufficient authority to rely upon. As far as Latin teachers of oratory, Cicero assures us that they began in the last days of Lucius Crassus. The most famous of these teachers was Plotius. (Quintilian 2.4.41–2)

Quintilian's narrative displaces onto Greece the same concerns with theatricality and loss of freedom expressed in the Roman narratives. Thus the birth of declamation is associated with the figure of Demetrius of Phalerum, an Athenian rhetorician with whom the Romans associated the beginning of the decline of Greek eloquence.[23] Demetrius was a key figure in the oligarchic government backed by the Macedonians and in 307 BCE was forced to flee to Egypt from Athens when Demetrius Poliorcetes restored democracy. Through the figure of Demetrius, therefore, declamation is associated not only with oratorical decline but also with loss of free speech. This cultural narrative focusing on declamation as a symptom of political decline is encapsulated in Tacitus' *Dialogus* in the figure of Messalla, who highlights the contrast between free orators such as Demosthenes and Aeschines and Greek *scholastici* such as Nicetes.[24]

To sum up, contrary to the standard perception (modern and ancient) of declamation as an Imperial phenomenon, rhetorical exercises had been practiced in Greece for centuries and were present in Rome from at least

---

[23] Quintilian 10.1.80 *Phalerea illum Demetrium, quamquam is primus inclinasse eloquentiam dicitur*, on which see Peterson (1981) 78; Cicero, *Brut.*37, 285; *De or.* 2.95; *Orat.* 91–2; *De off.* 1.3

[24] Tacitus, *Dial.* 15.1 *quia uideo etiam Graecis accidisse ut longius absit <ab> Aeschine et Demosthene Sacerdos ille Nicetes, et si quis alius Ephesum uel Mytilenas concentu scholasticorum et clamoribus quatit, quam Afer aut Africanus aut uos ipsi a Cicerone aut Asinio recessistis*. Nicetes is one of the Greek declaimers most criticized by Seneca: e.g. *Suas.* 3.6–7.

56 Seneca the Elder's *Controuersiae* and *Suasoriae*

the early first century BCE, not to mention the fact that Romans were exposed to declamation as part of their training in Greek letters. As we have seen, the cultural narrative that constructs the birth of declamation as contemporaneous with the death of Cicero develops in the Imperial period with writers such as Seneca, Quintilian, Tacitus and Suetonius but is firmly rooted in a deep-seated cultural prejudice against rhetoric that already informs Cicero's perspective on rhetorical education. According to this paradigm, declamation and rhetorical training are culturally inflected as Greek practices. Greek is constructed as the natural language for preparatory training, while Latin is privileged as the natural setting for "real-life" performance. Declamation can be practiced as a legitimate exercise but is no substitute for an active presence in the forum. Already in Cicero, declaimer and declamation are associated with political disfranchisement, old age and inaction and can be used as terms of abuse to denote that which is antithetical to the Roman orator's identity as a *uir bonus dicendi peritus*. This portrayal of declamatory practices is tendentious and culturally situated. Thus, as Michael Winterbottom has demonstrated, not only was Imperial declamation "a more realistic form of training than it is fashionable to think it" but Cicero's work already needs to be understood within the context of the schoolroom as Cicero himself was writing his speeches with an eye to how they would be read in the schools of rhetoric.[25]

Declamation as Poetic Discourse

Poetry and the poetic have an unusually important role in this moralistic discourse against rhetorical education. In attacking declamation as a movement away from and a perversion of traditional Roman oratory, Roman sources routinely blame declaimers for collapsing normative distinctions between oratory and poetry.[26] First, the idea that the decline of oratory was caused by declamation is ubiquitous in ancient sources. A key passage is the episode at the beginning of Petronius' *Satyricon* (1–5), in which Encolpius blames the shared decline of oratory, poetry and art on declaimers.

> Pace uestra liceat dixisse, primi omnium eloquentiam perdidistis. leuibus enim atque inanibus sonis ludibria quaedam excitando, effecistis ut corpus orationis eneruaretur et caderet. nondum iuuenes declamationibus continebantur, cum Sophocles aut Euripides inuenerunt uerba quibus deberent

---

[25] Winterbottom (1982) 68.   [26] See Berti (2007) 149–53 and Webb (1997) 349–50.

Declamation as Poetic Discourse

loqui. nondum umbraticus doctor ingenia deleuerat, cum Pindarus nouem-
que lyrici Homericis uersibus canere timuerunt. et ne poetas quidem ad
testimonium citem, certe neque Platona neque Demosthenen ad hoc genus
exercitationis accessisse uideo. grandis et, ut ita dicam, pudica oratio non est
maculosa nec turgida, sed naturali pulchritudine exsurgit. nuper uentosa
istaec et enormis loquacitas Athenas ex Asia commigrauit animosque
iuuenum ad magna surgentes ueluti pestilenti quodam sidere adflauit,
semelque corrupta regula eloquentia stetit et obmutuit. ad summam, quis
postea Thucydidis, quis Hyperidis ad famam processit? ac ne carmen
quidem sani coloris enituit, sed omnia quasi eodem cibo pasta non potuer-
unt usque ad senectutem canescere. pictura quoque non alium exitum fecit,
postquam Aegyptiorum audacia tam magnae artis compendiariam inuenit.

With your permission let me tell you that you [teachers] above anyone
have been the ruin of eloquence. By raising certain wantonness with
your lighthearted and empty sounds, you made it so that the body of
your speech was made effeminate and dies. Back when Sophocles or
Euripides found the words with which they ought to speak, young men
were not yet being confined to declamation. No idler of a professor had
yet ruined their brains when Pindar and the nine lyric poets were afraid
to sing Homer's lines. Not to cite the poets as evidence, I certainly do
not think that Plato or Demosthenes practiced this kind of exercise.
Great and, if I may say so, modest style, is never blotchy or bloated but
rather stands out by virtue of its natural beauty. Your flatulent and
bulky flow of words has emigrated just now from Asia to Athens and
like some destructive planet it poisoned the minds of ambitious young
men. Once corrupted, eloquence halted and grew dumb. In a word,
who after this rose to equal the glory of Thucydides or Hyperides? Even
poetry did not glow with a healthy complexion, but all artistic pursuits,
nourished on one and the same diet, lacked the vigour to last into old
age. The decadence in painting was no different, as soon as the boldness
of the Egyptians found a short way to this great art. (Petronius, *Sat.* 2,
trans. Heseltine)

Encolpius laments that, thanks to the declaimers (*pace uestra*), "an inflated
and bombastic garrulity from Asia" has infected the whole of *eloquentia*
including poetry, oratory and even art.[27] Encolpius, however, is hardly
a reliable character: despite his criticism of declamation, he admits that this
tirade is a declamatory performance (*Sat.* 3 *Non est passus Agamemnon me
diutius declamare in porticu*). Furthermore, his critique of Asianic influence is
full of outdated platitudes borrowed from Cicero's *Brutus* and is not
a genuine intellectual exchange but rather a ploy designed to attract the

---

[27] Kennedy (1978).

58   Seneca the Elder's *Controuersiae* and *Suasoriae*

attention of the rhetor Agamemnon.[28] Although Petronius' scene at the declamation school is clearly a parody of moralistic discourse on literary decline, it nevertheless highlights some important themes, not least the perceived connection between oratory and poetry and declamation's ability to corrupt both.

Moreover, in the ancient sources that discuss the decline of oratory, the deviance of declamation is repeatedly constructed as a dangerous approximation of the unnatural, ostentatious and pleasure-driven habits of poetry. Here, in defining declamation as a perversion of Roman oratory, critics invoke the normative opposition between poetic and rhetorical discourse found in rhetorical sources. For example, in the section on training under the rhetor in book 2 of the *Institutio Oratoria*, Quintilian defends declamation as a useful educational tool, especially if the subject matter can be brought to have some relevance to future practice in the forum.[29] Notwithstanding his positive approach, Quintilian recognizes that declamation is designed to draw attention to itself and to provide pleasure to the audience:

> si uero in ostentationem comparetur declamatio, sane paulum aliquid inclinare ad uoluptatem audientium debemus. nam et iis actionibus quae in aliqua sine dubio ueritate uersantur, sed sunt ad popularem aptatae delectationem, quales legimus panegyricos totumque hoc demonstratiuum genus, permittitur adhibere plus cultus, omnemque artem, quae latere plerumque in iudiciis debet, non confiteri modo sed ostentare etiam hominibus in hoc aduocatis. quare declamatio, quoniam est iudiciorum consiliorumque imago, similis esse debet ueritati, quoniam autem aliquid in se habet *epideiktikon*, nonnihil sibi nitoris adsumere.

> But if declamation is really for show, then we ought indeed to bend over somewhat to give the audience pleasure. For even in speeches which, though undoubtedly concerned with real events, are designed to entertain the people (such as Panegyrics which we read and the epideictic genre as a whole), it is permissible to introduce more ornament, and not only confess but actually display, before an audience assembled for this purpose, the art which in forensic oratory must generally be concealed. Thus declamation, inasmuch as it is the image of forensic and deliberative eloquence, must bear

---

[28] See Courtney (2001) 54–62 on Petronius' recasting of Cicero's language of decline in the *Brutus: Sat.* 3 *usque ad senectutem canescere – Brut.* 8 *ipsa oratio iam nostra canesceret haberetque suam quandam maturitatem et quasi senectutem.*

[29] See Winterbottom (1983) on Quintilian and declamation. In this way, Quintilian differs from the most extreme critics of declamation such as the orator Messala in Tacitus *Dialogus*. Quintilian's overall approach to oratorical decline was laid out in the now lost *De causis corruptae eloquentiae*, on which see Brink (1989).

Declamation as Poetic Discourse 59

a resemblance to real life; but inasmuch as it has an epideictic element, it must assume a degree of elegance. (Quintilian 2.10.10–13)

A key term in this moralistic critique is *ostentatio* or the idea that declamation, like poetry, is geared toward display and devoid of practical purpose. This critique harkens back to the notion that the *genus demonstratiuum* is closer to, and for some even includes, poetry and history.[30] Elsewhere Quintilian defines the epideictic genre as "the kind directed towards display [which] seeks only the pleasure of the audience" (8.3.11 *illud genus ostentationi compositum solam petit audientium uoluptatem*). As we hear in a later passage, poetry too is "a genre designed for display" (10.1.28 *genus ostentationi comparatum*). The pleasure of the audience (*audientum uoluptatem*), mentioned by Quintilian as the goal of every declaimer, is also often associated with poetry.[31] Thanks to these repeatedly found associations between declamation and the poetic, it is no surprise that, when he critiques declamation as a cause of literary decline, Quintilian stresses the poetic leanings of its practitioners. A singing intonation, appropriate to the stage or to revelers, is typical of the schools of declamation.[32] Excessive recourse to similes, which is a hallmark of poetry (cf. 8.3.73), is a fault of the declaimers.[33] The criticism of declamation as an unduly poetic form of discourse is reflected in contemporary complaints over the poetic coloring of modern oratory. In Tacitus' *Dialogus*, Aper complains that poetic ornamentation (20.5 *poeticus decor*) drawn from the likes of Virgil and Lucan is expected of today's *oratores*. The poeticisms to which he refers seem to be poetic citations and poetic vocabulary.[34] Aper here echoes Seneca the Younger's criticism of his contemporaries, who use nothing but splendid, resounding and poetic words and avoid nonmetaphorical daily words (*Ep.* 114.14 *utrumque diverso genere corruptum est, tam mehercules quam nolle nisi splendidis uti ac sonantibus et poeticis, necessaria atque in usu posita uitare*).[35]

---

[30] Cicero, *Orat.* 65–7; Hermogenes, *Id.* 2.10.231–80 and see Walker (2000) 302–10; Burgess (1902) 160–70.

[31] E.g. Quintilian 1.8.11 *poeticis uoluptatibus*; 8.6.17 *quod ea quae poetis, qui et omnia ad uoluptatem referunt*.

[32] Quintilian 11.3.57 *sed quodcumque ex his uitium magis tulerim quam, quo nunc maxime laboratur in causis omnibus scholasicis, cantandi, quod inutilius sit an foedius nescio. quid enim minus oratori conuenit quam modulatio scaenica et nonnumquam ebriorum aut comisantium licentiae similis?*

[33] Quintilian 8.3.76 *quod quidem genus a quibusdam declamatoria maxime licentia corruptum est: nam et falsis utuntur, nec illa iis quibus similia uideri uolunt adplicant.*

[34] On this passage, see Gudeman (1914) 338 *ad* 20.8, for whom *decor* refers not to citations but to the use of vocabulary; Norden (1898) 286–7. For a list of poetic vocabulary in Silver Latin prose, see Summers (1910) li–liv with the helpful correctives by Hine (2005).

[35] Bonner (1949) 74–5 argues that in this passage Seneca is criticizing declamatory style in imitation of his father. See also Leeman (1963) 313–14.

60 Seneca the Elder's *Controuersiae* and *Suasoriae*

Thus ancient critics repeatedly collapse declamation's ostentatious, performance-driven style, devoid of a practical function, with poetry written for art's sake. Being closer to epideictic than to the forensic or deliberative genres, declamation dangerously undermines the distinction between poetry, thought of as a vehicle for entertainment, and oratory, to which a political and practical purpose is traditionally assigned. The underlining connection between declamation and poetry is built into the etymology of the former:[36] the verb *declamare*, like the word *clamare* from which it derives, originally denoted a blustering or bawling vocal delivery appropriate to the stage. Indeed, the earliest occurrence of the word *declamatio* is in *Ad Herennium*, where it refers not to the rhetorical exercise but to the vocal exercise, in which reading out loud was to enhance vocal flexibility (3.20 *Mollitudinem uocis . . . maxime faciet exercitatio declamationis*). As Stanley Bonner has argued, "the early use of the term *declamatio* at Rome may have had a close connection with the stage."[37] It is well known that, in training the voice, orators were encouraged to imitate to some extent actors but, in the *De oratore*, Cicero chastises orators who "shout out" (*declamitant*) like tragic actors.[38] Although, as we have seen, *declamare* and *declamator* are sometimes used by Cicero in their technical sense as referring to the rhetorical exercise of declamation and to their practitioners, *declamo* is also used in the derogatory sense of a blustering rhetorical performance. So, in the *Verrines*, the shouting and ridiculously hysterical performance on Verres' behalf in front of the praetor of a Greek man nicknamed by the Syracusans "the God breaker" (Theoractus) is described as a form of *declamare*.[39] The man's foaming mouth, burning eyes and heightened voice combine to create an effective picture of a deranged performer (*Verr.* 2.4.148 *cum spumas ageret in ore, oculis arderet, uoce maxima uim me sibi adferre clamaret*). Although by the early Empire, the term *declamare* is almost exclusively restricted to the technical sense, these earlier semantic associations between declaiming and a ranting performance style appropriate to the performances of the theater always loom large, contributing to constructing declamation as an inherently theatrical, poetic and exasperated genre.

---

[36] Bonner (1949) 20–1, 28–31. [37] Bonner (1949) 21.

[38] Cicero, *De or.* 1.251 *quid est oratori tam necessarium quam uox? tamen me auctore nemo dicendi studiosus Graecorum more tragoedorum uoci seruiet, qui et annos compluris sedentes declamitant . . . hoc nos si facere uelimus, ante condemnentur ei, quorum causas receperimus, quam totiens, quotiens praescribitur, Paeanem aut hymnum recitarimus.* On the use of actors in training orators, see Quintilian 3.8.51; Macrobius, *Sat.* 3.14.12; and see further Fantham (2002).

[39] Cicero, *Verr.* 2.4.149 *ille autem insanus qui pro isto uehementissime contra me declamasset*). See further Cicero, *Rosc. Am.* 82; *Mur.* 44.

Poetry and Rhetoric: Fuscus and Latro

It is crucial to situate Seneca's presentation of Ovid as a student of rhetoric in the context of the role typically assigned to poetry in discussions of declamation and the decline of oratory. The first key passage regarding Ovid's rhetorical training comes in the second book of the *Controuersiae*. Before introducing Ovid's sample, Seneca presents the Augustan poet as a pupil of Fuscus and at the same time an admirer of Latro's *sententiae*:

> hanc controuersiam memini ab Ouidio Nasone declamari apud rhetorem Arellium Fuscum, cuius auditor fuit; nam[40] Latronis admirator erat, cum diuersum sequeretur dicendi genus. habebat ille comptum et decens et amabile ingenium. oratio eius iam tum nihil aliud poterat uideri quam solutum carmen. adeo autem studiose Latronem audit ut multas illius sententias in uersus suos transtulerit.

> I remember this controuersia being declaimed by Ovidius Naso at the school of the rhetor Arellius Fuscus – Ovid being his pupil. He was an admirer of Latro, though his style of speech was different. He had a neat, seemly and attractive talent. Even in those days his speech could be regarded as simply poetry put into prose. However, he was so keen a student of Latro that he transferred many epigrams of his to his own verse. (Seneca, *Controv.* 2.2.8)

To begin with, Seneca argues that even though he followed Fuscus' style, Ovid admired Latro to the point of imitating his *sententiae*, as, for example, in the Judgment of the Arms (*Met.* 13.121–2) and in the *Amores* (1.2.11–12). The choice of texts is highly significant: In the first instance, by borrowing from Latro, Ovid is implicitly acknowledging his indebtedness to the rhetorical sources that treat the episode of the Judgment of the Arms of Achilles.[41] In the second instance, the borrowing is parodic and shows how, while superficially an admirer of Latro's *sententia*, Ovid has fundamentally misunderstood its message – the topic of *Am.* 1.2. is the lover's inability to sleep due to *Amor*, a situation that reverses the Latronian original, which reads like an invective against a sloth.

Secondly, Arellius Fuscus and Porcius Latro, introduced here as Ovid's teacher and his secondary model respectively, function as an antithetical pair throughout Seneca's work. In book 10 of the *Controuersiae*, Seneca

---

[40] With Huelsenbeck I print *nam*, the reading of the transmitted text *pace* Fairweather (1981) 264–70, who sees a contradiction in the use of *nam* to link the sentence about Ovid's appreciation for Latro to the previous statement about Fuscus being his teacher. Huelsenbeck (2011) rightly argues in favor of the transmitted reading showing that *nam* is commonly used to highlight a contrast (as in this case) as opposed to an explanation.

[41] E.g. the *logoi* of Ajax and Odysseus by the fifth-century BCE sophist Antisthenes, on which see Russell (1983) 16–17.

singles out four declaimers as most eminent (*primum tetradeum*) – Latro, Arellius Fuscus, Albucius Silus and Junius Gallio (10.*Praef.*13). Three of the extant prefaces focus on professional declaimers and feature respectively Latro (book 1) and Albucius Silus (book 7), with the preface to book 10 referring to a number of figures, including the orator Aemilius Scaurus, the historian Titus Labienus and the Spanish advocates and declaimers Claudius Turrinus and Gavius Silo.[42] Moreover, the now-lost preface to the *Suasoriae* was probably dedicated to Arellius Fuscus, at least to judge from the frequency of his citation in the work and the relative scarcity of references to Latro, which contrasts with his overwhelming presence in the *Controuersiae*.[43] If so, the *Controuersiae* and *Suasoriae* opened with prefaces dedicated respectively to Seneca's hero (Latro) and to his antihero (Fuscus).

Already in the preface to book 1 of the *Controuersiae*, it is obvious that Porcius Latro functions as a projection and mirror image of Seneca, the author.[44] The two friends from childhood (1.*Praef.*13 *a prima pueritia usque ad ultimum eius diem perductam familiarem amicitiam*) were from Spain and had studied together under the rhetor Marullus (1.*Praef.*22 *cum condiscipuli essemus apud Marullum rhetorem*). The longest excerpt in the *Controuersiae* comes from Latro (2.7), whose *sententiae* are cited more often than those of any other declaimer.[45] As an acknowledgment of Latro's legacy, the preface to the last book of the *Controuersiae* ends with a complimentary reference to two Spanish orators who were also declaimers, Gavius Silo and Claudius Turrinus Senior. Another Spanish declaimer, Junius Gallio, cited by Seneca as most eminent together with Latro, Fuscus and Albucius, is the second most cited source after Latro.[46] In short, Seneca quite clearly promotes Latro and the rest of the Spanish school against the excesses of the rest of the declaimers. We occasionally hear complaints about Latro from other characters. Asinius Pollio thought that Latro betrayed himself (*deprehendi*) as a true schoolman nowhere more clearly than in his approach to

---

[42] On the Spanish school of Silo and Turrinus, see Mirmont (1910) 154–69.

[43] As demonstrated by Sussman (1977).   [44] Bloomer (1997a) 114–31.

[45] Sussman (1978) 58 n. 80; Bennett (2007) 7 shows that Latro is the most frequently and most extensively cited declaimer and concludes that "Latro emerges as Seneca's chief source of declamatory skill."

[46] On Gallio see *PIR* 4.757 and Bornecque (1902) 173–6. Gallio was a senator of Spanish origin (Statius, *Silv.* 2.7.30ff). He later adopted Seneca's eldest son (*Controv.* 10.*Praef.*16). Gallio was also a friend of Ovid (cf. Ovid, *Pont.* 4.11) and later fell out of favor with Tiberius (Tacitus, *Ann.* 6.3; Dio 58.18). On his style, see Tacitus, *Dial.* 26.1 (*tinnitus Gallionis*); Quintilian 9.2.91.

Poetry and Rhetoric: Fuscus and Latro

questions.[47] Montanus recalls an incident in which Latro supposedly went silent in court.[48] Yet, overall, Latro is clearly Seneca's top model.

The antithesis to Latro is the rhetor Arellius Fuscus. This antihero is introduced in the second book of the *Controuersiae*, where his style is first described.

> erat explicatio Fusci Arelli splendida quidem sed operosa et implicata, cultus nimis acquisitus, conpositio uerborum mollior quam ut illam tam sanctis fortibusque praeceptis praeparans se animus pati posset. summa inaequalitas orationis, quae modo exilis erat, modo nimia licentia uaga et effusa: principia, argumenta, narrationes aride dicebantur; in descriptionibus extra legem omnibus uerbis, dummodo niterent, permissa libertas. nihil acre, nihil solidum, nihil horridum: splendida oratio et magis lasciua quam laeta.

> Arellius Fuscus' developments were brilliant, but elaborate and involved, his ornament too contrived, his word arrangement more effeminate than could be tolerated by a mind in training for such chaste and rigorous precepts. His oratory was highly uneven, sometimes bare, sometimes because of its overfreedom wandering and discursive. Proems, arguments and narrations he spoke dryly, while in descriptions words were always granted a license that went beyond the rules – the only requirement was that they should shine. There was nothing sharp, hard or jagged. The style was brilliant, wanton rather than luxuriant. (Seneca, *Controv.* 2.*Praef.*1)

Unsurprisingly, Seneca's description of Fuscus' style is negatively inflected as "poetic."[49] Fuscus' *licentia* (cf. *extra legem . . . libertas*) echoes the notion of *poetica licentia*, the power generally granted to poets to depart from the rules of natural language. The splendor of his style (*splendida oratio*) echoes Quintilian's definition of the shining stylistic weapons of the poet (10.1). Latro's and Fuscus' styles are paired against one another using dichotomies that are traditionally found in discussions of the difference between the ornamental excesses of poetry and the appropriately restrained language of prose. Whereas Latro set out in neat order the points at issue in the *controuersia* he was about to declaim (*Controv.* 1.*Praef.*21), Fuscus wandered (*licentia uaga et effusa*). Whereas Latro's taste was restrained (*iudicium . . . strictius*) and his use of figurative language modest (*schema*

---

[47] Seneca, *Controv.* 2.3.13 *Pollio Asinius aiebat hoc Latronem uideri tamquam forensem facere, ut ineptas quaestiones circumcideret, sed in nulla magis filium re scholasticum deprehendi.*

[48] Seneca, *Controv.* 9.*Praef.*3 and see Quintilian 10.5.17–18

[49] Huelsenbeck (2018) 161–2 notes that the disparaging descriptions of Fuscus' style as poetic is also found in discussions of Asianism: e.g. Cicero, *Orat.* 230 *sunt etiam qui illo uitio, quod ab Hegesia maxume fluxit, infringendis concidendisque numeris in quoddam genus abiectum incidant uersiculorum simillimum.*

64 Seneca the Elder's *Controuersiae* and *Suasoriae*

negabat decoris causa inuentum), Fuscus' was ornate and luxuriant (*operosa et implicata*). Moreover, Seneca's complaint about Fuscus' excessively elaborate descriptions is also a traditional topic in denunciations of the over-poetic leanings of declaimers: *descriptiones* are especially considered a feature of poetry and history and Ps. Dionysius *Rhetoric* associates the penchant for descriptions in declamations with the undue influence of poetic models.[50]

Above all, Latro and Fuscus are *culturally* antithetical. Fuscus, we are told, declaimed in Greek as well as in Latin, incorporated Homeric lines into his declamations (*Suas.* 4.5) and imitated Greek declaimers such as Adaeus (9.1.13) and Hybreas (9.6.16). Whether Fuscus was born in Greece or Asia Minor is less clear: in a textually corrupt passage from book 9 of the *Controuersiae*, Seneca comments on Fuscus' translation of a Greek sententia by Hybreas stating that "it was not by chance (*casu*) that Arellius Fuscus spoke this epigram, for he was from Asia – but he translated it word for word" (*Controv.9.6.16 hanc sententiam Fuscus Arellius, cum esset ex Asia, non casu dixit, sed transtulit ad uerbum quidem*). While editors typically emend *ex Asia* ("being from Asia") to *ex Asianis* ("being one of the Asianists") in an effort to make better sense of the Latin, it is assumed that given his penchant for Greek declamation and his Asianism, Fuscus must have been Greek.[51] Since the label Asianist is clearly a tool of stylistic disparagement rather than an ethnic or aesthetic descriptor, the evidence is inconclusive.[52] Yet Fuscus' Hellenism is a mark not necessarily of his national origin but of his cultural identity as a connoisseur of Greek culture and a practitioner of the originally Greek genre of declamation. By contrast, while Latro was born in Spain, he is presented as the quintessential old-fashioned Roman among other things in that he "both despised the

---

[50] Cf. Pliny the Younger, *Ep.* 2.5.6 *nam descriptiones locorum, quae in hoc libro frequentiores erunt, non historice tantum sed prope poetice prosequi fas est*; Ps. Dionysius, *Ars Rhet.* 10.17 Radermacher εἰσερρύη δὲ τοῦτο τὸ ἁμάρτημα ἐν ταῖς μελέταις κατὰ ζῆλον τῆς ἱστορίας καὶ τῶν ποιημάτων. ἀγνοοῦμεν γὰρ ὡς ἔοικεν, ὅτι ἱστορία μὲν πεζῇ καὶ ποίησις γραφικὰς τὰς ὄψεις τῶν ἀναγκαίων τοῖς ἀκούουσιν παράγουσιν, ἀγὼν δὲ δικανικὸς μεμέτρηται πρὸς τὴν χρείαν. καὶ οἱ μὲν ποιηταὶ καὶ ἱστορικοὶ τὰ συμβεβηκότα τόποις τισὶ καὶ προσώποις ἐκτυποῦσιν, ὡς ἐγένετο.

[51] Fairweather (1981) 245–6; Berti (2007) 205 n. 1; Bornecque (1902) 150. Fuscus' name is not a giveaway as to his origin: *RE* ii 635–6 under Arellius. However, an inscription in Pompey from 34 CE speaks of an A. Arellius Graecus (*CIL* X.901) and see *PIR*2 A 1030 and 1031 on Fuscus' son mentioned by Pliny the Elder as being removed from the equestrian order (*HN* 33.152). We have no evidence that the painter Arellius, also mentioned by Pliny (*HN* 35.119) and the rich landowner of the same name mentioned by Horace (*Sat.* 2.6.78) were Greek.

[52] I agree with Huelsenbeck (2018) 159–65 that *pace* Norden (1898) and Fairweather (1981) 296–303 Asianism is a term of abuse, not a self-chosen label by the followers of Fuscus or the New Style. On the use of Asianism as a term of abuse, see Richlin (1997); Leeman (1963) 136–67.

Greeks and was ignorant of them" (*Controv.* 10.4.21 *Graecos enim et contemnebat et ignorabat*).

Following Tim Whitmarsh, we may approach Fuscus' "Greekness" and Latro's "Romanness" not as geopolitical descriptors but as markers of cultural and social values that function as "hypostatizations of Greece and Rome":[53] Latro's identity as a Spaniard is presented in ways that echo traditional Roman virtues, while Fuscus' character suffers from the faults typically associated with those from the East.[54] Thus, whereas Latro' Spanish rusticity and fortitude (*illum fortem et agrestem et Hispanae consuetudinis morem*) closely resemble the values of early Romans unadulterated by Greek culture, Fuscus is predictably described as effeminate (*mollior*), a fault typically associated with the negative influence of Greek culture.[55]

Moreover, Seneca exploits this dichotomy in constructing Latro's disinterest in public performance as "Roman" in opposition to Fuscus' corrupt and therefore "un-Roman" presence in the declamation halls. As is well known, Seneca is critical of declaimers who perform in public, showing a marked preference for those orators, like Asinius Pollio or Labienus, who declaimed in private or to a small audience.[56] By contrast, bad declaimers are always associated with public delivery.[57] Unsurprisingly, we learn that Latro declaimed in front of a selective audience (*Controv.* 2.4.12 Augustus and Agrippa; 2.4.8 Messalla) but never at dinner (10.*Praef.*15). Latro, we are told, "would never hear anyone declaim – he merely declaimed himself, saying he was a model, not a schoolteacher" (9.2.23 *neque enim illi mos erat quemquam audire declamantem; declamabat ipse tantum et aiebat se non esse magistrum sed exemplum*). Elsewhere in Seneca the Elder, the label *scholasticus* is always a dubious distinction, especially as opposed to a full-time public orator: according to Seneca, the orator Votienus Montanus, in whose mouth Seneca places one of the most scathing denunciations of declamation,

---

[53] Whitmarsh (2001) 21 and see further the important remarks on "Hellenization" in Wallace-Hadrill (1998), esp. 91 on "Greek" and "Roman" as "alternative *languages* [emphasis my own] in conscious juxtaposition with one another."

[54] On the construction of Roman identity in the Annaei, see the helpful analysis of Degl'Innocenti Pierini (2003).

[55] On the representation of the Spanish natives see Woolf (2011) esp. 24–31; Mirmont (1910) 341–52. On the link between Greekness and *mollitia*, see Edwards (1993) 63–97. On Fuscus' *mollitia*, see further Seneca, *Suas.* 2.23 *nimius cultus et fracta compositio*.

[56] Seneca, *Controv.* 4.*Praef.*2 *Pollio numquam admissa multitudine declamauit*; *Contr.* 10.*Praef.*4 *declamauit non quidem populo sed egregie*.

[57] E.g. Alfius Flavus *Controv.*1.1.22; Haterius 4.*Praef.*7; Albucius Silus 7.*Praef.*1.

66   Seneca the Elder's *Controuersiae* and *Suasoriae*

was so utterly a *scholasticus* that he enjoyed Vinicius' speech against him, scathing as it was, and quoted some of its witty epigrams.[58] Seneca's criticism is especially strong in his portrayal of Albucius Silus who divided his time between teaching and public oratory and who was "afraid of being thought a schoolman" (7.*Praef*.4 *timebat ne scholasticus uideretur … Albucius enim non quomodo non esset scholasticus quaerebat, sed quomodo non uideretur*).

In Seneca's text, declamation is tendentiously constructed around the traditional Roman practice of the *tirocinium fori*, in which a young man would follow a prominent orator in his daily work in the forum or Senate in preparation for public life.[59] This model of "nonperformative" declamation, which Seneca seeks to advance, is essentially a contradiction in terms. For, just as is the case with all forms of epideictic, in which "the object of evaluation is not the juridical or legislative issue (which constitutes the subject of the speech) but the speech itself," declamation is intrinsically tied to the notion of display.[60] By decoupling Latronian declamation from performance and inflecting the latter as corrupt and un-Roman, Seneca seeks to make rhetorical training more palatable to his Roman audience.

Seneca's presentation of Ovid in *Controv.* 2.2 as a student of Fuscus and an admirer of Latro must be understood in light not only of the role in which poetry and the poetic are traditionally found in discussions of the decline of oratory but also of Seneca's effort to promote Latronian rhetoric at the expense of Fuscus' Asianic style. Seneca's critique of Ovid's style in the section that follows the excerpt is clearly reminiscent both of his account of the excesses of the school of Fuscus and of the traditional construction of poetic language in rhetorical sources:

> declamabat autem Naso raro controuersias et non nisi ethicas. libentius dicebat suasorias. molesta illi erat omnis argumentatio. uerbis minime licenter usus est, nisi in carminibus, in quibus non ignorauit uitia sua sed amauit. manifestum potest esse, quod rogatus aliquando ab amicis suis, ut tolleret tres uersus, inuicem petit, ut ipse tres exciperet, in quos nihil illis liceret. aequa lex uisa est: scripserunt illi quos tolli uellent secreto, hic quos tutos esse uellet. in utrisque codicillis idem uersus erant, ex quibus primum fuisse narrabat Albinouanus Pedo, qui inter arbitros fuit:

---

[58] *Controv.* 7.5.12 *at Montanus adeo toto animo scholasticus era tut eodem die quo accusatus est a Vinicio diceret: 'delectauit me Vinici actio', et sententias eius referebat.*

[59] On the *tirocinium fori*, see Cicero, *Amic.* 1 (Scaeuola); Pliny, *Ep.* 2.14.10; Quintilian 10.5.19; Tacitus, *Dial.* 2.1 and 20.4.

[60] Lausberg (1998) 103.

Poetry and Rhetoric: Fuscus and Latro

semibouemque uirum semiuirumque bouem;

secundum:

et gelidum Borean egelidumque Notum.

ex quo apparet summi ingenii uiro non iudicium defuisse ad compescendam licentiam carminum suorum sed animum. aiebat interim decentiorem faciem esse, in qua aliquis naeuos esset.

However, Ovid rarely declaimed *controuersiae,* and only ones involving portrayal of character. He preferred *suasoriae,* finding all argumentation tiresome. He used language by no means over-freely except in his poetry, where he was well aware of his faults – and enjoyed them. What can make this clear is that once, when he was asked by his friends to suppress three of his lines, he asked in return to be allowed to make an exception of three over which they should have no rights. This seemed a fair condition. They wrote in private the lines they wanted removed, while he wrote the ones he wanted saved. The sheets of both contained the same verses. Albinovanus Pedo, who was among those present, tells that the first of them was:

"Half-bull man and half-man bull"

the second

"Freezing north wind and de-freezing south"

It is clear from this that the great man lacked not the judgment but the will to restrain the licence of his poetry. He used sometimes to say that a face is the more beautiful for some mole. (Seneca, *Controv.* 2.2.12)

First, Ovid's preference for the deliberative exercise of the *suasoria* matches Arellius Fuscus', who, as argued before, in all likelihood was the subject of the now-lost preface to the *Suasoriae.*[61] Such preference, as Seneca tells us, is due to the possibilities for poetic development that *suasoriae* provide and that are not present in *controuersiae*, in which reasoning (*argumentatio*) is instead paramount. This opposition between *suasoriae* and *controuersiae* based on the need for rationality and self-restraint is carried over in the contrast between poetry, in which Ovid's *licentia* is rife, and declamation, in which he showed more self-restraint (*minime licenter*). Seneca is here exploiting the traditional presentation of poetic language as licentious and an unabashed departure from the norms of everyday speaking.[62] The phrase *solutum carmen*, which characterizes Ovid's style (*oratio*), expresses the paradox of

---

[61] *Suas.* 4.5 *dicebat autem suasorias libentissime et frequentius Graecas quam Latinas.*

[62] On the *licentia* of poets, see Cicero, *De or.* 1.70; *Orat.* 68; Horace, *Ars P.* 9–10; Quintilian 2.4.3; 4.1.58 and see Lausberg (1998) 983 and further chap. 2.

68   Seneca the Elder's *Controuersiae* and *Suasoriae*

Ovid's "poetic" prose style: since the phrase *oratio soluta* is used to denote prose rhythm (*oratorius numerus*) as opposed to poetry, which is constrained by meter (e.g. Cicero, *De or.* 1.70 *numeris astrictior paulo*), the looseness (*solutum*) of Ovid's *oratio* can be read as referring to its freedom from metrical constrictions.[63] In describing Ovid's *oratio* as *solutum carmen*, Seneca echoes Ovid's own characterization in *Tr.* 4.10 of his attempts to practice "words free from rhythm" (*uerba soluta modis*) – that is, oratory – in his early youth when "all that [he] attempted to write came out as verse" (*quod temptabam scribere uersus erat*).[64] However, just as with the English translation, "looseness" can also be inflected negatively, both as a moral quality, referring to a slack, careless and weak personality, and as a trait of a disjointed, broken style.[65] Here, the looseness of Ovid's *oratio* is simultaneously a sign of its unmetrical character and of its self-indulgence.

Moreover, Seneca applies this moralistic discourse on poetic *licentia* to Ovid as well as to the other declaimers to whose style he objects. A case in point is represented by the sensational boy declaimer Alfius Flavus, whose natural talent "after many years, overwhelmed by idleness and weakened by indulgence in poetry, still retained its vigor" (*Controv.* 1.1.22 *naturalis tamen illa uis eminebat, quae post multos annos iam et desidia obruta et carminibus eneruata uigorem tamen suum tenuit*). Not only is poetry depicted as an emasculating force but we find out in a later passage that Alfius had a predilection for Ovidian elegy, which elicited the condemnation even of Cestius.[66] Similarly, in *Controv.* 9.5.17, Montanus, the orator who is really a *scholasticus* at heart, is negatively labeled "an Ovid among orators" (*inter oratores Ouidium*) by Scaurus in that neither Ovid nor Montanus could leave well enough alone (*nescit quod bene cessit relinquere*). Ovid's indulgence for his own vices (*non ignorauit uitia sua sed amauit*), incapsulated in the idea that a mole makes a face more attractive, is repeatedly directed at the declaimers whom Seneca labels as "decadent" and becomes a standard in Quintilian's representation of Ovidian style.[67]

---

[63] See *OLD* 9 and Lausberg (1998) 981. Cicero, *De or.* 3.184 already constructs the *oratio soluta* of Roman oratory moralistically as judicious freedom as opposed to unfettered *licentia: liberior est oratio* [sc. than poetry] *et plane, ut dicitur, sic est uere soluta, non ut fugiat aut erret, sed ut sine uinculis sibi ipsa moderetur.*

[64] Ovid, *Tr.* 4.10.23–6 *motus eram dictis, totoque Helicone relicto | scribere temptabam uerba soluta modis. | sponte sua carmen numeros ueniebat ad aptos, | et quod temptabam scribere uersus erat.*

[65] For *solutus* as morally slack see: *OLD* 6; Cicero, *Brut.* 225; Tacitus, *Dial.* 18.5; of style: Seneca, *Controv.* 9.*Praef.*5; Quintilian 8.5.27.

[66] *Controv.* 3.7.1 *Alfius Flauius hanc sententiam dixit: ipse sui et alimentum erat et damnum. hunc Cestius, quasi corrupte dixisset, obiurgans 'apparet' inquit 'te poetas studiose legere: iste sensus eius est, qui hoc saeculum amatoriis non artibus tantum sed sententiis impleuit.' Ouidius enim (in) libris metamorphoseon dicit* [Ovid, *Met.* 8.877–8.888]: *ipse suos artus lacero diuellere morsu | coepit et infelix minuendo corpus alebat.*

[67] Cestius: *Controv.* 9.6.11–12 *tantus autem error est in omnibus quidem studiis, maxime in eloquentia, cuius regula incerta est, ut uitia quidam sua et intellegant et ament* and *Suas.* 7.12 *nullius ingenii nisi sui*

Poetry and Rhetoric: Fuscus and Latro

In view of Seneca's disparaging treatment of Ovid's poetic self-indulgence, Latro's role in this passage as a model for the Augustan poet may come as a surprise. Nevertheless, it is important to note that Seneca's presentation of Latro highlights his exceptional status as the only declaimer who did not imitate poets but was rather imitated by them. As we have already seen, Latro presents himself self-consciously as an *exemplum* rather than a *magister* (*Controv.* 9.2.23) and is said to have been above suspicion when it came to the plagiarizing of Greek models (*Controv.* 10.4.21). In line with his presentation of Latro as a leader rather than a follower, Seneca stresses that it was the poets who held up Latro as a model. A key passage is *Suas.* 2.20, in which Seneca discusses the borrowing by two poets of the phrase *belli mora* coined by Latro:

> Postea memini auditorem Latronis Abronium Silonem, patrem huius Silonis qui pantomimis fabulas scripsit et ingenium grande non tantum deseruit sed polluit, recitare carmen in quo agnouimus sensum Latronis in his uersibus:
> > ite agite, <o> Danai, magnum paeana canentes
> > ite triumphantes: belli mora concidit Hector.
>
> tam diligentes tunc auditores erant, ne dicam tam maligni, ut unum uerbum surripi non posset; at nunc cuilibet orationes in Verrem tuto licet pro suis <dicere>. sed, ut sciatis sensum bene dictum dici tamen posse melius, notate prae ceteris quanto decentius Vergilius dixerit hoc quod ualde erat celebre, "belli mora concidit Hector":
> > quidquid ad aduersae cessatum est moenia Troiae
> > Hectoris Aeneaeque manu uictoria Graium
> > haesit.
>
> Messalla aiebat hic Vergilium debuisse desinere; quod sequitur
> > et in decimum uestigia rettulit annum
>
> explementum esse; Maecenas hoc etiam priori conparabat.

> Later I recall that Latro's pupil Abronius Silo, father of the Silo who wrote mime plays, thus profaning as well as neglecting his distinguished talents, recited a poem in which we recognized Latro's idea in the lines:
> > "Go forward, Greeks, singing a great paean; go in triumph. Hector, brake on war, has fallen."
>
> So assiduous (not to say carping) were audiences in those days that not even a single word could be plagiarized. Nowadays anyone can pass off the

---

amator; Albucius: Seneca *Controv. 7.Praef.4 et hoc aequale omnium est, ut uitia sua excusare malint quam effugere.* See further Berti (2007) 209–12. As Gibson (2003) 216 on Ovid, *Ars am.* 3.295 notes, the "paradoxical charm of *uitia*" is a topos of Ovidian poetry: cf. Ovid, *Am.* 3.1.10; *Fast.* 3.495 and also Cicero, *Nat. D.* 1.79. Quintilian calls Ovid *nimium amator ingenii suii* in 10.1.88; see also 10.1.98 on the *Medea* and 10.1.130 on Seneca. For Seneca, see *Ep.* 114.11 *sunt qui non usque ad uitium accedant ... sed qui ipsum uitium ament.*

Verrines for his own without being detected. But, to let you see how a well-expressed idea can all the same find a better expression, notice particularly how much more fittingly Virgil put this popular phrase: "Hector, brake on war, has fallen":

"Whatever pause there was by the walls of hostile Troy, it was by Hector's hand and Aeneas' that victory was stayed for the Greeks."

Messalla used to say that Virgil should have stopped there, and that what follows "and retreated from them till the tenth year" is merely a stopgap. Maecenas thought this as good as what goes before. (Seneca, *Suas.* 2.19–20)

Seneca offers two examples of reuses of one of Latro's phrases, "the brake of war" (*belli mora*). The first, involving a degenerate poet, is negative; the second, involving Virgil, is positive, but only measuredly so, especially if we assume that the comparison that Virgil has surpassed (*dici melius*) is Abronius Silo, not necessarily Latro himself.

Seneca's pronouncements on literary imitation are often read in a vacuum, as statements of literary theory and a manifesto for creative imitation. Yet Seneca's commendation for the creative emulation practices of Ovid and Virgil deserves to be explored as part and parcel of his overarching cultural goals. His praise for the two poets goes hand in hand with his condemnation of the imitative practices of declaimers such as Blandus, Sparsus, Cestius and Arellius Fuscus, who are chastised for their lack of originality in relation to Greek models. One of Seneca's most extensive meditations on plagiarism and originality occurs in the last book of the *Controuersiae*.[68] The theme of imitation is introduced in the preface to *Controv.* 10, in which Seneca disparages Sparsus' practice of imitating the ideas of Latro (10.*Praef.*11 *ad imitationem se Latronis derexerat, nec tamen umquam similis illi erat, nisi cum eadem diceret. utebatur sui uerbis, Latronis sententiis*). The fourth and fifth *Controuersiae* in book 10 contain extensive quotations from Greek rhetors and discussions of their adaptations by their Roman counterparts:[69] the Romans did not borrow but rather imitated the work of Greek declaimers (*Controv.* 10. 4.20 *hunc sensum quidam Latini dixerunt, sed sic ut putem illos non mutuatos esse hanc sententiam sed imitatos*); Latro represents the only positive exception, being above suspicion because of his ignorance of the Greeks' work (*Controv.*10.4.21 *hanc sententiam Latro Porcius uirilius dixit, qui non potest de furto suspectus esse*); Triarius stole from Greek declaimers (*Controv.* 10.5.20 *Triarius hoc ex aliqua parte, cum subriperet, inflexit*), and was in

---

[68] See McGill (2013) 146–77.

[69] This section is to be read closely in relation to *Controv.* 9.1.13–14 on Thucydidean *imitatio* in Sallust and Livy.

Poetry and Rhetoric: Fuscus and Latro

turn plagiarized by them (*Controv.* 10.5.21 *sed et Graeci illam subrupuerunt*); Cassius Severus used to say that people who behaved like Triarius were like thieves who changed the handle on other people's cups (*Controv.* 10.5.20 *similes sibi uideri furibus alienis poculis ansas mutantibus*). The section on the stealing of mottos by Greek and Latin declaimers in *Controv.* 10.5 is couched in the context of a case that involves the painter Parrhasius' faithful depiction of Prometheus, who became a benefactor of mankind after stealing fire from Zeus.[70] The final case of the *Controuersiae*, which we possess in excerpted form, is the only extant declamation theme in Seneca to focus on thievery. The case involves a man who accused another man of treason and proved his accusation by breaking into the latter's house and stealing letters from the enemy. The question for the performer is whether the man is guilty of theft (*furtum*) and whether the traitor can therefore sue him for damages. When Seneca rehearses the declaimers' approach to the questions such as whether property can be stolen if the owner is afraid to recognize it as his own (*Controv.* 10.6.1 *furtum est quod timet dominus agnosceret?*) or whether one can steal property that the owner denies is his (*furtum uocas quod qui perdiderat negabat suum?*), it is impossible not to read these statements as self-conscious references to the problem of originality in declamation that has been otherwise central to Seneca's work.

As these readings suggest, Seneca's comments on imitation are not unexpected when we consider that declamation is essentially characterized by endless reworkings of traditional *loci* and that plagiarism itself is often thematically at the center of these rhetorical exercises. In line with Seneca's stern condemnation of declamation as it was practiced by the Greeks, however, the declaimers' emulation is constantly portrayed in negative terms, as a sign and symptom of degeneration.[71] By contrast, Latro's status as a model for poets such as Virgil and Ovid clearly stands out as a sign of his prestige: that Virgil and Ovid borrowed from Latro is a sensationally unique event in Seneca's work, in which it is typically declaimers, and degenerate ones at that, who take from poets.

Not surprisingly, several anecdotes about imitation, all of them negative, focus on Arellius Fuscus who is otherwise known for his poetic style.[72] In *Suas.* 3.4, Seneca relates that Fuscus produced a second-rate imitation of Virgil's description of the moon rising in *G.* 1.427–33. Fuscus, however,

---

[70] The *controuersia* ends with a reference to the theft: *Controv.* 10.5.28. On the case in general, see Morales (1996).

[71] See Bloomer (1997a) 142–53 who notes (148) that "the thief is always a social inferior, predominantly a Greek and a freedman."

[72] On the traffic between Fuscus and Virgil, see Huelsenbeck (2011).

72   Seneca the Elder's *Controuersiae* and *Suasoriae*

had an ulterior motivation for taking from Virgil, Seneca adds, namely to please Maecenas (*Suas.* 3.5 *solebat autem Fuscus ex Virgilio multa trahere, ut Maecenati imputaret*). Furthermore, Fuscus' failed imitation of Virgil is contrasted with Ovid's creative borrowing in his *Medea* of the phrase *plena deo* not with the intention of stealing (*subripere*) but to borrow openly (*palam mutuandi*) with a desire for the borrowing to be recognized (*agnosci*).[73]

This passage is clearly connected both thematically and structurally to the one above from the preceding *Suasoria*, since a comparison of two poets' (Abronius Silo and Virgil) adaptations of a declaimer's (Latro) *sententia* in *Suas.* 2 is followed by discussion of the use by two declaimers (Fuscus and Gallio) and a poet (Ovid) of a line of the *Aeneid* in *Suas.* 3.[74] While in *Suas.* 2 Virgil is seen to best represent this idea of competitive engagement, in *Suas.* 3 the idea of open recognition is associated with Ovid. Fuscus continues to be associated with negative uses of poetic citations in the next *Suasoria*, in which it is said that he once cited a line from *Aen.* 4 (4.379–80) and later corrected one of his pupils who misused it in the *suasoria* on Alexander the Great, whereupon Fuscus pointed to another Virgilian line (*Aen.* 2.553) better suited to the context.

Probably like Fuscus, the other declaimer who is caught imitating poets is Greek: Cestius, who imitates not only Homer (*Controv.* 7.7.19) but also the Greek declaimer Damas (*Controv.* 10.4.21), is mocked by Seneca for his failure to live up to a Virgilian original:

> soleo dicere uobis Cestium Latinorum uerborum inopia <ut> hominem Graecum laborasse, sensibus abundasse; itaque, quotiens latius aliquid describere ausus est, totiens substitit, utique cum se ad imitationem magni alicuius ingeni derexerat, sicut in hac controuersia fecit. nam in narratione, cum fratrem traditum sibi describeret, placuit sibi in hac explicatione una et infelici: nox erat concubia, et omnia, iudices, canentia sub sideribus muta erant. Montanus Iulius, qui comes fuit <Tiberii>, egregius poeta, aiebat illum imitari uoluisse Vergili descriptionem:
>> nox erat et terras animalia fessa per omnis,
>> alituum pecudumque genus, sopor altus habebat.
> at Vergilio imitationem bene cessisse, qui illos optimos uersus Varronis expressisset in melius:
>> desierant latrare canes urbesque silebant;

---

[73] On the authorship and potential meaning of this phrase, which is not found in the Virgilian manuscript tradition, see Berti (2007) 282–90. I have discussed at length the discourse of "creative imitation" in this passage and elsewhere in Roman culture in Peirano (2013) on which this section is partially based.

[74] On this important passage, see McGill (2013) 167–73.

> omnia noctis erant placida composta quiete.
>
> solebat Ouidius de his uersibus dicere potuisse fieri longe meliores si secondi uersus ultima pars abscideretur et sic desineret:
>
> omnia noctis erant.
>
> Varro quem uoluit sensum optime explicuit, Ouidius in illius uersu suum sensum inuenit; aliud enim intercisus uersus significaturus est, aliud totus significat.

> I often tell you that Cestius, being a Greek, was handicapped by a lack of Latin words, while overflowing with ideas. And so, whenever he ventured on some more extravagant sweep of description, he would get stuck, especially when he had set himself to imitate some great genius. This is what happened in our present *controuersia*. In his narration, when he was describing how his brother was handed over to him, he was satisfied with this one unhappy vignette: "It was dead of night, and all singing things, judges, were silent beneath the stars." Julius Montanus, who was a friend of Tiberius and an outstanding poet, said that Cestius had intended to imitate Virgil's description:
>
> "It was night, and over all the earth tired creatures, birds and beasts, were held in deep sleep"
>
> Virgil, however, had (according to Montanus) been fortunate in his imitation, for he had rendered for the better those excellent lines of Varro:
>
> "Dogs had ceased to bark, the cities were still, everything was settled in the quiet calm of the night"
>
> Ovid used to say of these verses that they could have been much better if the last part of the second line were cut out and it finished thus:
>
> "Everything was of night"
>
> Varro developed the idea he wanted excellently, while Ovid found in Varro's verse an idea of his own. The abbreviated line will mean something different from the complete one. (Seneca, *Controv.* 7.1.27)

While Fuscus imitates Virgil to seek favor with Maecenas, Seneca ascribes Cestius' shameless borrowing to ignorance of the Latin language. Moreover, as in the cases of Virgil's adaptation of Varro (*Controv.* 7.1) and Ovid's creative imitation of the phrase *plena deo* (*Suas.* 3), Cestius' failed *imitatio* is contrasted with Virgil's improvement on Varro and Ovid's improvement on Virgil's take.

As we have seen, Seneca's approach to the poetic cannot be divorced from the use of this category in the tradition of moralistic critique of declamation as "poetically infected" discourse. In this reading, the poetic is a tool of abuse directed at corrupt rhetorical discourse, and Ovidian poetry is not so much a victim of rhetorical influence but rather a larger symptom of a dangerous collapsing of a series of culturally normative boundaries, including those between poetry and rhetoric, between

74 Seneca the Elder's *Controuersiae* and *Suasoriae*

epideictic and real life and between Greek and Roman. On the other hand, Seneca's account of the Augustan literary scene is subservient to his own goal of promoting Latronian rhetoric as an alternative to the degeneration that he is criticizing. As Seneca distances his Latronian model of rhetorical discourse from what he constructs as the moral and stylistic excesses of the poetic, he can evoke Roman poets as positive counterexamples to the slavish repetitious practice of the declaimers, as in the case of Ovid and Virgil in the *Suasoriae* examined in this section. In other words, when Ovid and Virgil are said to follow and imitate Porcius Latro, who is otherwise known to imitate no one, their literary and social prestige is employed in the service of Seneca's cultural agenda.

The *Controuersiae* as a Defense of Rhetorical Instruction

According to Seneca, declamation had only recently been accepted as an occupation worthy of an upper-class Roman.[75] Thus Rubellius Blandus, Papirius Fabianus' teacher, was the first Roman of equestrian rank to teach in Rome:

> habuit et Blandum rhetorem praeceptorem, qui <primus> eques Romanus Romae docuit; ante illum intra libertinos praeceptores pulcherrimae disciplinae continebantur, et minime probabili more turpe erat docere quod honestum erat discere.

> He also had the rhetorician Blandus for his teacher, the first Roman knight to teach in Rome. Before his time, the teaching of the most noble of subjects was restricted to freedmen and by quite an unsatisfactory custom it was accounted disgraceful to teach what it was honorable to learn. (Seneca, *Controv.* 2.*Praef.*5).

In presenting Blandus as a social exception, Seneca adopts Cicero's presentation in a crucial passage of the *Orator* of the hypocrisy of those who despised teachers of rhetoric while praising the value of what they taught.[76] Blandus, who was working in the early Augustan period, was from Tibur and evidently came from a prominent family since one of his sons would later marry Drusus' daughter Julia (Tacitus, *Ann.*

---

[75] There is no comprehensive study of the social status of rhetors in the early Empire equivalent to Kaster's work on the grammarians of late antiquity – see esp. Kaster (1988) 99–138 – but see McNelis (2007); Rawson (1985) 143–55; Griffin (1972); and Treggiari (1969) 117–19. Jullien (1885) 155–98 and Christes (1979) focus almost exclusively on *grammatici* who, however, initially also taught rhetoric.

[76] Cicero, *Orat.* 145 *num igitur aut latere eloquentia potest aut id quod dissimulat effugit aut est periculum ne quis putet in magna arte et gloriosa turpe esse docere alios id quod ipsi fuerit honestissimum discere?* On this passage and Cicero's defense of rhetorical education, see Dugan (2005) 259–61.

The Controuersiae *as a Defense of Rhetorical Instruction* 75

6.27).[77] It is instructive that, for Tacitus, the school constitutes a "humble beginning" (*obscura initia*) for a praetor, as he puts it in his description of the ascent to senator of the corrupt rhetor Iunius Otho under the auspices of Sejanus.[78] Pliny the Younger clearly thought of professional declamation as unsuited to a proper Roman: in *Ep.* 4.11, he mocks Valerius Licinianus who, once a prominent senator and advocate, is reduced to teaching rhetoric in Sicily.[79]

In his work, Seneca mentions 120 declaimers by name. Among these men, only a few are explicitly said to have their own schools in contrast to nonprofessional eminent Romans such as Votienus Montanus, Asinius Pollio, Titus Labienus, Haterius and Messalla, all of whom attended and practiced declamations only occasionally but were otherwise active as politicians and advocates. As expressed memorably by Syme, "of the performers registered by Seneca, the majority are small town careerists, with few senators or sons of senator."[80]

Moreover, the vast majority of the declaimers mentioned in Seneca were born outside Rome: Albucius Silus in Gallia Cisalpina; Latro, Marullus and quite likely Fulvius Sparsus in Spain; Cestius Pius and probably Arellius Fuscus were from Asia Minor; Hermagoras, Argentarius and Nicetes from Greece.[81] Only four Latin rhetors are mentioned by Seneca: Corvus, Buteon, Gargonius and Rubellius Blandus, the first teacher of equestrian status. Seneca may have selectively excluded some notable names.[82] None of the Latin rhetors he mentions were especially famous or well regarded: Corvus and Gargonius reap awards for stupidity (*Suas.* 2.21 *testimonium stuporis; Suas.* 7.14 *fatuorum amabilissimus*).[83] Gargonius was the successor at the school of Buteo (*Controv.* 1.7.18), whom Seneca mentions a few times but more often than not in a disapproving tone.[84] Nothing is known of his family background but Pliny the Elder tells us that

---

[77] Bornecque (1902) 194; *PIR* 7.108 and Syme (1982).

[78] Tacitus, *Ann.* 3.66 *Iunio Othoni litterarium ludum exercere uetus ars fuit: mox Seiani potentia senator obscura initia impudentibus ausis propolluebat.* On this figure, see also *Controv.* 2.1.33–7.

[79] Pliny, *Ep.* 4.11.1 *nunc eo decidit, ut exsul de senatore, rhetor de oratore fieret.*

[80] Syme (1986) 354 where he also lists great politicians of the Augustan age whose names are not found in the extant work of Seneca.

[81] Bornecque (1902) 139 and Edward (1996) xl–xliv. On Cestius and Argentarius, see Rochette (1997) 234–5; on Fuluius Sparsus, see *PIR* 3.560; Syme (1969) 232 n. 116 and Gómez-Pantoja (1987).

[82] No mention of Cassius Salanus, referred to by Ovid (*Pont.* 2.5) as Germanicus' rhetoric teacher, and of several authorities cited in Quintilian as, for example, Rutilius Lupus, Popilius Laenas and Cornelius Celsus: see Kaster (1995) 291. Did they not practice declamation?

[83] Of Corvus nothing is known; Gargonius could be a descendant of the equestrian Gaius Gargonius mentioned by Cicero at *Brut.* 180: see *PIR* 4.83. He may be the same Gargonius mentioned irreverently by Horace in *Sat.* 1.2.26–7 *facetus* | *pastillos Rufillus olet, Gargonius hircum.*

[84] *Controv.* 1.1.20 Latro disapproves of Buteo; 7.4.3 Buteo's question is too absurd to be refuted.

76 Seneca the Elder's *Controuersiae* and *Suasoriae*

Buteo was a cognomen of the Fabii (*HN* 10.21.6). It is surely significant that among the nine most cited declaimers in the *Controuersiae*, none is born in Rome.[85]

The picture painted by Suetonius is not substantially different. It is true that Suetonius is notable for his "Romanocentric point of view" (Kaster, xlv) and limited interest in the contribution of Greek scholars, failing to mention, for example, Gorgias of Athens, who had taught Cicero's son, or Augustus' Greek teacher Apollodorus of Pergamum, one of the leading rhetoricians of his generation and founder of an influential school.[86] On the whole, the fragmentary section of Suetonius' work devoted to the biographies of professional rhetors paints a picture of a profession essentially dominated by men of low social status born outside Rome.[87] Of the five rhetors whose biographies survive, two, Lucius Plotius Gallus and Albucius Silus (*Gram. et rhet.* 30.3), were from Gallia Cisalpina. Sextus Clodius, who was Antony's teacher, was born in Sicily and was probably a client of the *gens Claudia*. Of the remaining two, Manius Otacilius Pitholaus, who is said to have taught Pompey, was a former slave and possibly a Greek from Rhodes, if he is to be identified with the Pitholaus Rhodensis mentioned by Horace (*Sat.* 1.10.22).[88] Marcus Epidius, who, according to Suetonius, taught Augustus and Antony, was a Campanian from Nuceria. Unlike the rest, Marcus Epidius must have been a freeborn aristocrat since Suetonius relates that he was branded for false prosecution (*Gram. et rhet.* 28.1 *calumnia notatus*), which implies that he was practicing in the courts. Besides the Spaniards Porcius Latro (fr. 2), Gavius Silo and Claudius Turrinus, others like Statius Ursulus (fr. 3) and Clodius Quirinalis (fr. 4) were from Transalpine Gaul.

Limited though it may be, the evidence suggests that by the time Seneca was writing in the first half of the first century CE, the professional rhetor was a role adopted most often by provincials and men of lower social status, or suited to disfranchised Romans. As we have seen in the previous section,

---

[85] Bennett (2007) 8 table 2 lists in a descending order mirroring the length of their citations Latro, Gallio, Fuscus, Albucius Silus, Fulvius Sparsus, Papirius Fabianus, Cestius Pius, Capito and Clodius Turrinus.

[86] On Gorgias, see Cicero, *Fam.* 16.21 and Quintilian 9.2.102 and 9.3.89. On Apollodorus, see Suetonius, *Aug.* 89 and Quintilian 3.1.18. Others Greek rhetoricians in the imperial household include Tiberius' teacher, Theodorus of Gadara, and Nestor of Tarsus and Athenaeus of Cilician Seleucia, who had taught Marcellus. On Greek rhetoricians in Rome, see Bowersock (1965) 33–4; Kennedy (1972) 337–42.

[87] Treggiari (1969) 118 "the professional teaching of rhetoric in Rome was connected with freedmen and despised"; Bonner (1977) 69–75.

[88] I follow Kaster's reading of his name: Kaster (1995) 297 ad loc. Pitholaus is also known as a writer of scurrilous verses addressed to Caesar: Suetonius, *Iul.* 75.5; Macrobius, *Sat.* 2.2.13.

The Controuersiae *as a Defense of Rhetorical Instruction*   77

in response to this complex hybrid cultural landscape, in which socio-economic status, ethnicity, genre and style are read as mutually reinforcing symptoms of a larger pattern of decline, Seneca's strategy is to pit Arellius Fuscus as a representative of Greek rhetorical instruction against the up-and-coming Spanish school exemplified by Latro and his followers. While, in addressing an audience of Roman readers, Seneca is more than happy to exploit the cultural prejudices around declamation, his choice of Latro as a (Roman) paradigm for rhetorical instruction to rival and supplant inherited Greek paradigms goes hand in hand with a shrewd response to the negative perception surrounding rhetorical instruction. By foisting onto Arellius the decadent traits – be they social, ethnic, stylistic or moral – associated with declamation, Seneca implicitly offers Latro and his school as a wholesome, traditional Roman alternative to the alleged degeneration of the declaimers. Latro's Spanish identity is an asset to Seneca's project as Seneca consistently portrays his provincial characters as true inheritors of traditional Roman values that have since left the mainstream of Roman society.

In selecting as a topic for his work a relatively new and ambiguously perceived cultural phenomenon, Seneca's line could not but be defensive. His apologetic stance begins with his choice of authorial persona. As scholars point out, although Seneca is often dubbed "the Rhetor" to distinguish him from his son Lucius Annaeus Seneca Iunior, the Stoic philosopher, he nowhere in his work describes his own occupation as a teacher of rhetoric and generally tells us virtually nothing of his life.[89] Seneca and Latro, we are informed, attended the school of Marullus, another Spaniard, but it is not clear whether that was in Rome or Corduba.[90] Furthermore, in presenting his own work as an answer to his sons' curiosity about the sayings of declaimers, Seneca repeatedly refers to declamation as a "pursuit" or "object of studies" of his former years (*Controv.* 1.*Praef.*1 *iucundum mihi redire in antiqua studia*; 1.*Praef.*5 *necesse est enim per omnia studia mea errem*; 10.*Praef.*1 *ab istis iuuenilibus studiis*; 10. *Praef.*1 *scholasticorum studia*). Seneca describes attending declamation as "the happiest time of his life" (*Controv.* 10.*Praef.*1 *optimam uitae meae partem*) but clearly continued to attend rhetorical performances into his

---

[89] Bornecque (1902) 9–15; Degl'Innocenti Pierini (2003). Griffin (1972) 6 concludes that there is not "the slightest reason to believe that he taught rhetoric at Rome."

[90] Seneca,*Controv.* 1.*Praef.*22. On Marullus and his school, see Griffin (1972) 6. See Keay (1988) 85–6 on the evidence for education in Roman Spain, which goes back to the early first century BCE when Asclepiades of Myrleia from Asia Minor taught Greek grammar in Hispania Ulterior: Strabo 3.4.3 and see Woolf (2011) 24–5.

78 Seneca the Elder's *Controuersiae* and *Suasoriae*

more mature years.[91] More details about Seneca's life can be extrapolated from other sources: from Tacitus' memorable portrayal of his son, we know that Seneca was an *eques* from Corduba, one of the wealthiest towns in wealthy Baetica.[92] On the basis of Seneca's intimacy with the likes of Pollio (*Controv.* 4.*Praef.*3), Cassius Seuerus, who declaimed only "rarely and if obliged by friends" (3.*Praef.*7 *raro ... et non nisi ab amicis coactus*), Labienus, who shunned the public (10.*Praef.*4), Maecenas and Messalla and on that of the autobiographical information in his son's works, we can deduce that the Annaei were a rich and well-connected family.[93] Seneca the father continued to maintain strong ties with Spain as is made clear by his friendship with Spanish declaimers Gavius Silo and Claudius Turrinus, both of whom lived not in Rome but in Spain. Seneca the philosopher tells us that, in his old age, his father wrote a work of historiography, which was published posthumously if it was published at all.[94]

The *Controuersiae* are divided into ten books, each of which was originally introduced by a preface. Books 5, 6 and 8, however, are missing their prefaces and that to book 9 is fragmentary. Books 3–6 and 8 are known only from an excerpted version and are missing attribution of the *sententiae* and *colores*. As we have seen, the preface to book 1 introduces Porcius Latro, whose work is the most extensively quoted in the collection. The preface to the second book is formally structured as an exhortation to rhetoric addressed to the would-be philosopher Mela, but, through the character of the philosopher Papirius Fabianus, Seneca introduces the main challenger to Latro, the Greek Arellius Fuscus, who was one of Fabianus' teachers (*Controv.* 2.*Praef.*1). A passage from this preface to the second book of the *Controuersiae* is often cited as evidence that Seneca did not have a career either as a teacher or as a politician:[95]

---

[91] The latest datable performance is Scaurus' declamation in the house of Marcus Lepidus, which had recently happened (*nouissime*): Seneca, *Controv.* 10.*Praef.*3 *declamantem audiuimus et nouissime quidem M. Lepido*. This was probably the Marcus Lepidus cos. 6 CE who died in 33 CE. As Seneca writes of Tiberius implying that he is dead, his work must have been composed after 37 CE but before 41 CE, the year of his son's exile, when Seneca tells us that his father was already dead (*Helv.* 4–5 *carissimum uirum, ex quo mater trium liberorum eras, extulisti. Lugenti tibi luctus nuntiatus est omnibus quidem absentibus liberis*).

[92] Tacitus, *Ann.* 14.53 *egone, equestri et prouinciali loco ortus, proceribus ciuitatis adnumeror?*

[93] Griffin (1972) 5 points out that Seneca's connections in Rome may have been facilitated by Asinius Pollio who spent the summer of 43 BCE in Corduba (Cicero, *Fam.* 10.31–3) and may well have been introduced to Seneca's family then. On this correspondence, see Fletcher (2016). I thank one of the anonymous readers for the Press for this helpful reference.

[94] Peter, *HRRel.* vol. 2. The narrative of Tiberius' death attributed by Suetonius to "Seneca" may belong to this work: Suetonius, *Tib.* 73.2.

[95] Fairweather (1981) 11–14.

The Controuersiae as a Defense of Rhetorical Instruction 79

haec eo libentius, Mela, fili carissime, refero, quia uideo animum tuum a ciuilibus officiis abhorrentem et ab omni ambitu auersum hoc unum concupiscentem, nihil concupiscere , ut eloquentiae tamen studeas. facilis ab hac in omnes artes discursus est; instruit etiam quos non sibi exercet. nec est, quod insidias tibi putes fieri, quasi id agam, ut te bene cedentis studii fauor teneat; ego uero non sum bonae mentis impedimentum: perge quo inclinat animus, et paterno contentus ordine subduc fortunae magnam tui partem. erat quidem tibi maius ingenium quam fratribus tuis, omnium bonarum artium capacissimum; est et hoc ipsum melioris ingenii pignus non corrumpi bonitate eius, ut illo male utaris. sed quoniam fratribus tuis ambitiosa curae sunt foroque se et honoribus parant, in quibus ipsa quae sperantur timenda sunt, ego quoque, eius alioqui processus auidus et hortator laudatorque uel periculosae dum honestae modo industriae, duobus filiis nauigantibus te in portu retineo.

I am the more happy to relate this, my dear son Mela, because I see that your mind, shrinking from political office and averse from all ambition, has only one desire – to have no desires. But do study eloquence. You can easily pass from this art to all others; it equips even those whom it does not train for its own ends. There is no reason for you to think plots are being laid for you, as if I were planning that you should be held tight by enthusiasm for a study that goes well. No, I am no obstacle to a good mind; go where your inclination takes you, and, content with your father's rank, withdraw a great part of yourself from the reach of fortune. You had a greater intellect than your brothers, completely capable of grasping all honorable arts. And this is in itself the guarantee of a superior mind, not to be corrupted by its good quality into using it ill. But since your brothers care for ambitious goals and set themselves for the forum and a political career, where even what one hopes for is to be feared, even I, who otherwise am eager for such advancement and encourage and praise such efforts (their dangers don't matter, provided they are honorable), even I keep you in port while your two brothers voyage out. (Seneca, Controv. 2.Praef.3–4)

This passage forms part of Seneca's attempt to recommend declamation not as specialized training but as a helpful activity no matter what the aspirations of the student. Seneca here contrasts his two eldest sons, who care about the forum and a political career (*foroque et honoribus*), with his youngest son Mela, who abhors political office and like his father is content with his (equestrian) rank (*paterno contentus ordine*).

In line with his self-presentation in this passage, in the rest of his work Seneca refers to the *scholastici* as an alien class and depicts declamation as a phenomenon he observed from the margins rather than one in which he participated. In general, his comments are addressed to the reader, and his autoptic narratives do not include comments and reactions he shared with the participants at the time. The only exceptions are the quoted responses to Cassius Seuerus and Votienus Montanus, who are directly answering Seneca's inquiry.[96]

Curiously, however, one piece of evidence for Seneca's participation in declamation is often neglected: Quintilian cites a passage from a *controuersia* by Seneca on the topic of a father who catches his son and his stepmother in adultery and kills them.[97] While it is theoretically possible that the passage belongs to a section of the *Controuersiae* now lost, it is unlikely that Seneca violated his practice by citing his own treatments. It is rather more likely that Quintilian is citing Seneca by memory or through a collection other than the *Controuersiae*.[98] Moreover, it is significant that the cited passage is meant to illustrate the use of *euidentia* by declaimers (9.2.42 *noui uero et praecipue declamatores audacius nec mehercule sine motu quodam imaginantur, ut Seneca in controuersia . . .*), among whom Seneca is included. Despite their vagueness, Seneca's references to declamation as a *studium* when combined with Quintilian's reference to Seneca's *controuersiae* suggest that Seneca's involvement with the declaimers was more direct than he explicitly admits in his work.

We are left with a curious problem of authorial self-definition: if Seneca had taught or even practiced declamation, he purposefully elided any references to his experience, choosing instead to portray himself overwhelmingly as a detached and even casual observer. This disavowal of direct participation is in stark contrast with the typical authorial stance of using one's direct experience as a way to confer authority and credibility to the narrative and must be accounted for as an *authorial* strategy.[99] The ambivalence of Romans toward declamation may explain why Seneca adopted an "oblique" authorial persona. Seneca appeals to those who view declamation suspiciously by distancing himself from the professionals. The narrative framework of the work, in which declamation is viewed as a temporary object of study to be supplanted by more mature interests, further appeals to the prejudicial attitude toward rhetorical instruction of his intended audience.

---

[96] Seneca, *Controv.* 3.*Praef.*8 *quaerenti mihi quare in declamationibus impar sibi esset, haec aiebat*; 9. *Praef.*1 *rationem quaerenti mihi ait.*

[97] Quintilian 9.2.42–3 = Seneca fr. 1 Winterbottom. And see also 9.2.95, which summarizes *Controv.* 7. *Praef.*6.

[98] Thus returning the favor, since it is likely that the *Quintilianus senex* cited by Seneca at *Controv.* 10. *Praef.*2 was the rhetorician's father. It should also be noted that Quintilian elsewhere acknowledges the speaker even when he gives lines also known from Seneca's collection: e.g. 9.2.91 (Gallio and Latro) – *Controv.* 2.3.6.

[99] On the value of autopsy to bolster the authority of narratives, see Marincola (1997) 63–86.

The Controuersiae *as a Defense of Rhetorical Instruction*   81

An important way through which Seneca distances himself further from the professionals, whom he calls *"scholastici,"* is by his privileging of non-professional voices, Roman orators who occasionally declaimed but were not professional teachers, throughout several of the prefaces of the *Controuersiae*. These opinions of eminent Romans in the prefaces are alluded and responded to in the treatment sections of each *controuersia*, in which samples of declamation mostly by professionals are also given. The preface to book 3 is devoted to the career orator Cassius Seuerus, whose opinions on declamation Seneca reports in direct speech. Seuerus' words have come to epitomize the moralistic condemnation of declamation (modern and ancient).

> ego tamen et propriam causam uideor posse reddere: adsueui non auditorem spectare sed iudicem; adsueui non mihi respondere sed aduersario; non minus deuito superuacua dicere quam contraria. in scholastica quid non superuacuum est, cum ipsa superuacua sit? indicabo tibi affectum meum: cum in foro dico, aliquid ago; cum declamo, id quod bellissime Censorinus aiebat de his qui honores in municipiis ambitiose peterent, uideor mihi in somniis laborare. deinde res ipsa diuersa est: totum aliud est pugnare, aliud uentilare. hoc ita semper habitum est, scholam quasi ludum esse, forum arenam; et ideo ille primum in foro uerba facturus tiro dictus est. agedum istos declamatores produc in senatum, in forum: cum loco mutabuntur; uelut adsueta clause et delicatae umbrae corpora sub diuo stare non possunt, non imbrem ferre, non solem sciunt, uix se inueniunt; adsuerunt enim suo arbitrio diserti esse. non est quod oratorem in hac puerili exercitatione spectes. quid si uelis gubernatorem in piscina aestimare?

> However, I may be able to give you a reason peculiar to me. I am used to keeping my eye on the judge, not the audience. I am used to replying to my opponents, not to myself. I avoid the superfluous as well as what tells against myself. Everything is superfluous in a declamation: declamation is superfluous. I will tell you what I feel. When I speak in the forum, I am doing something. When I declaim, I feel. To use Censorinus' excellent phrase of zealous candidates for local office, that I am struggling in a dream. Again, the two things are quite different: it is one thing to fight, quite another to shadow-box. The school has always been taken to be a sort of school for gladiators, the forum as an arena – hence the word tiro for the man who is going to make his first speech in the courts. Come on, bring your declaimers into senate and forum! With their surroundings they will change their character. They are like bodies used to the closet and the luxury of the shade, unable to stand in the open and put up with rain and sun. They scarcely know where they are; they are used to being clever at their own rating. There is no point trying to test an orator amid these childish pursuits. You might as well judge a helmsman on a fishpond. (Seneca, *Controv.* 3. *Praef.*12–14)

82   Seneca the Elder's *Controuersiae* and *Suasoriae*

Seuerus' speech is a scathing indictment of declamatory exercises as a superfluous (*superuacuua*), self-indulgent and childish activity (*puerilis exercitatio*) and of the low standards of modern audiences who prefer the declaimer Cestius to Cicero (3.*Praef*.15–17). Just as one would not test a helmsman in a small pond, claims Seuerus, so one is not to assess an orator's competence based on his performance in the artificial setting of the declamation schools.

In assessing Seuerus' contribution in the overall plan of the *Controuersiae* and *Suasoriae*, one must resist the temptation to read his words out of context, as evidence for Seneca's own views on the subject. To begin with, although Seneca praises the orator's competent control of the emotions of the audience, his *grauitas* and hard work, he carefully sets up Seuerus' speech as a self-defense to his own questions about Seuerus' failure as a declaimer (*Controv.* 3.*Praef*.8 *sed quaerenti mihi quare in declamationibus impar sibi esset . . .*). His self-defense opens with an elaborately rhetorical priamel in which he lists other writers who are good at one genre and not good at another, and animals who excel in one area and not another, before finally moving on to his own failing – declamation. The speech of self-defense then turns into an attack on the schools, an attack to which Seneca does not respond in the preface.

Crucially, however, the rhetorical context of the attack is already suspicious, as the speaker whose poor performance is being questioned has a clear motive for trivializing declamation. Moreover, in his introduction, Seneca reminds us of this point when he elaborates on Seuerus' extraordinary talent for self-defense (*Controv.* 3.*Praef*.5 *nec tamen scio quem reum illi defendere nisi se contigerit; adeo nusquam rerum ullam materiam dicendi nisi in periculis suis habuit*). At the same time, it is hard not to take Seneca's stance here as tongue-in-cheek: Seneca's remark is a veiled allusion to Seuerus' reputation as a vicious prosecutor.[100] Although Quintilian (10.1.116–17) and Aper in the *Dialogus* (19) have some praise for Seuerus' oratorical style, ancient historians, including most extensively Tacitus in the *Annales*, tell of his venomous prosecutions and dubious character, which for Quintilian included a "passion for accusation" (11.1.57 *accusandi uoluptate*).[101] When Augustus had enough of his impudent attacks, Cassius

---

[100] On Cassius Seuerus, see *PIR* 2 C 522; Rutledge (2001) 209–12; Winterbottom (1964) 90–2; Bornecque (1902) 157–9. A reference to Cassius Seuerus' hatred toward Labienus appears later in the preface to book 10 of the *Controuersiae* (10.*Praef*.8): *Cassi Seueri, hominis Labieno inuisissimi.*

[101] See also Messalla's characterization of Seuerus as representing the beginning of decline in Tacitus, *Dial.* 26.5: *primus enim contempto ordine rerum, omissa modestia ac pudore uerborum, ipsis etiam quibus utitur armis incompositus et studio feriendi plerumque deiectus, non pugnat, sed rixatur.*

The Controuersiae *as a Defense of Rhetorical Instruction* 83

Seuerus was put on trial and exiled, first to Crete and then to Seriphus where he spent his old age.[102] In the preface to book 3 of the *Controuersiae*, Seuerus relates the story of his prosecution of the Greek declaimer Cestius Pius, who had written replies to Cicero's speeches. Outraged by Cestius' arrogance, Seuerus dragged him to court on a succession of outlandish charges until, at last, he let go but not before trying to force Cestius to swear that he, Cestius, was inferior to Cicero.[103] Seneca the Elder elsewhere attests to Cestius' mordacity and comments that Cicero's son, Marcus, was justified in flogging Cestius when, at a dinner party at which they were both present, he heard that the declaimer despised his father's achievement (*Suas.* 7.13). Cestius, a Greek speaker and native of Asia Minor, was an easy target of abuse.[104] Nevertheless, Seuerus' narrative of his encounter with Cestius highlights the former's propensity for pointless litigation, which is also attested in other sources.

To sum up, by the time Seneca was writing some time between 37 CE and 41 CE, Cassius Seuerus was a disgraced and dead *delator*. Seneca's placement of this indictment of declamatory practice in the mouth of such a questionable character is an oblique response to the standard complaints against declamatory nonsense: by associating such moralistic discourse with moral decadence, Seneca subtly attempts to distance the Roman reader from the typical Roman suspicion of declamation toward a more positive view of the role of rhetorical training.

Unfortunately, the remainder of book 3 has survived only in excerpted form and we have therefore most likely lost precious parts of Seneca's discussion of Seuerus' take on declamatory topics. The preface to book 9, however, which is dedicated to the orator Votienus Montanus, mirrors closely that of book 3; unlike the latter, book 9 is preserved in its entirety, allowing us to compare Votienus' words with Seneca's direct assessment of his style and technique. Montanus' response to Seneca's questioning of his lack of interest in practicing declamation is cited directly, just as Seuerus' was in the preface to book 3. Montanus echoes Seuerus in contrasting the rigorous preparation required in court with the artificial environment of the schoolroom where no one is interrupted (*Controv.* 9.*Praef.*2–5). The conclusion of the preface is lost, but a response to Montanus' point is made in the fifth *controuersia* of the book, where a long excerpt of his is cited along with Seneca's assessment:

---

[102] Tacitus, *Ann.* 1.72 *procacibus scriptis*; Dio 55.4; 56.27. On his trial, see Tacitus, *Ann.* 4.21.
[103] See also Suetonius, *Gram. et rhet.* 22.
[104] Seneca, *Controv.* 7.*Praef.*8 *mordacissimi hominis*; 9.3.13 *contumeliose multa interponebat.*

84   Seneca the Elder's *Controuersiae* and *Suasoriae*

> Montanus Votienus, homo rarissumi etiamsi non emendatissimi ingeni, uitium suum, quod in orationibus non euitat, in scholasticis quoque euitare non potuit; sed in orationibus, quia laxatior est materia, minus [ex] earundem rerum adnotatur iteratio. in scholasticis si eadem sunt quae dicuntur, quia pauca sunt, notantur.

> Votienus Montanus, a man of rare though not faultless talent, could not avoid in school either the fault that waylays him in his speeches; but in his speeches, the material being more diffuse, one notices repetition less: in declamation, if the same things get said again, it shows, just because there are few things said. (Seneca, *Controv.* 9.5.15)

Implicitly rebutting Montanus' attack on the artificiality of declamation, Seneca points out that the declamation halls are a less forgiving setting than the forum, in that the exercises are more compressed than the diffuse legal speeches.[105] In what follows, Seneca further responds to Montanus' criticism by incorporating Aemilius Scaurus' negative assessment of Montanus' style as an Ovid who cannot leave well alone. This criticism is significant in two respects. First, Aemilius Scaurus is a powerful Roman senator and one of the most notable orators of his generation.[106] Secondly, although Montanus enjoyed a good reputation (Tacitus, *Ann.* 4.42 *celebris ingenii uiro*), he too was not an altogether successful case: originally from Narbo in southern France (Martial 8.72.5–6), he was an eminent lawyer but was convicted of treason under Tiberius and exiled (Tacitus, *Ann.* 4.42). Finally, an anecdote related in an earlier passage undermines Montanus' self-presentation: Seneca tells us that, when sued by Vinicius, Montanus was so utterly enthralled by his accuser's rhetorical performance that, as the "utter schoolman" that he was, he enjoyed his accuser's speech (*Controv.* 7.5.12 *adeo toto animo scholasticus erat*).

The preface to book 4 continues this trend of discussing the views of prominent Roman orators on declamation. Specifically, Seneca discusses Asinius Pollio, who "never let a crowd in when he declaimed" (*Controv.* 4. *Praef.2 numquam admissa multitudine declamauit*) because as the distinguished orator that he was he "regarded this occupation as unworthy of his talents, and, while prepared to get exercise from it, scorned to make a parade of it" (4.*Praef.2 tantus orator inferius id opus ingenio suo duxit, et exerceri quidem illo uolebat, gloriari fastidiebat*). Asinius Pollio's ability to

---

[105] We are reminded of Seneca's criticism of Paulus Fabius Maximus, the consul of 11 BCE and dedicatee of Horace, *Carm.* 4.1. According to Seneca, Fabius Maximus was the first to introduce the vice of tricola in the courts: *Controv.* 2.4.12. See Fairweather (1981) 139.

[106] Seneca,*Controv.* 1.2.22 *disertissimus homo*; Tacitus, *Ann.* 3.331 *oratorum aetate uberrimus*, 6.29 *insignis nobilitate et orandis causis*.

The Controuersiae *as a Defense of Rhetorical Instruction* 85

declaim in Seneca's presence (4.*Praef.*4 *declamare nobis*) three days after losing his son is contrasted with the lack of self-control of Quintus Haterius, another distinguished Roman orator of Senatorial rank, who died in 26 CE.[107] Tacitus memorably praises Haterius' oratory for its force rather than sophistication (*Ann.* 4.61 *scilicet impetu magis quam cura uigebat*). Unlike Asinius who practices sparingly and only privately, Haterius was in the habit of declaiming extemporaneously in front of a large crowd (*Controv.* 4.*Praef.*7 *declamabat autem Haterius admisso populo ex tempore*) and is praised for translating the skills of the Greeks into Latin. Seneca criticizes Haterius for his lack of control, exemplified by his employment of a freedman to direct him into making a transition while giving a speech. Haterius and Pollio are both practitioners of declamation but differ in the degree to which they embrace the public dimension of performance to which the schoolmen are committed. Yet, once again, Seneca's tone is one of measured deference toward these eminent Roman orators but of exculpation in relation to the professionals:[108] lest we should think of Haterius as a schoolman, we are reminded that, in structuring his *controuersiae*, "he did not regulate himself by the rules of declamation" (*Controv.* 4.*Praef.*9 *non dirigebat se ad declamatoriam legem*) and instead moved as his "flow of language dictated" (*Controv.* 4.*Praef.*9 *is illi erat ordo quem impetus dederat*). Haterius' lack of restraint and passion for display, Seneca seems to be saying, were those of the worst of the schoolmen, but otherwise he had no command of the art.

Seneca's approach to rhetorical instruction is twofold. On the one hand, he rehearses the traditional moralistic discourse on declamation as a cause and symptom of decline. On the other hand, in an effort to rehabilitate declamation, Seneca subtly promotes Latro and the other Spanish declaimers as the true alternative to the vices of the Asianic school and therefore as true heirs to traditional Roman values. Furthermore, Seneca resists traditional Roman attacks on declamation by alternating between giving the floor to distinguished nonprofessional Roman critics in the prefaces and to declaimers, whose *sententiae* and treatments are cited in the remainder of the book. Seneca incorporates the views of respected Romans only to debunk their arguments obliquely. This authorial strategy of oblique

---

[107] See Tacitus, *Ann.* 4.61 *Q. Haterius, familia senatoria, eloquentiae quoad vixit celebratae.* On Haterius see *PIR* 4.24.

[108] Seneca may also be exploiting the fact that Haterius enjoyed a mixed reputation: Tacitus, *Ann.* 1.13 and *Ann.* 3.57 on his adulation for Tiberius: *at Q. Haterius cum eius diei senatus consulta aureis litteris figenda in curia censuisset deridiculo fuit senex foedissimae adulationis tantum infamia usurus.*

criticism is a function not only of the negative perceptions surrounding declamation but also of Seneca's cultural status:[109] as an outsider from Spain, Seneca does not have the authority to confront the suspicious attitudes of this educated audience of upper-class Romans but must instead resort to more subtle means to elicit this audience's support.

Conclusion

Seneca's aim in the *Controuersiae* and *Suasoriae* is to adhere to and yet subtly resist the traditional Roman condemnation of declamation as the root cause of literary decline. Seneca's choice to efface his own involvement in the scene of declamation is a deliberate authorial strategy designed to co-opt but not challenge his Roman audience. Making recourse to traditional oppositions such as Roman/Greek, free/slave, male/female, real life/performance, he constructs the Spanish school of Latro, to which he implicitly aligns himself, as a restrained, Roman alternative to the excesses of Hellenizing declaimers. His representation of Ovid and Virgil is closely bound up with this ambitious cultural project: on the one hand, Seneca exploits the cultural capital of these Augustan poets when he makes them followers and imitators of his own hero, Latro. On the other, rehearsing a well-established discourse of condemnation of declamation qua poetic distortion of Roman oratory, he aligns poetry and the poetic with the excesses and ornateness of declamation.

In examining the often-cited cameo appearances of Ovid and Virgil in Seneca's text as part of the wider evocation of the divide between poetry and rhetoric in Imperial culture, we have had to read the *Controuersiae* and *Suasoriae* in a different light, not simply as sources for excerptible anecdotes. Seneca's account of Ovid's relationship to the declaimers has typically been used to corroborate the existence of a cultural and literary traffic between declamation and poetry. In this reading, Seneca's text is treated as transparent evidence for the literary phenomenon of "rhetorical influence." Yet, when examined closely, Seneca's representation of the literary scene of declamation is more opaque than it might appear at first. Far from being an innocent cultural spectator, Seneca has a stake in defining both poetry and the category of the poetic and in using them to foreground his own version

---

[109] In this way, my reading of Seneca as a provincial critic seeking to establish his authority in front of a Roman audience is inspired by Nino Luraghi's approach to Dionysius of Halicarnassus as a covert critic of Roman morality: see Luraghi (2003) and see further Weaire (2005).

of a wholesome and restrained model of rhetorical education. Rehearsing a well-established strategy of rhetorical sources, Seneca's approach in rehabilitating declamation is to conflate the debased with the poetic. Poetry therefore is not simply an activity to be observed but a tool of criticism that can be polemically aimed at corrupt discourse.

CHAPTER 3

The Orator and the Poet in Quintilian's
Institutio Oratoria

Quintilian's *Institutio Oratoria* – "The training of the orator" – is the largest and among the most influential sources on rhetorical theory and instruction to have survived, if not from Classical antiquity, at least from the early Roman Empire.[1] Poetry and the analysis thereof are naturally at the heart of the project of the *Institutio Oratoria* by virtue of the dominant role of poetic texts in the educational curriculum.[2] On the most basic level, poetry's function in Quintilian's work is to furnish stylistic exempla and thus to demonstrate rhetorical features deemed desirable in oratory. In particular, poetry is used to exemplify and illustrate the discussion of *elocutio* ("style") centered on tropes and figures in books 8 and 9. On a practical level, not only does Quintilian overwhelmingly demonstrate his precepts with exempla drawn from poetry but also more than two-thirds of the poetic citations in the *Institutio Oratoria* occur in these books.[3] As we have seen, this use of poetic examples to illustrate style goes back to Aristotle's *Rhetoric* and was, by Quintilian's time, standard: in the preface to his fourth book devoted to style (*elocutio*), the *Ad Herennium* states that ornaments of style are typically illustrated with reference to poetry (e.g. Ennius) or oratory, with no clear preference between them (4.1, 4.2, 4.7, etc.).[4] In the tenth book, a section of the work that I will analyze in more detail, Quintilian states that Homer provided "an example and a starting point for all parts of eloquence" (10.1.46 *omnibus eloquentiae partibus*

---

[1] Gunderson (2009) is the starting point for any discussion of *Institutio Oratoria* as text. On the reception of Quintilian, see Ward (1995). For general treatments, see Cousin (1967), Seel (1977) and Zundel (1981). For commentaries, see Colson (1924) and Ax (2011) on book 1, Reinhardt and Winterbottom (2006) on book 2, Adamietz (1966) on book 3, Peterson (1981) on book 10 and Austin (1954) on book 12. Unless otherwise noted, text and translation of the *Institutio* is from D. A. Russell's Loeb edition.

[2] On poetry in the school of the *grammaticus*, see Bonner (1977) 212–49 and, on poetry in the training of the orator, see North (1952).

[3] On the use of poetic citations in the *Institutio*, see Joly (1979), Odgers (1933) and Cole (1906).

[4] *Rhet. Her.* 4.1 *compluribus de causis putant oportere cum ipsi praeceperint quo pacto oporteat ornare elocutionem, unius cuiusque generis ab oratore aut poeta probate sumptum ponere exemplum.*

88

exemplum et ortum dedit). This position reflects the deeply held belief that Homer preceded prose writers in his use of artistic devices of style.[5]

However, traditional as it may be, this use of poetic citations to illustrate style in the context of the *Institutio* generates a number of interesting tensions that will form the subject of this chapter. For while endowed with exemplary status, poetry is at the same time subtly portrayed as excessive and unnatural in comparison to oratory, both explicitly in the sections of the work in which poetry and rhetoric are compared and implicitly in the rhetorical presentation of poetic exempla. Thus Quintilian's definition of the appropriate rhetorical style hinges on a judicious and selective imitation of the poetic register and, as a result, portrays rhetoric as a more natural alternative to the poetic medium.

However, as I argue, Quintilian's struggle to undermine the role of poetic texts must be read side by side with his elaborate deployment of poetic metaphors to represent both his work and that of the orator. In this way, a far more complex picture emerges, one in which poetry is not simply a repository of phrases to be judiciously imitated but a source of cultural authority to be competed with and yet ultimately appropriated. In this reading, the *Institutio* becomes an ambitiously complex and deeply emulative text through which Quintilian seeks to present his own version of the *uir bonus dicendi peritus* as capable of contesting and ultimately surpassing the authority of the poets. The discussion of the boundaries between poetry and rhetoric is thus not an innocent theoretical debate but an important part of a historically situated cultural struggle to rebuild the authority of the rhetorical medium in response to the perceived decline of oratory in the early Empire.

Licentia poetarum

Poetry and its function in the training of the orator are introduced right in the first book of the *Institutio*, which is devoted to elementary instruction under the *grammaticus* (1.4.2). There, Quintilian describes grammar as comprising two parts: the study of correctness of speech (*recte loquendi scientia*) and the interpretation of poets (*poetarum enarratio*). The purpose of the latter is to provide a platform for the study of tropes, figures of speech and figures of style, which he will discuss in books 8 and 9.

---

[5] See pp. 28–9.

90 The Orator and the Poet in Quintilian's *Institutio Oratoria*

in praelegendo grammaticus et illa quidem minora praestare debebit, ut partes orationis reddi sibi soluto uersu desideret et pedum proprietates, quae adeo debent esse notae in carminibus ut etiam in oratoria compositione desiderentur. deprendat quae barbara, quae inpropria, quae contra legem loquendi sint posita, non ut ex his utique improbentur poetae (quibus, quia plerumque seruire metro coguntur, adeo ignoscitur ut uitia ipsa aliis in carmine appellationibus nominentur: metaplasmus enim et schematismus seu schemata, ut dixi, uocamus et laudem uirtutis necessitati damus), sed ut commoneat artificialium et memoriam agitet. id quoque inter prima rudimenta non inutile demonstrare, quot quaeque uerba modis intellegenda sint. circa glossemata etiam, id est uoces minus usitatas, non ultima eius professionis diligentia est. enimuero iam maiore cura doceat tropos omnes, quibus praecipue non poema modo sed etiam oratio ornatur, schemata utraque, id est figuras, quaeque lexeos quaeque dianoeas uocantur: quorum ego sicut troporum tractatum in eum locum differo quo mihi de ornatu orationis dicendum erit.

In expounding the text, the *grammaticus* must also deal with more elementary matters. He must ask the pupils to break up the verse and give the parts of speech and the qualities of the metrical feet, which need to become so familiar in poetry that the need for them is felt also in rhetorical composition. He must point out barbarisms, improper usages, and anything contrary to the laws of speech, not by way of censuring the poets for these (for poets are often forced to be the slaves of meter, and are so far forgiven that the faults themselves have other names when they occur in poetry; we call them, as I said, metaplasms, schematisms, schemata, and make a virtue of necessity), but to remind the pupil of technical rules and activate his memory of them. [The *grammatici*], however, should take great care in teaching all the tropes, which are the main ornaments not only of poetry but also of oratory, and both kinds of schemata – that is to say, figures of speech and of thought, as they are called; these like the tropes I postpone until I come to deal with the ornaments of style. (Quintilian 1.8.13–16)

As Quintilian describes, the *grammaticus* gave preliminary readings (*praelectiones*) of poetry followed by expositions (*enarrationes*) pointing out issues of pronunciation, meter, vocabulary and grammar.[6] However, one of his most important tasks was that of outlining the use of figures of speech, which are viewed as sources of *ornatus* in both prose and poetry and which Quintilian promises to discuss later in the work under the heading of style.

It is important to note here the rhetoric of Quintilian's presentation of poetry: in this passage, rhetorical norms and rhetorically appropriate style

---

[6] On *praelectio*, see Suetonius, *Gram. et rhet.* 1.2 with Kaster (1995) 54 ad loc. and Bonner (1977) 225–6.

Licentia poetarum 91

are to be grounded in and illustrated from poetic texts, with the result that the latter are presented as repositories of technical knowledge for the orator. At the same time, the vocabulary of criticism is heavily moralizing, constructing poetry as a deviant whose breach of the law must be tolerated and excused. While it is used to furnish exempla of rhetorically effective language, poetry is also simultaneously disavowed as unnatural and unabashed. Thus, following Aristotle, Quintilian characterizes poetry and poetic language as essentially deviating from linguistic and stylistic norms.[7] In Quintilian's presentation, poetry goes against stylistic rules (*contra legem loquendi*) and is therefore potentially subject to reproach: were it not for the allowance (*ignoscitur*) normally given to poets in light of the restrictions placed on them by the adoption of meter, their twisted use of language would be deemed a vice (*uitia*). Thus tropes (*tropos*) and figures (*schemata*), which are mentioned here as the greatest ornaments of both prose and poetry, are exemplified by the figure of *metaplasmus*, the technical Greek term for divergence from the rules of correct language tolerated because of the requirements of meter.[8] Like other figures, solecism, which belongs to the category of *metaplasmus*, is characterized earlier in the book as "typical of poets but also allowed to orators" (1.5.52–3 *schemata igitur nominabuntur, frequentiora quidem apud poetas, sed oratoribus quoque permissa*).[9]

Elsewhere Quintilian refers to this allowance granted to poets to deviate from natural language as *licentia poetarum*, as for example in the discussion of *exordium* in book 4, once again in conjunction with the use of solecism (4.1.58 *Illud ex praeceptis ueteribus manet, ne quod insolens uerbum, ne audacius tralatum, ne aut ab obsoleta uetustate aut poetica licentia sumptum in principio deprehendatur*).[10] What counts here is the use to which Quintilian has put this traditional opposition between oratorical and

---

[7] Aristotle, *Poet.* 1460b11–13 "the narration of these involves verbal expression, including the use of dialect terms and metaphor and many abnormal elements of expression, as these are licenses we allow poets" (trans. Hubbard in Russell and Winterbottom (1972)) (ταῦτα δ᾽ ἐξαγγέλλεται λέξει ἐν ᾗ καὶ γλῶτται καὶ μεταφοραὶ καὶ πολλὰ πάθη τῆς λέξεώς ἐστι· δίδομεν γὰρ ταῦτα τοῖς ποιηταῖς). See pp. 35–7. On the history of this distinction in Greece, see Graff (2005).

[8] Lausberg (1998) § 479–95.

[9] The discussion of solecisms under the heading of figures of speech (*schemata lexeōs*) occurs in Quintilian 9.3.2–27.

[10] For the characterization of solecism as an instance of poetic license, see Cicero, *De or.* 3.153 *inusitata sunt prisca fere ac uetustate ab usu cotidiani sermonis iam diu intermissa, quae sunt poetarum licentiae liberiora quam nostrae; Orat.* 68 *ego autem, etiam si quorundam grandis et ornata uox est poetarum, tamen in ea cum licentiam statuo maiorem esse quam in nobis faciendorum iungendorumque uerborum, tum etiam non nulli eorum uoluntati uocibus magis quam rebus inseruiunt.* On poetic license in Quintilian, see Dozier (2012).

92   The Orator and the Poet in Quintilian's *Institutio Oratoria*

poetic language: while the pupil is invited to behave like a condescending censor (*deprehendat, improbentur*), able to detect the deviant language of poets and yet abstain from censure, poets are characterized as slaves both of meter (*seruire metro*) and of necessity (*necessitati*), which they are forced to obey by breaking up the natural word order. Here, style and morals are clearly interconnected: in Quintilian's presentation, far from being a purely stylistic phenomenon, the *licentia* of poets is invested with the negative connotations associated with servility, lack of control and enslavement to pleasure, which the rhetor seeks to prevent in his budding orator.[11]

This contrast between the orator's restrained use of everyday language and the poet's self-indulgent deviation from linguistic and stylistic norms recurs throughout the *Institutio*. In book 2, the discussion of the preliminary exercise (*progymnasma*) known as *narratio* warns against "indulg[ing] in descriptions (2.4.3) dragged into the text into which very many are led by imitation of *poetica licentia*."[12] The *licentia* of poets is also invoked in relation to the misuse of the fabulous by Greek historians (2.4.19) according to the standard argument that poets are allowed to engage creatively with historical facts.[13]

In this respect, although he reuses a traditional opposition between prose and poetry based on the latter's departure from the norm that goes back to Aristotle's *Rhetoric*, Quintilian takes this distinction further to highlight rhetoric's superiority over the poetic medium in striking and innovative ways. For example, he returns several times to the notion that meter acts as a constraint on the poet, forcing him to bend and twist language.[14] This idea of meter as a constraint is traditional: in the famous *synkrisis* of poetry and rhetoric in book 1 of the *De oratore*, Cicero had already linked the *licentia* of poetry to the constrictions of meter, arguing that the poet is "more restricted by the use of meter and more free in relation to license with words" (*De or.* 1.70 *numeris astrictior paulo, uerborum autem licentia liberior*). Moreover, the use of meter as a yardstick to measure the difference between prose and poetry is found already in

---

[11] For the use of the language of freedom and self-mastery elsewhere in Roman rhetoric, see Gunderson (2000) 87–122.

[12] Quintilian 2.4.3 *neque rursus sinuosa et arcessitis descriptionibus, in quas plerique imitatione poeticae licentiae ducuntur, lasciuiat.*

[13] Going back to Aristotle, *Poet.* 1415a36–b5. See also Ovid, *Am.* 3.12.41; Seneca, *QNat.* 2.44.1; Columella 9.2.2. For this comparison between historiography and poetry cf. Quintilian 10.1.31 *[historia] est … proxima poetis, et quodam modo carmen solutum est*, on which, see Woodman (1988) 98–101.

[14] Quintilian 1.8.14 *quia plerumque seruire metro coguntur*; 1.6.2 *poetas metri necessitates excusat*; 8.6.17 *plurima uertere etiam ipsa metri necessitate coguntur*; 10.1.28 *alligata ad certam pedum necessitatem.*

Licentia poetarum   93

Rhetoric book 3, where Aristotle asserts that in prose "the form of the language should be neither metrical nor unrhythmical" (*Rh.* 3.8.1408b21–2).[15] At the basis of this distinction is the notion that the naturally alternating sequences of long and short syllables give rise to rhythm (Gr. *rhythmos*/Lt. *numerus*) in prose, whereas the predictable succession of the same feet in poetry is called meter (Gr. *metron*/Lt. *metrum*). Prose and poetry use the same metrical feet but, for Aristotle, the ideal oratorical rhythm stays away from the predictability of poetry (*metron*) and from the arbitrariness of artless *rhythmos*: "thus speech should have rhythm but not meter; for the latter will be a poem" (*Rh.* 3.8.1408b28–31). While he discourages the use of dactylic hexameter as overtly dignified and of iambics as too conversational, Aristotle endorses the paean as the ideal oratorical clausula (*Rh.* 3.8.1409a).

This characterization of the proper oratorical rhythm as the mean between *natura* (naturally occurring *numerus*) and *ars* (the craft of poetic *metra*) becomes traditional in subsequent discussions of prose rhythm.[16] According to Cicero, Theophrastus "believes that speeches, at least those that are in any way shaped and polished, should be rhythmical, not rigidly but somewhat loosely" (*De or.* 3.184 *qui putat orationem, quae quidem sit polita atque facta quodam modo, non astricte, sed remissius numerosam esse oportere*). The idea that the use of recognizable metrical units is poetic and therefore not at home in prose is also found in Cicero, Demetrius and Dionysius of Halicarnassus, although the last, while professing to follow Aristotle's distinction, is in fact far more accepting of meter in oratory and presents Demosthenes as the representative of a style of poetic prose.[17] Similarly, paraphrasing Cicero's position, Quintilian declares that prose rhythm should be "not unrhythmical (that would be inartistic and coarse) rather than rhythmical, this being a feature of poetry" (9.4.56 *magis non arrhythmum, quod esset inscitum atque agreste, quam enrhythmum, quod*

---

[15] The advantages and limitations of using meter as the hallmark of poetry are widely discussed topics in ancient theory: thus, somewhat in contrast to his pronouncement in the *Rhetoric*, in *Poet.* 9 (1451b1–11) Aristotle insists that mimesis, not meter is the defining characteristic of poetry. Cf. also Horace, *Sat.* 1.4.45–62.

[16] Lausberg (1998) § 977–1054.

[17] Cicero, *Orat.* 67 *quicquid est enim quod sub aurium mensuram aliquam cadit, etiam si abest a uersu – nam id quidem orationis est uitium – numerus uocatur, qui Graece rhythmos dicitur*; *De or.* 3.182–6; Demetrius, *De el.* 116 "verse in prose is out of place and frigid as lines in verse with excess syllables"; Dionysius of Halicarnassus, *Comp.* 25 "mere prose cannot come to resemble metrical and lyrical writing unless it contains meters and rhythms that have been introduced into it unobtrusively. It is not appropriate, however, for it to appear to be in meter or in rhythm (for in that case it will be a poem and a lyric) . . . in this way it may be poetical, though not actually a poem, and lyrical, but without being lyric," and, on this section of the work, see Jonge (2008) 348–61.

94   The Orator and the Poet in Quintilian's *Institutio Oratoria*

poeticum est, esse compositionem uelit). Although prose uses the same feet as poetry, Quintilian insists that orators should not use entire verses in prose (9.4.72–111), especially at the beginning and at the close of a sentence, so that, for example, poetic *clausulae* (closing rhythmical effects) such as the sequence dactyl spondee borrowed from poetry must be avoided (9.4.102).

This setting of rhetorical discourse against both excessive *ars* represented by poetry and uncultivated *natura* represented by the natural, untrained rhythm of everyday speech fulfills an important intellectual function, helping to construct oratorical style as an ideal mean. However, this freedom from metrical constraints of oratorical discourse is exploited in different ways by different writers. In the section of the *De oratore* dealing with prose rhythm (3.182–6), Cicero states that prose speech (*oratio*) is more free (*liberior*) and capable of setting its own limits, whereas poets are forced by necessity to fit their words into metrical units:

> neque uero haec tam acrem curam diligentiamque desiderant, quam est illa poetarum; quos necessitas cogit et ipsi numeri ac modi sic uerba uersu includere, ut nihil sit ne spiritu quidem minimo breuius aut longius, quam necesse est. liberior est oratio et plane, ut dicitur, sic est uere soluta, non ut fugiat tamen aut erret, sed ut sine uinculis sibi ipsa moderetur.

> Certainly all this does not call for the painstaking care and diligence demanded of the poets. They are compelled by the constraints of their very rhythms and cadences to fit their words into verse in such a way that nothing is longer or shorter than required, even by the smallest breath. Prose speech is freer and indeed unbound, as it is called, though not so much that it will slip away or wander, but that without being chained, it will set its own limits. (Cicero, *De or.* 3.184, trans. May and Wisse)

In Cicero, the common phrase *oratio soluta* employed to denote prose is a true testament to the freedom (*soluta/soluere*) of the orator, whose task is therefore lighter than that of the poet.

In a surprising move, however, Quintilian reverses Cicero's position, presenting the orator's freedom as technically more demanding than the easy repetitive work of the poet. Thus, in the discussion of rhythm in the *Institutio*, Quintilian argues that prose rhythm is more difficult than poetic meter both because it necessitates constant adaptability and variation as opposed to the predictability of meter and because of the length of periods:

> ratio uero pedum in oratione est multo quam in uersu difficilior: primum quod uersus paucis continetur, oratio longiores habet saepe circumitus, deinde quod uersus semper similis sibi est et una ratione decurrit, orationis

Ornatus: *Poetic Tropes and Figures*

compositio, nisi uaria est, et offendit similitudine et in adfectatione deprenditur.

> The principles relating to feet are much more difficult in prose than in verse, first because a verse is limited to a few feet, whereas prose often has quite long periods, and secondly because verse is always uniform and proceeds on a single principle, whereas oratorical composition, unless it is varied, gives offence by its uniformity, and is seen to be contrived. (Quintilian 9.4.60)

Having already insisted on prose's "freedom," Quintilian here uses meter to demonstrate that prose is also technically more demanding, thus reversing Cicero's pronouncements. Prose discourse (*oratio*) is represented as an athlete who in order not to be caught (*deprehenditur*) must run longer distances (*circumitus*) in contrast to the poet who can simply hasten down (*decurrit*) with his verses.

Thus the introduction of poetic texts in the first book as sources for the teaching of *ornatus* reveals the limited extent of poetry's exemplary function. While the grammarian (and later the *rhetor*) is told to use poetic texts to illustrate tropes and figures and familiarize the pupil with the metrical units of Latin rhythm, he is also to point to the foreign nature of poetic style in so far as the latter twists, modifies and subverts language to serve the requirements of meter. In this way, poetry is portrayed as a tool to be judiciously exploited and simultaneously criticized as different.

Ornatus: Poetic Tropes and Figures

This programmatic distancing of rhetoric from the poetic medium is evident throughout Quintilian's work but nowhere more so than in books 8 and 9, where the topic of discussion is style (*elocutio*). Quintilian's account follows Cicero's and the Aristotelian treatment of the topic around four virtues: correctness, clarity, ornament and propriety.[18] Of these, correctness (*Latinitas*) and clarity (*luciditas*) occupy the first three chapters of book 8, while ornament (*ornatus*) takes up by far the bulk of this book as well as the entirety of the following one. The discussion of ornament resumes at the beginning of book 11 with a brief account of propriety (*decorum*) after a digression on the means to acquire facility in speaking that occupies the entirety of book 10 and that, as we will see, is in fact an integral part of Quintilian's account of style.

---

[18] On virtues of style in Aristotle and the subsequent development of this theory, see Solmsen (1941) 43–50.

96   The Orator and the Poet in Quintilian's *Institutio Oratoria*

In the course of the discussion of *ornatus* in books 8 and 9, Quintilian returns several times to the notion that the appropriate oratorical style is not one and the same as the poetic. It is crucial to note, however, that the gap between the poetic and the prosaic is seldom represented neutrally as an intrinsic distance or dissimilarity between different generic media but is rather constantly inflected along ethical lines, much to the detriment of poetry. Thus, in its distance from the everyday, poetry is aligned now with decadence, now with obscurity, now with linguistic irregularity. In the preface to book 8, the present decline in oratory is explained by the tendency on the part of his contemporaries to use words that depart from natural language and instead opt for metaphorical language, "borrowing figures or metaphors from the most decadent of poets" (8.pr.5 *a corruptissimo quoque poetarum figuras seu tralationes mutuamur*), as it were causing the crop that is their speech to be suffocated by luxuriant growth. Oratory strives for clarity while poets are allowed obscurity. Therefore, in similes, "what is selected to illustrate something else needs to be clearer than the thing it illustrates" (8.3.73), and to poets alone must be permitted what Virgil did in *Aen.* 4.143–4, when he compared Aeneas before the hunt to Apollo, thus daring to explain by analogy to something even more obscure than the concept in need of explanation. In metonymy, poets "dare" to indicate the container by reference to that which is contained (8.6.25: the example provided comes from Virgil *Aen.* 2.311–12, where *proximus ardet | Ucalegon* means "Ucalegon's *house* was on fire nearby"). In short, the evocation of the divide between rhetoric and poetry is polemically driven and typically geared toward representing rhetorical discourse as the more restrained and natural of the two.

The emulative spirit of Quintilian's project is evident in his treatment of poetic exempla, which he uses constantly despite his equally frequent warnings about the danger of poeticism. Certainly, poetic passages, the vast majority of which are drawn from Virgilian epic, are held up as a model for the orator. However, a more in-depth exploration of the use of poetic citations in these sections of the *Institutio* reveals not only that Quintilian is carefully presenting prose as an equally deserving exemplary model but also that poetic citations are frequently used in a subtly polemical vein.

To begin with, within the discussion of *ornatus*, poetic citations occur with greatest frequency in the section on tropes, which are most closely associated with poetry. However, while making use of poetic models, Quintilian strives to complement poetic exempla (mostly from Virgil) with prosaic ones (drawn overwhelmingly from Cicero). This point is

Ornatus: *Poetic Tropes and Figures* 97

stated explicitly in book 8, where he declares that, while he could find many worthy examples of similes in Virgil, he must seek his illustrations in oratory (8.3.79 *oratoriis potius utendum est*) and thereby suggests to his reader an implicit hierarchy of worthy models. The majority of the illustrations of tropes follow a specific pattern: poetic, and specifically Virgilian, quotations are first introduced to illustrate a stylistic device, but Ciceronian models are quickly brought in to illustrate that prose has the same, if not a bigger, range than poetry.

The discussion of metaphor in book 8 is to a great extent paradigmatic of Quintilian's method. Quintilian follows a fourfold classification of metaphors based on whether the substitution occurs between animate or inanimate things. The four types are all exemplified by poetry, respectively Ennius (*Ann.* 486), Virgil (*Aen.* 6.1 and 2.307–8) and an unknown tragedian, while all along Quintilian is paraphrasing Cicero's treatment of the same topic in *De or.* 3. Yet Quintilian's favorite metaphor defies this divide:

> praecipueque ex his oritur mira sublimitas quae audaci et proxime periculum tralatione tolluntur, cum rebus sensu carentibus actum quendam et animos damus, qualis est "pontem indignatus Araxes" et illa Ciceronis: "Quid enim tuus ille, Tubero, destrictus in acie Pharsalica gladius agebat? cuius latus ille mucro petebat? qui sensus erat armorum tuorum"?

> In particular, a wonderfully sublime effect is produced if the subject is elevated by a bold and hazardous metaphor, when we attribute some sort of action and feeling to senseless objects: "Araxes who spurns bridges"; or Cicero's "What was that sword of yours doing, Tubero, the sword you drew on the field of Pharsalus? At whose body was that sword pointed? What was the meaning of your appearing under arms?" (Quintilian 8.6.11–12)

Quintilian's penchant for emotional amplification and sublimity of thought is reflected in his choice of passages, respectively the depiction of the river Araxes' defiant spurning of bridges from Aeneas' shield in *Aen.* 8 (8.728) and Cicero's accusation against Tubero from the *Pro Ligario* (9). The arrangement is deliberately climactic: after the rather mechanical exposition of categories has been illustrated with poetic examples, two outstanding passages (one from poetry and one from prose) are brought in to exemplify the recommended style; more attention is drawn to the prose passage, which is longer and consequently acts as a cap to the whole section.

Next, Quintilian discusses which metaphors are appropriate in oratory. According to Quintilian, the type most recommended in prose is especially associated with necessary metaphors, as opposed to ornamental "poetic" metaphors. This division essentially goes back to Aristotle's treatment of

98   The Orator and the Poet in Quintilian's *Institutio Oratoria*

metaphor in *Rhetoric* book 3. Whereas, in the *Poetics*, Aristotle asserted that the metaphorical is the most important thing in poetry, in the *Rhetoric* we encounter the surprising notion that "a word in its prevailing and native meaning and metaphor are alone useful in the *lexis* of prose" (3.2.1404b31–3 τὸ δὲ κύριον καὶ τὸ οἰκεῖον καὶ μεταφορὰ μόνα χρήσιμα πρὸς τὴν τῶν ψιλῶν λόγων λέξιν). However, already in *Poet.* 22, Aristotle had argued that expressions like metaphor are those best suited to ordinary speech and therefore to iambus, which closely resembles it (1459a9–13).[19] More specifically, in the *Rhetoric*, Aristotle identifies the laughable and tragic kinds of metaphors as "poetic" and unbecoming (3.3.1406b) and recommends instead *metaphorai* based on analogy (3.2.1405b10–11 δεῖ δὲ καὶ τὰ ἐπίθετα καὶ τὰς μεταφορὰς ἁρμοττούσας λέγειν. τοῦτο δ' ἔσται ἐκ τοῦ ἀνάλογον·), a type that corresponds closely to the common notion of metaphor and is discussed at more length at 3.10.1411a, where the examples provided are similes and metaphors.[20] This apparent inconsistency – metaphor as both a device for ornamentation and a feature of everyday speech – is explained by its being a highly prized intellectual ability to detect likeness in things that are very different.[21] In addition, metaphor is also a natural feature of language and language expansion, so that Aristotle claims that "all people carry on their conversations with metaphors" (3.2.1404b34). Although Aristotle does not elaborate on this insight, later theorists such as Quintilian distinguish between unnecessary and necessary metaphors. The latter are known as *catachreseis* (*abusiones*: Quintilian 8.6.34) and borrow from an extraneous semantic field to fill a deficiency in the language, as when the vine bud is referred to as a "jewel" (*gemma*) or the parched harvest as "thirsty" (*sitire segetes*) (8.6.6). While language naturally extends the meaning of words to fill in for a concept to which no word corresponds, according to Quintilian, "the poets are in the habit of using closely related words catachrestically even for things which do have names of their own" (8.6.35 *nam poetae solent abusiue etiam in iis rebus quibus nomina sua sunt uicinis potius uti*).

This polarity between natural/necessary and artificial/ornamental reinscribes the fundamental distinction between the natural authenticity of

---

[19] Cf. *Rh.* 3.1.1404a34ff, where Aristotle asserts that poetry evolved toward a more restrained, "prosaic" style closer to everyday language with tragedy's iambics. For this tendency on the part of Aristotle to conflate appropriate and desirable prosaic style with tragedy at the expense of epic poetry, see Halliwell (1986) 347–8.

[20] On analogical metaphors, see Aristotle, *Poet.* 1457b16–33.

[21] Hence Aristotle sees a connection between metaphor and philosophy: "as in philosophy too, it is characteristic of a well-directed mind to observe the likeness even in things very different" (*Rh.* 3.11.1412a12–13). On the tension between the poetic and the everyday in Aristotle's theory of metaphor, see Kirby (1997) 534 and 541–7.

Ornatus: *Poetic Tropes and Figures* 99

prose and the artificiality of poetry, which is explored in the remainder of the section. The last quotation in the chapter is from Furius Bibaculus, already criticized by Horace in *Sat.* 2.5.40, and thus a decisively negative model. This quotation is followed by an elaborate passage on the inappropriateness of imitating the poets in their use of tropes. Calling on the traditional dichotomy between pleasure and utility, freedom and constraint in the definition of prose and poetry, Quintilian argues that it is a mistake to use metaphors in the same way in the two genres.

> in illo uero plurimum erroris, quod ea quae poetis, qui et omnia ad uoluptatem referunt et plurima uertere etiam ipsa metri necessitate coguntur, permissa sunt conuenire quidam etiam prorsae putant. at ego in agendo nec "pastorem populi" auctore Homero dixerim nec uolucres per aera "nare," licet hoc Vergilius in apibus ac Daedalo speciosissime sit usus. metaphora enim aut uacantem locum occupare debet aut, si in alienum uenit, plus ualere eo quod expellit.

> The biggest mistake, however, is made by those who believe that everything is appropriate in prose which is permitted to the poets, whose only standard is pleasure and who are often forced into Tropes by the necessities of metre. Personally, I would not say "shepherd of the people" on Homer's authority in a speech, nor speak of birds "swimming" through the air, though Virgil uses this very beautifully for the bees and for Daedalus [*G.* 4.59; *Aen.* 6.16]. Metaphor ought either to occupy a vacant space or, if it replaces something else, to be more effective than the word it banishes. (Quintilian 8.6.17–18)

While poetic metaphor aims at pleasure, prosaic metaphor is driven by utility. Thus the apt metaphor in prose will either occupy a "vacant space" (*uacantem locum*), that is will be necessary, or serve the purpose of expressing a concept "with more force" (*plus ualere*). This latter category is obviously vague and highly subjective. Yet what counts here once again is the way in which these distinctions color the representation of prose and poetry. Prosaic metaphor is represented as a settler who occupies unclaimed space, as opposed to poetic metaphor, whose right to occupy someone else's space is problematic and contingent on its force.

In this respect, Quintilian's concern over the danger of poeticism is a striking departure from Cicero's treatment of the same topic in *De oratore* book 3.[22] Cicero's account of metaphor is similarly structured around an evolutionary movement from necessity to art: at first, poverty and shortage

---

[22] For other passages denouncing the dangers of poeticism in the use of metaphor, see Demetrius, *Eloc.* 78: "[metaphors] must not occur too frequently or we find ourselves writing dithyrambic poetry instead of prose."

gave rise to metaphor, which was later made popular by pleasantness and charm (3.155). There are thus two kinds of metaphors: those "metaphors which are almost borrowings, since you take that which you do not have from some other source, and then there are those bolder ones, which do not point to a shortage, but rather bring some splendor to a speech" (3.156 *ergo hae translationes quasi mutuationes sunt, cum quod non habeas aliunde sumas, illae paulo audaciores, quae non inopiam indicant, sed orationi splendoris aliquid arcessunt*). Although Cicero warns about metaphor needing not to be more elevated than the subject requires (3.164 *maius quam res postulet*) and to be bashful (3.165 *uerecunda*), he is on the whole unconcerned with over-poeticism.[23] On the contrary, the example he gives of a praiseworthy metaphor used to illuminate style (3.157 *quae clariorem rem faciunt*) is an elaborate fragment from a Pacuvian tragedy describing a storm (411–16 Ribbeck and see further p. 151). Cicero's own version of the storm metaphor in the *Pro Murena* (36), comparing the storms in electoral assemblies to unpredictable weather phenomena, is described by Quintilian in our section as "almost endowed with poetic inspiration" (8.3.80 *paene poetico spiritu*).

By contrast, in those sections where Quintilian is limiting himself to poetic examples, his tone is often critical: thus two Virgilian passages are used to illustrate the vice of obscurity (8.2.15: *Aen.* 1.109, *G.* 3.79–84). In the discussion of similes referred to above, he gives several examples drawn from Virgil's *Aeneid* in order to provide initial categorizations (8.3.72–8) but also criticizes Virgil for using a simile that has no term of reference in the narrative (8.3.78–9) – the technical term employed is *antapodosis*, lit. "repayment." Amplification, which is treated in book 8.4, stands out for being the only section from book 8 in which all but two examples are drawn from Ciceronian speeches. This is not surprising in view of the fact that amplification is a central virtue of rhetorical style and in the section of his work dealing with the topic, Longinus declares Cicero the unchallenged champion of amplification (*Subl.* 12).

The section on figures in book 9 – figures of thought (9.2) and figures of speech (9.3) – is overall more independent from poetry. Cicero in the *Orator* had already deemed figures of thought the greatest ornament to public speech and reports that Demosthenes was considered by many to be particularly admirable on the basis of his use of these figures (*Orat.* 136). Naturally then, Ciceronian *exempla* as well as passages drawn from

---

[23] Innes (1988) 315–20. Along the same lines, see Cicero, *Orat.* 81 *in transferendis uerecundus et parcus*; Longinus *Subl.* 32 on the need to curb the excesses of natural language; Demetrius, *Eloc.* 83–4.

Poetry and the Orator: Understanding Book 10   101

otherwise unattested Roman orators abound in this section, which turns out to be a priceless source for the history of Roman oratory. It is also interesting to note that Virgilian citations most often are excerpted from speeches of various characters, most notably Dido's and Aeneas' speeches in book 4 of the *Aeneid*.[24] The balance of poetic and prosaic citations is higher in the section on figures of speech, but yet again the use of poetry is pointed: figures based on variations in grammatical form (gender, number, verb, tense, solecisms etc.) are illustrated almost exclusively from poetry (9.3.1–27). Prose, especially oratory, and poetry are cited interchangeably in the section on figures based on addition (9.3.28–57) and in the section on figures based on subtraction (9.3.58–65) and the one on figures based on sound (9.3.66–86), but with some provisos: some types of anaphora are found mostly in poetry (9.3.44) and less so in oratory, while balance in sound is to be avoided as too Gorgianic and suited to poetry (9.3.74).

Poetry and the Orator: Understanding Book 10

It is with an appreciation of Quintilian's emulative spirit in mind that we should approach the tenth book of the *Institutio Oratoria* and its discussion of poetry's role in the training of the orator. Although the section containing Quintilian's "reading list" is without question the most widely read part of the work, it is also the hardest to understand in its complex relation to the surrounding narrative. Full of memorable sententious pronouncements easy to quote on the style of all major Roman writers, this section of the work seems to encourage a piecemeal approach that neglects not just the place of the book in the *Institutio* but also the role of the reading list proper in the context of book 10.[25]

The topic of this book is facility in speaking (*facilitas*), without which, according to Quintilian, the rules of rhetoric (*praecepta eloquendi*) discussed in the previous books carry no force. Technically, the book as a whole is a digression from the main topic in this section of the work, namely *elocutio* (style) which, as we have seen, occupies books 8 and 9 (on tropes and figures), book 10 on training and book 11, which begins with a section on decorum in *elocutio* before moving on to the remaining two of the five parts of rhetoric, namely *memoria* and *actio*. This digression is distinctively innovative and serves several purposes in the project of the

---

[24] For the rhetorical value of this book, see Servius *ad Aen.* 4.pr. *sane totus in consiliis et subtilitatibus est.* 4.173ff. ~ 9.2.36; 4.425–6 ~ 9.2.39; 4.379 ~ 9.2.50; 4.381 ~ 9.2.48; 4.550–1 ~ 9.2.644; 4.592 ~ 9.2.11; 595 ~ 9.3.25.
[25] See, however, helpful remarks in Schneider (1983).

102   The Orator and the Poet in Quintilian's *Institutio Oratoria*

Institutio:[26] while it is technically still part of the discussion of style, by virtue of its focus on the orator's training, book 10 actually picks up on the discussion of education left off at the end of book 2 and only resumed at the end of book 12 when Quintilian addresses the needs of the fully fledged, mature *orator*. Thus the discussion of imitation and of the appropriate balance between poetry and prose in the training of the orator in this book are bound up in important ways with Quintilian's unique authorial self-presentation as an educator. To support this claim, it is enough to look at *Ad Herennium*'s treatment of the same topic perfunctorily left to the very last sentence of the treatise and unsurprisingly so given that *Ad Herennium*'s authorial persona is that of a public man (1.1 *etsi negotiis familiaribus impediti uix satis otium studio suppeditare possumus . . .*).[27]

Secondly, in harking back to books 1 and 2 through the lens of education, book 10 with its digression on *facilitas* breaches the traditional handbook structure that dominates books 3–11. This arrangement goes back to Aristotle's *Rhetoric* and was based on the five parts, or *officia*, of rhetoric: *inuentio, dispositio, elocutio, memoria* and *actio*. In broad terms, the *Ad Herennium* and Cicero, *De inuentione* and *De oratore* follow this principle of arrangement. The first two combine this division with a treatment of the three kinds of causes (deliberative, forensic and epideictic).[28] Quintilian distinctly innovates on this organizational principle in the first place by bookending the traditional discussion of the five parts of rhetoric with two long sections, books 1–2 and book 12 respectively.[29] Prefaced by a letter to the bookseller Trypho, who has been soliciting the publication of the work, books 1 (dealing with elementary education under the *grammaticus*) and 2 (on education under the rhetor) function as an introduction to the handbook proper and its fivefold topical division over the central books (3–11). The handbook section of the *Institutio* (3–11) is then followed by book 12, whose topic is the mature orator and which deals respectively with the *opus* (12.1–9), that is oratory, and the *artifex* (12.10–end).[30] In turn, these two

---

[26] Comparable lists are Theon, *Progymnasmata* 13; Dio Chrysostomus, *Or.* 18; Hermogenes, *Id.* 395–413. See Rutherford (1992), esp. 359–63.

[27] *Rhet. Her.* 4.56.69 *Haec omnia adipiscemur, si rationes praeceptionis diligentia consequemur exercitationis.*

[28] For example, books 1 and 2 of the *Ad Herennium* focus on judicial and deliberative causes; book 3 deals with the epideictic type before moving into the *officia* of rhetoric (*dispositio, actio, memoria*); book 4 is devoted to *elocutio*. *De oratore*: book 2 *inuentio, dispositio, memoria*; book 3: *elocutio*. On status theory and its development, see Calboli Montefusco (1986) and on status theory in the *Institutio* see Adamietz (1966) 14–21.

[29] The plan is laid out in the preface to book 1: Quintilian 1.pr.21–5.

[30] In so doing, Quintilian eschews the treatment of the three causes as a principle of arrangement although the epideictic and deliberative types are dealt with extensively in the discussion of

Poetry and the Orator: Understanding Book 10   103

sections are balanced by the previous eleven books, which together form a unity, the subject of which is rhetorical *ars* (see Figure 1).

Behind this division of the *Institutio* in three parts – *ars* (books 1–11), *opus* (12.1–9) and *artifex* (12.10–end), however, is an implicit chronological arrangement, as Quintilian's work reflects and captures the educational path of his student from the school of the *grammaticus* (books 1–2), to rhetorical school (books 3–11), to the fully fledged orator's practice in the courts (book 12).[31] Quintilian's persona as an educator thus prevails over the dry structuring principle of the parts of rhetoric derived from the handbook tradition.

Thus, although it is often referred to as a "handbook," the *Institutio* is a grand literary and cultural project that spans several genres such as the treatise, which is especially important for books 1–2 and 12, and the rhetorical manual, the main frame of reference for books 3–11.[32] In addition, an important model in book 10 is Cicero's *Brutus*, whose historical survey of Roman oratory is influential for Quintilian's list.[33] Indeed, the reading list proper opens with an elaborate *recusatio* in which Quintilian invokes Cicero's selective approach in the *Brutus*, where contemporary orators are excluded from the survey:

> credo exacturos plerosque, cum tantum esse utilitatis in legendo iudicemus, ut id quoque adiungamus operi, qui sint legendi, quae in auctore quoque praecipua uirtus. sed persequi singulos infiniti fuerit operis. quippe cum in Bruto M. Tullius tot milibus uersuum de Romanis tantum oratoribus loquatur et tamen de omnibus aetatis suae, qui quidem tum uiuebant, exceptis Caesare atque Marcello, silentium egerit: quis erit modus si et illos et qui postea fuerunt et Graecos omnis et philosophos <et poetas et historicos persequamur>? Fuit igitur breuitas illa tutissima quae est apud Liuium in epistula ad filium scripta, legendos Demosthenen atque Ciceronem, tum ita ut quisque esset Demostheni et Ciceroni simillimus.

> In view of the fact that I consider reading to be so useful, I expect most of my readers will want me to add a statement of what authors are to be read and the special virtues of each. But it would be an endless task to go through them one

---

invention in book three (3.7 epideictic; 3.8 forensic). Another noticeable innovation is the displacement of the discussion of the three styles (grand, middle, low) from the section on *elocutio* (cf. *Rhet. Her.* 4) to the section on *opus* in book 12 (12.10): Russell (2001b) vol. 1, 10–12.

[31] Quintilian 1.pr.6 *non inutiles fore libri uidebantur quos ab ipsis dicendi uelut incunabulis per omnes quae modo aliquid oratori futuro conferant artis ad summum eius operis perducere festinabimus.*

[32] Colson (1924) xviii–xlii.

[33] Other historical surveys in the *Institutio* for which the *Brutus* is an important model are 3.1–2 on the history of rhetoric and 12.10 on development of style. A study of the reception of the *Brutus* in the *Institutio* is sorely needed but is beyond the scope of this book.

QUITILIAN'S *INSTITUTIO ORATORIA*											
1	2	3	4	5	**6**	7	8	9	10	11	12
Grammaticus	Rhetor	Status theory Three Genres: epideictic, deliberative, forensic	Parts of forensic causes: proemia, narrative, digressions, etc.	Proofs and Refutations	***Proem in the middle*** **The Emotions**	Division	*Ornatus* : figures and tropes		*Facilitas*	*Decorum in elocutio* 11.3 *Memoria* 11.2 *Actio* 11.3	12.1–9 *uir bonus dicendi peritus* 12.10 Types of style 12.11 Conclusion
The orator's education		*INVENTIO*				*DISPOSITIO*	*ELOCUTIO*			*ELOCUTIO* continued-*MEMORIA-ACTIO*	The finished orator
ARS										12.1–9 *ARTIFEX*	
										12.10–11 *OPUS*	

Figure 1 Plan of the *Institutio Oratoria*

Poetry and the Orator: Understanding Book 10   105

by one. Cicero, in the *Brutus*, writes thousands of lines just about Roman orators, yet without saying anything of his contemporaries, those at least who were alive at the time, except for Caesar and Marcellus; where will be the limit, then, if I try to include these and their successors, all the Greeks, and the philosophers, the poets and the historians? Safest is the brief advice given by Livy in his letter to his son, to read Demosthenes and Cicero, and then others as they are most like Demosthenes and Cicero. (Quintilian 10.1.37–9)

This passage exhibits several features typical of prefaces:[34] the idea that the present writing is in response to a reader's request (*exacturos*) echoes the prefatory epistle as well as the introduction and is a staple of the prefatory genre. Connected to the *topos* of the reader's request is the humble tone with which Quintilian declares his inability to write about the whole of Greco-Roman literature. In an elaborate rhetorical question, Quintilian doubts whether, if Cicero in thousands of lines was only able to write about dead Roman orators, he would be able to encompass the whole of Greco-Roman literature. Should he perhaps not restrict himself to Livy's advice to read Cicero and Demosthenes and whoever is closest to them? Quintilian is selective in his choice of representative figures: later in the section on Greek poetry, he once again affirms that quality is the most important factor: "while we are still striving for that assured facility of which I spoke, it is the best writers to whom we must become accustomed" (10.1.59 *sed dum adsequimur illam firmam, ut dixi, facilitatem, optimis adsuescendum est et multa magis quam multorum lectione formanda mens et ducendus color*). However, Quintilian's list is also remarkably ambitious, encompassing as it does all known genres and both literatures and the implied comparison with the *Brutus* is disinguous, since Quintilian's list famously extends to contemporaries, most notably Domitian (10.1.91) and near contemporaries such as Seneca the Younger and Persius.

As Quintilian tells us in the opening lines of the book, as necessary as rhetorical precepts are, they are not sufficient for oratorical force unless they are accompanied by facility that is arrived at by reading and writing (10.1.1). The book as a whole then traces the role of these two activities in developing style: chapters 1 and 2 tackle respectively reading, which texts are best suited to develop style and the best practices in imitation, while the remainder of the book (10.3–7) focuses on writing. As Elaine Fantham notes in her study of theories of imitation, it is important to bear in mind that the reading list serves a limited purpose, discussing not the best writers in general but the best models for the orator.[35] Quintilian emphasizes this

---

[34] Janson (1964) 117–34.   [35] Fantham (1978) 103.

106   The Orator and the Poet in Quintilian's *Institutio Oratoria*

point repeatedly in the list – for example, in refusing to decide whether Sophocles or Euripides is the better poet (10.1.67). There is much dispute, he argues, as to which is the better but the question has nothing to do with his subject. What matters, according to Quintilian, is that "Euripides will be much the more useful to persons preparing themselves to plead in court" (10.1.67 *iis qui se ad agendum comparant utiliorem longe fore Euripiden*). Underlining this distinction between the "best" and the "best for the orator" is perhaps a polemical attempt by Quintilian to differentiate himself from the Hellenistic canon traditions exemplified by Aristarchus' list of lyric poets (10.1.59) and the canon of ten Attic orators (10.1.76).[36]

The limited scope of Quintilian's approach to literature as a source for facility in oratory is confirmed by the preliminary discussion of the main four genres – oratory (10.1.20–6), poetry (10.1.27–30), history (10.1.31–4) and philosophy (10.1.35–6) – and their contribution to the mastery of style. The order of presentation is far from random: what we have is a pointed hierarchical structure in which poetry is presented as the greatest asset to the orator after oratory itself. Crucially, however, Quintilian endorses poetry as a model for the orator only to a limited extent. Rehearsing arguments that are by now familiar to us, Quintilian argues that poetry is different from oratory in that it is designed for display (*ostentatio*) and pleasure (*uoluptas*) and is constrained to use metaphorical expression by its use of meter (*ad certam pedum necessitatem*) and should therefore not be followed in every respect, especially in its freedom of vocabulary and license to develop figures (10.1.28 *meminerimus tamen non per omnia poetas esse oratori sequendos, nec libertate uerborum nec licentia figurarum*).

In the preface to the reading list, poetry is followed by history, which is defined as "very close to the poets and almost a poem written in prose" (10.1.31 *est enim proxima poetis, et quodam modo carmen solutum est*). The lowest space on the scale is occupied by philosophy, whose only rationale for being on the list at all is the decadence of modern oratory that no longer deals with philosophical subject matter (10.1.35).

As we approach the discussion of the role of poetry in the reading-list section of book 10, it is important to read the author's explicit message – his measured approach to the usefulness of poetry – against the implicit rhetorical emphasis accorded to poetry in this generic hierarchy. The pride of place in the reading list goes to Homer, whose priority forms the subject of the opening section of the list:

---

[36] Cf. Quintilian's ironic presentation of the job of the old *grammatici* in 1.4.3. On Quintilian and the canon, see Douglas (1956); Rutherford (1992) 361–2.

Poetry and the Orator: Understanding Book 10   107

igitur, ut Aratus ab Ioue incipiendum putat, ita nos rite coepturi ab Homero uidemur. hic enim, quem ad modum ex Oceano dicit ipse omnium amnium fontiumque cursus initium capere, omnibus eloquentiae partibus exemplum et ortum dedit. hunc nemo in magnis rebus sublimitate, in paruis proprietate superauerit. idem laetus ac pressus, iucundus et grauis, tum copia tum breuitate mirabilis, nec poetica modo sed oratoria uirtute eminentissimus.

Therefore, as Aratus says "let us begin with Zeus," so the proper place for us to begin is with Homer. Like his own Ocean, which he says is the source of every river and spring, Homer provides the model and the origin of every department of eloquence. No one surely surpassed him in sublimity in great themes, or in propriety in small. He is at once luxuriant and concise, charming and grave, marvelous in his fullness and in his brevity, supreme not only in poetic but in oratorical excellence. (Quintilian 10.1.46)

The allegorical use of the passage about Oceanus in *Il.* 21.195–7, in the context of the celebration of Homer as the supreme model for both orator and poet, is by Quintilian's time a *topos*.[37] Just as Oceanus is hailed in Homer as the father of all rivers, so Homer is celebrated as the spring of all parts of *eloquentia*, and in what follows he is said to exemplify among other things not only the three styles of oratory but also the handling of emotions, the parts of a speech (e.g. *proemium*), figures and arrangement. Despite the fact that Quintilian can talk of a poetic kind of *uirtus* as distinct from a rhetorical type, the implication of this aetiology of rhetoric is that poetry is the overarching source of both. This account is thus close to the one found in Strabo (see p. 40–1), according to whom poetry is constructed as "the source and origin of style, that is, ornate, or rhetorical, style" (πηγὴ καὶ ἀρχὴ φράσεως κατεσκευασμένης καὶ ῥητορικῆς ὑπῆρξεν ἡ ποιητική 1.2.6).

Furthermore, Quintilian restates the contiguity of the two media in a later passage from book 10 in which the subject is propriety in imitation:

id quoque uitandum, in quo magna pars errat, ne in oratione poetas nobis et historicos, in illis operibus oratores aut declamatores imitandos putemus. sua cuique proposito lex, suus decor est: nec comoedia in coturnos adsurgit, nec contra tragoedia socco ingreditur. habet tamen omnis eloquentia aliquid commune: id imitemur quod commune est.

We must also avoid this mistake, into which many fall, of imitating poets and historians in speeches, and orators or declaimers in history and poetry. Each genre has its own law, and its own standards of appropriateness. Comedy does not walk tall in tragedy's high boots, nor tragedy amble on

---

[37] Dionysius of Halicarnassus, *Comp.* 24; Ovid, *Am.* 3.9.25.

108 The Orator and the Poet in Quintilian's *Institutio Oratoria*

> in comedy's slippers. Still, all eloquence has something in common, and it is this common element that we should imitate. (Quintilian 10.2.21–2)

This use of the word *eloquentia* in the context of book 10 to describe, in Roland Mayer's words, "the artistic use of language" or the idea of "language as an artifact" is not limited to Quintilian.[38] What counts here is that the aetiological derivation of rhetoric from the spring of Homeric poetry forms an important backdrop to Quintilian's own rhetoric in the list: the selection of poetic models and treatment thereof are heavily influenced by their potential as rhetorical sources of instruction. Thus, in the preliminary discussion of the role of poetry in 10.1.27–30, citing Theophrastus, Quintilian states that poetry is a source of *sublimitas* in style and is suitable for learning techniques of emotional arousal (*in adfectibus motus omnis*) and decorum in characterization (*in personis decorum*).[39] The usefulness of poetic models on these three grounds is confirmed in the list proper, where, besides Homer, Euripides and Menander receive the highest praise. All three are celebrated as the best models for the orator on account of their handling of *adfectus*, while Aratus is predictably criticized for lacking *uarietas, adfectus* and *persona*.[40] Moreover, Menander, who is characterized as the best model for the orator together with Homer, is praised for his handling of persona and referred to for that reason as a suitable model for declaimers.[41]

The preferences expressed in the poetry list reflect these overarching priorities and are confirmed by the frequency of poetic, especially Virgilian, citations in book 6, the section of the work devoted to the emotions. Crucially, while the section on laughter (6.3) uses several Ciceronian examples drawn both from his oratory and from his theoretical writing, the section on pathos (6.2) – by far the most important emotion in oratory (6.2.7 *adeo uelut spiritus operis huius* [i.e. oratory] *atque animus est in adfectibus*) – is illustrated almost exclusively with passages from the *Aeneid*. Even before the discussion begins, the Sibyl's warning to Aeneas at the beginning of book 6 – *hoc opus, hic labor est* (6.129) – is quoted to invite

---

[38] Mayer (2001) 118 *ad* Tacitus, *Dial.* 10.4–5; Gudeman (1914) 206 *ad Dial.* 4.4.

[39] The connection between poets and orators on the grounds of a shared interest in the emotion is nothing new: e.g. Ovid, *Pont.* 2.5.65–70, discussed on p. 20, *distat opus nostrum, sed fontibus exit ab isdem | artis et ingenuae cultor uterque sumus. | Thyrsus abest a te gustata et laurea nobis, | sed tamen ambobus debet inesse calor, | utque meis numeris tua dat facundia neruos, | sic uenit a nobis in tua uerba nitor*; Cicero, *De or.* 2.193–4; *Tusc.* 1.64.

[40] Quintilian 10.1.55 *Arati materia motu caret, ut in qua nulla uarietas, nullus adfectus, nulla persona, nulla cuiusquam sit oratio.*

[41] Quintilian 10.1.69 *ita omnem uitae imaginem expressit, tanta in eo inueniendi copia et eloquendi facultas, ita est omnibus rebus personis adfectibus accommodatus.*

Poetry and the Orator: Understanding Book 10 109

the orator to keep a firm focus on *adfectus*, just as Aeneas is summoned to make his journey to and from the Underworld. Andromache's opening words in *Aen.* 3.321–2 – *o felix una ante alias Priameia uirgo . . .* – display fear (6.2.21–2); the reaction of Euryalus' mother to his death as she lets the shuttle fly from her hand at *Aen.* 9.476, Pallas' "gaping wound on his smooth breast" (*leuique patens in pectore uulnus*) at *Aen.* 11.40, and his horse "his trappings laid aside" (*positis insignibus*) at *Aen.* 11.89 and finally Antenor's dying thoughts at *Aen.* 10.782 exemplify *euidentia/enargeia*, the orator's ability to exhibit rather than describe pathetic scenes.

Quintilian's list as a whole is divided into two chronological and geographical halves: the first focuses on Greek literature down to the second century BCE, while the latter is occupied by a discussion of Roman models (10.1.85–131). The internal arrangement of the Greek list is mirrored by that of the Roman list. However, when we compare the internal order of both lists with the theoretical discussion that precedes it (10.1.20–36), it is impossible not to notice that the hierarchy we first encounter in the book is upset in the reading list proper. In the theoretical discussion, oratory stood at the top, followed by poetry, its twin, history, and philosophy. This order, however, is interestingly modified in both the Greek and the Roman reading lists, where poetry is followed by history, and then oratory and philosophy. The discussion of Greek poetry that opens the section is arranged in a ring composition structure, beginning and ending with the two most influential poetic models, namely Homer and Menander. In the Greek reading list, Thucydides and Herodotus are the primary models among the historians (10.1.73–5), Demosthenes the undiscussed champion among the vast army of orators (10.1.76–80), while the section on philosophers is almost entirely occupied by a series of elaborate rhetorical questions highlighting the sublimity of Plato's style (10.1.81–2). Here, it is to be noted that while philosophy has displaced oratory in the emphatic last position of the catalogue, Plato is described as "soaring high above prose" (*multo enim supra prorsam orationem . . . surgit*) and endowed with Homeric gifts of style (*eloquendi facultate diuina quadam et Homerica*).

The Roman list begins with the emphatic statement that Quintilian will follow the same order in this section as he did in the Greek catalogue (10.1.85). Thus the list begins with the canonical comparison between Homer and Virgil, the *Homerus Romanus*. Though this section of the work is among the most cited, it contains some peculiar assertions. To begin with, the rhetorical emphasis of the Roman list is different from that of the Greek section: whereas in the latter the main criterion is excellence

110   The Orator and the Poet in Quintilian's *Institutio Oratoria*

and suitability for the would-be orator, the paramount question in the former is the ability to challenge the Greeks. Virgil trails just behind Homer, being, however, closer to first than to third (10.1.86 *propior tamen primo quam tertio*); in Elegy too, Romans challenge (but tellingly do not surpass) the Greeks (10.1.93 *elegia quoque Graecos prouocamus*), while in comedy Romans "barely achieve a faint shadow" (10.1.100 *uix leuem consequimur umbram*). In addition, satire is distinctively Roman (10.1.93 *satura quidem tota nostra est*), while Roman history does not yield the prize to the Greeks (10.1.101 *at non historia cesserit Graecis*).[42]

It is not hard to detect the payoff of Quintilian's rhetorical presentation: his point, and the climax of his argument, is the contention that it is only in oratory that the Romans have been able to rival the Greeks: "it is our orators above all who enable us to put Roman *eloquentia* on equal terms with Greek: I would happily pit Cicero against any of the Greeks" (10.1.105 *oratores uero uel praecipue Latinam eloquentiam parem facere Graecae possunt: nam Ciceronem cuicumque eorum fortiter opposuerim*). This is indeed a striking departure from the vigorous plea on behalf of contemporary poets by Horace in the *Epistle to Augustus*. Quintilian's position, however, is not archaizing: on the contrary, with the exception of Lucilius, he characterizes older Roman poetry as relatively useless to the orator in training: Ennius' poetry (10.1.88) is to be worshipped for its sanctity (*religio*) rather than imitated for its beauty (*species*); Accius and Pacuvius lack polish and finishing touches and not even Plautus and Terence, whose work is much quoted by Quintilian, compete with Menander and old Comedy (10.1.99–100).

Far from an innocent exposition of the relative merits of the different genres for the training of the orator, the reading list has a precise rhetorical function stemming from Quintilian's intellectual agenda. For, while Homer is the source of *eloquentia* and Roman poetry discounted as altogether inferior to the Greek with the exception of Virgil, the Romans are said to tower over the Greeks in the field of oratory. Thus the presentation of poetry's role in the training of the orator throughout the first ten books of the *Institutio* is confirmed by the implicit rhetoric of the reading list: excellence for the Romans lies in oratory.

This point is driven home aggressively already in the treatment of Roman poetry, where all poets are said to trail far behind Virgil who is already second to Homer (10.1.87). This lukewarm depiction of the most-cited author in the *Institutio* after Cicero is striking: unlike Propertius, who

---

[42] For the digression on *satura* and Quintilian's engagement with Horace, see p. 113.

Poetry and the Orator: Understanding Book 10

famously hails the *Aeneid* as superior to the *Iliad* (2.34.66 *nescio quid maius nascitur Iliade*), Quintilian believes that Virgil trails behind Homer's immortal *natura* but surpasses him in *labor*. This contrast between *ars* and *natura* is far from flattering: one need only compare Ovid's famous assessment of Callimachus in *Am.* 1.15.13–14, where he states that "the son of Battus is sung throughout the world, although he is not strong for his talent, he is strong for his art" (*Battiades semper toto cantabitur orbe/ quamuis ingenio non ualet, arte ualet*). In addition, the contrast returns in the *synkrisis* of Demosthenes and Cicero, where the *ars* of the former is set side by side with the superior *natura* of the latter, and, while Quintilian is reticent, it is pretty clear that his preference is with Cicero.[43] Not only is Quintilian confident about Cicero's achievement vis-à-vis the Greeks but he boldly asserts Cicero's claim to subsume the best of Demosthenes, Plato and Isocrates (10.1.108–9).

An interesting case is represented by Lucan, the poet who receives arguably the highest commendation after Virgil. Generations of readers have puzzled over the meaning of Quintilian's assertion that Lucan's ardent and passionate style, distinguished for his *sententiae*, is to be imitated by orators more than by poets (10.1.90 *Lucanus ardens, concitatus, et sententiis clarissimus et, ut dicam quod sentio, magis oratoribus quam poetis imitandus*).[44] The development of *sententiae* was isolated as a feature of the new oratorical style by Quintilian back in 8.5, where the topic of *sententiae* is somewhat oddly introduced in the discussion of tropes. Thus the mention of Lucan's *sententiae* might explain the recommendation that the text be imitated by orators. However the case may be, the point about *sententiae* is not ultimately solid ground for praise, especially when read against the background of Quintilian's denunciation of the broken style of speech characterized by overuse of *sententiae* in 8.5.25–31 and his later dismissal of Seneca's excessively broken style full of distinguished *minutissimae sententiae* (10.1.129–30). This point is also confirmed by the fact that Quintilian never cites Lucan in the *Institutio*, although citations of his contemporary, Persius, abound.

Finally, modern poetry is characterized by loss of talent – the death of Valerius Flaccus (10.1.90); the unavailability of the emperor Domitian (10.1.91); Pomponius Secundus, whose talent is not, however, universally agreed on (10.1.98) – whereas, under Quintilian's expert guidance, oratory

---

[43] Quintilian 10.1.106 *curae plus in illo, in hoc naturae*. On this passage and the use of the *natura/ars* opposition in Quintilian, see Fantham (1995), esp. 131; Varwig (1976).

[44] See Ahl (2010).

112 The Orator and the Poet in Quintilian's *Institutio Oratoria*

has promise: "those who write about orators in the future will find ample material for genuine praise in those who are now in their prime, for the talents who grace the courts today are very great" (10.1.122 *habebunt qui post nos de oratoribus scribent magnam eos qui nunc uigent materiam uere laudandi: sunt enim summa hodie quibus inlustratur forum ingenia*).

Just as the Greek list ended with the philosophers, the Roman reading list culminates with an overview of Roman philosophical writing that ends with a digression on Seneca. I have noted earlier in this section that Quintilian modifies the hierarchy of genres – oratory, poetry, history, philosophy – announced at the beginning. In addition, as Ian Rutherford has noted, this peculiar arrangement is also a striking departure from Dionysius *Peri mimēseōs*, which may well have been one of Quintilian's sources in this book and placed oratory last, complementing the treatment of poetry in the first place.[45] Here, however, it is not hard to see how Quintilian has exploited this displacement of philosophy: To begin with, Quintilian's positioning of philosophy last allows him to claim Cicero as a supreme model for both the orator (an *alter* Demosthenes) and the philosopher (an *alter* Plato). In addition, the reading list ends not with the discussion of philosophy but with a long digression on Seneca the Younger, which provides a meaningful transition to the next section on imitation and acts as a conclusion to the list. Quintilian's ostensible reason for delaying discussion of Seneca is that he needs the space to respond to his critics who accused him of partiality when he, Quintilian, condemned Seneca's style as decadent in the now lost *De causis corruptae eloquentiae*.[46] However, Seneca is, in many ways, an apt figure with which to end the discussion: as Quintilian says, he attempted almost every genre (10.1.129 *tractauit etiam omnem fere studiorum materiam*), including oratory, poems, letters and dialogues. More importantly, the discussion of Seneca's style acts as a powerful bridge to the next chapter (10.2), which deals with imitation: echoing Seneca's own discussion of imitation in *Ep.* 114, Quintilian asserts that the youth crazy about Seneca's style liked only his faults. Because Seneca had talent (*ingenium*) but no judgment (*iudicium*), he is recommended reading only for the trained and mature orator who already knows how to use judgment and discretion. Crucially, selectivity and judgment are key points in the ensuing discussion of *imitatio* (see especially 10.2.14–26).[47]

---

[45] Rutherford (1992) 360. On Dionysius and Quintilian, see Peterson (1981) xxx–xxxiv.
[46] On this work, see Brink (1989) and, on Seneca in Quintilian's, see Taoka (2011).
[47] For the importance of these concepts in other ancient discussions of *imitatio*, see Russell (1979).

Poetry and the Orator: Understanding Book 10

To conclude, with its memorable pronouncements, Quintilian's list is often read as a document of literary history useful for reconstructing the reception of authors and texts in the early Roman Empire. In my reading, I have stressed the role of this section of the work in the overall presentation of the topic of style in the *Institutio*. Seemingly tucked away as a digression, book 10 is in fact pivotal to the project of the work, helping to establish a strong case for the rhetorical medium. While it begins with what appears to be a straightforward catalogue of top reading choices for the would-be orator, the list subtly mutates into a plea for modern-day oratory that more than holds its own against poetry.

One striking exception in the treatment of poetry is the status accorded to satire, the only poetic field that still produces talents who will one day be famous (10.1.94 *sunt clari hodieque et qui olim nominabuntur*), and, in what follows, I examine this much-quoted passage of the *Institutio* in light of Quintilian's discussion of style. In order to unravel the significance of this discussion and its role in the *Institutio*, it is necessary to examine Quintilian's discussion of *satura* in light of his use of Horace elsewhere in the work. I have noted above how the *Institutio*, which is typically dismissed as a rhetorical manual, is in fact a work of ambitious literary breadth encompassing the handbook, the history and the treatise. Yet another important but underacknowledged source of influence behind the literary structure of the work is provided by didactic poetry, specifically the Horatian discussions of literature in the *Ars Poetica*, *Epistles* and *Sermones*. The *Ars Poetica* is in fact already invoked as an implicit model in the epistle to the bookseller Trypho which prefaces the work:

> EPISTVLA I. M. FABIVS QVINTILIANVS TRYPHONI SVO SALVTEM. efflagitasti cotidiano conuicio ut libros quos ad Marcellum meum de institutione oratoria scripseram iam emittere inciperem. nam ipse eos nondum opinabar satis maturuisse, quibus componendis, ut scis, paulo plus quam biennium tot alioqui negotiis districtus inpendi: quod tempus non tam stilo quam inquisitioni operis prope infiniti et legendis auctoribus, qui sunt innumerabiles, datum est. usus deinde Horati consilio, qui in arte poetica suadet ne praecipitetur editio "nonumque prematur in annum," dabam his otium, ut refrigerato inuentionis amore diligentius repetitos tamquam lector perpenderem. sed si tantopere efflagitantur quam tu adfirmas, permittamus uela uentis et oram soluentibus bene precemur. multum autem in tua quoque fide ac diligentia positum est, ut in manus hominum quam emendatissimi ueniant. uale.

> You have been pressing me every day, with great insistence, to start publishing the books on "the orator's education" which I had written for my friend

114   The Orator and the Poet in Quintilian's *Institutio Oratoria*

> Marcellus. My own view was that they had not yet matured enough. As you know, I spent a little more than two years on composing them, at a time when I was anyway distracted by much business. The time has been spent not so much on the actual writing as on the research required by a work of almost infinite scope, and on reading the countless authorities. Since then, following the advice of Horace, who, in the *Ars Poetica*, urges that publication should not be hurried but "kept in store till the ninth year comes round," I have been giving them a rest, to let my satisfaction in my own productions cool, so as to go over them again more carefully, with a reader's eyes. But if they are called for as urgently as you allege, let us spread our sails before the wind and pray for a good voyage as we cast off. But it depends very much on your own loyal care also to see that they come into people's hands in as correct a form as possible. (Quintilian, Ep. ad Tryph.)

In this preface, Quintilian uses a quotation from the *Ars Poetica* to justify the length of time he took to complete the work. In explaining his reluctance to send Trypho the *Institutio Oratoria*, Quintilian protests that he has been following "the advice of Horace, who, in the *Ars Poetica* [v. 388], urges that publication should not be hurried but 'kept in store until the ninth year comes around'."

Quintilian's use of the Horatian quote at the onset of his work is clearly programmatic. To begin with, the Horatian quote claims for the *Institutio* the literary refinement of poetry, the image of the nine years of labor being a reference to Catullus 95, a poem that celebrates Cinna's publication of the *Zmyrna* nine summers and nine winters after it began to be written.[48] Having thus presented his work as deserving of the same *labor limae* as neoteric poetry, Quintilian uses the epic image of the sea voyage to represent the process of literary composition: "let us entrust our sails to the winds and as we cast off let us pray that it turns out well" (*permittamus uela uentis et oram soluentibus bene precemur*). This image recurs in the last book of the work, in a passage that, as we will see, exploits the presentation of the orator as an epic hero.[49] Elsewhere, Quintilian's programmatic language about his own work is redolent of metaphors that have a long association with poetic craft: his assertion of literary originality at the beginning of book 1 – 1.pr.3 *ne uulgarem uiam ingressus alienis demum*

---

[48] Catullus 95.1–2 *Zmyrna mei Cinnae nonam post denique messem | quam coepta est nonamque edita post hiemem.*

[49] Quintilian 12.pr.2 *mox uelut aura sollicitante prouecti longius ... nec adhuc a litore procul uidebamur ...* ; 12.11.4 *receptui canet et in portum integra naue perueniet.* Cf. Propertius 3.9.3 *quid me scribendi tam uastum mittis in aequor?*; Horace, *Carm.* 4.15.3–4 *ne parua Tyrrhenum per aequor | uela darem; Georg.* 2.41 *pelagoque uolans da uela patenti*; Cicero, *Orat.* 75; Livy 31.1.5, and see further Assfahl (1932) 66–9.

Poetry and the Orator: Understanding Book 10   115

uestigiis insisterem – is modeled on Horace's claim in *Ep.* 1.19.21–2 *libera per uacuum posui uestigia princeps, | non aliena meo pressi pede.* Book 4, whose topic is parts of speech, begins with a discussion of proemia. Yet this discussion is anticipated by an elaborate proemium to the book in which Quintilian, who is now a third into his project, cites delayed invocations to the Muses by poets (e.g. Homer, *Il.* 2.485ff.) as a model for his renewed prayer to Domitian.

Secondly, the reference to the Horatian passage situates the *Institutio* within the prestigious tradition of literary and rhetorical criticism that the *Ars Poetica* exemplified. The importance of Horace as a model for Quintilian's criticism is confirmed by the occurrence of citations of his works – *Sat.* 1.1, 1.4, 1.10, *Epistles* and, above all, *Ars Poetica* – a frequency only surpassed among the poets by Virgil.[50] Crucially, Quintilian uses Horace to back his own contentions, for example in the discussion of diction in 8.3.60, which ends with Quintilian's citing of the human–horse monster from the beginning of the *Ars Poetica* to exemplify the mumble-jumble mixture of different kinds of diction that characterizes *kakozelia*. Moreover, in book 10, Quintilian reuses two Horatian lines: in 10.1.25, he supports his discussion of the need for selectivity in imitation with the famous Horatian line from *Ars Poetica* – v. 359 *quandoque bonus dormitat Homerus* – about Homer nodding off to sleep; in 10.1.65, it is Horace's contention that Tyrtaeus comes next to Homer that is at issue.

The erudite digression on the origin of satire in book 10 fits well into this trend to appropriate and reuse Horatian critical discourse. As we saw earlier, the rhetorical drift of the argument in this section has moved away from reading toward the topic of emulation, the emphasis being no longer on the models for imitation but rather on the fields in which emulation will pay off. Quintilian's much-quoted statement "*satura qui-dem tota nostra est*" (10.1.93) fits in with this attempt to highlight Roman literary accomplishments. Moreover, four figures are mentioned: Lucilius, Horace, Persius and Varro. Of these, Horace is praised as the most eminent, followed by Persius, who is in fact cited several times by Quintilian. Quintilian's praise of Lucilius and Varro is more ambiguous: though he rejects Horace's criticism of Lucilius's muddy style, he does not agree that Horace is the best. Here, although Quintilian distances himself from Horace, he also praises him as a beloved model (*nisi labor eius amore*).

---

[50] E.g. *Ars P.* 311 – Quintilian 1.5.2; *Ars P.* 359 – Quintilian 10.1.24; *Ars P.* 402 – Quintilian 10.1.56. On Horace's role in Quintilian, see Calboli (1995).

116   The Orator and the Poet in Quintilian's *Institutio Oratoria*

Furthermore, while he praises Varro he considers him a model not of *eloquentia* but of *eruditio*.[51]

Quintilian's open challenge to Horace's evaluation of Lucilius and his derivation of Lucilian satire from Greek Old Comedy (*Sat.* 1.4.1–6) must be read in the context not only of Quintilian's interest in Roman accomplishments but also of his own *aemulatio* of Horace elsewhere in the *Institutio*. Quintilian's critical pose in this passage allows him to stake a claim as a writer in the tradition of Horatian literary criticism and put forward a competitive account of the history of the genre.

Quintilian's Epic Performances: The Orator and the Hero in Book 12

With Quintilian's emulation of Horace as a literary critic in the *Epistle to Trypho* and beyond, and the strategic evocation of the poetic language of *labor limae*, we have hit on a different and rarely studied aspect of Quintilian's literary project and its relation to poetry. Quintilian's use of poetry in these examples is significantly different from his frequent recourse to Virgilian citations to illustrate a grammatical point or rhetorical figure, a habit that was the focus of my discussion earlier. Whereas in those instances, poetry is used as a source of examples, albeit a problematic one, in these other cases the poetic model functions as an intertext, becoming part of the fabric of the argument and, as it were, being appropriated and subsumed by Quintilian's voice. This tendency on the part of Quintilian's text to incorporate poetry should not be surprising in view of what Gregory Hutchinson has described as the "two-way traffic" between didactic prose and poetry after the second century BCE.[52] As Hutchinson shows in relation to Lucretius and Virgil, not only does didactic poetry seek to appropriate the characteristics of technical prose but the commonly held view of didactic prose writers as dull sources whose material is brought alive by poets is contradicted by the ambitiousness and multilayered nature of the work of writers such as Varro, Vitruvius and Columella.

Similarly, Quintilian's work evokes the tradition of Lucretian and Virgilian didactic poetry as a parallel for his own didactic venture. In the proem to book 3, for example, as he moves on from the treatment of education to the technical section of his work, Quintilian evokes the example of Lucretius' "honey on the cup" (*DNR* 1.936–8) as a model for

---

[51] On the significance of Varro in this list, see Freudenburg (2013) esp. 298–300.
[52] Hutchinson (2009) and (2008) 230–50.

The Orator and the Hero in Book 12

delaying the dry and arid handbook sections until after books 1 and 2 (3.1.4 and cf. 1.4.5). More to the point, Quintilian frequently alludes to Virgil's *Georgics* in constructing his own didactic practices. It is well recognized that Quintilian frequently adopts agricultural metaphors to illustrate the process of oratorical training, especially in the first two books of the work where the subject is education:[53] young children will imitate their peers, just as vines climb by supporting themselves on the lower ones (1.2.26); precocious intellects of children are like seeds scattered on the surface of the soil with no real strong roots and shallow growth (1.3.5); education is compared to the training of young vines (1.3.12); a dry teacher should be avoided as much as a dry field (2.4.8); just as farmers avoid applying the pruning hook to the tender leaves, so too the teacher should avoid harsh punishment of young students (2.4.11). This comparison between agriculture and oratorical training is already found pervasively in the *De oratore*, and, in book 2, Quintilian explicitly acknowledges Cicero as a source for this metaphor, quoting Antonius' remark on Sulpicius' fertile style in his youth (Cicero, *De or.* 2.88 "I like fecundity to run riot in a young man": *uolo enim se efferat in adulescente fecunditas*).[54]

Crucially, however, in Quintilian the agricultural metaphor, familiar as it may have been in Ciceronian rhetorical writing, is now filtered and understood through the didactic tradition of Virgil's *Georgics*, whose discussion of vine growing in book 2.226–370 informs Quintilian's treatment of rhetorical training.[55] In 1.3.13, for example, the subject of which is how to train the gifts of young children, Quintilian summarizes his position by quoting a line from Virgil's description of soil preparation – *G.* 2.272 *adeo in teneris consuescere multum est*, "so strong is the habit in the tender plant" – to prove that important habits are formed in childhood.[56] The second book of the *Georgics* is again an important model in book 2 in the discussion of *progymnasmata*. After quoting Cicero's statement in the *De oratore* about the *fecunditas* of the young, Quintilian goes on to elaborate on the comparison, paraphrasing Virgil's description of pruning in *G.* 2:[57]

---

[53] Connors (1997) 77–81; Assfahl (1932) 44–5; Reinhardt and Winterbottom (2006) 91 on 2.4.11 and, on *natura* in the *Institutio*, see also Fantham (1995).

[54] Quintilian 2.4.8 *quod me de his aetatibus sentire minus mirabitur qui apud Ciceronem legerit: "uolo enim se efferat in adulescente fecunditas"* [*De or.* 2.88]. On this digression in *De oratore* and the use of the pruning metaphor, see Fantham (1972) 145–6.

[55] Mynors (1990) 144–5 *ad* Virgil, *G.* 2.362–70; Colson (1924) 33 on Quintilian 1.3.5.

[56] It should also be noted that Virgil is already casting trees metaphorically as young children: e.g. *G.* 2.268 *mutatam . . . matrem* with Thomas (1988) 205 ad loc.

[57] Reinhardt and Winterbottom (2006) 91 ad loc.

118   The Orator and the Poet in Quintilian's *Institutio Oratoria*

ne illud quidem quod admoneamus indignum est, ingenia puerorum nimia interim emendationis seueritate deficere; nam et desperant et dolent et nouissime oderunt et, quod maxime nocet, dum omnia timent nihil conantur. quod etiam rusticis notum est, qui frondibus teneris non putant adhibendam esse falcem, quia reformidare ferrum uidentur et nondum cicatricem pati posse.

It is worth noting too that boys' minds sometimes cannot stand up to undue severity in correction. They despair, they feel hurt, they come ultimately to hate the work, and (most damaging of all) they make no effort because they are frightened of everything. Farmers know this: they do not believe in applying the pruning hook to the tender leaves, because these seem to be afraid of the knife and not yet able to bear a scar. (Quintilian 2.4.10–12)

Quintilian's point is that, at an early stage, teachers should be kind, just like farmers who wait to prune the young leaves, which are scared of the knife and unable to bear a scar. Quintilian has here adapted Virgil's personification of the leaves shrinking from growth because of aggressive pruning:

> ac dum prima nouis adolescit frondibus aetas,
> parcendum teneris, et dum se laetus ad auras
> palmes agit laxis per purum immissus habenis,
> ipsa acie nondum falcis temptanda, sed uncis   365
> carpendae manibus frondes interque legendae.
> inde ubi iam ualidis amplexae stirpibus ulmos
> exierint, tum stringe comas, tum bracchia tonde
> (ante reformidant ferrum), tum denique dura
> exerce imperia et ramos compesce fluentis.

While they are growing new leaves in their tender age, you must spare the tender ones and while the young vine branch shoots towards the sky cheerfully sent through the void with free rein it must not be assailed by the very sharpness of the sickle but the leaves are to be plucked and thinned out with bent fingers. But when they come out and embrace the elm trees with sturdy stems, then crop the foliage, then prune the branches (before this time they are afraid of iron), then practice a harsh discipline and cut back the spread out branches. (Virgil, *G.* 2.362–70)

Similarly, agriculture, with its appropriate balance of utility and beauty, functions as a metaphor for rhetoric in the section that prefaces the discussion of *ornatus* in books 8 and 9. While, as we have seen, Quintilian disavows the excessive use of poeticism, his own discussion of tropes and figures is prefaced by an elaborately metaphorical crescendo of rhetorical questions. Having just preached (8.3.6) that ornament must be virile (*uirilis*), strong (*fortis*) and chaste (*sanctus*), he illustrates his point with a vivid diatribe:

> quare nemo ex corruptis dicat me inimicum esse culte dicentibus: non hanc esse uirtutem nego, sed illis eam non tribuo. an ego fundum cultiorem putem in quo mihi quis ostenderit lilia et uiolas et anemonas sponte surgentes quam ubi plena messis aut graues fructu uites erunt? sterilem platanum tonsasque myrtos quam maritam ulmum et uberes oleas praeoptauerim? habeant illa diuites licet: quid essent si aliud nihil haberent? nullusne ergo etiam frugiferis adhibendus est decor? quis negat? nam et in ordinem certaque interualla redigam meas arbores. quid illo quincunce speciosius, qui in quamcumque partem spectaueris rectus est?

> Therefore I do not want any of our decadents to say that I am against elegant speakers. I do not deny that elegance is a virtue; but I do not find it in them. Am I to regard a farm where I am shown lilies and violets and anemones freely springing up as better cultivated than one where there is a full harvest and vines laden with fruit? Am I to prefer the barren plane and clipped myrtle to the vine-supporting elm and fruitful olive? Rich men may be allowed these luxuries: but what would they be if they had nothing else? "Are we not to lend beauty to the fruit trees also?" Of course. I shall plant my trees in order and at fixed distances apart. What can be more handsome than the quincunx, which presents straight lines whichever way you look? (Quintilian 8.3.7–9)

The real cultivated speakers (*culte dicentes*) will model themselves on well-cultivated farms (*fundus cultus*) that have useful plants such as olive trees and vine plants, as opposed to the purely ornamental lilies and violets. Here, Quintilian's diatribe against the barren plane (*sterilem platanum*) echoes Horace, *Carm.* 2.15.4–8, in which the poet complains that the unmarried plane tree will soon prevail over the elm trees and the violets and myrtle and a vast abundance of sweet-smelling flowers scatter their scent throughout the olive groves that bore fruit to the previous owner (*platanusque caelebs | euincet ulmos; tum uiolaria et | myrtus et omnis copia narium | spargent oliuetis odorem | fertilibus domino priori*).[58]

However, Quintilian's point is that utility need not be divorced from beauty: here, alluding to a famous anecdote on Cyrus' well-ordered but fragrant garden narrated in Xenophon, *Oeconomicus* (4.21) and translated by Cicero in *Sen.* 59, Quintilian praises the beautiful look of trees planted at regular intervals in the Roman pattern based on five-twelfths known as

---

[58] Nisbet and Hubbard (1978) 242.

120   The Orator and the Poet in Quintilian's *Institutio Oratoria*

the *quincunx*.[59] The reference to the latter also exploits an analogy between the orderly formation of trees and battle lines, a comparison elaborately developed in a Virgilian passage from the same arboricultural section of book 2 of the *Georgics* not directly alluded to here by Quintilian.[60]

Quintilian's excursus on properly cultivated speech stands out for the complexity of its metaphors and its intersection with the tradition of didactic poetry. It is instructive to compare Quintilian's treatment of the topic in the passage above with Cicero's discussion of the same issue – the appropriate balance of beauty and utility – in *De or.* 3.178–81. While Quintilian stays with the agricultural metaphor and develops it at length into a self-standing digression, Cicero moves quickly between a series of pointed exempla: the shape of heavenly bodies is both beautiful and functional (178); the human body and trees are made only of functional parts but are nevertheless beautiful (179); in the realm of art, ships and columns are similarly indispensable structures that are also alluring (179–80). Finally, Cicero concludes that "the same phenomenon occurs in the case of all elements of speech: their utility, which virtually amounts to necessity, results into a certain kind of attractiveness and charm" (181 *hoc in omnibus item partibus orationis euenit, ut utilitatem ac prope necessitatem suauitas quaedam et lepos consequatur*).

Cicero's pioneering development of figurative language in the *De oratore*, which has been well studied by Elaine Fantham, is an important model for Quintilian. Yet Quintilian's penchant for elaborate metaphorical digressions is exuberant: according to Gerard Assfahl, Quintilian uses more metaphors than Cicero or any other prose writer in the Latin and Greek language, being surpassed only by Longinus.[61]

Moreover, his figurative *ornatus* is deeply implicated with poetic discourse in several ways. To begin with, Quintilian's ornate digression on arboriculture provides an example of the kind of ornamentation equally distant from the effeminate elaboration of poetic discourse and the naked simplicity of everyday language that Quintilian advocates in the preceding section as the most appropriate for prose (8.3.6–7). The exemplary function of Quintilian's passage is confirmed by the fact that, later in the same book, Quintilian lists metaphors of style such as "thunderbolts of eloquence" (*fulmina eloquentiae*) and "highlight of style" (*lumen orationis*) among the ones he discusses as particularly ornate (8.6.7 *ad ornatum*), as

---

[59] See Varro, *Rust.* 1.7.2; 1.23.4; Columella 3.13.4; 15.1; Pliny the Elder, *HN* 17.78.
[60] Virgil, *G.* 2.279–83, in which vines show the same beautiful regularity of cohorts, on which, see Mynors (1990) 135–6.
[61] Assfahl (1932) 139–41.

The Orator and the Hero in Book 12

opposed to the natural or necessary kind. Needless to say, the use of metaphor *ornandi causa* is singled out as a feature of poetic language that is discouraged in prose (8.6.18 *metaphora enim aut uacantem locum occupare debet aut si in alienum uenit, plus ualere eo quod expellit*).[62] Quintilian's penchant for elaborate metaphorical constructs throughout the work is thus in tension with his own characterization of metaphorical language as poetic and his calls for restrained usage of metaphors.

Moreover, Virgilian epic is undoubtedly one of Quintilian's greatest resources in developing his figurative language. This poetic coloring is especially evident in the use of metaphors from the sphere of war, which implicitly presents the orator as a warrior.[63] If agricultural imagery from the world of the *Georgics* structured the discussion of early education in book 1, the implied comparison between war and oratory pervades the discussion of oratorical training in book 2. There, Quintilian compares the budding orator to a general leading his troops to victory and his own project to a military manual whose precepts cannot supersede the general's experience on the field.[64] Here, the comparison between war and oratory stresses the flexibility of rhetorical precepts and the need for the orator to adapt rhetorical rules according to the circumstances at hand. This point is developed more fully in a later section of the book in which military strategy is used again to stress the need for flexibility on the part of the orator:

> atque ideo res in oratore praecipua consilium est, quia uarie et ad rerum momenta conuertitur. quid si enim praecipias imperatori, quotiens aciem instruet derigat frontem, cornua utrimque promoueat, equites pro cornibus locet? erit haec quidem rectissima fortasse ratio quotiens licebit, sed mutabit natura loci, si mons occurret, si flumen obstabit, si collibus siluis asperitate alia prohibebitur. mutabit hostium genus, mutabit praesentis condicio discriminis: nunc acie derecta, nunc cuneis, nunc auxiliis, nunc legione pugnabitur, nonnumquam terga etiam dedisse simulata fuga proderit.

> Hence an especially important feature in an orator is prudent planning, because this adjusts itself in various ways to the trend of events. Suppose you

---

[62] Cf. 12.10.42, in which Quintilian reports the opinion that oratory developed into something that is more akin to poetry when speakers employed words metaphorically: "each of the earliest orators spoke according to nature, and later speakers arose very similar to poets, and albeit more cautiously, nevertheless regarded invented or metaphorical expressions in a similar way as a virtue" (*denique antiquissimum quemque maxime secundum naturam dixisse contendunt: mox poetis similiores extitisse, etiam si parcius, simili tamen ratione facta et inpropria pro uirtute ducentis*).

[63] Assfahl (1932) 85–98.

[64] Quintilian 2.5.15 *sicut de re militari quamquam sunt tradita quaedam praecepta communia, magis tamen proderit scire qua ducum quisque ratione in quali re tempore loco sit sapienter usus aut contra: nam in omnibus fere minus ualent praecepta quam experimenta.*

122   The Orator and the Poet in Quintilian's *Institutio Oratoria*

were to advise a general, every time he draws up his troops for battle, to keep the line straight, advance the two wings, and position the cavalry on the flanks. This may indeed be the best plan, when it is feasible; but the nature of the terrain will force a change, if there is a mountain ahead or a river in the way, or if he is held up by hills or woods or other unfavorable features. The character of the enemy will also force a change, so will the nature of the immediate danger. The battle will sometimes be fought in line, sometimes in column, with the auxiliaries or with the legions; it will even be a good plan sometimes to feign flight and turn your back on the enemy. (Quintilian 2.13.3)

Quintilian argues that it is not possible to give a uniform set of instructions (*praecipias*) as the terrain (*natura loci*), the character of the enemy (*hostium genus*) and the nature of the imminent danger (*praesentis condicio discriminis*) will affect the choice of strategy. Finally, military history provides an exemplum for the appropriate use of deception in rhetorical discourse as Quintilian cites two examples of generals who used tricks to deceive the enemy: Fabius' use of the trick of the oxen to defeat Hannibal (cf. Livy 22.16) and Theopompus' escape from custody dressed like a woman.[65]

The military metaphor is used again in book 7 in the section that marks the ending of Quintilian's discussion of *inuentio* and *dispositio* that started in book 1. Quintilian's claim is similar to the point stressed in book 2: theoretical instruction can only go so far and must be complemented by experience and careful use of resources. Thus some things, Quintilian says, depend on the student, not the teacher (7.10.10 *quaedam uero non docentium sunt sed discentium*). Whether a *proemium* is needed or not, whether to refute the other side's argument as a whole or not, what order should be followed and so on, are examples of issues that must be left to the orator's assessment of the situation at hand, just as the general "keeps back part of his forces to meet the contingencies of battle, and detaches other parts to defend forts and guard cities, ensure supplies, block roads, and indeed serve either at sea or on land" (7.10.13 *haec est uelut imperatoria uirtus copias suas partim ad casus proeliorum retinentis, partim per castella tuenda custodiendasue urbes, petendos commeatus, obsidenda itinera, mari denique ac terra diuidentis*).

This metaphorical use of the language of warfare to describe oratory is by no means exclusive to Quintilian. As Elaine Fantham has demonstrated in her analysis of Cicero, *De oratore*, because the metaphor of war informs the representation of the legal justice system – the trial as a military

---

[65] Quintilian 2.17.19–20. Cf. 10.1.114, where Caesar is said to "have spoken as he fought" (*eodem animo dixisse quo bellauit*).

The Orator and the Hero in Book 12   123

encounter – "two basic metaphors, that of the orator as a combatant and that of the speech as a body, run through the [*De oratore*]."[66] As Fantham shows, the recurrent use of the implicit comparison between the orator and the soldier is a peculiarly Roman spin on the widespread Greek use of gladiatorial and athletic metaphors to denote the work of public speakers.[67] Moreover, the figurative language of combat is particularly associated with Antonius in book 2 (2.292–303; cf. *Brut.* 139), and it is no surprise that, in Tacitus' *Dialogus*, Aper, who is in many ways modeled on Antonius, uses the imagery to support his praise of the orator's role as an armed defender (Tacitus, *Dial.* 5.5–7).[68]

In the *Institutio*, however, this metaphor not only assumes unusual prominence but also is mediated by and expressed through the resources of Virgilian epic, beginning with the discussion of *elocutio* in book 8. In the preface to the book, Quintilian defined a speech without adequate style as a sword stuck in its sheath (8.pr.15 *similia gladio condito atque intra uaginam suam haerenti*).[69] This metaphor implying a connection between ornament and armament is supported by the standard usage of the word *ornamentum* to denote weapons as well as ornaments of style.[70] Indeed, Quintilian makes the connection explicit in a brief digression on *ornamentum* at the end of book 5 (5.14.33–5). There he praises Cicero's use of metaphor (*tralatio*) in "the laws are silent amidst the arms" (*silere leges inter arma, Mil.* 11) and "the laws themselves sometimes put a sword in our hand" (*gladium nobis interim ab ipsis porrigi legibus, Mil.* 9) and concludes by stating that "the criterion in these matters, however, must be that they are conducive to ornamentation, not to hindrance" (5.14.35 *ut sint ornamento, non impedimento*). The Ciceronian examples are clearly a case of "punning trespass" between theory and *exemplum*:[71] the sword of the law is an example of the kind of ornament – a sword/metaphor – that will not hinder but rather adorn the orator/warrior.

Continuing this comparison of style to the weapon of the orator in book 8, Quintilian likens ornaments of style to the shine of the orator's weapons, which need to be not only effective but also gleaming: "but with elegance and ornament, the orator is out to recommend himself as well as his

---

[66] Fantham (1972) 186; Mastrorosa (2000).   [67] Fantham (1972) 155–8; Van Hook (1905) 23–6.

[68] Goldberg (1999) esp. 229–30 and Mayer (2001) 102 ad loc.

[69] Cf. 4.2.2, in which Quintilian compares the invention of rhetoric to the building of the first sword for self-defense.

[70] *TLL* 9.2.1010.9–23 and see Vickers (1988a) 314. Varro supports the connection between *ornamentum* and verbal art by etymologizing the former as a derivative of *os: Ling.* 6.76.

[71] For this phenomenon, whereby quotations are seen to contain punning references to the theory they are meant to illustrate, see Innes (1994).

124   The Orator and the Poet in Quintilian's *Institutio Oratoria*

cause ... and is fighting with weapons that are not only strong but gleaming" (8.3.2 *cultu uero atque ornatu se quoque commendat ipse qui dicit ... nec fortibus modo sed etiam fulgentibus armis proeliatur*). In this way, the orator can frighten us with his flash just as lightning does (8.3.5 *et fulmina ipsa non tam nos confunderent si uis eorum tantum, non etiam ipse fulgor timeretur*). The phrase *fulgentibus armis*, used by Quintilian to denote the arms of the orator, is a favorite Virgilian epic formula of possible Ennian origin.[72]

The use of *fulgor* recurs in the extended discussion of the difference between poetic and prosaic language in book 10, where poetry is represented as guerrilla-style warfare having to resort to diversions (*deuerticula*). By contrast, the orator is represented as a courageous warrior (*armatos*) standing in the first line of battle (*stare in acie*) ready to fight. Moreover, the style of oratory is compared to weapons made not of silver or gold but of gleaming iron (*fulgorem ferri*), of the sort that might frighten the enemy:

> meminerimus tamen non per omnia poetas esse oratori sequendos, nec libertate uerborum nec licentia figurarum: genus ostentationi comparatum, et, praeter id quod solam petit uoluptatem eamque fingendo non falsa modo sed etiam quaedam incredibilia sectatur, patrocinio quoque aliquo iuuari: quod alligata ad certam pedum necessitatem non semper uti propriis possit, sed depulsa recta uia necessario ad eloquendi quaedam deuerticula confugiat, nec mutare modo uerba, sed extendere corripere conuertere diuidere cogatur: nos uero armatos stare in acie et summis de rebus decernere et ad uictoriam niti. neque ego arma squalere situ ac robigine uelim, sed fulgorem in iis esse qui terreat qualis est ferri, quo mens simul uisusque praestringitur, non qualis auri argentique, inbellis et potius habenti periculosus.

But let us remember that the orator should not follow the poet in everything – neither in his freedom of vocabulary, nor in his license to develop Figures – and that poetry is designed for display. Quite apart from the fact that it aims exclusively for pleasure and pursues this by inventing things that are not only untrue but unbelievable, it also has a special defense for its license, namely that it is bound by metrical constraints and so cannot always use the literal expressions, but it is driven by necessity off the straight path into certain byways of language; it is obliged, therefore, not only to change words but to extend, shorten, transpose, and divide them. But we, let us not forget, stand armed in the front line, fight for high stakes, and strive for victory. And I should not wish our weapons to be foul with neglect and rust; they should have the brilliance that strikes terror, the brilliance of steel that

---

[72] A *uox epica* according to Zaffagno (1988) and see further Horsfall (2003) *ad Aen.* 11.749. I owe this observation to Ben Jerue.

The Orator and the Hero in Book 12

dazzles both mind and eye, not that of gold and silver, which is unwarlike and more dangerous to its possessor than to the foe. (Quintilian 10.1.28–30)

The dazzle of the army is a *topos* in epic and historiography.[73] Moreover, the image of the rust growing on weapons recalls Catullus' depiction of the abandoned landscape of Thessaly in contrast to the splendor of the royal palace on the occasion of the wedding of Thetis and Peleus in poem 64:[74]

> squalida desertis rubigo infertur aratris.
> ipsius at sedes, quacumque opulenta recessit
> regia, fulgenti splendent auro atque argento.
> candet ebur soliis, collucent pocula mensae,
> tota domus gaudet regali splendida gaza.

Squalid rust moves over the abandoned ploughs. But this mansion, in all its royal and opulent innermost corners, is bright with gleaming gold and silver. The ivory makes the seats white, the cups shine on the table, the whole house rejoices and glitters with royal treasures. (Catullus 64.42–6)

The rusty weapons that are to be avoided by the orator also recall Virgilian depictions of decay after the civil wars in the first book of the *Georgics* where the poet predicts that a farmer will one day discover "javelins eaten by rough rust" (*G.* 1.495 *exesa inueniet scabra robigine pila*). The use of the word *situs* to indicate "rust and mould that comes from being let alone (*sino*)" is also poetic in coloring and used several times by Virgil with this meaning.[75]

More to the point, the danger posed to the warrior who wears enticing armor made of gold (*habenti periculosus*) is familiar from history: in Livy book 9, Alexander conquers Darius, whose purple and gold make him booty rather than an enemy (9.17.16 *praedam uerius quam hostem*).[76] By contrast, in the same book, the Romans are aware that the soldier must be bristling, not covered in gold and silver but relying on iron and his courage (9.40.4 *horridum militem esse debere, non caelatum auro et argento sed ferro et*

---

[73] Homer, *Il.* 11.83 χαλκοῦ τε στεροπήν (cf. *Od.* 4.72 where the gleam of bronze is domestic); Horace, *Carm.* 2.1.19 *fulgor armorum fugacis | terret equos equitumque uoltus* (of Pollio's work); Lucan 7.214–6; Livy 22.28.8 *fulgor armorum*; Tacitus, *Ann.* 1.68.4 *fulgor armorum, Agr.* 33 *armorum fulgores.* Cf. *TLL* 6.1.1516.55–9 and Nisbet and Hubbard (1978) 19–20 *ad Carm.* 2.1.19.

[74] The image of the rust and decay of weapons is also familiar from military history: Flor. 1.19 *ne robiginem ac situm scilicet arma sentirent*; Veg. *Mil.* 2.14 *plurimum enim terroris hostibus armorum splendor inportat. quis credat militem bellicosum, cuius dissimulatione situ ac robigine arma foedantur?*

[75] Peterson (1981) 33 *ad loc.* Cf. Virgil, *G.* 1.72 *segnem patiere situ durescere campum*; *Aen.* 6.462 *loca senta situ*; *Aen.* 7.440 *senectus uicta situ.*

[76] Cf. Curtius Rufus 3.10 *aciem hostium auro purpuraque fulgentem intueri iubebat, praedam non arma gestantem: irent, et inbellibus feminis aurum uiri eriperent*; Justinus, *Epit.* 9.13.11.

126   The Orator and the Poet in Quintilian's *Institutio Oratoria*

animis fretum). The danger of gleaming weapons is also an epic motif: it is the reflection of the light on Euryalus' helmet that betrays him in the night expedition in book 9 of the *Aeneid* (*Aen.* 9.373–4 *et galea Euryalum sublustri noctis in umbra | prodidit immemorem radiisque aduersa refulsit*).

The difference between poetry and oratory is thus illustrated by way of an elaborate comparison equating poetic discourse with cowardly guerrilla warfare and inappropriate displays of wealth in armament on the one hand and rhetorical practice with epic combat and flashing manly weapons on the other. Yet while Quintilian constructs poetic practice as a decadent antihero, his image of the orator as a courageous warrior evokes epic codes and models of fighting heroes.

As I have argued, poetry is an important model for Quintilian's presentation not just of his didactic project but also of his model orator as a whole. This tendency on the part of Quintilian to invest the orator with heroic qualities associated with epic is nowhere more visible than in what is perhaps the most complex book of the *Institutio Oratoria* – book 12, which concludes the work as a whole, treating the subjects of the *artifex* and the *opus*. In book 2, Quintilian announced a tripartite division for his work:[77] the majority of the *Institutio* is devoted to *ars*, the treatment of which spans books 3–11 and follows the traditional fivefold handbook division. By book 11, however, Quintilian has concluded the discussion of *ars* and devotes the majority of book 12 (chs. 1–9) to discussion of the *artifex*: in this first section, he goes through his moral as well as physical qualities (5), when he should start arguing causes (6), what kind of causes he should pick up (7), how he should go about the process of discovery (8) and, finally, how he should argue his cases (9). The final section (12.10) is devoted to the last of the three divisions, namely *opus*, and contains an elaborate discussion of style of oratory by way of a series of *synkriseis* between oratorical style and styles of painting and statuary (12.10.10–15), between Attic and Asianic manner (12.10.16–26) and Latin and Greek eloquence (12.10.27–39) and the three styles of oratory (12.10.58–72). The book, which begins with the *perfectus orator*, ends with a chapter on retirement from public speaking (12.11).

The preface begins with an explicit echo of the image of spreading sails and the casting of the literary work as an epic journey of sorts found in the

---

[77] Quintilian 2.14.5 "rhetoric then . . . will be best, in my view, divided into (1) art, (2) the artist, (3) the work. (1) The art (*ars*) is what is to be acquired by study: it is the science of speaking well. (2) The (*artifex*) artist is the man who has acquired the art, that is, the orator, whose goal is to speak well. (3) The work (*opus*) is what the orator produces, that is, a good speech." On this passage and the *ars/artifex/opus* distinction, see Reinhardt and Winterbottom (2006) 224 ad loc. For a discussion of the *ars/artifex* distinction in Horace, *Ars Poetica*, see Norden (1905).

Epistula to Trypho at the beginning of the *Institutio* (*Ep. ad Tryph.* 3.1 *permittamus uela uentis et oram soluentibus bene precemur*). In book 12, the author frames his groundbreaking exploration of the role of the *artifex* as a lonely journey in treacherous, open waters:

> postquam uero nobis ille quem instituebamus orator, a dicendi magistris dimissus, aut suo iam impetu fertur aut maiora sibi auxilia ex ipsis sapientiae penetralibus petit, quam in altum simus ablati sentire coepimus. nunc "caelum undique et undique pontus." unum modo in illa immensa uastitate cernere uidemur M. Tullium, qui tamen ipse, quamuis tanta atque ita instructa naue hoc mare ingressus, contrahit uela inhibetque remos et de ipso demum genere dicendi quo sit usurus perfectus orator satis habet dicere.

> And finally, now that the orator I was educating has been dismissed by his teachers and is either proceeding under his own power or seeking greater assistance from the innermost shrine of philosophy, I begin to feel how far I have been swept out to sea. Now I have "sky all around, and all around the deep" [*Aen.* 3.193]. Only one man can I see in all the boundless waste of waters, Marcus Tullius, and even he, though he entered this sea with such a great and finely equipped ship, shortens sail and checks his stroke, content to speak merely about the type of style which his ideal orator is to use. (Quintilian 12.pr.2–3)

This last phrase ("*caelum undique et undique pontus*") is a quotation from book 3 of the *Aeneid*, taken from Aeneas' narrative of the terrifying storm after the Trojans' departure from Crete. Quintilian's perception of the danger threatening his voyage in the sea of rhetorical theory is expressed through the words of Aeneas. Although Quintilian is claiming to surpass him, Cicero too is here portrayed as an Aeneadic epic hero, especially if we consider that *in illa uastitate cernere* must be picking up on the image of the heroes "scattered and tossed about in the vast raging abyss" – "*dispersi iactamur gurgite uasto*" (*Aen.* 3.197) – which follows the quotation in the Virgilian text.

The long section on the *artifex* is framed by two elaborate metaphors comparing the orator who has been formed through Quintilian's precepts to a *miles*: first, the section on the *artifex* opens with Quintilian stating that, if the orator is not a *uir bonus*, then he, Quintilian, will have supplied weapons to a brigand rather than a soldier (12.1.1 *pessime mereamur de rebus humanis si latroni comparamus haec arma non militi*). Moreover, "the orator must know his adversaries' plans as the general does the enemy's" (12.1.35 *debent ergo oratori sic esse aduersariorum nota consilia ut hostium imperatori*). The tools of the orator, which include poetic *exempla* (12.4) as well as

128   The Orator and the Poet in Quintilian's *Institutio Oratoria*

figures, *inuentio* and *dispositio*, are the weapons of the soldier (12.5.1 *haec arma habere ad manum, horum scientia debet esse succinctus*). The final image of the *artifex* is that of a soldier always armed and, as it were, in battle order (12.9.21 *armatum semper ac uelut in procinctu stantem*).

Furthermore, the section on the *artifex* (12.1–9) contains two key passages exploiting the relationship between epic and oratory. As his journey through the book begins, Quintilian links his self-presentation as an epic hero with that of the orator by using the famous Virgilian simile comparing Neptune's calming of the sea storm in which the Trojans are caught at the beginning of book 1 to the soothing words of a statesman who addresses an angry rabble (*Aen.* 1.148–53). In Quintilian's presentation, the Virgilian orator *pietate grauis ac meritis* exemplifies the Ciceronian ideal of the *uir bonus* who is also *dicendi peritus*, an ideal that he espouses in book 12:

> an non talem quendam uidetur finxisse Vergilius, quem in seditione uulgi iam faces et saxa iaculantis moderatorem dedit: "tum pietate grauem ac meritis si forte uirum quem conspexere, silent arrectisque auribus adstant"? Habemus igitur ante omnia uirum bonum: post hoc adiciet dicendi peritum: "ille regit dictis animos et pectora mulcet."
>
> It was surely some such man as this whom Virgil imagined, and whom he shows taking control when the rioting crowd hurls torches and stones: "then if they chance to see a man whose deeds and virtues have authority, silent they stand, and with attentive ears." Here then we have first and foremost a good man; the poet will then go on to say that he is an able speaker: "he rules their minds with speech and soothes their passions" [*Aen.* 1.151–3]. (Quintilian 12.1.27–8)

There is a lot to say about how the statesman in the very first simile of the *Aeneid* functions in the original Virgilian context as a foil for rhetoric, poetry's generic rival (see chapter 4). The use of the Virgilian simile in this central section of Quintilian's final book, however, is part and parcel of his strategic recourse to references to epic in order to flesh out the portrayal of the orator and of his professional domain.

The most interesting development of the image of the orator as a general, however, comes at the beginning of section 9, which concludes the discussion of the *artifex*. Although by his own admission Quintilian has offered plenty of advice on composing speeches in the course of the work, he returns here to some crucial issues that are part of the speaker's duty. First among them is the need to adapt to the requirements of the situation and to use strategy to confront the opponent:

The Orator and the Hero in Book 12

nam ut gerentibus bella non semper exercitus per plana et amoena ducendus est, sed adeundi plerumque asperi colles, expugnandae ciuitates quamlibet praecisis impositae rupibus aut operum mole difficiles, ita oratio gaudebit quidem occasione laetius decurrendi et aequo congressa campo totas uires populariter explicabit: at si iuris anfractus aut eruendae ueritatis latebras adire cogetur, non obequitabit nec illis uibrantibus concitatisque sententiis uelut missilibus utetur, sed operibus et cuniculis et insidiis et occultis artibus rem geret.

It is not always the lot of generals in a war to lead their armies through level, pleasant country; rugged hills often have to be climbed, cities stormed even if they are perched on top of sheer cliffs or made impregnable by massive fortifications. Similarly, oratory will enjoy its opportunities of sweeping freely along and deploying its whole strength with popular approval in an open field of battle; but if it is forced to enter the defiles of the law or the dark places from which truth must be unearthed, it will not ride up to challenge the foe or launch its favourite missiles, those quivering, quick *sententiae*; it will fight its war with siege works, mines, ambushes, and secret skills. (Quintilian 12.9.2–4)

In this passage, the usual comparison between the orator and the general (*bella gerentes*) takes an atypical shape. While Quintilian has used the analogy to highlight the need for tactical flexibility earlier in the work (esp. 2.13.3 *si flumen obstabit, si collibus siluis asperitate alia prohibebitur*), the stress on the use of siege works, mines, ambushes and other secret skills (*occultis artibus*) as opposed to open field battle (*aequo congressa campo*) inverts the earlier distinction found in book 10 between poetry, which must seek refuge in the "byways of language" (10.1.29 *ad eloquendi quaedam deuerticula confugiat*), and oratory, which can withstand battle on an open field (10.1.29 *nos uero armatos stare in acie et summis de rebus decernere et ad uictoriam niti*).[78] In this passage, on the other hand, just like poetry, oratory is said to be obliged (*cogetur*) from time to time to "enter the defiles of the law or dark places for the purpose of unearthing the truth" and resort to secret skills. Predictably, this perplexing invitation to pursue the *deuerticula eloquentiae* is expressed with metaphorical language deeply indebted to both epic and historiography.[79]

---

[78] Although it can be used of literary digressions (e.g. Livy 9.17.1), the word *deuerticulum* implies a negative diversion: *TLL* V.1.854.25–66; cf. also Quintilian 9.2.78 and 12.3.11.

[79] E.g. *praecisis impositae rupibus*: cf. Virgil, *G. 2.156 congesta manu praeruptis oppida saxis;* Livy 21.32.7 *tecta informia imposita rupibus,* 32.4.6 *nec altitudine solum tuta urbs sed quod saxo undique absciso rupibus imposita est; aequo congressa campo*: the expression is found six times in Livy (2.50.2 and 64.5; 21.5.11; 24.48.12; 27.18.8; 32.33.11; 36.17.10) and once in Virgil (*Aen.* 9.56); *latebras adire*: Virgil, *Aen.* 2.38 *temptare latebras* and 2.55 *foedare latebras* (of the Trojan horse). *Obequitare* is a favorite word of Livy.

130   The Orator and the Poet in Quintilian's *Institutio Oratoria*

Book 12 concludes with a highly developed section on the last of the three main divisions – the *opus* ("work").[80] After a comparison between the development of art and the history of oratory, Quintilian outlines his own version of the theory of the three styles (grand, middle and plain).[81] Unlike Cicero, who stresses the need for the orator to master all three of the styles depending on context (*Orat.* 69–99), Quintilian privileges the grand type, stating that it is both the "most powerful" (12.10.63 *ualidissimum*) and "the best suited to the most important causes" (12.10.63 *maximis quibusque causis accomodatissiumum*). The grand style is described metaphorically, like a river bursting through its bank, with recourse to Virgil's depiction of another body of water, the river Araxes in book 8 of the *Aeneid* (12.10.61 *At ille qui saxa deuoluat et "pontem indignetur" et ripas sibi faciat multus et torrens iudicem uel nitentem contra feret, cogetque ire qua rapiet*).[82] As is characteristic for Quintilian, the poetic exemplum of the high style is followed by more extensive citations from Cicero but paradoxically these too evoke epic, for Quintilian praises Cicero's reference to Antony as the Homeric monster Charybdis and Oceanus in the *Second Philippic* (*Phil.* 2.67) as well as the invocation of the Alban hills in the *Pro Milone* (*Mil.* 81). Furthermore, each of the styles is associated with a different Homeric hero: Menelaus with the plain style, Nestor with the middle style and Ulysses with the grand style. While this comparison is found in other sources, in alluding to Homer, Quintilian is also putting into practice the advice he offered earlier in the book (12.4) when he stated that poetic exempla are to be preferred to historical ones as they are sanctioned by antiquity.[83] Furthermore, although the text is corrupt, it seems fairly certain that Quintilian is citing a Homeric simile linking the vehemence of Odysseus' eloquence to the snow in the middle of a winter storm (12.10.64 *uim orationis niuibus hibernis copia uerborum atque impetu parem tribuit* – *Il.* 3.221–3 ἀλλ' ὅτε δὴ ὄπα τε μεγάλην ἐκ στήθεος εἵη | καὶ ἔπεα νιφάδεσσιν ἐοικότα χειμερίῃσιν, | οὐκ ἂν ἔπειτ' Ὀδυσῆϊ γ' ἐρίσσειε βροτὸς ἄλλος, see further p. 175). Crucially, while the Homeric hero functions as a foil for the orator, Quintilian models his evocation of a natural event – the bursting Araxes – as *comparandum* for style after Homer's recourse to the image of the winter storm to illustrate Odysseus' oratory.

---

[80] On this section, see Cousin (1967) 658–75; Austin (1944).

[81] For an overview of the theory of the three styles, see Rutherford (1998) 10–18, and Innes (1985).

[82] Quintilian is perhaps here enlarging on an implied comparison between the grand style and the rushing of water in Cicero, *Orat.* 97 *hanc eloquentiam quae cursu magno sonituque ferretur.*

[83] Quintilian 12.4.2 *haec quoque aut uetustatis fide tuta sun taut ab hominibus magnis praeceptorum loco ficta creduntur.* For a parallel use of the matching of styles of oratory with different Homeric heroes, see Pliny, *Ep.* 1.20; Gellius 6.14.7.

The Orator and the Hero in Book 12   131

As the *Institutio* comes to a close, its last chapter brings together the epic imagery of the sea voyage and the military campaign. Thus Quintilian warns the retiring orator not to fall into the ambush set by old age but rather to sing his retreat when he still can and bring the ship unharmed to harbor (12.11.4 *quare antequam in has aetatis ueniat insidias, receptui canet et in portum integra naue perueniet*), teaching young men like a veteran pilot (*uetus gubernator*) showing the inner movements of winds and the perils of the coast (12.11.5 *hos ille formabit quasi eloquentiae parens, et ut uetus gubernator litora et portus et quae tempestatium signa, quid secundis flatibus quid aduersis ratio poscat docebit*).

Quintilian's final exhortation to his reader takes us back to the comparison between rhetoric and poetry that opened the work:

> nam et poesis ab Homero et Vergilio tantum fastigium accepit et eloquentia a Demosthene atque Cicerone … Neque enim si quis Achillis gloriam in rebus bellicis consequi non potest, Aiacis aut Diomedis laudem aspernabitur, nec qui Homeri non fuerunt <aemuli, non fuerunt Tyrtaei>. quin immo si hanc cogitationem homines habuissent, ut nemo se meliorem fore eo qui optimus fuisset arbitraretur, ii ipsi qui sunt optimi non fuissent, nec post Lucretium ac Macrum Vergilius nec post Crassum et Hortensium Cicero, sed nec illi qui post eos fuerunt.

> Poetry reached its great heights with Homer and Virgil, oratory with Demosthenes and Cicero … If a soldier cannot attain the glory of Achilles in war, he will not despise the reputation of an Ajax or Diomedes, nor did those who could not rival Homer fail to rival Tyrtaeus. Indeed, if men had thought that no one should expect to be better than the best so far, there would have been no Virgil to follow Lucretius and Macer, no Cicero to follow Crassus and Hortensius, let alone their later successors. (Quintilian 12.11.26–7)

Quintilian's comparison between Cicero and Virgil on the one hand and Demosthenes and Homer on the other comes as the culmination of his extensive engagement with Cicero's *Brutus* in this last section of book 12, beginning with chapter 10 and its survey of artistic and verbal styles (cf. *Brut.* 70) and implicit polemic against the Atticists (cf. *Brut.* 284–91). Cicero prefaced his survey of Roman oratory with a comparison between Greek and Roman literature and cited the existence of pre-Homeric poets as evidence that perfection in art comes with time.[84] Similarly, exhorting his orator to emulate his predecessors, Quintilian insists that without

---

[84] Cicero, *Brut.* 71 *et nescio an reliquis in rebus omnibus idem eueniat: nihil est enim simul et inuentum et perfectum; nec dubitari debet quin fuerint ante Homerum poetae.*

132   The Orator and the Poet in Quintilian's *Institutio Oratoria*

a desire to compete with the past, there would have been no Cicero and Virgil after Crassus, Hortensius, Macer and Lucretius. Whereas, in book 1, poetry had an important but seemingly limited and conflicted function for the orator, in this final passage it is portrayed as fully complementary to oratory in its aim and in the forms of its historical development. However, although poetry and rhetoric are nominally paired against one another and each is endowed with exemplary figures, it is poetry that ultimately provides an exemplum of conduct in Ajax and Diomedes who are show-cased as models of behavior for the orator.

To sum up, Quintilian's discussion of the appropriate rhetorical style in the *Institutio Oratoria* is characterized by a series of productive tensions. On the one hand, Quintilian repeatedly claims that appropriate speech requires a measure of distance from poetry, as, for example, in the discussions of metaphor (book 8) and reading and imitation (book 10). In Quintilian's hands, the assumed stylistic gap between rhetoric and poetry is used polemically as a tool of criticism of the latter, both implicitly, in the choice and rhetorical emphasis given to poetic exempla in the discussion of *ornatus*, and explicitly, through the negative evaluation of Roman poetry in the reading list. On the other hand, the commonality of intent between Quintilian's orator and the poet is inescapable: not only is *elocutio*, and especially tropes, illustrated from poetry but stylistic ornamentation is essentially characterized as a judicious foray into the freedoms allowed to poets to depart from speech in its natural state.

In addition, it is impossible to ignore the fact that despite Quintilian's polemical effort to distance rhetoric from poetry, his teacher and orator are largely constructed through poetic models and his authorial persona is that not just of a Virgilian critic but of a Virgilian emulator. When set in the context of the history of rhetorical theory, Quintilian's treatment of the poetic reveals an important intellectual agenda: the evocation of the boundaries between poetry and rhetoric and Quintilian's showcasing of the possibilities of the rhetorical medium expose a deep-seated anxiety about the commonality of the two genres as well as an energetic claim to encompass and subsume the authority of poetic, especially Virgilian, texts.

PART II

Oratory in Epic

CHAPTER 4

The Orator in the Storm

Introduction

Scholarship on the relationship between Roman epic and rhetoric has traditionally focused on mapping and documenting the presence of rhetorical features in epic, the basic assumption being that these are "elements of an alien discursive system that have somehow made their way into the epic genre."[1] Scholars have especially focused on speeches in the poems, proving beyond doubt that Roman poets, as early as Virgil, employed techniques of style, composition and arrangement known from the rhetorical tradition.[2] Typically, the presence of "rhetorical influence" is used to construct an aesthetic hierarchy in which texts that are deemed "rhetorical" are simultaneously branded as derivative and aesthetically inferior. This historiographical model, which I have discussed at greater length in the Introduction, essentially constructs the history of Latin poetry as an unstoppable movement away from a Republican and early Augustan "pre-rhetorical" style to the rhetorical corruption of the Silver age.[3]

Moving away from this traditional focus on stylistic typologies, in this part of the book, I explore the relationship between rhetoric and epic, with an emphasis not on literary form, as is typically done, but on "generic interaction."[4] Now that we have examined how rhetoric's similarity to and difference from poetry are used as key tools of self-definition in rhetorical theory, it is time to map how epic confronts and incorporates rhetoric as a "generic guest." Thus, in what follows, my focus will be the representation of the rhetorical medium in Roman epic: how do Roman poets

---

[1] Farrell (1997) 131.
[2] See Helzle (1996); Heinze (1993) 330–2; Billmayer (1932); Clarke (1949); Highet (1972) on Virgil; Higham (1958); Kenney (2002) and Auhagen (2007) on Ovid; Bonner (1966); Morford (1967a); Hübner (1972) and Hübner (1975) on Lucan; Dominik (1994) on Statius, *Thebaid*.
[3] Williams (1980).
[4] Along these lines, see Hardie (2012) 126–49; Feeney (1983). For the notion of "generic interaction," see Harrison (2007) 1–33, esp. 12–13.

represent rhetoric? What role do they assign to rhetorical performance in their poems? What commentary do the epics provide on rhetoric and its relationship to poetry? Thus, rather than tracing the extent to which poets make use of specific devices that may be labeled "rhetorical," I am interested in the poets' own perspective on the role of the rhetorical medium in the economy of their poems.

My analysis of the self-conscious generic interaction between epic and rhetoric will be carried out through select case studies of key type-scenes in the epics involving orators. I argue that, through the embedded rhetorical performances assigned to these characters, poets can be seen to provide a self-conscious, ironic and deeply nuanced commentary on rhetoric's relation to poetry. This chapter and the next then track specifically two type-scenes representative of generic interaction both of which involve *oratores* but in different settings:[5] in this chapter, I analyze the storm as a setting for rhetorical performance in Roman epic starting from Virgil's seminal comparison between Neptune's calming of the storm and an orator's exertion of control over a crowd through rhetoric in the first simile of the *Aeneid* (1.148–56) and moving on to the reception of this key scene in post-Virgilian epic. The orator's presence in this prominent place in Virgil's epic is far from random: rather, Virgil is inserting himself into a rich tradition of rhetorical reading of epic poetry in which figures of orators are singled out as foils for both the author and the orator for whom poetry is a source of rhetorical instruction.

At the same time, because tempestuous natural phenomena feature prominently in descriptions of the grand style in ancient literary criticism, these scenes of oratory in the storm are crucial self-conscious moments for exploring the tension between rhetorical performance and the epic genre. Ironically, in Virgil and Silius, the orator's rhetorical performance is associated with a calming effect that moves the epic narrative away from scenes of epic grandeur. But it is Lucan who, in his reworking of the Virgilian scene in books 5 and 9 of the *Bellum Ciuile*, brings out even further its ironic potential. In Caesar's and Cato's carefully crafted rhetorical performances in the storms respectively of the Adriatic and of the Libyan desert, the focus on the indifference of the epic environment to the orators and on the corresponding mismatch between the rhetorical intentions of the characters and their inefficacy activates an ironic reading in which oratory is represented as overwhelmed by epic and unable to match its intensity. The orator in the storm of Roman epic becomes a key figure

---

[5] Calboli (1987) is the only treatment of these figures in epic that I have been able to find.

The Orator 137

through whom poets playfully question rhetoric's claim to have mastered the grand style.

My next chapter moves to the orator in the assembly, focusing on scenes of deliberative oratory in Roman epic. On the one hand, the Homeric poems present effective speaking as an essential component of the epic hero. On the other, through figures such as Thersites (*Il.* 2) and Drances (*Aen.* 11), the epic tradition insists that persuasion not backed by action is unheroic and thus generically suspect. These scenes in which epic action degenerates into fruitless debate populate the Greek epic cycle, as is the case with the narrative of the judgment of Achilles' arms in the *Aethiopis* and *Little Iliad*, where the inability of characters to live up to epic standards becomes a self-conscious vehicle for exploring the derivativeness of post-Homeric epic and its sense of "coming after." Roman poets pick up on this self-conscious reading of the role of rhetoric into the poems and reimagine Homeric debates by polemically inserting aspects of contemporary rhetoric into them, often contrasting a stereotypical epic hero with an "over-rhetorical" demagogic type (e.g. Odysseus in Ovid's *Met.* 13; Cicero and Lentulus in Lucan's *Bellum Ciuile*, Varro in Silius' *Punica*). These epic demagogues, however, are deeply ambivalent figures: they embody a breach of the epic code, yet in clinging to words as opposed to deeds they become, in effect, tropes for the epic poet's own verbal performance and for the derivativeness of the Roman epic tradition as a whole.

In moving through these different scenes of embedded rhetorical performance, my aim is to shed light on the dynamics through which Roman poets confronted, commented on and, at times, challenged the claims of rhetoricians. Throughout my analysis, my objective is not to establish clear lines of demarcation between what counts as poetic and what as rhetorical; rather, I want to bring out how even definitions of rhetoric and poetry that we take for granted and boundaries now accepted as normative were fluid and contested in Roman Imperial culture.

The *Orator*

Before beginning our analysis of scenes of rhetorical performance, a word about my selection criteria is in order. As we have seen from Quintilian's discussion of Homer in book 10 of the *Institutio Oratoria*, by the first century CE it was common to construct Homer retrospectively as the inventor of rhetoric.[6] The detailed demonstration of Homer's mastery of rhetoric focused

---

[6] According to Kennedy (1957) 23, Cicero, *Brut.* 40 and 50 is the earliest attestation of this belief. See further Keith (2000) 8–35.

138 The Orator in the Storm

on character, diction, *inuentio* and arrangement, and it mines both speeches and narrative for rhetorical exempla.[7] In these readings, Homer is often presented as a teacher of rhetoric who illustrates aspects of his art through expert deployment of rhetorical figures and principles of arrangement.[8] For example, when in book 1 of the *Iliad* Achilles asks his goddess mother, Thetis, why she wants to hear from him a tale that she knows already and then proceeds to tell the story (*Il.* 1.365ff.), the scholiast remarks that this section of the speech to his mother exemplifies the trope of *anakephalaiosis* ("recapitulation"): "the poet being rhetorical and wanting to teach us the trope of recapitulation he narrates everything from the beginning" (*Schol. bT in Il.* 1.366a *ex.* ῥητορικὸς ὢν ὁ ποιητὴς καὶ τρόπον ἀνακεφαλαιώσεως βουλόμενος διδάξαι ἡμᾶς ταὐτὰ πάλιν ἐξ ἀρχῆς διηγεῖται).

This interest in the epics as sources of rhetorical instruction is also evident in the Roman exegetical tradition. In Chapter 3, we have seen how Quintilian's discussion of tropes and figures is heavily illustrated through poetry, but already Cicero's discussion of tropes in *De oratore* book 3 (166–72) includes citations from Ennius' *Annales*, Accius and Lucilius. Furthermore, the Servian commentaries use the adverb *rhetorice* ("rhetorically") eleven times, mostly to highlight aspects of a character's artfully constructed speech.[9] However, the poet's own verbal performance is also labeled as "rhetorical," as is the case for the panegyric of the *puer* in *Ecl.* 4 and the proem to *G.* 4, in which, "although Virgil is going to speak of minor things, he promises great things in a rhetorical fashion so as to elevate a light subject matter and make his listener more intent" (Servius *ad G.* 4.1 *rhetorice dicturus de minoribus rebus magna promittit, ut et leuem materiam subleuet et attentum faciat auditorem*). One could therefore argue that, from the perspective of these ancient critics, the *whole* texture of the epics is rhetorically inflected.[10]

However, since the art of rhetoric was meant to prepare students to become public speakers (*rhetores* or *oratores*), speeches delivered by Homeric heroes in the assembly (*Il.* 1, 2 and 7) or in the context of an embassy (*Il.* 9) are particularly suited to rhetorical analysis because, albeit *in nuce*, they already exemplify the public and political contexts in which pupils would be expected to implement rhetorical instruction. In line with

---

[7] See Richardson (1980); Nünlist (2009) index rhetoric and esp. 218–21.
[8] Porter (2016) 85–7.
[9] Servius *ad Aen.* 1.265 (Jupiter); *Servius Dan. ad Aen.* 2.657 (Aeneas); Servius *ad Aen.* 3.616 (Achaemenides), *ad Aen.* 6.875 (Anchises), *ad Aen.* 11.243 (Diomedes); *ad Aen.* 11.343 and 378 (Drances and Turnus). But see Servius *ad Aen.* 7.535 of Virgil's description.
[10] See Whittington (2016) 60–8 on reading as a form of "rhetorical supplication" in the *Aeneid*.

The Orator 139

the general tendency to view Homer as the father of all inventions, the three branches of oratory – deliberative, forensic and epideictic – were all traced back to the Homeric poems. The deliberative genus was grounded in the assembly scene in *Il.* 2. There, after Odysseus intervenes violently to stop Thersites and prevent the disbandment of the army, the scholia refer to his speech in front of his fellow Achaeans as an instance of deliberative rhetoric:

> τρία ῥητορικῆς εἴδη· συμβουλευτικόν, ὅ ἐστιν ἐκ προτροπῆς καὶ ἀποτροπῆς, ὡς νῦν· δικανικὸν ἐκ κατηγορίας καὶ ἀπολογίας, ὡς "δύο δ' ἄνδρες
> ἐνείκεον εἵνεκα ποινῆς"· πανηγυρικὸν ἐξ ἐγκωμίου καὶ ψόγου,
> ὡς "ὦ μάκαρ Ἀτρείδη", "οἰνοβαρές, κυνὸς ὄμματ' ἔχων"

> There are three kinds of rhetoric: the deliberative kind, which is used for promoting or discouraging a course of action as in the present passage; the forensic kind used for accusation and defense as in "two men were quarreling because of a blood payment" [*Il.* 18.498], and epideictic used for praise and blame as in "Oh blessed son of Atreus" [*Il.* 3.182] and "drunkard, dog-face" [*Il.* 1.225]. (*Schol. AbT.* in *Il.* 2.283 *ex*)

While Odysseus' performance in the assembly is considered an example of deliberative oratory (συμβουλευτικόν), the description of the trial scene on the shield of Achilles is read as a reference to judicial oratory, while two lines from *Il.* 3 and 1 exemplify the epideictic genre. Similarly, Ps. Plutarch's *On the Life and Poetry of Homer* insists that Homer is above all the father of deliberative oratory: "political discourse is a function of the craft of rhetoric, which Homer seems to have been the first to understand" (161, text and trans. Keaney and Lamberton), and the bulk of his analysis (169–70) focuses on the use of rhetorical technique in the embassy scene in *Il.* 9.[11]

Moreover, critics focus their attention on Homeric passages that can be retrospectively read as suggesting that Homer knew about the value of rhetorical instruction. One such passage comes in *Il.* 9.442–3: Phoenix, Achilles' tutor, describes how he was asked by Peleus to instruct Achilles in all things, to be "both a speaker of words and a doer of things" (τοὔνεκά με προέηκε διδασκέμεναι τάδε πάντα, μύθων τε ῥητῆρ' ἔμεναι πρηκτῆρά τε ἔργων). As we will see in the next chapter, Phoenix' *sententia* comes to exemplify the appropriate balance between words and deeds expected of the Homeric hero. At the same time, his strikingly contemporary use of key

---

[11] Keaney and Lamberton (1996).

140   The Orator in the Storm

terms in rhetorical instruction such as *rhet(e)r* and *didaskein* compels the
scholiast to see Phoenix as a proto-teacher of rhetoric and Achilles as
a proto-*rhetor*. Thus the bT scholion to *Il.* 9.443 comments: "it is clear
that he knows the name of rhetoric" (φαίνεται οὖν καὶ τὸ τῆς ῥητορικῆς
ὄνομα εἰδώς).

Another Homeric passage that features prominently in rhetorical readings of epic is the section of the *teikhoskopia* in *Il.* 3 in which Antenor recalls
the embassy of Odysseus and Menelaus to Troy before the start of the war
and describes the different styles of speaking of the Greek leaders. This
embedded embassy scene becomes a key passage in which to ground the
theory of the three styles – grand, middle and low – that are to be employed
in rhetorical discourse.[12] For example, Quintilian offers an outline of the
theory built from a patchwork translation of Homeric texts that include
Antenor's speech, Homer's introduction of Nestor and Odysseus' implied
comparison between himself and a public speaker in *Od.* 8:

> nam et Homerus breuem quidem cum iucunditate et propriam (id enim est
> non deerrare uerbis) et carentem superuacuis eloquentiam Menelao dedit,
> quae sunt uirtutes generis illius primi, et ex ore Nestoris dixit dulciorem
> melle profluere sermonem, qua certe delectatione nihil fingi maius potest;
> sed summam expressurus in Ulixe facundiam et magnitudinem illi uocis et
> uim orationis niuibus hibernis copia uerborum atque impetu parem tribuit.
> cum hoc igitur nemo mortalium contendet, hunc ut deum homines intue-
> buntur. hanc uim et celeritatem in Pericle miratur Eupolis, hanc fulminibus
> Aristophanes comparat, haec est uere dicendi facultas.

> Homer gave Menelaus an eloquence which is concise, pleasing and precise
> (this is what he means by "not straying in speech" [*Il.* 3.215 οὐδ'
> ἀφαμαρτοεπής]) and without any superfluities: these are the virtues of the
> first type. From Nestor's lips, he tells us, "flowed speech sweeter than
> honey" [*Il.* 1.249 τοῦ καὶ ἀπὸ γλώσσης μέλιτος γλυκίων ῥέεν αὐδή]; we
> can conceive no greater pleasure. But when he comes to express the supreme
> eloquence, in Ulysses, he gives him a mighty voice, and a force of speech
> "like a winter blizzard" [*Il.* 3.222 ἔπεα νιφάδεσσιν ἐοικότα χειμερίῃσιν] in its
> volume and violence. So "no mortal will contend with him" [*Il.* 3.223 οὐκ ἂν
> ἔπειτ' Ὀδυσῆΐ γ' ἐρίσσειε βροτὸς ἄλλος], and men "will look upon him as
> a god" [*Od.* 8.173 θεὸν ὣς εἰσορόωσιν]. (Quintilian 12.10.64)

Repeating an argument already found in the Homeric scholia, he argues
that Menelaus represents the low style and Nestor the middle style, while

---

[12] On the origin and history of this theory, see Innes (1985); Kennedy (1957); Hendrickson (1904) and
see further *Rhet. Her.* 4.11–16; Cicero, *Brut.* 40 and *Orat.* 69–112; Dionysius of Halicarnassus, *Dem.* 1;
Gellius 6.14.7; Ps. Plutarch, *Life and Poetry of Homer* 172; Libanius, *Decl.* 3 and 4.

The Orator 141

Odysseus is the representative of the grand style, and the orator will use all three of these *genera* depending on the occasion (12.10.69 *utetur enim, ut res exiget, omnibus, nec pro causa modo sed pro partibus causae*).[13] Crucially, therefore, when epic was read and interpreted through a rhetorical lens, oratorical activity in the poems that prefigured the work of the future orator naturally attracted considerable attention.[14] As we will see, all these Homeric scenes of public speech are prominent intertexts in representations of rhetorical performance in Roman epic, and their place in discussion of rhetorical theory provides an essential background to our understanding of how Roman poets use figures of orators in their works.

However, scenes of public speech in poetry warrant our attention not just because they can read and were read (sometimes anachronistically) as anticipating "rhetorical" performance in real-life contexts. It is also crucial to note that, in the exegetical tradition, proficient orators are often seen as foils for the poet. Phoenix, who, as we have seen, is presented as a proto-teacher of rhetoric, is not explicitly compared to Homer in the scholia but the reading of *Il.* 9.442–3 surely informs the biographical tradition in which the poet is portrayed as a teacher of small children.[15] The most obvious overlap between poet and orator is represented by Odysseus, who in the *Odyssey* is both compared to a bard several times and praised as a consummate rhetorical performer.[16] A quotation from the late fifth-century sophist Antisthenes preserved by Porphyry and cited in a scholion to *Odyssey* 1 constructs Odysseus' famous *polutropia* as a reference to his use of tropes and hence to his rhetorical ability:

> μήποτε οὖν τρόπος τὸ μέν τι σημαίνει τὸ ἦθος, τὸ δέ τι σημαίνει τὴν τοῦ λόγου χρῆσιν· εὔτροπος γὰρ ἀνὴρ ὁ τὸ ἦθος ἔχων εἰς τὸ εὖ τετραμμένον. τρόποι δὲ λόγων †αἴτιοι αἴ† πλάσεις· καὶ χρῆται τῷ τρόπῳ καὶ ἐπὶ φωνῆς καὶ ἐπὶ μελῶν ἐξαλλαγῆς, ὡς ἐπὶ τῆς ἀηδόνος "ἥ τε θαμὰ τρωπῶσα χέει πολυηχέα φωνήν"

> Perhaps the word *tropos* does not refer to character but rather to his acquaintance with speech. A man is called *eutropos* if he has a character turned towards the good. But in relation to speeches *tropoi* are styles. And Homer uses *tropos* also of the voice and varied songs, as in the case of the

---

[13] *Schol. AbT in Il.* 3.212 *ex.* See also Seneca, *Ep.* 40.2.

[14] See Pernot (2005) 3–6 for a list of other relevant passages.

[15] Ps. Herodotus, *Vita Homeri* 25 χρόνου δὲ προϊόντος δεηθεὶς τοῦ Χίου πορεῖσαι αὐτὸν εἰς τὴν Χίον ἀπίκετο εἰς τὴν πόλιν· καὶ διδασκαλεῖον κατασκευασάμενος ἐδίδασκε παῖδας τὰ ἔπεα.

[16] See esp. Homer, *Od.* 11.368 with *Schol.* ad loc ἐπιστημόνως κατέλεξας πάντων Ἀργείων σέο τ' αὐτοῦ κήδεα λυγρά, ὡς μῦθον ἀοιδός. Καὶ ἄλλως. οὐ γὰρ ἄνευ μύθων οἴονται εἶναι ποιητικήν; 21.405–9 and see Goldhill (1991) 66–8.

142 The Orator in the Storm

nightingale "who changing often pours forth her many-toned voice" (*Schol. Od.* 1.1.12–16 Pontani)

Nestor is another rhetorical figure whose verbal competence is read as reflecting the poet's art. When he first enters the scene, in *Il.* 1.247–9, he is praised above all for his eloquence: "among them sweet-speaking Nestor rose up, the clear-sounding orator of the Pylians, from whose tongue flew speech sweeter than honey" (1.247–9 τοῖσι δὲ Νέστωρ | ἡδυεπὴς ἀνόρουσε λιγὺς Πυλίων ἀγορητής | τοῦ καὶ ἀπὸ γλώσσης μέλιτος γλυκίων ῥέεν αὐδή). Tellingly, the scholia read this praise of sweet speech as a self-reference on the part of Homer to his own poetry:

> ἔοικε δὲ ἀποτείνεσθαι εἰς ἑαυτὸν ὁ κατὰ συλλογισμὸν ἔπαινος
>
> It seems as if this subtle praise refers to himself. (*Schol. Ab* in Hom. *Il.* 1.249 *ex.*)

When he chooses an orator as the subject of the first simile of his poem, Virgil is inserting himself in this hermeneutical tradition: on the one hand, because of their verbal dexterity, orators can be read as representing the poet; on the other, precisely because of their ability to speak, they prefigure contemporary orators and thus invest rhetoric with the cultural capital associated with the epic tradition.

A fragment from Ennius' *Annales* quoted by Cicero in the *Brutus* (57) describes Marcus Cornelius Cethegus, cos. 204 BCE, as "an orator with a sweet-speaking mouth" (*Ann.* 304 *orator Cornelius suauiloquenti | ore*), where the adjective *suauiloquens* translates Homer's description of Nestor as ἡδυεπὴς in *Il.* 1.248. A famous fragment transmitted by Gellius pits war against oratory and equates the beginning of the hostilities (probably before Cannae) to the end of activities for the *orator*: "the good orator is despised, the fierce soldier is loved, no longer vying with learned words or offensive remarks, they mix among themselves carrying out their enmity."[17] Yet another fragment cited by Gellius contains a portrayal of Seruilius Geminus' trusted companion, whom the early first-century phi-lologist Aelius Stilo identified as a self-portrayal by Ennius.[18] It has often been remarked that Ennius' companion passage informs Horace's descrip-tion of his relationship to Maecenas. Less obvious but no less significant for

---

[17] Ennius, *Ann.* 248–51 *pellitur e medio sapientia, ui geritur res; | spernitur orator bonus, horridus miles amatur; | haud doctis dictis certantes, nec maledictis | miscent inter sese inimicitias agitantes.* See page. 219.

[18] Gellius 12.5 *L. Aelium Stilonem dicere solitum ferunt Q. Ennium de semet ipso haec scripsisse pictur-amque istam morum et ingenii ipsius Q. Ennii factam esse.*

The Orator   143

the purposes of our discussion is the emphasis on the companion's mastery of speech complementing Geminus' portrayal as an orator:[19]

> haece locutus uocat quocum bene saepe libenter
> mensam sermonesque suos rerumque suarum
> consilium partit, magnam quom lassus diei   270
> partem fuisset de summis rebus regundis
> consilio indu foro lato sanctoque senatu;
> quoi res audacter magnas paruasque iocumque
> eloqueretur †et cuncta† malaque et bona dictu
> euomeret si qui uellet tutoque locaret;   275
>   quocum multa uolup
> gaudia clamque palamque;
> ingenium quoi nulla malum sententia suadet
> ut faceret facinus leuis aut mala: doctus, fidelis,
> suauis homo, iucundus, suo contentus, beatus,   280
> scitus, secunda loquens in tempore, commodus, uerbum
> paucum, multa tenens antiqua, sepulta uetustas
> quae facit, et mores ueteresque nouosque †tenentem
> multorum ueterum leges diuomque hominumque
> prudentem qui dicta loquiue tacereue posset: 285
> hunc inter pugnas conpellat Seruilius sic.

Having spoken thus, he calls one with whom he often shared gladly and with pleasure his table, talk and advice on his own affairs when he was tired from managing the most important affairs for the greatest part of the day by counsel in the forum and holy Senate. One to whom he would often talk boldly of great things and small trifles and blurt out both good and bad things if he wished at all and would store them up safely. One with whom he could share agreeably many joys both openly and secretly, whose nature was not swayed by any lighthearted or evil thought to do a bad deed: a learned, trustworthy and agreeable man, pleasant, happy with his own lot, blessed, knowledgeable, one who knows how to say the appropriate things at the right time, obliging, of few words, with much knowledge of antiquities to which a long-buried generation gave rise, keeping many old and new customs, many old laws divine and human, a prudent man one who can speak out or keep silent. Him did Servilius summon thus in the midst of battle. (Ennius, *Ann.* 268–86 Skutsch)

In this passage, Geminus follows up his day activity as an orator in the forum and senate (272 *foro . . . senatu*) with an evening spent in conversation (v. 269 *sermones*) with the companion.[20] In turn, Geminus' oratorical

---

[19] The text of this fragment is hopelessly corrupt. I have followed Skutsch (1985) unless otherwise noted.

[20] Although I have adopted Skutsch's text *de summis rebus regundis* in v. 271, I wonder whether *regundis* should be emended to *agundis* as in the common expression *res agere* "to proceed with a case" see

The Orator in the Storm

performance (v. 268 *locutus*), whatever its occasion may have been, is matched not only by the intimate dinner conversation but also by the companion's own verbal dexterity, referred to by the verb *eloqui* in v. 274 (v. 274 *eloqueretur*), which can point specifically to an orator's speech or performance.[21] The companion's *suauitas* (v. 280 *suauis*) may also point to the use of *suauis* to characterize the eloquent speech of Marcus Cethegus in the fragment we analyzed earlier (*Ann.* 304). Indeed, the companion's portrait insists repeatedly on his rhetorical ability: although initially his characterization as a man of few words (v. 281–2 *uerbum paucum*) may suggest a humbling contrast with Geminus, the public speaker, on further inspection the companion's ability to persuade (v. 278 *suadet*) but never instigate bad deeds, his knowledge of how to speak to the requirements of the occasion (v. 281 *secunda loquens in tempore*), as well as to withhold speech if appropriate (v. 285 *qui dicta loquiue tacereue posset*), and his familiarity with the law and antiquities make him an ideal match, if not rival, to the orator Geminus. This is all the more so if, pace Skutsch, we retain the manuscripts' *facundus* instead of the editor's *iocundus* in v. 280.[22]

While it is hard to recover the original context of Ennius' fragment, Stilo's identification of the rhetorically gifted companion with the poet may be significant. Suetonius names Stilo as one of the earliest commentators of poetry in Rome (*Gram. et rhet.* 2), but it is clear that, although Stilo was not himself an orator, he was known from writing *orationes* for others: Suetonius explains his nickname (Stilo) as originating from his activity as a writer (cf. *stilus*: "writing instrument").[23] The fact that Stilo singled out this passage, in which the poet's mastery of rhetorical performance is supposedly contrasted with Geminus' role as a public speaker, may reflect his own interests in combining the reading and explication of poetry with rhetorical practice.

To conclude, our analysis of epic's response to rhetoric will focus on the literary representations of performances by *oratores*, both as "ambassadors"

    OLD 11b and Plautus, *Poen.* 599 and Sallust, *Iug.* 103.3. Unlike *regund-, agund-* is attested in Ennius, *Ann.* 374, Plautus, Lucretius and Sallust.

[21] See Skutsch (1985) 449 for discussion of the possible contexts for Geminus' speech, probably not the battle of Cannae where he sided with Aemilius in the debates over military strategy (Appian, *Hann.* 18). He participated in the battle at lake Trasimene (Silius 5.94, 114) but no speeches of his appear in Polybius, Livy or Silius.

[22] Skutsch's argument ad loc. p. 459 that *facundus* seats oddly with *uerbum paucum* could be countered by the many instances in which *paucis uerbis* is used in Latin to refer to pointed rhetorical performance, e.g. Livy 10.24, Lucan 9.188.

[23] Suetonius, *Gram. et rhet.* 3 *et Stilo, quod orationes nobilissimo cuique scribere solebat*; Cicero, *Brut.* 205–7, esp. 206 *sed idem Aelius Stoicus <esse> uoluit, orator autem nec studuit unquam nec fuit. scribebat tamen orationes, quas alii dicerent.* The nickname, however, was not used by either Cicero or Varro: see Kaster (1995) 76 ad loc. and see further Rawson (1985) 120, 269, 270 and 273.

or "envoys" (*OLD* 1) and in the more common meaning of the word *orator*, as a speaker or orator (*OLD* 2) in a public assembly. Although these characters and the type-scenes in which they appear are by no means the *only* moments in epic that are construable as "rhetorical," they are nevertheless the ones that anticipate and best mirror the *opus oratorium* in action. Furthermore, Roman poets were well aware of the role played by epic poetry's *oratores* in rhetorical theory, and the representation of rhetorical performance in their poems is informed by and responds to the rhetoricians' reading of those scenes as proto-versions of their art. Just as scenes that feature poets and poetic performance in epic are often read as programmatic authorial statements, orators and scenes of public oratory can be read as self-conscious poetic engagements with the rhetorical medium and thus offer a privileged vantage point from which to observe the complex dynamic interaction between the genres and poetry's response to the claims of rhetorical writers.

The Orator at Sea

> sic ait, et dicto citius tumida aequora placat
> collectasque fugat nubes solemque reducit.
> Cymothoe simul et Triton adnixus acuto
> detrudunt nauis scopulo; leuat ipse tridenti   145
> et uastas aperit Syrtis et temperat aequor
> atque rotis summas leuibus perlabitur undas.
> ac ueluti magno in populo cum saepe coorta est
> seditio saeuitque animis ignobile uulgus
> iamque faces et saxa uolant, furor arma ministrat;   150
> tum, pietate grauem ac meritis si forte uirum quem
> conspexere, silent arrectisque auribus astant;
> ille regit dictis animos et pectora mulcet:
> sic cunctus pelagi cecidit fragor, aequora postquam
> prospiciens genitor caeloque inuectus aperto   155
> flectit equos curruque uolans dat lora secundo.

So he spoke and quicker than his word he placates the swollen sea, disperses the gathered clouds and brings back the sun. Cymothoe and Triton with effort together push down the ships from the sharp rock; the king himself with his trident lifts and opens up the vast Syrtes and calms the sea and with his lightweight chariot he glides over the crest of the waves. As it often happens amid a great mob when an insurrection arises and the anonymous masses rage within and already fire and stones are flying around and mad rage is at the service of the weapons. Then if by any chance they catch sight

146 The Orator in the Storm

of a man of authority on account of his virtue and merits, they are suddenly silent and stand with attentive ears. That man rules their minds with words and soothes their hearts. In this way, the sea's uproar ceased completely after the father looking at the sea and riding in the open sky drove his horses and flying through gave free reins to the obedient chariot. (Virgil, *Aen.* 1.142–56)

The first simile of the *Aeneid* has often been read as "programmatic." To readers interested in the politics of Virgil's poem, the statesman *pietate grauis ac meritis*, who both dominates (*regit*) and soothes (*mulcet*) the tumultuous crowd with his skillful speech, has seemed to allude to Augustus' establishment of the *pax Augusta*.[24] This political reading is set up in the previous lines, in which the unleashing of the winds at Juno's bequest is represented by Neptune in political terms as a coup d'état (v. 138 *non illi imperium pelagi*; v. 141 *regnet*) and is reinforced by the allegorical tradition of interpreting the quelling of cosmic upheaval as a metaphor for the establishment of political order. In his assertion of control over the weather, Neptune, to whom Augustus victorious at Actium compared himself, prefigures the future emperor's ability to end the series of turbid political upheavals of the late Republic.[25] Indeed, the Virgilian simile plays with the comparisons of the mob to the swollen sea and of popular unrest to a storm that have a long history in political theory, dating back to Homer, *Il.* 2.144–9, in which the Greeks' unrest following Agamemnon's seditious remarks is compared to a storm at sea.[26] In the simile, however, politics is in the foreground with nature (the swollen sea) functioning instead as the metaphor's tenor.

There is, however, another important programmatic layer in this simile: coming as conspicuously as they do at the beginning of the poem, the lines set up the *dicta* of the orator as a potential parallel for the words of the poet. As we have seen, the possibility of reading orators in epic as allegories of the author was already a familiar interpretative strategy in the Homeric scholia. Moreover, it has been suggested that the simile as a whole is "anti-

---

[24] See Cairns (1989) 93–5; Hardie (1986) 204–6; Quint (2011) 288–92; Feeney (2014) 213–21; Freudenburg (2018). On Valerius Flaccus' rendering of the political interpretation of this simile, see Stover (2012) 79–112.

[25] Some commentators even see an allusion to a specific occasion in which Cato the Younger controlled an angry crowd, told in Plutarch, *Cat. Min.* 44: Pöschl (1962) 20–2. Other possibilities include Popillius Laenas: Galinsky (1996) 26; Menenius Agrippa: Morwood (1998).

[26] See Servius *ad Aen.* 1.148 *iste tempestati populi motum comparat, Tullius populo tempestatem: pro Milone "equidem ceteras tempestates et procellas in illis dumtaxat fluctibus contionum"; Servius Dan.* ad loc *ita et Homerus seditioni tempestatem* κινήθη δ' ἀγορὴ ὡς κύματα μακρὰ θαλάσσης; cf. Herodotus 7.16; Polybius 11.29.10–11 (from Scipio's speech to his rebellious soldiers) is picked up by Livy 28.27.11 *sed multitudo omnis sicut natura maris per se immobilis est, [et] uenti et aurae cient; ita aut tranquillum aut procellae in uobis sunt*; Nepos, *Att.* 6; Cicero, *Clu.* 138.

The Orator at Sea

rhetorical." As Sarah Spence has noted, Virgil is responding to the Ciceronian claim about the civilizing power of rhetoric in the *Inv. rhet.* 1.2 (cf. also *De or.* 1.30–5). In this grand narrative, rhetoric has the power to quell violence and elevate man over beast. By contrast, Spence sees the first simile of the *Aeneid* as a powerful contestation of the claim of rhetoric to bring about order. By juxtaposing good orderly speech of the orator in the simile with Juno's seductive speech to Aeolus in which she lures him to calm the storm with the promise of a nymph, Virgil is inviting us to "rethink the assumptions of the rhetorical tradition."[27] While Servius was the first to suggest that the comparison of political upheaval to the storm is suggestive both of Homer and of Cicero, I would like to suggest that the Roman atmosphere of the simile ultimately takes us back to Cicero's account of the rise of Roman rhetoric in the *Brutus*.[28] There, through a sustained comparison between Greek and Roman rhetoric, Cicero argues that oratory is an essential engine of peace, "the companion of peace, ally of tranquility and the offspring so to speak of a well-governed state" (*Brut.* 45 *pacis est comes otique socia et iam bene constitutae civitatis quasi alumna quaedam eloquentia*) – a point later mocked by Tacitus in the *Dialogus* (40). More to the point, Cicero's account of the rise of rhetoric centers on successive *exempla* illustrating the power of the orator to control the seditious tendencies of the masses. From its earliest beginnings, persuasion is a critical element in the development of the Roman state: Lucius Brutus could not have accomplished the overthrow of the monarchy "without the persuasion of oratory" (*Brut.* 54 *nisi esset oratione persuasum*); next Marcus Valerius the dictator appeased the discord of the plebeians by his eloquence (*Brut.* 54 *dicendo sedauisse discordias*);[29] Lucius Valerius "assuaged the passions of the common people" (*Brut.* 54 *plebem in patres incitatam ... mitigauerit*);[30] Marcus Popilius "came to the assembly and by the authority of his presence as well as by his words appeased the rebellion" (*Brut.* 56 *uenit in contionem seditionemque cum auctoritate tum oratione sedauit*). In the discussion of constitutional models in book 1 of the *De Republica*, Scipio warns against thinking that "any huge ocean or fire is harder to calm than the violence of the mob out of control" (Cicero, *Rep.* 1.65 *caue putes aut[em] mare ullum aut flammam esse tantam, quam non facilius sit*

---

[27] Spence (1988) 21. See also the points raised by Feeney (2014) 218, when he notes that Neptune's reliance on the trident (*saeuum ... tridentem*) and his acting "more quickly than words" (1.142 *dicto citius*) point us away from the orator's words and back to the pragmatic role of the Homeric scepter in ensuring order.

[28] See Feeney (2014) 215–6. [29] See Livy 2.33 and Morwood (1998). [30] See Livy 3.55.

148　　The Orator in the Storm

sedare quam effrenatam insolentia multitudinem, trans. Zetzel).[31] Virgil's orator does not refer to any one of these specific cases as much as it alludes to the Ciceronian etiology of rhetorical power only to contest it implicitly in the context of the narrative.

Moreover, this contestation of the Ciceronian narrative of the primacy of rhetoric is also activated intertextually by reference to a well-known text that highlights the relation between the language of politicians and the language of poets: S. J. Harrison noted that Virgil's description of the statesman owes much to the beginning of Hesiod's *Theogony* (84–90) and its description of the speech of kings:[32]

> οἱ δέ νυ λαοὶ
> πάντες ἐς αὐτὸν ὁρῶσι διακρίνοντα θέμιστας　　　　85
> ἰθείῃσι δίκῃσιν· ὁ δ' ἀσφαλέως ἀγορεύων
> αἶψά τι καὶ μέγα νεῖκος ἐπισταμένως κατέπαυσε·
> τοὔνεκα γὰρ βασιλῆες ἐχέφρονες, οὕνεκα λαοῖς
> βλαπτομένοις ἀγορῆφι μετάτροπα ἔργα τελεῦσι　　　90
> ῥηιδίως, μαλακοῖσι παραιφάμενοι ἐπέεσσιν.
> ἐρχόμενον δ' ἀν' ἀγῶνα θεὸν ὣς ἱλάσκονται
> αἰδοῖ μειλιχίῃ, μετὰ δὲ πρέπει ἀγρομένοισι

All the populace look to him as he decides disputes with straight judgments; and speaking publicly without erring, he quickly ends even a great quarrel by his skill. For this is why kings are wise, because when the populace is being harmed in the assembly they easily manage to turn the deeds around, effecting persuasion with mild words; and as he goes up to the gathering they seek his favor like a god with soothing reverence, and he is conspicuous among the assembled people. (Hesiod, *Theog.* 84–92, trans. Most)

The *seditio* in Virgil's text translates Hesiod's "great strife" (v. 87 μέγα νεῖκος), while the description of the orator's words at line 153 – *regit dictis animos et pectora mulcet* – unites two concepts found in the Hesiodic passage: the emphasis on the straightness of justice (v. 86 ἰθείῃσι δίκῃσιν ⁓ *regit*) and the soothing words of v. 90 (μαλακοῖσι ... ἐπέεσσιν ⁓ *mulcet*). The setting of the Virgilian simile – the "great crowd" of v. 148 (*magno in populo*) – also "corrects" an ancient *crux* in the Hesiodic tradition, which, as the scholia report, transmitted two separate readings for v. 91: one in which the king walks up "to the city" (ἀνὰ ἄστυ) and one, adopted by West, in which he

---

[31] Servius *ad Aen.* 1.149 on *seditio* also cites Cicero, *Rep.* 6 fr. 3. The now-lost beginning of that book dealt with the issue of sedition: see esp. fr. 6 (*qui contuderit eius uim et ecfrenatam illam ferociam*).
[32] Harrison (1988).

The Orator at Sea

goes to a gathering (ἀν' ἀγῶνα).[33] As the scholium ad loc. comments: "up to a gathering" (ἀν' ἀγῶνα) can be understood in three different ways as the place itself, as the crowd in it or as both as when we say 'the city'" (*Schol. ad Hes. Theog.* 91b ed. Di Gregorio: λέγεται δὲ τριχῶς, αὐτὸ τὸ χωρίον καὶ ὁ ἐν αὐτῷ ὄχλος καὶ τὸ ξυναμφότερον, ὥσπερ καὶ πόλις).

The prominently enjambed *conspexere* in the Virgilian text (1.152) alludes not only to the Hesiodic mob watching the king administer justice – v. 85 πάντες ἐς αὐτὸν ὁρῶσι διακρίνοντα θέμιστας – but also to another text that scholars have long recognized as related to the *Theogony* passage: in *Od.* 8.167–77, Odysseus responds to Euryalus' taunts with an elaborate description of the man on whom the gods confer the gift of speech, stating that "men look upon him with delight, and he speaks on unfalteringly with sweet modesty, and is conspicuous among the gathered people, and as he goes through the city men gaze upon him as upon a god (θεὸν ὣς εἰσορόωσιν)" (*Od.* 8.170–3).

That Virgil is clearly alluding to both texts is evident not only from his translation of *conspexere* but also from the fact that the Homeric intertext provides an essential background to the simile in the *Aeneid*. Readers have pointed out that the Virgilian simile is a conspicuous reversal of the typical situation in which human actions are explained by reference to natural phenomena. Indeed, the closest Homeric equivalent to our passage is a simile from *Il.* 2.144–9 in which the Greeks' unrest following Agamemnon's seditious remarks is compared to a storm at sea. However, Virgil's comparison between the god and the effective speaker in the simile is explained by the context of the *Odyssey* passage, in which the effective orator is looked on *as a god*.

Virgil's adaptation of Hesiod's simile contains a striking omission. The speech of kings in Hesiod is part of an elaborate and somewhat obscure comparison between the gifts the Muses bestow on kings and those they bestow on poets.[34] Hesiod seems to be setting up a link between kings and poets based on their relationship to the Muses: while the power of kings comes from Zeus and that of poets from the Muses, the former will be blessed if the Muses "pour sweet dew upon their tongue and their words flow soothingly from his mouth" (83–4). The scholia understand the comparison as an affirmation on Hesiod's part that the eloquence of kings is like poetry a gift of the Muses: "the race of kings does not descend

---

[33] West (1966) 185 *ad Theog.* 91 takes ἀνὰ ἄστυ as an interpolation from *Od.* 8.173 (ἐρχόμενον δ' ἀνὰ ἄστυ).

[34] For discussion of the relation between the two passages, see Walker (2000) 3–10; Stoddard (2003); Martin (1984); Duban (1980); and Solmsen (1954).

150 The Orator in the Storm

from the Muses, but rather from Zeus. The Muses only provide kings with the capacity for speaking well (τὸ εὔγλωττον)" (*Schol. ad Hes. Theog.* 93). Although Virgil omits the reference to the poet found in the *Theogony*, the rhetorical context of the source text, in which a comparison is established between poetry and public speech, looms large in the *Aeneid* and provides an interpretative frame through which we are invited to analyze the simile as a self-conscious assessment of poetry's relation to rhetoric.

The Storm between Epic and Rhetoric: The *genus grande*

If we pursue this "meta-generic" reading of Virgil's simile, we can detect a further level of irony. Take, for example, Juvenal's prelude to his satirical rewriting of a shipwreck scene in *Satire* 12. Juvenal's friend Catullus, whose story he is about to tell, has survived not just a storm but also a lightning strike:

> densae caelum abscondere tenebrae
> nube una subitusque antemnas inpulit ignis,
> cum se quisque illo percussum crederet et mox   20
> attonitus nullum conferri posse putaret
> naufragium uelis ardentibus. omnia fiunt
> talia, tam grauiter, si quando poetica surgit
> tempestas. genus ecce aliud discriminis audi

> Thick darkness hides the sky with one cover of clouds and all of the sudden fire struck the mast, when everyone thought that they had been struck and in shock reckoned that no ship-wreck can compare to sails on fire. Everything happens just like that, everything is just as somber as whenever a poetic storm blows up. But here it comes: listen to a different kind of danger (Juvenal 12.18–24)

By cutting short his description of the storm, which had begun in line 18, Juvenal here stresses that storm scenes are part of the traditional apparatus of Roman poetry, while at the same time signaling to his reader the novelty of his satirical reinterpretation of the conventional poetic storm (*poetica tempestas*).[35] Indeed it is not hard to notice that, following Virgil's storm scene in *Aen.* 1, the storm at sea becomes a conventional epic beginning: from the storm sent to punish mortals at Ovid, *Met.* 1.262ff., to the storm that surprises Polynices in the forest in *Thebaid* (1.339–82), to the storm in Valerius Flaccus' *Argonautica* (1.578ff.), descriptions of storms are a sine

---

[35] On storms in Roman literature, see Manolaraki (2008); Morford (1967a) 20–36; Huxley (1952).

The Storm between Epic and Rhetoric: The genus grande   151

qua non of Roman epic beginnings. No surprise then that, in an ironic twist, the storm is the site of composition of Eumolpus' epic *Bellum Ciuile* in Petronius, *Satyricon*. That poem is, however, left unfinished because the boat on which the characters are traveling is wrecked. As Encolpius and Gyton struggle to save Eumolpus, who has been jotting down verses through the storm, the poet demands to be allowed to "finish [his] thought" (*Sat.* 115 *sinite me sententiam explere*). As Catherine Connors has argued, not only is there a match between the metaphorical shipwreck of Eumolpus' epic project and the literal shipwreck he suffers but the storm itself embodies Eumolpus' epic ambitions and is thus an apt setting for the composition of his poem.[36]

Yet the storm not only is a symbol of the epic tradition but also, together with other spectacular natural phenomena such as fire, thunder and lightning, is often used as a metaphor for the grand style.[37] In book 12 of the *Institutio Oratoria*, Quintilian describes this grand style as being like a river bursting through its banks with recourse to Virgil's depiction of another uncontrollable body of water, the river Araxes in *Aen.* 8.728 (12.10.61 *At ille qui saxa deuoluat et "pontem indignetur" et ripas sibi faciat multus et torrens iudicem uel nitentem contra feret, cogetque ire qua rapiet*). The storm stands for the *genus grande* in the *Ars Poetica*, where Horace refers to the writer who seeks to stay away from the grand style (but ends up with a style that is too close to the ground) as "afraid of a tempest" (*Ars P.* 28 *timidusque procellae*). Thus, citing the *Acharnians* (vv. 530–1), in the *Orator*, Cicero reminds us that "if Pericles had employed the slender style (*genus tenue*), he would have never been said by Aristophanes to have lightened, thundered, and confounded Greece" (*Orat.* 29 *si tenui genere uteretur, numquam ab Aristophane poeta fulgere tonare permiscere Graeciam dictus esset*). In the discussion of metaphor in book 3 of Cicero's *De oratore* (3.157), a fragment from a tragedy by Pacuvius containing a description of a raging sea storm illustrates the kind of ornamentation that adds splendor (3.156 *splendoris aliquis*) to the style. In Longinus, scenes of a storm from *Od.* 15.624ff. and of a shipwreck from Archilochus illustrate how selection and organization of material can contribute to the sublime (*Subl.* 10.4–7), while the sea is used as a prime metaphor for the sublime itself.[38] In Hermogenes, the second class of solemn or grand subject matter embraces "earthquakes, the flood and ebb of water [and] the impact of thunderbolts" (*On Types of Style*, 1.6.28–30

---

[36] Connors (1998) 141–6.   [37] See Van Hook (1905) 12–15.

[38] See esp. *Subl.* 12.2–3 "spreads out richly as a sea into an open sea of grandeur" (πλουσιώτατα, καθάπερ τι πέλαγος, εἰς ἀναπεπταμένον κέχυται πολλαχῆ μέγεθος). On the use of epic forces of nature to capture the sublime, see the important remarks in Segal (1987) 210–11.

Rabe).[39] Indeed, the origin of the comparison of the orator with a storm is traced by rhetorical writers all the way to Homer himself. In *Il.* 3, Antenor describes Odysseus' words as being "like snow in a winter-storm" (*Il.* 3.222 ἔπεα νιφάδεσσιν ἐοικότα χειμερίῃσιν). The scholia explains how the image "compares [the blizzard] to the swiftness of rhetoric, through its mass it elucidates the compression of speech, clarity through its white color, the fear of the listeners through the snow" (*Schol. b in Il.* 3.222a1 *ex*).

Scholars have long debated the origin of ancient theories of style and the extent to which the formulation of the three styles found in its earliest attestation in the *Ad Herennium* was a Peripatetic invention.[40] Whatever their origins, however, it is reasonably clear that the theory of the three styles and the later theory of types (*ideai*) found in Hermogenes and Aristides are developed by rhetorical writers in parallel to, if not in imitation of, discussions of the hierarchy of poetic genres.[41] Thus the grand style with its emphasis on emotional arousal maps onto (and is largely illustrated with reference to) epic and tragedy, while the middle style invites a parallel with comedy.[42] Aristophanes' critique of tragic language in the *Frogs* already sets up the opposition between a grand, magniloquent style geared toward emotional arousal and a slender, intellectual style suited to persuasion and argument, which is found in different forms throughout the history of Greco-Roman rhetorical theory and its discussion of stylistic categories. This distinction is echoed in Cicero's *Brutus*, where the juxtaposition of Cotta's simple and concise style (*Brut.* 201 *attenuate presseque*) and Sulpicius' elevated and abundant speech (*Brut.* 201 *sublate ampleque*) is built on an opposition between the logical and the tragic, so that Sulpicius is defined as "a grand and so to speak tragic orator" (*Brut.* 203 *grandis et, ut ita dicam, tragicus orator*). Furthermore, the relationship between rhetorical styles and poetic genres is affirmed implicitly in the *officia* assigned to the different styles.[43] According to Cicero's outline of the theory in *Orat.* 69, the goal of the grand style is emotional arousal (*flectere*), that of the middle style is entertainment (*delectare*) and that of slender style is proof (*probare*). In this categorization, the *genus grande* and *genus medium* map easily onto tragedy and comedy, and it is in light of this easily available

---

[39] Hermogenes, *On Types of Style* 1.6.40–6 Rabe ποῦ δ' αὖ λόγου πολιτικοῦ τὸ ζητεῖν, ὅπως κινεῖται γῆ, καὶ ὅτι ἐπικλύσει ἢ ὑπονοστήσει ὕδατος, ἢ πάλιν περὶ σκηπτῶν φορᾶς ἢ τὰ τοιαῦτα; ταῦτ' οὖν ὅπερ ἔφην εἰ μὲν οὕτως ἐξετάζοιτο, σεμνὸν μόνον, οὐ μὴν πολιτικὸν ποιεῖ τὸν λόγον· διὸ καὶ μετὰ τὰς πρώτας σεμνότητος ἐννοίας εὐθύς εἰσιν αὗται δεύτεραι.

[40] See esp. Hendrickson (1904).

[41] On the development of theories of style, see Russell (1981) 129–47, esp. 138 where the connection with genre theory is briefly discussed. On the notion of genre hierarchy, see Farrell (2002) 27–34.

[42] Leigh (2004) 326. [43] Lausberg (1998) 1078–82; Hendrickson (1905) 267–8.

The Storm between Epic and Rhetoric: The genus grande   153

connection that we should read Cicero's comparison of himself to a poet who can write both tragedies and comedies and has the full stylistic range of an epic poet such as Homer and Ennius.[44] A like image is found in the discussion of deliberative oratory in book 2 of the *De oratore* (2.337–8), where Cicero lists emotional control of the crowd as the orator's main task and similarly defines the grand style as tragic.[45] Aulus Gellius uses the same stylistic taxonomy grounded in Homeric poetry that we found in Quintilian to describe the three styles stating that they apply both to prose and to poetry.[46]

Although Cicero and other rhetorical writers repeatedly stress that the orator needs to have a command of all three styles, an orator's claim to fame rests on his ability to master the grand style when the occasion calls for it. Though the orator who can speak only in this grand manner will be considered raving mad, one who can speak only cleverly will never achieve greatness (*Orat.* 69–112). In his discussion of the grand style (ὁ μεγαλοπρεπὴς λόγος), Demetrius equates the latter to the essence of good speech, calling it "the quality which men now term true eloquence" (*Eloc.* 37, trans. Innes: ὅνπερ νῦν λόγιον ὀνομάζουσιν). In the words of G. L. Hendrickson, "the grand style is rhetoric itself in the original conception of it as an instrument of emotional transport."[47]

In tracing the history of the metaphor of the storm, my intention has been to show how the standard narrative, which constructs rhetoric as exerting undue influence over poetry, fails to take into account the extent to which rhetorical writers employ and in essence "take over" poetic imagery in defining their art. Thus the *genus grande*, which constitutes the greatest test of an orator's ability, is not only described by recourse to sublime natural phenomena that find their home in epic but also derives its prestige from epic's place in the hierarchy of genres. Ultimately, rhetoric itself can be defined as an epic journey over the stormy waters of the grand style:[48]

> haec autem, ut ex Appennino fluminum, sic ex communi sapientiae iugo
> sunt doctrinarum facta diuortia, ut philosophi tamquam in superum mare

---

[44] Cicero, *Orat.* 109 *an ego Homero, Ennio, reliquis poetis et maxime tragicis concederem ut ne omnibus locis eadem contentione uterentur crebroque mutarent, non numquam etiam ad cotidianum genus sermonis accederent: ipse numquam ab illa acerrima contentione discederem?*

[45] Cf. *De or.* 1.31 *[quid] tam potens tamque magnificum quam populi motus, iudicum religiones, senatus grauitatem unius oratione conuerti?* See Chapter 5 for discussion of *De or.* 2 337–8.

[46] Gellius 6.14.1 *et in carmine et in soluta oratione genera dicendi probabilia sunt tria . . .* Cf. Demetrius, *Eloc.* 37.

[47] Hendrickson (1905) 290.

[48] My thanks to Chris Kraus for supplying the reference to this passage.

[Ionium] defluerent Graecum quoddam et portuosum, oratores autem in inferum hoc, Tuscum et barbarum, scopulosum atque infestum laberentur, in quo etiam ipse Ulixes errasset.

So, just as the rivers part at the watershed of the Apennines, the disciplines parted when flowing down from the common ridge of wisdom. The philosophers flowed into the Ionian Sea on the East, as it were, which is Greek and well provided with harbors, while the orators came down into our barbarian Tyrrhenian Sea on the West, which is full of reefs and dangers, and where even Ulyxes himself had lost his way. (Cicero, *De or.* 3.69, trans. May and Wisse)

In Crassus' description, the orator is a Ulysses traveling in the same dangerous choppy waters of epic, while the philosopher's journey takes place in the safe environment of Ionic stillness. As we track the image of the storm as a trope for the grand style from epic to rhetorical texts, the notion of rhetorical influence appears more and more inadequate to capture the dynamic intellectual traffic between the two media. For, as we have seen, the storm of the grand style is an image that refuses to be labeled as either "rhetorical" or "poetic." On the one hand, as this last example reveals, rhetoric itself uses the cultural and meta-phorical resources of poetry to define its emotional and stylistic power. On the other, the orator in the storm of *Aen.* 1 deserves to be read in the context of the rhetorical discussions of the *genus grande* of public oratory and the role of epic in the construction of this style. As I have argued, the intertextual reference to Hesiod's comparison of the language of kings to that of singers encourages the reader to expect an implied contrast between the orator and the poet. Furthermore, when we read the Virgilian simile with an awareness of rheto-rical debates over rhetoric's power to match or imitate epic in the *genus grande*, we are in a better position to appreciate an ironic subtext: given that the storm symbolizes the epic tradition and the grand style, from a generic point of view, the orator's entrance onto the epic stage marks the scene of grandeur, to which, according to Cicero and others, orators should aspire. Yet, from a narrative standpoint, it also brings it paradoxically to a close in that the orator's *dicta* (v. 153 *dictis*) are responsible for engineering the end of the scene.

In this respect, Virgil's description of the effects of the orator's speech as "soothing" (v. 153 *pectora mulcet*) is markedly ironic. The word *mulcere*, like its more prosaic counterpart *permulcere*, recuperates the vocabulary of the Platonic critique of poetry as a form of magic that soothes the soul and caters to its most irrational elements.[49] Echoing Gorgias' claims about the

---

[49] Plato, *Rep.* 3.413d and 10.602d. In turn, Plato is responding to Gorgias' claim about the magical quality of *logos*: Gorgias, *Hel.* 8–14; Aristophanes, *Ran.* 909–10, 961–2.

The Orator at Sea after Virgil | 155

soothing qualities of speech, Horace, for example, speaks of the tragic poet as one who "causes irrational pain to the heart, stirs, soothes, fills with false fears as a magician, and transports me now to Thebes, now to Athens" (*Ep.* 2.1.211–13 *qui pectus inaniter angit, | inritat, mulcet, falsis terroribus implet, | ut magus, et modo me Thebis, modo ponit Athenis*). These morally dubious calming effects are associated with the mythical, prehistorical poetry of Orpheus in *G.* 4 (4.510 *mulcentem tigres*) and with the enchanted song of the healer priest Umbro (7.754–5 *spargere qui somnos cantuque manuque solebat | mulcebatque iras*) in the *Aeneid*.[50] It is also significant that the *uir pietate grauis* of the simile foreshadows Aeneas. Unsurprisingly, the phrase *pectora mulcet* occurs only one other time in the *Aeneid*, in the later scene in book 1, where it introduces Aeneas' words of exhortation to his comrades after the storm (1.197 *dictis maerentia pectora mulcet*). Crucially, however, soothing speech has a morally ambiguous connotation. In the case of Aeneas, for instance, it points to the contrast between the positive tone of his remarks and his real feelings of despair (1.209 *spem uultu simulat, premit altum corde dolorem*). In general, *mulcere* and *permulcere* denote speech that seeks to provide pleasure and that is manipulative in nature.[51] Not only are the words of the orator presented as morally dubious but they are also invested with attributes that traditionally receive a negative assessment in philosophical critiques of poetry.

The Orator at Sea after Virgil

In post-Virgilian epic, the Virgilian image of the orator at sea becomes a *locus classicus* for exploring the relationship between poetry and rhetoric. The most explicit engagement with this Virgilian passage occurs in book 7 of Silius Italicus' *Punica*, where, faced by a mutiny of the soldiers, who want to fight and are opposed to his delaying tactic, Quintus Fabius Maximus delivers an impassioned speech in defense of his policy.[52] Introduced by an epic appeal to the Muse to "surrender the man to glory" (7.217 *da famae, da, Musa, uirum*), the calming effect of the harangue on the angry and dissatisfied crowd of soldiers is compared to Neptune's pacifying of the stormy winds at sea, a clear allusion to the

---

[50] Dinter (2005) 166–7 and see further Putnam (1992). Cf. Canens in Ovid, *Met.* 13.339 and Quintilian 1.10.9.7.

[51] e.g. Quintilian 2.12.6.6; 11.3.60.5; Seneca, *Suas.* 1.6.3 *ut multa adulatione animus eius permulceretur.*

[52] Livy 22.14 is one of Silius' sources for this episode. In Livy, however, the speech of the seditious Marcus Minucius Rufus is not answered by Fabius. For Silius' use of Livy, see Littlewood (2011) 110 *ad* 7.217–18, 116 *ad* 7.235–6.

156   The Orator in the Storm

Virgilian simile of the statesman.[53] A passage in Fabius' speech anticipates the meteorological setting of the simile:

> fortunae Libys incumbit flatuque secundo
> fidit agens puppim. dum desinat aura sinusque
> destituat tumidos subducto flamine uentus,
> in rem cunctari fuerit.

> The Libyan leans on his good fortune and in driving his ship puts his confidence in a favorable wind. Until the breeze ceases and the wind subsides and abandons his now swelling sails it will be to our advantage to delay. (Silius Italicus, *Pun.* 7.241–4)

Reworking Ennius' epigrammatic assessment of Fabius' strategy, Silius' Fabius argues that it will be advantageous to delay (*cunctari*) until the favorable wind that is propelling Hannibal's (*Libys*) fortune subsides.

As scholars have argued, whether Fabius' policy of delaying engagement with the enemy resembles too closely Hannibal's tactics (Livy 22.16.5 *nec Hannibalem fefellit suis se artibus peti*), and whether such a policy constitutes a breach in the Roman code of conduct, is precisely what is at stake in the narrative of the Second Punic War in both Livy and Silius.[54] From a narrative standpoint, however, it is clear that the speech with which Fabius urges his men to stop has the effect of stalling the epic narrative.[55] The simile makes clear that Hannibal alone will take advantage of the winds, while the storm foretold by the soldiers' discontent is curtailed by the speech of the general:

> his dictis fractus furor et rabida arma quierunt:
> ut, cum turbatis placidum caput extulit undis
> Neptunus totumque uidet totique uidetur   255
> regnator ponto, saeui fera murmura uenti
> dimittunt nullasque mouent in frontibus alas,
> tum sensim infusa tranquilla per aequora pace
> languentes tacito lucent in litore fluctus.

---

[53] See esp. v. 254 *turbatis placidum caput extulit undis* – *Aen.* 1.127 *summa placidum caput extulit unda*; the aposiopesis in 248–9 *modo qui – sed parcere dictis | sit melius* – *Aen.* 1.135 *quos ego.* Livy's comparison (22.14.15) of Minucius to a general haranguing his soldiers (*contionanti*) and of the soldiers to a multitude asked to vote (*si militaris suffragi res esset*) may have inspired Silius' use of the Virgilian image of the *orator*.

[54] See Elliott (2009); Rossi (2004); Levene (2010) esp. 228–36. Cf. the narrator's presentation of Silius at *Pun.* 7.1–19 and of Fabius again 7.91–2 *arte bellandi lento similis* "in the art of war similar to a sluggish person."

[55] So Hannibal's appeal to his men to stop in their tracks – v. 234 *state uiri* – repeats Volcens' cry to Euryalus and Nisus in *Aen.* 9 – 9.376 *state, uiri. quae causa uiae? quiue estis in armis?* – which results in the end of their epic *aristeia*. By contrast, while the Romans are stopped from action, the epic night raid is carried out by Hannibal (see 7.282–366).

The Orator at Sea after Virgil   157

By these words, frenzy was broken and the angry weapons were calmed. As when Neptune the ruler raises his peaceful head above the stormy waves and sees the whole expanse of the sea and is seen by it, the fierce winds let go of their savage howling and do not stir their wings on their foreheads; then little by little with peace spreading over the tranquil sea, the waves, decreasing in intensity, shine along the silent shore. (Silius Italicus, *Pun.* 7.253–9)

Thus the *quies* (v. 253 *quierunt*) and *pax* (v. 258 *infusa pace*) engendered by the speech sway the plot away from the much more epic outcomes of *furor* and *arma* (v. 253). Furthermore, the description of the sea pacified by Neptune's appearance hints at the stalling of epic action: the wings (v. 257 *alas*) of the winds' foreheads evoke the *alae* of the army, while the peaceful plains (v. 257 *tranquilla per aequora*) allude simultaneously to the sea and to the plain that is the theater of war. Finally, the concluding image of the light shining on the waves at peace (v. 258 *languentes . . . lucent . . . fluctus*) may recall the epic flash of weapons.[56]

By using the storm at sea as an image for political turmoil, Silius inverts the choice of tenor and vehicle found in Virgil, thus restoring the traditional method found in Homer of illustrating human phenomena by appeal to nature. In other ways, however, Silius follows Virgil in using the image of the orator in the metaphorical sea of epic as a vehicle for exploring the tension that occurs when rhetoric takes over the epic space. Furthermore, his collapsing of Fabius' rhetorical prowess and epic inaction can also be read as an ironic critique of rhetoric's ability to inhabit the epic space.

The narrative significance of Fabius' quelling of the storm in Neptunian fashion is all the more apparent when we consider that the storm – *procella* – is repeatedly used throughout the *Punica* as a metaphor for battle.[57] In his final appearance in the poem, the now-aged Fabius makes his last attempt to stall epic action with his proverbial delay (cf. 16.670 *moras*), opposing in a debate in the Senate Scipio the Younger's plan to invade and destroy Carthage (16.604–44). Though the old senators approve of Fabius' caution (16.644 *seniorque manus paria ore fremebat*), Scipio's rhetoric eventually sways the assembly of the fathers, paving the way for the general's victory at Zama, with which the poem ends.[58] The

---

[56] Cf. Silius 7.97 *fulsitque nouis exercitus armis* and 12.11 *at Libyci ducis ut fulserunt signa per agros*.

[57] Silius 1.506 *auerte procellam* (of Hannibal's attack); 3.227–8 *non ulla nec umquam | saeuior it trucibus iacta procellis* introducing the catalogue of Carthaginians; 4.296 the battle at Ticinum; 5.538 *tempestas acta procella*; 9.283, 313, 516 battle of Cannae; 11.91 *belli . . . procella*; 12.334.

[58] Silius omits Scipio's previous speech to the Senate by which the command of troops in Spain was awarded to him, saying only that "he climbed the high Rostrum" (15.131 *ardua rostra petit*).

158   The Orator in the Storm

Punica ends with another noteworthy allusion to the storm that opens Virgil's *Aeneid*: the last book contrasts Scipio's uneventful and thus successful crossings to (17.47–58) and from (17.627) Africa with the storm that Hannibal encounters when he attempts to sail back to Italy (17.218–91) and that occupies the bulk of the book. In a striking inversion of his model, Silius assigns the role of Aeneas in the storm to his antihero Hannibal.[59] But while Hannibal is saved from the sea storm by Venus, worried that a death at sea would diminish the glory of the Romans, he does not survive the real storm represented by Scipio, who is explicitly defined as a "coming tempest" (17.59 *tanta . . . ueniente procella*). If Fabius' first placating speech is aligned with a stalling of the epic onslaught, his second one fails to prevent the unleashing of the storm that will eventually seal the enemy's fate.

The choice of the storm as a setting and foil for oratorical performance is thus not random: rather, the stormy sea, the symbol par excellence of epic and the grand style, is used to test rhetoric's ability to inhabit the space of epic. In Virgil and Silius, the association between rhetorical performance and appeasement is used as an ironic tool to challenge rhetoric's claim to match epic grandeur. Continuing this exploration of rhetorical performance in Roman epic, my next case study – Lucan's *Bellum Ciuile* – is not only a notoriously "rhetorical" poem but also a text where storms abound and function as one of the many symbols of cosmic disorder and upheaval that permeate the poem's narrative.[60] Here by contrast, the poem's *oratores* are seemingly at ease in the grand environment of the epic storm. However, Lucan polemically underlines a mismatch between the orators' intent to control the elements and their indifference to rhetorical showcasing. The orator who is expected to quell a seditious storm with his *grauitas* is instead prey to the elements. In Lucan, the orator in the storm can thus be read as an ironic figure embodying the collapse and failure of Republican oratory.

The question of how to define the "rhetorical" nature of Lucan's epic has been central in modern scholarship in light of Quintilian's recommendation that the *Bellum Ciuile* should be imitated by orators rather than poets (10.1.90 *magis oratoribus quam poetis imitandus*).[61] Critics have pointed to many rhetorical elements, ranging from Lucan's use of declamatory topics to his exploitation of rhetorical figures and *sententiae* and even his

---

[59] See esp. Silius 17.260–7 where Hannibal's opening *felix, o frater* echoes Aeneas' *terque quaterque beati*.
[60] Lapidge (1979) esp. 364–6.
[61] For recent discussions see Ahl (2010) and Narducci (2007) and see further Bonner (1966); Morford (1967a); Goebel (1981); Rutz (1970).

The Orator at Sea after Virgil

historiographical subject matter, which makes him an ideal model for the orator. What is beyond question is that of the poem's protagonists, Caesar and Cato were known as two of the greatest orators of their generation.[62] It may be with a hint of sarcasm that Cicero praises Cato's oratory as powerful in spite of his Stoic influences (*Brut.* 118), but, in his famous comparison of the two in the *Bellum Catilinae*, Sallust weighed them as "almost equal in eloquence."[63] By contrast, despite the fact that the real Pompey received some praise from Cicero (*Brut.* 239) and Tacitus (*Dial.* 37.2–3) for his eloquence in the public assemblies, Velleius Paterculus reckoned his oratorical talent as moderate (2.29.3–4 *eloquentia medius*) and Suetonius reports that, during the civil wars, Pompey practiced declamation to sharpen his ability to counter Curio's eloquence (*Rhet.* 25).[64] Unsurprisingly, then, in the *Bellum Ciuile*, Pompey is portrayed as a largely ineffective speaker: in contrast to Caesar's forceful address to his troops at Ariminum in book 1, Pompey's speech in book 2 fails to engage his soldiers.[65] His only other speech to his troops is on the eve of battle at Pharsalus (7.342–82) and is at least successful in kindling the soldiers' spirits (7.383 *flagrant animi*) but in tone (7.382 *maesta*) it is oddly structured not as an *exhortatio* but as a *supplicatio* in that Pompey literally begs (7.381 *deprecor*) the soldiers to avert exile and slavery in old age from himself and his family. In the *Bellum Ciuile*, Pompey delivers only two speeches to his fellow senators, before and after Pharsalus, and both fail to convince the audience: in the first instance, Lucan actually stresses that the speech is responsible for unleashing the civil war that it sought to prevent, while, in the second case, we witness Pompey's realization that his speech has failed.[66] However, while Caesar is seen only in his public persona, Pompey's rhetoric comes to life in the private exchanges with his wife (5.722ff. and 8.1–108).[67] Given Pompey's ineffectiveness as a public speaker, it is no surprise that in the *Bellum Ciuile*, Caesar's oratory finds its match not in Pompey's but in Cato's. This juxtaposition of the two characters qua orators, taken over from Sallust's *Bellum Catilinae*, is

---

[62] See Stem (2005).

[63] Sallust, *Cat.* 54 *Igitur iis genus, aetas, eloquentia prope aequalia fuere, magnitudo animi par, item gloria, sed alia alii.* For Cato see Cicero, *Brut.* 118 *unum excipio Catonem, in quo perfectissumo Stoico summam eloquentiam non desiderem; Paradoxa Stoicorum* 1–3; Quintilian 11.1.36, where he is defined as an *eloquens senator.* For Caesar, see *Brut.* 251–5.

[64] See Van Der Blom (2011).

[65] Lucan 2.596–7 *uerba ducis nullo partes clamore secuntur* | *nec matura petunt promissae classica pugnae.*

[66] Before Pharsalus: Lucan 7.123–5 *sic fatur et arma* | *permittit populis frenosque furentibus ira* | *laxat.* After Pharsalus: Lucan 8.327–8 *sic fatus murmure sensit* | *consilium damnasse uiros.*

[67] Fantham (2010) 54–7.

160   The Orator in the Storm

achieved by the pointed correspondences between books 5 and 9, which, as scholars have long noticed, are structurally and thematically related, featuring respectively Caesar and Cato first quelling a mutiny in the army with a powerful speech (5.237–373; 9.215–93) and then embarking on treacherous journeys that will take the former across the stormy waters of the Adriatic Sea (5.374–677) and the latter through the sandy but similarly stormy landscape of the Libyan Syrtes (9.294–949).[68]

Before we begin to examine what happens when the rhetorical performances of these two characters are made to inhabit not their customary environment of the forum but the world of epic, it is necessary to establish the particular role played by storms and weather-related disasters as engineers of epic action in the narrative economy of this particular poem.[69] Caesar's epic action is initiated by a series of crossings, the first and most famous of which marks the conclusion of Lucan's proem and the beginning of the narrative: *iam gelidas Caesar cursu superauerat Alpes | ingentesque animo motus bellumque futurum | ceperat. ut uentum est parui Rubiconis ad undas* (Lucan 1.183–5). The crossing of the Alps, in itself an ominous reenactment of Hannibal's hostile invasion of Italy, is followed by the passage over the Rubicon. But, if the Rubicon is first referred to as small (*parui*), by the time Lucan describes the crossing, the river has swollen (1.204 *tumidumque per amnem*) and a complex simile is used to describe the event:

> inde moras soluit belli tumidumque per
> amnem
> signa tulit propere: sicut squalentibus aruis   205
> aestiferae Libyes uiso leo comminus hoste
> subsedit dubius, totam dum colligit iram;
> mox, ubi se saeuae stimulauit uerbere caudae
> erexitque iubam et uasto graue murmur hiatu
> infremuit, tum torta leuis si lancea Mauri   210
> haereat aut latum subeant uenabula pectus,
> per ferrum tanti securus uolneris exit.

Then he loosened the delays of war and swiftly brought his standards across the swollen river: just as on the abandoned fields of scorching Libya, after it has seen an enemy close by, a lion crouches in hesitation, while he gathers all the rage he has; presently, after he has roused himself with the leash of his cruel tail and raised up his mane and groaned with a deep roar from the vast gap of his mouth, then if the light spear thrown by a Moor happens to stick and the hunting spear enters his broad chest, unconcerned with such a big wound, the lion goes through the spear. (Lucan 1.204–12)

---

[68] Ahl (2010) 252–79; Morford (1967b).   [69] Morford (1967a) 20–36 is a classic starting point.

The Orator at Sea after Virgil 161

The immediate point of reference for the lion of the simile is Caesar: the loosening of the delays of war on his part in the narrative corresponds to the pause of the beast as he gathers his anger. The identification of the lion with the general is pushed to its limits in the striking hypallage that concludes the simile, in which the lion is shown as "going through the spear" that wounds him (v. 212 *per ferrum . . . exit*) just as Caesar moves through the Rubicon (v. 204 *tumidumque per amnem . . . tulit*). In a striking inversion, the lion, which stands for Caesar, has taken on the characteristics of the light, swift weapon with which the proverbially fast leader is associated just a few lines below (cf. 1.228–30). The simile assimilates Caesar even further with the action of the crossing in that the lion who "groans with a deep roar from the large gap [of his mouth]" (209–10 *uasto graue murmur hiatu | infremuit*) echoes the gaping, roaring watery stretch of the Rubicon that the general is about to traverse.

Crossings over turbid waters continue to mark key points in the narrative: while Caesar enters the story with the crossing of the Rubicon, Pompey begins his epic exploit by fleeing from his rival, eventually arriving in Brundisium. Despite Caesar's blocking of the harbor, Pompey is able to escape and his departure from Italy is marked by a description of his crossing to Epirus over the stormy Adriatic Sea (2.680–736). While the two enemies do not engage in battle until Pharsalus in book 7, the siege of Massilia culminates in the first battle, a naval clash that both recalls Actium and anticipates Pharsalus (3.298–762). However, the first clash between Caesar and Pompeian forces, at the Spanish town of Ilerda, is not until book 4, which is therefore explicitly presented as a new beginning for the poem (e.g. 4.23 *prima dies belli*). This new phase of the narrative is marked by sudden rain that floods or, better still, shipwrecks, Caesar's camp: 4.87–89 *iam naufraga campo Caesaris arma natant, impulsaque gurgite multo | castra labant*. This new phase in the poem is marked by allusion to the flood that begins the action in Ovid's *Metamorphoses* book 1 as well as to the storm that shipwrecks Aeneas in *Aen.* 1.[70] As Jamie Masters has argued, the weather upheavals are "simply an alternative version of war, replacing the *motus* of war with the *motus* of winds" (see esp. 4.48–9 *hactenus armorum discrimina; cetera bello | fata dedit uariis incertus motibus aer*).[71]

---

[70] Thompson and Bruere (1970) 153 on Lucan 4.77–8 *nec seruant fulmina flammas | quamuis crebra micent. exstinguunt fulgura nimbi* and *Aen.* 1.90 *crebris micat ignibus aether.* Masters (1992) 58–70; Tarrant (2002) 357–8; and, on Ovid and Lucan, see also Wheeler (2002): see esp. Ovid, *Met.* 1.291–2 (*iamque mare et tellus nullum discrimen habebant: | omnia pontus erant, derant quoque litora ponto*) and Lucan 4.104–5 (*rerum discrimina miscet | deformis caeli facies iunctaeque tenebrae*).

[71] Masters (1992) 60–1.

162   The Orator in the Storm

After Caesar's victory and the surrender of the Pompeian forces (4.337–401), the second half of book 4 focuses on the war in Illyria and Libya. The book ends with the exploits and death of Caesar's lieutenant, Curio (5.4.581–824). When we encounter Caesar again, he is returning victorious from Spain only to face a mutiny of his troops.[72] A speech by the mutineers (5.261–95) is followed by one from Caesar (5.319–64) that results in a march to Brundisium (5.374–402) where, undeterred by the stormy winter weather, Caesar makes yet another momentous crossing, this time through a strangely idle Adriatic Sea (5.403–61) and encamps right opposite Pompey. However, Antony's reluctance to cross over with the remaining troops causes the impatient Caesar to retrace his steps and cross again the Adriatic, on his own.[73] The central part of the book is taken by Caesar's second crossing: a night visit to the humble hut of the fisherman Amyclas, whom Caesar persuades to take him to Italy despite the inauspicious weather. During the stormy crossing, Caesar pronounces two defiant speeches (5.577–93 and 5.653–71) and is miraculously delivered on the shore where he is greeted by his anxious soldiers who then prepare to carry out the third crossing of the Adriatic Sea in the book (5.703–21).

As Elaine Fantham has argued, book 5 alternates different types of storms with periods of calm, with the result that a parallel is established between "the metaphorical storm of Caesar's mutineers and the real tempest of the Adriatic."[74] Thus Fantham points to the connection between the metaphorical storm caused by Caesar's mutineers (5.300 *quem non ille ducem potuit terrere tumultum*) and the actual storm faced by Caesar on his second crossing of the Adriatic in 5.504–653 (5.592 *pelagi caelique tumultum*), between the growling of the mutineers (5.255 *non pauidum iam murmur erat*) and the sound produced by the sea (5.571 *murmura ponti*). Moreover, Caesar's fearless response to the human storm is matched by his exceptional defiance in the face of the swollen sea in his second crossing.[75] Indeed, his lack of concern for the dangers of

---

[72] See Fantham (1985) and Ahl (1976) 202–9 for essential discussion of the episode and, for its relation to book 4, see Leigh (1997) 68–76. The episode of the mutiny at Placentia is not in Caesar or Livy, *Periochae* but is mentioned in Suetonius (*Iul.* 69–70), Appian (2.47) and Dio (41.27–35).

[73] For detailed commentary of this episode of Caesar in the storm, see Matthews (2008) and see further Martindale (1976) 48–51.

[74] Fantham (1985) 121.

[75] So, as he prepares to respond to the mutineers, Caesar is depicted as "undismayed in his appearance and in his fearlessness he deserved to be feared" (Lucan 5.316–7 *intrepidus uoltu meruitque timeri | non metuens*). Similarly, in the storm "he trusts that all dangers would make way for him" (5.577 *fisus cuncta sibi cessura pericula*) and is content to die as sea knowing provided that he is the object of universal fear (5.671 *dum metuar semper terraque expecter ab omni*).

The Orator at Sea after Virgil

nature embodies his confident trust in his own good Fortune. But throughout the story Lucan also assimilates Caesar to the tempestuous upheaval of the civil war, which he is made to embody.[76] Thus, in his own speech to the unruly crowd of soldiers, he compares the threat posed to his power by the mutiny to that suffered by the bottomless sea: *ueluti si cuncta minentur | flumina quos miscent pelago subducere fontes | non magis ablatis umquam descenderit aequor | quam nunc crescit aquis* (5.336–9). The threatening tone of his speeches to the soldiers (5.364 *saeua sub uoce minantis*) and to Antony (5.480 *minis Caesar precibusque morantem*) is matched by the threats of the sea (5.578 *sperne minas . . . pelagi*).

These political and meteorological convulsions are the setting for several speeches by Caesar, who delivers more lines of direct discourse in this book than in any other. Repeatedly throughout the narrative, Lucan alludes to the storms faced in books 1 and 5 by Aeneas, whose speeches are evoked, albeit antiphrastically, by Caesar.[77] In addition, the placement at the beginning of the line of the word *seditio* in reference to the mutiny (5.322–3 *detegit inbelles animas nil fortiter ausa | seditio*) strongly evokes the statesman simile in which the same word is similarly placed (1.148–9 *cum saepe coorta est | seditio*).

Furthermore, Caesar's speech to the mutineers echoes Neptune's words in *Aen.* 1. In his belief that he can control the sea, Caesar takes on not just Jovian traits but also a Neptunian flavor. Yet, throughout the narrative of book 5, Lucan underscores a mismatch between the controlling intent of Caesar's rhetoric and its actual effect on the narrative. While peace (*quies*) is reestablished by his address to the soldiers in Neptunian fashion, the subsequent events belie his Neptunian ability to control through speech.[78] Thus, when he first arrives at Brundisium, Caesar finds the sea "closed by winter winds" (5.407 *clausas uentis brumalibus undas*). His speech to the soldiers who have no experience of the sea (5.412 *expertes animos pelagi*) fills them with the courage to face the perils of the stormy Adriatic in the winter.[79] But Caesar and his men find instead a chillingly flat sea, so much so that they are forced to hope for a shipwreck (5.455 *naufragii spes*). Here the savage quietness of the sea (5.442 *saeua quies pelagi*) not only contradicts

---

[76] Cf. Caesar's earlier characterization of himself as a destructive fire in his speech at Massilia: Lucan 3.362–6. On Caesar's tendency to take on speed, fire and lightning, which are also attributes that characterize Lucan's epic, see Henderson (1998a) 176–86.

[77] Lucan 5.577–93 ~ *Aen.* 5.26–31, Lucan 5.653–71 ~ *Aen.* 1.92–101, see Thompson and Bruere (1968) 10–16.

[78] Lucan 5.372–3 *tam diri foederis ictu | parta quies, poenaque redit placate iuuentus.*

[79] On the perils of the stormy Adriatic, see Horace, *Carm.* 3.9.23 with Nisbet and Rudd (2004) 140 ad loc.

164   The Orator in the Storm

Caesar's prognostication but ironically reenacts the silence (5.373 *quies*) brought about by his earlier speech and threatens the end of his epic journey.

No sooner has Caesar arrived in Epirus than in the face of Antony's reluctance to cross he decides to make his way back on his own. In a manner that is reminiscent of Euryalus and Nisus' night expedition in *Aen.* 9, he evades his own troops in the dead of the night and enlists the help of the fisherman Amyclas. The beginning of the episode conveys at once Caesar's inability to understand the generic expectations of the epic scene:

> rectorem dominumque ratis secura tenebat
> haud procul inde domus, non ullo robore fulta
> sed sterili iunco cannaque intexta palustri
> et latus inuersa nudum munita phaselo.
> haec Caesar bis terque manu quassantia tectum
> limina commouit. molli consurgit Amyclas   520
> quem dabat alga toro.

> The helmsman and lord of the boat lived not far from there in a safe house, built not with hard wood but wove together with barren rush and reed from the marshes and its exposed side was protected by a light vessel turned upside down. Over and over again Caesar shook up the hut with its roof. Amyclas rose from his soft bed provided by seaweed. (Lucan 5.515–21)

The world of Amyclas is the slender domain of Callimachean epic – this type of encounter between a god or semi-god and a poor man is found, for example, in Callimachus *Hecale*, in the story of the hospitality given by Hecale to Theseus, who just like Caesar was caught in a storm. In addition, Lucan can here be seen to allude to Ovid's adaptation of the story in the episode of Baucis and Philemon in *Met.* 8.[80] The *phaselus* that protects the hut is reminiscent of Catullus' metapoetic boat (also a *phaselus*) in poem 4, while the "soft bed" (*molli . . . toro*) from which Amyclas rises evokes the use of the category of the soft and slender to describe refined poetry. Caesar's commotion and repeated banging on the door not only cast the statesman as a destructive force of nature but also highlight his lack of comprehension of generic codes: the orator whose speech fills his men with *robur* (5.412 *sic robore conplet*) does not know how to approach this hut that lacks any *robur* (5.516 *non ullo robore fulta*).

---

[80] See Aeneas' visit to Evander in *Aen.* 8 (Lucan 5.539 *tum pauper Amyclas - Aen.* 8.359–60 *ad tecta subibant | pauperis Euandri*) and the Baucis and Philemon episode in Ovid, *Met.* 8 (Lucan 5.517 *cannaque intexta palustri - Met.* 8.630 *canna tecta palustri*; Lucan 5.523 *casae - Met.* 8.699; Lucan 5.523–5 the fire - *Met.* 8.641) and see Matthews (2008) 89–90.

The Orator at Sea after Virgil   165

Unsurprisingly, then, in his encounter with Amyclas, Caesar perverts the traditional expectation of narratives of theoxeny on which the episode is built: most blatantly of all, instead of the divine figure experiencing the poverty of his host, Caesar promises wealth in return for safe passage (5.535–8). Furthermore, in stories of theoxeny, the god's divine identity must first be hidden from his guests.[81] By contrast, Lucan's sarcastic comment on Caesar's first speech to Amyclas highlights the statesman's inability to stay in character:[82]

> sic fatur, quamquam plebeio tectus amictu,
> indocilis priuata loqui

> So he spoke, for although he was dressed in plebeian clothes, he did not know how to speak like a private citizen. (Lucan 5.538–9)

In pointing out the contrast between the general's garb and his manner of speech, the authorial voice faults Caesar for being unable to adjust his speech to the requirements of the occasion, a skill expected of the orator. But the comment also reflects self-consciously on the orator's inability to keep pace with the requirements of Lucan's narrative: Caesar's monotonic battlefield oratory will not be able to live up to what is required of the epic hero.

Lucan's subsequent narrative continues to undermine Caesar's overwhelming confidence in his ability to exercise control over political as well as meteorological *tumultus*. In a striking inversion of Aeneas' actions when he heeds Palinurus' advice to follow the coast in the midst of the storm, Caesar orders Amyclas to "burst through the middle of the storm, safe with my protection" (5.583 *medias perrumpe procellas | tutela secure mea*).[83] This statement echoes the narrator's assessment earlier in the book that Caesar does not wait for the anger of the seditious mob to die down but rather "hastens to defy fury at its height" (5.304 *medios properat temptare furores*). But far from being controlled by Caesar's rhetoric, nature unleashes a tempest, which, Lucan makes a point of saying, is second to none of those depicted by his epic predecessors.[84] In describing the epic

---

[81] So, in Ovid, *Met.* 8.626, Jupiter appears to Baucis and Philemon *specie mortali*: see Hollis (1970) 113 ad loc.

[82] On this line, see Helzle (1994) who argues that Caesar's relentless use of imperatives in the speech constitute his inability to "speak like a private citizen."

[83] So, at Lucan 5.579–80 *Italiam si caelo auctore recusas | me pete*, Caesar actively defies Palinurus' words at *Aen.* 5.17–18 *non si mihi Iuppiter auctor | spondeat hoc sperem Italiam contingere caelo*.

[84] Hence I read his reference to Jupiter's punishment of mankind through the flood at Lucan 5.620–4 as an implicit reference to Ovid's treatment of the story in *Met.* 1.243–312 but also see the reference to

166 The Orator in the Storm

storm in such manner, one of Lucan's aims is no doubt to advertise the novelty of his own text. However, the poetic storm can also be seen as a rival to the orator's verbosity and perceived ability to command through speech, as Caesar's flood of words is no match for the epic tempest. Caesar may think he can command the crowd with his rhetoric like the Virgilian orator in *Aeneid* 1 but, unlike the Virgilian Neptune, he is unable to put in check the elements.

Lucan self-consciously comments on the incommensurable gap between the power of the epic inspiration and rhetoric in 5.645–6, where he points out that "fear prevailed over the aid derived from skill, and the helmsman does not know which wave to break and to which to yield" (*artis opem uicere metus, nescitque magister, | quam frangat, cui cedat aquae*). As commentators have observed, the phrase *artis opem* is Ovidian, as is the emphasis on the failure of the *ars* of navigation in the face of natural disaster.[85] This comment alludes indirectly to the long-standing debate over the relative merits of art and nature in literature but inverts its current wisdom: while Horace and Longinus (to name but two) argue that each needs the help (*opem*) of the other, here overwhelming nature is said to preclude the assistance (*opem*) of *ars*.[86] Thus, while the failure is imputed to the art of navigation, it is hard in this context not to think of another kind of *ars* to which navigation is often compared, namely the *ars rhetorica*.[87] The double meaning of the word *magister*, which can signify in nautical terms a helmsman as well as a professional teacher, aids the ambiguity. Furthermore, the helmsman and navigation are two of Cicero's favorite metaphors to describe his role as a public figure and are applied antiphrastically to Caesar by the narrator in book 1, where the escape of the citizens from Rome on news of his crossing of the Rubicon is compared to the

---

cape Leucate at 5.638 and *Aen.* 8.676–7 *totumque instructo Marte uideres | feruere Leucaten auroque effulgere fluctus; Met.* 11.503–4.

[85] For the phrase *artis opem*, see esp. Ovid, *Tr.* 1.11.21–2 *ipse gubernator tollens ad sidera palmas exposcit uotis, immemor artis, opem;Tr.* 5.6.12 *promissam medicae non tulit artis opem; Ars am.* 3.257 *formosae non artis opem praeceptaque quaerunt; Rem. am* 16; *Fast.* 6.760. For the *topos* of the failure of *ars* in the storm, see *Tr.* 1.2.32 *ambiguis ars stupet ipsa malis* where, as Ingleheart notes, the *ars* can be understood as an oblique reference to the *Ars Amatoria*: Ingleheart (2006) 88; *Fast.* 3.593; Ovid, *Met.* 11.492–4; Statius,*Theb.* 3.29; Manilius 1.887; Seneca, *Ag.* 507 with Tarrant (1976) 272 ad loc.

[86] See Brink (1963) 394–7 on Horace, *Ars P.* 408–11 *natura fieret laudabile carmen an arte, | quaesitum est; ego nec studium sine diuite uena | nec rude quid prosit uideo ingenium; alterius sic | altera poscit opem res et coniurat amice*; Longinus *Subl.* 36.4 προσήκει δ' ὅμως . . . βοήθημα τῇ φύσει πάντη πορίζεσθαι τὴν τέχνην· ἡ γὰρ ἀλληλουχία τούτων ἴσως γένοιτ' ἂν τὸ τέλειον. On the debate, see further Quintilian 2.19 with Reinhardt and Winterbottom (2006) 357–8 ad loc. And Ennius, *Ann.* 508 Skutsch quoted by Quintilian at 2.17.24. Lurking in the background is also the use of helmsmanship and medicine in Stoic arguments over the essence of *uirtus*: Seneca, *Ep.* 85.30–7.

[87] For the comparison, see Varro F268 Funaioli; Quintilian 2.17.24; 12.11.4.

The Orator at Sea after Virgil   167

shipwreck of a boat whose *magister* jumped into the waves (1.498–504).[88] Given the widespread analogy between navigation, political leadership and the art of oratory, the poet's declaration of the failure of *ars gubernatoris* has meta-literary implications that extend beyond the framework of the narrative.

In line with his refusal to engage the traditional divine apparatus of epic, Lucan does not mention why the storm eventually stops but simply describes the process by which a tenth wave miraculously lands Caesar on a strip of land clear of rocks:

> haec fatum decimus, dictu mirabile, fluctus
> inualida cum puppe leuat, nec rursus ab alto
> aggere deiecit pelagi sed pertulit unda
> scruposisque angusta uacant ubi litora saxis   675
> inposuit terrae. pariter tot regna, tot urbes
> fortunamque suam tacta tellure recepit.

> As he spoke these words, a tenth wave, amazing to tell, lifts him up together with the weak boat, nor did the tide throw him back again from the high mound of the sea but carried him and laid him out on the land where a narrow stretch of shore is free from ragged rocks. Having touched the land, he recovered at once so many kingdoms, so many cities and his own Fortune. (Lucan 5.672–7)

The striking metaphorical expression *ab alto aggere pelagi* in vv. 673–4 (lit. "from the high mound of the sea"), referring to the crest of the wave, takes us back to the mound (*agger*) that was the appropriate setting for Caesar's speech to the mutineers (5.316–18 *stetit aggere fulti caespitis intrepidus uoltu ... atque haec ira dictante profatur*). The repetition calls attention to the inappropriately public tone of Caesar's rhetorical performance in the storm, connecting it to his speech to the soldiers earlier in the book.

The narrator continues to use irony to undermine Caesar's rhetoric and character. First, it is well recognized that Caesar's third and final speech (5.654–71) inverts Aeneas' speech in the storm at *Aen.* 1.92–101. In particular, Caesar's claim that he needs no burial (5.668–71) reverses Aeneas' fear of death at sea (1.92–101). More to the point, Caesar's self-composed epitaph in this speech recalls that of Dido in *Aen.* 4, a character who is caught in an emotional storm from which she cannot be saved and that is famously described in vividly

---

[88] Cicero, *Fam.* 9.15.3 *sedebamus enim in puppi et clauum tenebamus; Att.* 2.7.4 *iam pridem gubernare me taedebat* and see *Sen.* 17.

168   The Orator in the Storm

meteorological terms.[89] Though he seems convinced that he can outdo the storm, Caesar's own rhetoric reveals that he is doomed to succumb eventually, as did the character of Dido, with whom he is aligned intertextually.

Furthermore, it has been noticed that Amyclas' well-founded warning to Caesar not to trust the weather (5.540–56) reworks Virgil's catalogue of weather signs in *G.* 1.[90] Thus his opening line, for example – 5.540 *multa quidem prohibent nocturno credere ponto*, "many things prevent one from trusting the sea at night" – reworks Virgil's warning at *G.* 1.456–7 (*non illa quisquam me nocte per altum | ire neque a terra moneat conuellere funem*). The signs mentioned by Amyclas are almost all found in Virgil's *G.* 1.351–464.[91] Crucially, however, in Virgil, the discussion of weather signs is followed by the narrative of how portentous phenomena attended the death of Caesar and foreshadowed civil war:[92]

> solem quis dicere falsum
> audeat? ille etiam caecos instare tumultus
> saepe monet fraudemque et operta tumescere bella;   465
> ille etiam exstincto miseratus Caesare Romam,
> cum caput obscura nitidum ferrugine texit
> impiaque aeternam timuerunt saecula noctem.

> Who would dare to call the sun a liar? He often even warns that there are impending hidden commotions and that deceit and wars are fermenting in secret; taking pity on Rome when Caesar was killed he even covered his brilliant head with dark iron-rust and the impious generations feared the eternal night. (Virgil, *G. 1.463–8*)

Virgil is the source for Lucan's use of the word tumultus to indicate the upheavals (both meteorological and political) portended by the signs. But in alluding to the passage on weather signs from *G.* 1, Lucan also adds an ironic twist: Caesar's refusal to accept Amyclas' reading of the weather *signa*, which in Virgil attend Caesar's death, foreshadows the protagonist's failure later in life to foresee the political storm that will result in his death at the hands of the conspirators. Through the Virgilian intertext, Lucan alludes to events outside the narrative to suggest that, if Caesar

---

[89] See esp. Virgil, *Aen.* 4.532 *saeuit amor magnoque irarum fluctuat aestu*; 4.564 *uariosque irarum concitat aestus*.

[90] See Thompson and Bruere (1968) 12–15.

[91] See esp. the pale sun (Lucan 5.544–5) and *G.* 1.441–4; the moon (Lucan 5.546–7) and *G.* 1.427–9; the forest (Lucan 5.551–2) and *G.* 1.357–9; the birds (Lucan 5.553–4) and *G.* 1.360–4.

[92] For discussion of the relation between this Virgilian depiction of *bellum ciuile* from the *Georgics* and the proem to Lucan's *Bellum Ciuile*, see Casali (2010) 85–6.

The Orator at Sea after Virgil

miraculously survived this storm, he would not survive the next big destructive wave that is destined to kill him.

Caesar's peripeteia at sea has its counterpart in Cato's epic march through the Libyan desert in book 9.[93] Following the death of Pompey, the epic narrative switches its focus onto Cato, whose first action is to quell a mutiny of his men with a speech (9.256–84). Despite its anti-tyrannical rhetoric, Cato's speech displays disturbing resemblances to and verbal echoes of Caesar's words to his rebellious soldiers in book 5.237–373.[94] Lucan then uses a simile to illustrate the effect of Cato's words on the soldiers, who are compared to bees returning to their hives at the sound of Phrygian brass:

> dixit, et omnes
> haud aliter medio reuocauit ab aequore puppes
> quam, simul effetas linquunt examina ceras   285
> atque oblita faui non miscent nexibus alas
> sed sibi quaeque uolat nec iam degustat amarum
> desidiosa thymum, Phrygii sonus increpat aeris,
> attonitae posuere fugam studiumque laboris
> floriferi repetunt et sparsi mellis amorem: 290
> gaudet in Hyblaeo securus gramine pastor
> diuitias seruasse casae. sic uoce Catonis
> inculcata uiris iusti patientia Martis.

He spoke and thus called back all the ships from the mid sea. When the swarms leave the wax cells that have given birth and forgetful of the honeycomb no longer entwine their wings but each flies by itself and in its idleness no longer tastes bitter thyme, but if the sound of the Phrygian brass rattles them, stunned they halt their flight and seek again the pursuit of hard work that bears flowers and their love for scattered honey. Untroubled, the shepherd on the pasture of Hybla rejoices that the wealth of his hut has been preserved. Thus through Cato's speech endurance of just war is forced upon the men. (Lucan 9.283–93)

This passage is deeply indebted to Virgil's description of the bees in *G*. 4. In particular, the reference to the Phrygian brass blends two distinct passages

---

[93] This episode is narrated in Livy, *Per.* 112; Plutarch, *Cat Min.* 56; Seneca, *Ep.* 104.33 but not in Dio 42.13 or Appian 2.87. For discussion of Lucan book 9, see Morford (1967b); Ahl (1976) 268–74; Thomas (1982?) c.5; Fantham (1992); Leigh (1997) 265–82; Wick (2004) vol. 1, 1–32.

[94] Both speeches are answers to remarks by soldiers (at Lucan 5.262–95 and 9.227–51), although the latter is preceded by Cato's scolding of the instigator of the mutiny, the Cilician king Tarcondimotus at 9.222–3. For specific resemblances, see esp. 5.325 *uadite* ~ 9.272 *uadite securi*; 5.280 *mercede* ~ 9.281–2 *pretio meritum*. See also 9.293 *patientia Martis* with 1.361 and 5.369 on the *patientia* of Caesar's army as noticed by Fantham (1985) 126.

from *G*. 4 where the effect of sound on bees is described: first, the Phrygian origin of the brass recalls *G*. 4.64, where the *tinnitus* of the Phrygian cymbals is said to cause the bees to return to their hives.[95] But the martial tone of the sound (v. 288 *increpat*) suggests a later passage where the bees, their hearts trembling with war (*G*. 4.69–70 *trepidantia bello | corda*), are summoned to battle by hoarse brass (*G*. 4.71 *Martius ille aeris rauci canor increpat*). Thus, although the simile seems to suggest a comparison between the shepherd and Cato based on their ability to restrain, the bees in the model are predisposed instead to fight. Lucan also alludes ironically to the bee simile of *Il*. 2.87–91, in which the buzzing bees represent the Achaeans gathering in assembly. In the *Iliad*, the Greeks will be tested by Agamemnon's speech that provokes unrest and sedition in the army. Thus the Homeric model already casts doubts on the effectiveness of Cato's speech and questions his ability to control the soldiers.

Next, Cato attempts to reach Libya and King Juba from Cyrene (Lucan 9.300–2). At first, Cato attempts the journey by boat across the proverbially dangerous gulf of Syrtis (9.303–67).[96] The landscape of Cato's journey is highly significant: to begin with, the locale helps to construct a comparison between Cato's and Caesar's journeys. When Caesar was trying to persuade the reluctant Antony to cross the Adriatic, he had sarcastically stated that "Libya broken up by the stormy Syrtes does not stand between us with its unreliable currents" (5.484–5 *non rupta uadosis | Syrtibus incerto Libye nos diuidit aestu*). Crucially, the Syrtes are also the site of the storm that swept Aeneas to the shores of Carthage in *Aen*. 1 and it is the Syrtes over which Neptune asserts his control (*et uastas aperit Syrtis et temperat aequor*), so that Caesar's comment ironically sets up his voyage as a perverse repetition of Aeneas'.[97]

Cato's journey, however, takes the Stoic hero to the very sea in which Aeneas shipwrecked. Predictably, this sea crossing ends in disaster. Cato then attempts an equally dangerous crossing by land through the desert and reaches Leptis after a march of two months that causes him to visit the oracle of Jupiter at Hammonium (9.511–86) and to confront the dangers posed by venomous desert snakes (9.604–937). This march is advertised by

---

[95] Virgil, *G*. 4.64 *tinnitusque cie et Matris quate cymbala circum*.

[96] Sallust, *Iug*. 78.2–4; Strabo 17.20; Pomponius Mela 1.35; Pliny the Elder, *HN* 5.26.

[97] Given the geographical proximity of Carthage and the Syrtes, it seems inevitable that *pace* Austin Syrtes should here be capitalized as indeed at Virgil, *Aen*. 4.41 (*et Numidae infreni cingunt et inhospita Syrtis*); 5.192 (*nunc animos, quibus in Gaetulis Syrtibus usi*); 6.60 (*Massylum gentis praetentaque Syrtibus arua*). For other poetic instances of the Syrtes, see Apollonius Rhodius, *Argon*. 4.1237–49, 1264–71; Statius, *Theb*. 8.409–11.

The Orator at Sea after Virgil 171

Cato himself as a test of Stoic endurance and of his men's devotion to the fatherland.[98] Furthermore, Lucan makes a point of drawing a connection between Cato's march on land and Caesar's storm at sea when he states that "the youth unconcerned with winds and fearing no storms from the land suffered fears that belong to the water. For the Syrtis receives the south Wind more violently on the dry shore than on the sea and it is much more harmful to the land" (9.445–9 *illic secura iuuentus | uentorum nullasque timens tellure procellas | aequoreos est passa metus. nam litore sicco, | quam pelago, Syrtis uiolentius excipit Austrum, | et terrae magis ille nocens*). Indeed, the troops are not only swept away by the gales but are also forced to find their way by observing the stars as if at sea (9.494–5). While Cato does not talk during the unsuccessful sea crossing, he is given two speeches during the march, matching Caesar's two speeches in the storm of book 5. The first speech comes before the march when nature unleashes her brutality (9.379–406), while the second comes as Cato spurns the precious gift of water offered by a thirsty centurion (9.505–9) and mirrors Caesar's scolding of Amyclas' advice. Furthermore, like Caesar, Cato despises the dangers ahead of him, but, in his case, the reason is the Stoic belief that endurance of hardship is a source of pleasure for the sage (9.402–3 *serpens, sitis, ardor harenae | dulcia uirtuti gaudet patientia duris*). In the case of both characters, the poet mocks the orators' illusion that they can control the events through their rhetoric. I have noted on p. 167 how the supposedly Neptunian calm imposed by Caesar's speech is frustrated first by the quietness of the sea and then by the epic grandiosity of the storm unleashed by Lucan. In a similar fashion, Cato's speech is said to "fire up with virtue and love of toil their fearful souls" (9.406–7 *sic ille pauentes incendit uirtute animos et amore laborum*). The line seemingly celebrates the effectiveness of Cato's rhetoric on his men via a reference to the effects on Aeneas of Anchises' speech in *Aen.* 6, which, as we are told, "inflames [Aeneas'] soul with love for the glory to come" (6.889 *incenditque animum famae uenientis amore*). Lucan, however, has added an ironic twist since the men are literally set on fire by Cato's directive, as they venture into the scorching heat of the desert's sun (9.499 *incensus dies*) and the burning poison of its snakes (9.742 *incendit uiscera tabe*).[99]

Cato's rhetoric, like Caesar's, takes on the frightening attributes of the environment it seeks to control. The juxtaposition is parodic and pointed:

---

[98] Cato characterizes the march thus: "hard is the path to legality and to the love of our falling fatherland" (Lucan 9.385 *durum iter ad leges patriaeque ruentis amorem*). See Seneca, *Ep.* 104.32–3.

[99] Lucan may be alluding to the Stoic principle that hunger and thirst should be avoided: Seneca, *De Ira* 9.4 *fames quoque et sitis ex isdem causis uitanda est: exasperat et incendit animos*.

172 The Orator in the Storm

on the one hand, the style of speech of Caesar and Cato is described metaphorically with reference to the sweeping forces of fire, stormy winds and high waters that embody the grand style they aspire to employ in their rhetoric. On the other, this resemblance becomes more and more eerie as the characters eventually become prey to rather than masters of those epic forces.

Conclusion

Stylistic and compositional elements in poetry such as speeches that are artfully constructed according to principles found in rhetorical handbooks, pointed *sententiae* and "rhetorical" figures are typically spotlighted as off-shoots of a process of discursive corruption. This approach, which constructs and justifies the presence of "rhetorical" elements in poetry as the product of "rhetorical influence," is based on a number of presuppositions, first among which is the existence of a definable direction of intellectual traffic: to invoke a somewhat distant cultural paradigm, one might say that rhetoric is viewed as the offending party, the colonizer of a pristine native land represented by poetry.

This model, however, is open to several objections. To begin with, the notion of "rhetorical influence" fails to take into account the extent to which rhetorical theorists exploit poetry, and especially epic, as a source of cultural capital in constructing their *ars rhetorica*. In this chapter, for example, we have seen how, in its different instantiations, ancient stylistic theory lays out and ranks the stylistic qualities that an orator should deploy depending on the occasion and task according to an order that mirrors the traditional hierarchy of poetic genres. As a result, the grand style is described by reference to epic phenomena such as thunder and storms, which come to represent it. This recourse to shared metaphors in the representation of stylistic taxonomies is a revealing symptom: By using epic categories to construct the grand style, rhetorical writers implicitly claim for oratory the cultural status of epic. What is more, by requiring orators to have full command of all the different styles, they present the rhetorical medium as subsuming different poetic genres, thus implicitly staking a claim of superiority. At the same time, by constructing the theory of style in parallel to and even in imitation of poetry, rhetoricians ignite the debate about the boundaries between the poetic and the rhetorical.

Secondly, viewing rhetoric not as a taxonomy of stylistic and persuasive strategies employed in poetry but as a generic guest and rival has revealed that far, from being seduced or victimized by colonization, poets are aware of and react to the cultural narratives found in rhetorical texts. Thus Virgil uses the first simile of his epic to dramatize the question of rhetoric's difference from

Conclusion 173

and similarity to poetry not only by alluding to Hesiod's discussion of the issue in the *Theogony* but also by creating an ironic contrast between the rhetorical aims of the orator and the requirements of the epic narrative. This irony is picked up and enlarged on by Lucan, who uses the uncontrollable epic elements of fire and water to undercut his characters' intent to assert control through speech. In the end, this staging of rhetorical performance in the epic narrative questions rhetoric's claim to reproduce and even embody the emotional and literary effects of epic. In the process, we witness a debate about whether rhetorical theory preceded or followed poetry and a dynamic confrontation about the very origin of rhetoric and the grand style.

CHAPTER 5

Epic Demagoguery

The previous chapter has traced the image of the orator in the first simile of *Aen.* 1, arguing that the setting of the storm provides a self-conscious medium for exploring the origins of rhetoric and the grand style in the poem. The focus now shifts from oratory as contained in the metaphorical space of a simile to epic politics, with an analysis of key scenes of deliberative oratory in Virgil and Ovid – the council of the Latins in *Aen.* 11 and the debate over the arms of Achilles in *Met.* 13 – and their reception in post-Augustan epic. My objective is to show the ways in which these scenes of debate and the demagogues that inhabit them channel not just traditional Roman critiques of rhetoric but also more broadly leverage a strategic appeal to rhetoric to explore the tension between originality and derivativeness in a literary context. Roman poets latched onto a number of critiques of rhetoric – from Plato's to Cicero's and Sallust's – in the context of creating narratives that are suspended between the Homeric tradition, the not-so-distant Roman Republican past and the new political realities of the empire. While council scenes echo these critiques of rhetoric, in my reading the demagogue is not a figure of the poet's disapproval of the rhetorical discourse. Rather, the demagogue is a "generic guest" who leverages anti-rhetorical discourse but ultimately profoundly disturbs the fluid boundaries between the rhetorical and the poetic, at times becoming one with the epic mission.

As rhetorical performances embedded in a poem, council scenes are in some way an obvious vantage point from which to observe the poet's relationship with the rhetorical tradition. As we have seen in the previous chapter, the assembly is a type-scene in the Homeric epics, repeatedly analyzed for rhetorical organization by the scholia and read as an early manifestation of what will later become known as the *genus deliberativum.* For example, in this letter on conciseness (*breuitas*) by Pliny the Younger to his orator friend Tacitus, it is Eupolis, Aristophanes and Homer who are cited as examples of appropriate rhetorical style:

Epic Demagoguery

adde quae de eodem Pericle comicus alter:

"ἤστραπτ', ἐβρόντα, συνεκύκα τὴν ... Ἑλλάδα"

non enim amputata oratio et abscisa, sed lata et magnifica et
excelsa tonat fulgurat, omnia denique perturbat ac miscet ... nec
uero cum haec dico illum Homericum ἀμετροεπῆ probo, sed hunc:

"καὶ ἔπεα νιφάδεσσιν ἐοικότα χειμερίησιν,"

non quia non et ille mihi ualdissime placeat:

"παῦρα μέν, ἀλλὰ μάλα λιγέως"

si tamen detur electio, illam orationem similem niuibus hibernis, id
est crebram et assiduam sed et largam, postremo diuinam et caelestem uolo.

Add to this what the other comic poet said, also about Pericles: "His
lightning and his thunder shattered Greece" [*Acharnians* 531]. It is not
a disconnected and broken style of speaking, but one which is broad,
magnificent, and sublime which thunders and lightens, which in short
confounds and mixes up the entire world ... In saying this, I am not
approving the character whom Homer describes as "unmeasured in
words" [*Il.* 2.212], but rather the one who spoke "words which fall like
snowflakes in the wintertime" [*Il.* 3.222]. Not that the one who speaks "few
words but with the utmost clarity" [*Il.* 3.214] fails to please me very much.
But if given a choice, I prefer an utterance resembling winter snow, that is
copious and continuous but also abundant, in short divine and heavenly.
(Pliny, *Ep.* 1.20.19, 22–3)

Thersites' verbosity – his "unmeasured words" ἀμετροεπῆ (*Il.* 2.212) –
exemplifies the style to avoid, while Odysseus' snow-like words, falling
abundantly and frequently, embody the most positive model, followed
by Menelaus' "few words but of the utmost clarity." Viewed in the light
of this tradition, the Roman poets' recreation of the Homeric assembly
is always in some way "rhetorical" in so far as it implies engagement
with the appropriation of Homer as a proto-rhetorician by rhetorical
writers.

Yet, within this context, some specific trends emerge. The assembly is
a key feature of the Homeric poems, providing a stage for heroes to
showcase their counsel. In Homer, word and action, the ability to speak
and fight, are inextricably linked. Peleus' instructions to Phoenix to teach
Achilles "to be a speaker of words and a doer of deeds" (9.443 μύθων τε
ῥητῆρ' ἔμεναι πρηκτῆρά τε ἔργων) are interpreted by later writers as
symptomatic of the importance attached to rhetoric by the poet.[1] Nestor
praises Achilles and Agamemnon as excelling among the Achaeans "in both

---

[1] The scholia interprets this as a reference to rhetoric: *Schol. bT in Il.* 9.443 φαίνεται οὖν καὶ τὸ τῆς
ῥητορικῆς ὄνομα εἰδώς. And see Ps. Plutarch, *Life and Poetry of Homer* 170 citing this passage as

counsel and fighting" (1.258 οἳ περὶ μὲν βουλὴν Δαναῶν, περὶ δ᾽ ἐστὲ μάχεσθαι; cf. 9.53–4 Τυδεΐδη πέρι μὲν πολέμῳ ἔνι καρτερός ἐσσι, | καὶ βουλῇ μετὰ πάντας ὁμήλικας ἔπλευ ἄριστος); in his rage, Achilles is said to no longer be going "to the assembly that confers glory to men or to war" (1.490–1 οὔτε ποτ᾽ εἰς ἀγορὴν πωλέσκετο κυδιάνειραν | οὔτε ποτ᾽ ἐς πόλεμον). Given the prominence of public speaking in the characterization of the epic protagonists, the assembly scene becomes an important lens through which to analyze the poet's view of the role of rhetoric in the definition of heroism.

By contrast, not only are council scenes, as well as direct speech in general, drastically reduced in number in Virgil's *Aeneid* but the traditional balance of word and deed, which is a cornerstone of epic heroism, has now been compromised. This transfiguration of the Homeric assembly relies on the increased role assigned to the character of the demagogue, the antecedent of which is traced to the figure of Thersites, the ugly man of the people who challenges Agamemnon and gets silenced with violence by Odysseus in *Il.* 2. Whereas the Homeric Thersites' defiant and unbecoming words are squashed by the socially dominant and rhetorically superior Odysseus, Drances, the demagogue of *Aen.* 11, now constructed through the prism of the partisan upheaval of the late Republic, is a more ambiguous figure who implodes the Homeric balance between words and action.

Typically, the demagogue is seen as an "anti-rhetorical" figure through whom Virgil is engaged in a distancing act in which poetry is aligned with truth and rhetoric with falsity, partisanship and distortion.[2] Yet the dichotomy between *res* and *uerba*, around which the conflict of the council of the Latins is structured, is itself a rhetorical rendering of what are two inextricably linked qualities in Homer. This antithesis is ultimately unraveled as unsustainable in the context of a narrative that is itself consciously rhetoricized.[3] Virgil's translation of the Homeric council scene is not a wholesale rejection of rhetoric but rather reflects a Roman tradition of which Cicero, among others, partakes, of criticizing Greek political habits of free speech. In this discourse, rhetoric in the hands of the masses is already associated with political and cultural decline. Instead of the council, Virgil assigns to the future Romans the restricted *boulē* and the embassy, forms of rhetorical performance that are more archaic, more controlled and more quintessentially Roman.

---

evidence that, according to Homer, "it is preeminently the power of eloquence that makes men great."

[2] Feeney (1983); Highet (1972) 283–5. [3] Hardie (2012).

Finally, the crucial intermediary role of the Homeric cycle in the construction of the figure of the demagogue cannot be overstated. The inability of characters to live up to balance between deed and word, which characterizes the ideal of epic heroism, is itself a self-conscious means for exploring the derivativeness of the post-Homeric epic voice in the episode of the debate over the arms of Achilles. There was a tradition of using the character of the demagogue as a tool for exploring the sense of "coming after Homer" both in the cycle and in tragedy, where the debate over the arms of Achilles turns into a reflection over the meaning of heroism and epos in the shadow of Troy's ruins and the role of audiences in adjudicating literary merit. Thus Virgil and Ovid are latching onto an already established literary tradition of using the tension between word and action as a self-conscious exploration of the epic tradition. The result of this complex mediation is that the figure of the demagogue is both a symbol of political corruption and a trope for the belatedness of Roman epic, and hence implicitly a figure for the poet's own work. The limits of such dichotomy between word and action are evident in the history of the reception of the main debate scene in the *Aeneid*, the council of the Latins in *Aen.* 11. Though the voice of the poet follows his Homeric predecessor in opposing the demagogic voice of Drances, subsequent adaptations of the scene in Lucan and Silius tellingly deconstruct the opposition between word (Drances) and deed (Turnus) and consistently highlight the potential for Turnus to be read as a demagogic figure, while simultaneously aligning the out-of-control voice of the demagogue with war, destruction and, ultimately, the epic voice. The critique of rhetoric in the poem, that is, invests not just the discourse about politics and morality but also the epic author's attempt to write epic after Homer.

The Roman Assembly and Its Greek Counterparts

In the Homeric poems, the assembly (*agorē*) is the prime venue for speeches and a recurrent type-scene through which key developments in the poem are introduced.[4] In creating their own scenes of assembly, Virgil and Ovid are responding first and foremost to the tradition of reading the Homeric assemblies as proto-examples of political institutions and customs that postdate them. In Ps. Plutarch's essay *Life and Poetry of Homer*, Homer

---

[4] See Barker (2009) 31–134; Hammer (2002) esp. 144–69; Hölkeskamp (1997); Schofield (1986). The *boulē* – the restricted council of elite leaders – is another typology of assembly that I will discuss below.

178   Epic Demagoguery

is said to have been the first to "speak analytically of matters pertaining
to government" (176 τὰ τῆς πολιτείας διεῖλεν). He is the first to speak of
a deliberative council (*boulē*) that meets before the people (*dēmos*) is
assembled (177) and the first to speak of the need for the king to be
concerned with the safety of all and the obligation of subjects to obey
those in power (178).[5] According to Ps. Plutarch, Homer knows all three
forms of constitution (monarchy, aristocracy, democracy) and their
degenerated counterparts (tyranny, oligarchy and mob rule) (182–3).[6]
According to the pseudo-Aristotelian *Constitution of the Athenians*
(Plutarch, *Thes.* 25), Homer seems to have been aware of the democratic
inclinations of the Athenians, whose ruler Theseus is the only one who
in the Catalogue of the Ships is explicitly said to be leading a *dēmos* (*Il.*
2.547). In the previous chapter, we have seen how Odysseus' speech in
the assembly of *Il.* 2 is regarded as a proto-example of deliberative
oratory (συμβουλευτικόν).[7] The assembly in *Il.* 2 offered an especially
rich repository of information regarding Homer's view of the best forms
of political government. In Ps. Plutarch (*Life and Poetry of Homer* 182),
Homer is said to have praised monarchy when he referred to Zeus' love
for kings (*Il.* 2.196–7). Quoting *Il.* 2.391, Aristotle argues that although
Homer allowed kings to be reviled in the context of the assembly, he
believed in the absolute power over their military troops (*Pol.* 1285a).
The testing of the troops is also read as typifying a perverse demagogic
experiment. For Aristotle, Odysseus' statement according to which "the
lordship of the many is not a good thing" (*Il.* 2.204) is a condemnation
of democracy (*Pol.* 1292a13–15). In the *Nicomachean Ethics* (1113a),
Aristotle argues that the *agorai* were designed as a venue for the aristo-
crats to announce their decisions to the people. By contrast, in the
Roman sources, Thersites is held up as a paradigm for outspokenness
against autocratic rule.[8] In Seneca, *De Ira*, the restraint of rulers in the
face of the *contumelia* of the Greeks is exemplified by two stories: one
involving Timagenes' offensive remarks against Augustus, the other the
impudence of one Demokhares, nephew of Demosthenes, nicknamed
"Free speech" (Parrhesiastes), at the expense of Alexander the Great (*De
Ira* 4.23). Demokhares' response to the question of what the king could

---

[5] The assembly in book 2 and the speeches by Agamemnon and Odysseus are used to illustrate the
point.
[6] See Aristotle, *Pol.* 1279a–b.   [7] *Schol. AbT in Il.* 2.283 *ex.*
[8] On the reception of Thersites, see further Gebhard (1934); Elmer (2013) 93–7; and Hunter
(2009) 87–9.

The Roman Assembly and Its Greek Counterparts 179

do for the Athenians – "go hang yourself" was his answer – earned him the title of Thersites.[9]

While the emphasis in the reception of the Homeric poems continues to be on nondemocratic forms of government, the assemblies are clearly seen to prefigure idealized forms of healthy democratic behavior in the scholia. For example, the scholia regularly refer to the speakers in the assemblies as "haranguing the demos" (δημηγορεῖν), as when, in book 9, Diomedes' frankness is described as exemplifying the freedom of speech (παρρησία) of the democratic assembly.[10] Polydamas' advice to Hector in book 12 is similarly described as embodying *Greek* freedom of speech.[11] Nestor speaks with more *parrhesia* on account of his old age.[12] Moreover, there is a visible effort to "other" the Trojans along political lines.[13] While it is true that in Ps. Plutarch (*Life and Poetry of Homer* 182), for example, the (Greek) suitors exemplify oligarchy and Aegisthus the character of the tyrant, the Trojans offer a paradigm of mob rule in that "all are accomplices of Paris." This theme is also found in the scholia, as, for example, when the *dēmēgoriai* of Hector and Menelaus in book 17 are said to exemplify respectively the stupidity of the barbarians and the order of the Greeks.[14]

This retrospective political reading of the Homeric assembly is a crucial context for Roman rewritings of these scenes. For, in reading the Homeric assembly against the background of late Republican history, Virgil is also participating in a debate about Greek political institutions, such as democracy and free speech, which were retrojected onto the Homeric poems. Here, the popular assembly (*contio*), viewed through the distorted lens of the Homeric past, functions as a locus for stating a claim about the uniqueness of the Roman political system.[15] For example, in a passage from the *Pro Flacco*, Cicero explains the difference between the Roman

[9] For this use of Thersites as a paradigm for rebellious speech, see Freudenburg (2018) 304 and Casali (1997) 100–1 on Ovid, *Met.* 13.232–33 . . . *et ausus erat reges incessere dictis | Thersites; etiam per me haud impune proteruus.* On the Roman reception of Thersites, see further Spina (1984).

[10] *Scholia A in Il.* 9.33a *Nicander* ὡς νόμος ἐστὶν – ἐν δημοκρατίᾳ, bT *ex.* θέμις δὲ τῆς δημηγορίας τὸ τὸ δοκοῦν παρρησιάζεσθαι. Cf. Ps. Plutarch, *Life and Poetry of Homer* 168.

[11] *Scholia bT in Il.* 12.215a *ex.* τὰ δὲ Ἑλληνικὰ πλησίον δημοκρατίας, καὶ παρρησία πολλὴ τοῖς ἡγεμόσι. And cf. *Scholia bT in Il.* 16.33 *ex.* and *Scholia bT in Il.* 16.273–4 *ex.* (of Patroclus). *Scholia T in Il.* 19.167 *ex.* compares Odysseus' description of a man with a fierceless heart to Plato's *Laws* 1.649a9 on *parrhesia*. On *parrhesia*, see Raaflaub (2004).

[12] *Scholia bT in Il.* 2.336–59 *ex.* παρρησιαστικὸς δὲ διὰ τὸ γῆρας ὁ Νέστωρ.

[13] For the disorderly nature of the Trojan assemblies, see Mackie (1996) 22–3; on Hector's behavior as a proto-demagogue in the Trojan *agorai*, see Elmer (2013) 132–45.

[14] *Scholia bT in Il.* 17.248–55 *ex.* τεθεῖσα ἐκ παραλλήλου ἡ δημηγορία αὕτη τῇ τοῦ Ἕκτορος ἤλεγξε μὲν τὸ τῶν βαρβάρων ἀνόητον, ἔδειξε δὲ τὴν Ἑλληνικὴν σύνεσιν.

[15] Gellius' definition of the contio (13.16.3) is often cited: *contionem habere est uerba facere ad populum sine ulla rogatione.*

Epic Demagoguery

system in which the *contio,* the popular assembly in which speeches were heard, was separated from the voting process (*comitia*), and the Greek custom of holding open debate and vote:

> Graecorum autem totae res publicae sedentis contionis temeritate administrantur. itaque ut hanc Graeciam quae iam diu suis consiliis perculsa et adflicta est omittam, illa uetus quae quondam opibus, imperio, gloria floruit hoc uno malo concidit, libertate immoderata ac licentia contionum. cum in theatro imperiti homines rerum omnium rudes ignarique consederant, tum bella inutilia suscipiebant, tum seditiosos homines rei publicae praeficebant, tum optime meritos ciuis e ciuitate eiciebant.

> But all the republics of the Greeks are governed by the foolhardiness of the sitting popular assembly. Therefore, to say no more of this Greece, which has for a long time been beaten down and crushed by its own counsels; that ancient civilization, which once flourished with wealth, power, and glory, fell on account of that one evil, namely unrestrained liberty and licentiousness of the popular assemblies. When men who are inexperienced, unskilled and ignorant of all things, sat down in the theatre, then they undertook useless wars; then they appointed seditious men to head the state; then they banished from the city the most deserving citizens. (Cicero, *Flac.* 16)

The passage presents the Greeks as confusing the boundaries between theater and politics, which was at the heart of Plato's critique of rhetoric in the Gorgias where poetry was defined as "a form of *dēmēgoria*" (*Grg* 502c12; see Chapter 1, p. 32). The men are in the theater (*in theatro*) in the seated position suitable for viewing audiences. The crowd is presented as imbued with natural force (*uis*) and the inability to control its destructiveness is singled out as the cause of the political decline of the Greek world. Cicero comes back to the fickleness of the mob and the distinction between the Greek democratic institution of the assembly and the orderly dealings in the Roman forum, in which, despite the Senate's check on the unruly behavior of the mob, the waves of the *contio* can still be seen swelling (*Flac.* 57 *cum speculatur atque obsidet rostra uindex temeritatis et moderatrix officii curia, tamen quantos fluctus excitari contionum uidetis*). By contrast, the levity of the Greeks creates a chaotic environment in which "seditious speech exercises its power" (*Flac.* 57 *quid in contione seditiosa ualeat oratio*). In this idealized reading, the gap between the Greek *agorē* and the Roman *contio,* to which Virgil will return, generates a powerful debate about the nature of Roman political institutions.

The Roman Assembly and Its Greek Counterparts

Cicero comes back to the crucial distinction between Greek and Roman political assemblies in *De Republica* book 1.[16] Arguing that every commonwealth needs to be ruled by some sort of deliberation (1.41 *omnis res publica, quae, ut dixi, populi res est, consilio quodam regenda est*), which can be entrusted either to an individual, to a select few or to the mob, Cicero singles out Athens as an example of a government in which the people's control of all things turned into madness and license of the mob (1.44 *Iam Atheniensium populi potestatem omnium rerum ipsi, ne alios requiramus, ad furorem multitudinis licentiamque conuersam pesti*). By contrast, as an advocate of democracy, Scipio summarizes the unique curtailing of the power of public deliberation by the crowds in what has been interpreted as a representation of the Roman constitution (*Rep.* 1.47). The people are free only in name in this system. They vote but "give what must be given even if they are unwilling" (*ea dant, quae, etiamsi nolint, danda sint*) and "they have no share in power, in public deliberation, or in the panels of select judges, all of which are apportioned on the basis of pedigree or wealth" (*expertes imperii, consilii publici, iudicii delectorum iudicum, quae familiarum uetustatibus aut pecuniis ponderantur*).

While Cicero's presentation of the *contio* in the *Pro Flacco* may well be tendentious, what interests us here is not only the polemical emphasis on unrestrained speech as an engine of political and cultural decline but above all the potential for speech in the assembly to be construed as spectacle.[17] The point is emphasized very clearly in the section of the *De oratore* book 2 dealing with the *genus deliberatiuum*. Here, Antonius argues it is one thing to argue in front of the Senate, a "wise council" (*sapiens consilium* 333), in which ostentation must be avoided, and another to speak in a public assembly (*contio*), which "gives scope for all the force of oratory, and requires dignity and variety" (334 *contio capit omnem uim orationis et grauitatem uarietatemque desiderat*). The force of the speech has to match the strength of the passion and the mutability of the crowd, with a full range of stylistic options being deployed:

> ad dicendum uero probabiliter nosse mores ciuitatis, qui quia crebro mutantur, genus quoque orationis est saepe mutandum; et quamquam una fere uis est eloquentiae, tamen quia summa dignitas est populi, grauissima causa rei publicae, maximi motus multitudinis, genus quoque dicendi grandius quoddam et inlustrius esse adhibendum uidetur; maximaque pars orationis admouenda est ad animorum motus non numquam aut

---

[16] On this passage see Arena (2012) 116–24 and Asmis (2005).
[17] Millar (1998) 220–6 on the idealizing picture offered by Cicero in this passage.

cohortatione aut commemoratione aliqua aut in spem aut in metum aut ad cupiditatem aut ad gloriam concitandos, saepe etiam a temeritate, iracundia, spe, iniuria, inuidia, crudelitate reuocandos fit autem ut, quia maxima quasi oratoris scaena uideatur contionis esse, natura ipsa ad ornatius dicendi genus excitemur; habet enim multitudo uim quandam talem, ut, quem ad modum tibicen sine tibiis canere, sic orator sine multitudine audiente eloquens esse non possit.

And yet although we may say that eloquentia is essentially a unity, yet, because of the unsurpassable dignity of the people, the high importance of the interests of the State, and the passionate emotions of the crowd, it seems that here we must employ some grandeur, some more brilliant mode of oratory. Indeed, the greater part of a speech must be devoted to exciting the emotions of the audience, at times inciting them, by direct exhortation or by some reminder, to hope or to fear or to be partial or to have high aspirations, often also calling them back from recklessness, anger, hope, injustice, envy, or cruelty. It actually happens quite naturally that we are stirred to employ a more distinguished mode of oratory, because a public meeting provides what might be called the orator's greatest stage. For, just as a flute player cannot play without a flute, the crowd has a certain power that makes it impossible for an orator to be eloquent unless a crowd is listening. (Cicero, *De or.* 2.337–8 trans. May and Wisse)

As Cicero points out, the setting of the *contio* and the powerful manipulation of the crowd's emotions call for the employment of a grander style (*genus . . . grandius . . . et illustrius*).[18] The metaphor of the *contio* as the orator's stage (*scaena*) used by Cicero further suggests a comparison between the handling of emotions by tragedians and the orator's hold on the crowd. This process is theatrical, turning the orator into a stage performer, reduced to a flute player without his instrument, if he cannot engage his audience. The comparison of the *contio* to a stage (*scaena*) brings to mind an earlier passage in book 2 in which the power of the orator's speech to appeal through the emotions is conjured up through a tragic quotation from Pacuvius (177 Ribbeck):[19]

sed tantam uim habet illa, quae recte a bono poeta dicta est "flexanima atque omnium regina rerum oratio", ut non modo inclinantem excipere aut stantem inclinare, sed etiam aduersantem ac repugnantem, ut imperator fortis ac bonus, capere possit.

But such enormous power is wielded by what one of our good poets rightly describes as "soul bending, the queen of all the world-speech", that it cannot

---

[18] See Arena (2013) on passions and reason in this model of deliberation sketched out by Cicero. See further Connolly (2007a) 231–6 on the orator's control of the crowd in Cicero.

[19] The fragment is a close translation of Euripides, *Hec.* 816.

Rewriting the Homeric Assembly: concilia *in the* Aeneid   183

only straighten up someone who is bending over and bend over someone who is standing, but also like a good and brave general, take prisoner someone who is offering resistance and is fighting back. (Cicero, *De or.* 2.187 trans. May and Wisse)

While Cicero plays on the equation between tragic and rhetorical pathos, he also compares the orator's swaying of a resistant or oppositional crowd to a general's capture of the enemy.[20] Unlike Thersites, whose rhetoric is foreign to the epic, the orator qua demagogue in Cicero is already a figure close to epic paradigms stylistically and generically.

Whether or not the *contio* functioned as a proto-democratic institution has been vigorously debated by scholars of the Roman Republic.[21] What counts for our purposes is that the assembly is a locus in which the Romans' relationship to the Greek democratic past is actively negotiated and the emotional power of rhetoric tested and scrutinized. In creating scenes of deliberation modeled on the Homeric *agorai* that nevertheless incorporate and, in so doing, profoundly *distort* elements of Roman assemblies, Virgil is actively responding to the Ciceronian critique of Greek *dēmēgoria*. Moreover, in approaching the assembly as an embedded rhetorical performance, it is crucial to remember that the orator's attempt to capture the emotions of the audience is already conjured up through epic poetry's hold on the emotions.

Rewriting the Homeric Assembly: *concilia* in the *Aeneid*

When it comes to the oratory of the Trojans qua future Romans, Virgil's reception of the Homeric assembly involves, from the start, a suppression of the most criticized aspects of the Greek assembly and an emphasis instead on archaic and more intrinsically Roman forms of rhetorical performance. This archaizing of rhetoric is evident, for example, in the increased role of the embassy over the council as a site for embedding rhetorical discourse. In the poem, there are three embassy scenes: the ones by Ilioneus, who acts as the Trojan envoy in book 1 to Dido (1.520–60) and book 7 to Latinus (7.212–48), and that of Drances and the *oratores* (11.100) sent by Latinus to negotiate the burial truce (11.100–21).[22] In developing

---

[20] On the close relationship between acting and oratory, see Fantham (2002).

[21] On oratory in the Roman *contio*, see Mouritsen (2017) 15–21; Morstein-Marx (2004) 35–67; Hölkeskamp (2004) 219–56; Fantham (1997) 111–15. On the question of the power of the *contio*, see Mouritsen (2001) 46–54; Millar (1998).

[22] Cf. *Aen.* 11.331 where Latinus proposes to send a hundred *oratores* to ask for peace. Venulus is also an ambassador but his role is described as that of a *legatus*: 11.227, 239, 296.

184 Epic Demagoguery

these figures, Virgil may well be following Ennius' focus on scenes of diplomacy. In what is left of his discussion of Latin poetic language in book 7 of the *De lingua latina*, Varro discusses the word *orator*:

> apud Ennium: Orator sine pace redit regique refert rem.
>   orator dictus ab oratione: qui enim uerba haberet publice aduersus eum quo legabatur, ab oratione orator dictus; cum res maior erat actioni, legebantur potissimum qui causam commodissime orare poterant. itaque Ennius ait: Oratores doctiloqui

> In Ennius we find: "The spokesman comes back without peace and relates the matter to the king" [*Ann.* 202]. The spokesman (*orator*) is called this way from the speech (*oratio*): for he who speaks in public before one to whom he was sent as a spokesperson, is called spokesman from the speech. When there was a matter of greater import, men were selected who could plead the case (*causam orare*) most aptly. Therefore, Ennius says: "spokesmen skilled in speaking" [*Ann.* 593 sed. inc.]. (Varro, *Ling.* 7.41)

Varro seems to outline two etymologies for *orator*: one that derives the noun from *oratio* and one that connects it with the verb *orare*, meaning to plead or beg. The latter etymology is alluded to by Virgil in his portrayal of Ilioneus. First, as Servius mentions (*ad Aen.* 1.520), the choice of Ilioneus as an *orator* is highly significant as in Homer his father Phorbas is a favorite of Hermes whose Roman counterpart, Mercury, is known for his eloquence.[23] The name Ilioneus further suggests a connection not just with Ilium (ʼΊλιον) but also, conceivably, with navigation (νηῦς), an art to which, as we have seen, rhetoric is often compared.[24] Furthermore, although Ilioneus is not explicitly called an *orator*, his first words, in which he represents the Trojans as beggars (1.525 *oramus* and cf. 1.519 *orantes ueniam*), allude to the etymological connection between *orator* and *orare*.

As Varro points out, the use of the word *orator* to indicate an envoy or legate, as well as the standard meaning of orator or advocate, is found in Ennius, who uses the word five times in our extant corpus, and in other early Roman writers.[25] Like Varro, Festus considered the use of *orator* to

---

[23] Homer, *Il.* 14.489–90. For Mercury as *facundus*, see Horace, *Carm.* 1.10.1 cited by Servius; Martial 7.74.1.
[24] See Paschalis (1997) 58 who also notes Ilioneus' reworking of the shipwreck's narrative at *Aen.* 1.535–8 and 7.213–15.
[25] For *orator* as envoy see Ennius, *Ann.* 202; Plautus, *Stich.* 290; Cato, *Orat.* 130.3 Malcovati; *Orig.* 22. For *orator* as speaker or advocate, see Terence, *Heaut.* 11; *Hec.* 9 where the poet and actor compares the prologues to the plays to defense speeches. See further Neuhauser (1958) 139–52.

Rewriting the Homeric Assembly: concilia *in the* Aeneid   185

refer to an envoy an archaism, and it probably has an archaic flavor when it is employed with reference to spokesmen in an embassy in Roman epic.[26]

Ilioneus, the character who acts as Aeneas' ambassador (*orator*) in two strategically matched scenes respectively in book 1, where he speaks to Dido, and in book 7, where he is sent to Latinus' palace, embodies not the stormy epic grandeur of the *genus deliberativum* but a soothing middle style.[27] The Trojan ambassador's countenance in his first speech is described as "appeasing" – *Aen.* 1.521 *maximus Ilioneus placido sic pectore coepit* "greatest Ilioneus thus began with appeasing spirit." The expression connects Ilioneus to Neptune, whose placating effects on the sea (1.127 *placidum caput* and 1.142 *placat*) trigger the comparison with the orator in the simile.[28] It is significant that the speech of Ilioneus, together with Drances, one of only two *oratores* who speak in the *Aeneid*, is characterized as having a placating rather than an arousing effect. It is true that orators need to be able to both stir and soothe the emotions; in addition, a placating effect is a feature of the middle style and is particularly appropriate to proemia.[29] This reframing of the *orator* in archaizing terms as a diplomat rather than as a Ciceronian politician is marked: unlike the *genus grande*, with its capacity for emotional arousal, Ilioneus polemically channels and showcases the appeasing effects of the middle style.

When it comes to public oratory in the conventional sense of the word, the first striking aspect of Virgil's treatment of Homeric assembly scenes in the *Aeneid* is their marked suppression and deferral. First, council scenes are reduced in number when compared to the Homeric epics: the council of the Trojans in book 5 and that of the Latins in book 11.[30] Additionally, the night council of the Trojans in book 9 represents an adaptation of the Homeric *boulē*, a more restricted council of the best, which can meet separately, before or after an *agorē*. This curtailing of scenes of public debate follows a well-known trend on the part of Virgil of limiting all

---

[26] Festus *Gloss. Lat.* Lindsay 182.30–46; 199.30–3 and see Neuhauser (1958) 150–1. For the *orator* as an envoy in Roman epic, see Virgil, *Aen.* 7.153; 8.505; 11.100; 11.331; Lucan 10.472; Silius 2.272; Ovid, *Met.* 13.196. For *orator* in this meaning outside of epic, see Sallust, *Iug.* 108.1; Tacitus, *Ann.* 13.37, and Livy (42x).

[27] On Ilioneus' speech, see Milanese (1985).

[28] *Servius Dan. ad Aen.* 1.520 notes in relation to *placido ore* that "it is the definition of the task of the orator who must make himself feel what he wants the judge to feel."

[29] On the orator's need to soothe and placate, especially in the proemium, see Cicero, *De or.* 2.315 *eum qui audit permulcere atque allicere;* Quintilian 2.5.8 *quibus uiribus inspiret qua iucundidate permulceat;* 6.1.11 *concitare adfectus et componere.*

[30] In the interests of space, I am excluding from discussion the council of the Gods in *Aen.* 10: although I consider divine rhetoric distinct from human rhetorical discourse, representations of *concilia deorum* raise parallel questions: see Barchiesi (2009b).

186   Epic Demagoguery

types of direct speech in his poem.[31] The diminished role of direct speech has been repeatedly analyzed biographically as a manifestation of Virgil's deep antipathy toward rhetoric viewed in opposition to unadulterated truth.[32] Yet, by analyzing these scenes both against the Roman critique of Greek politics and against the tradition of Homeric commentary, what emerges is Virgil's engagement with a much richer critique of rhetoric as an inherent cause of political decline.

While the action of the *Iliad* begins with an assembly scene (*Il.* 1.57 οἳ δ' ἐπεὶ οὖν ἤγερθεν ὁμηγερέες τε γένοντο), the first of such gatherings in the *Aeneid* does not come until book 5: Aeneas calls his companions to an assembly (5.43–4 *socios in coetum litore ab omni | aduocat Aeneas tumulique ex aggere fatur*) in order to announce the funeral games in honor of his father.[33] The location of the speech – by the shore and on the funeral mound of Anchises – blends the ambience for Homeric and Roman speech-making. The shore is the setting of a number of Iliadic *agorai*, while the *agger*, as we have seen in the previous chapter, is the typical setting for a *cohortatio*, a general's address to his troops.[34] At the conclusion of his announcement, his temples adorned with myrtle, Aeneas moves from the council (5.75 *e concilio multis cum milibus*) with the many thousands who attended to worship at his father's tomb.

In this scene, the literary trope of the Greek *agorē* intermeshes with the Roman *contio*. The assembly is first introduced as an informal "gathering" (*coetus*) but later described more formally as a *concilium*, the technical word for plebeian legislative assemblies from Cicero onward.[35] In signaling that Aeneas is summoning the assembly (*coetus . . . aduocat*), Virgil is hinting at the popular etymology of *concilium* from *concalare* (Gr. *kalein*).[36] Moreover, the *concilium* was marked as a gathering aimed at deliberation by a process of folk etymology that connected it with *consilium* – the two words are often found interchangeably in the manuscript tradition.[37]

---

[31] Laird (1999) 153–208; Farrell (1997); Heinze (1993) 315–18.

[32] Feeney (1983); Highet (1972) 22–5.   [33] Cairns (1989) 58–9.

[34] Thus Servius commenting on the phrase *ad Aen.* 5.43 *proprie enim aduocata contio dicitur*. For the setting of the Homeric assembly by the shore, see *Il.* 2.92–3 ἠϊόνος προπάροιθε βαθείης ἐστιχόωντο | ἰλαδὸν εἰς ἀγορήν; *Il.* 19.40 παρὰ θῖνα θαλάσσης with Seymour (1914) 107.

[35] See Taylor (1966) 138–9. *Concilium* is the word used of the assembly of the gods in book *Aen.* 10.2, the council of the Latins in *Aen.* 11.234, 304, 460, 469. See Fratantuono and Smith (2015) 182 *ad Aen.* 5.75.

[36] Paschalis (1997) 145 *ad Aen.* 3.679. See Isidore, *Etym.* 6.16.12; Festus, *Gloss. Lat.* Lindsay 33.26 *concilium dicitur a concalando, id est uocando*.

[37] Varro, *Ling.* 6.43 *a cogitatione concilium (inde consilium)*. See Botsford (1909) 135–6 and Horsfall (2008) 116 *ad Aen.* 2.88 on *conciliis regum* of the Greeks assemblies at Troy.

Rewriting the Homeric Assembly: concilia in the Aeneid   187

By contrast, this first Virgilian assembly is lacking in debate or in a response from the crowd, both features of Homeric *agorai*. Instead, the mute procession following the *concilium* in *Aen.* 5 recalls the *agorē* of the Phaeacians at the beginning of *Od.* 8 (8.12 εἰς ἀγορὴν ἰέναι). As has been noted, the Phaeacian assemblies are conspicuous for their lack of debate.[38] In this *agorē*, summoned by Athena, Alcinous announces his intention of providing the yet to be named Odysseus with an escort. This assembly closes with the scepter-bearing aristocracy following the king and executing his orders.[39] At the same time, the orderly crowd movement in *Aen.* 5 recalls the crowds of the Republican *concilium plebis*. But, in the representation of the crowd of a thousand men accompanying Pallas' funeral (11.60–1 *et toto lectos ex agmine mittit | mille uiros qui supremum comitentur honorem*), Virgil is also playing with the image of the Roman funeral, which Polybius saw as a pivotal moment in Roman political discourse comparable to the *contio* in its capacity to affect the masses.[40] The political dimension of the *concilium* in *Aeneid* 5 is reaffirmed in the following line where the followers are described as a *magna ... comitante caterua* (5.76), a phrase that denotes the retinue of political leaders and other powerful figures with ominous resonances.[41]

The second council scene in the *Aeneid* underscores the complex effect of the interweaving of Homeric rhetoric with the contemporary political vocabulary of Roman institutions. As the night draws on, the Trojan leaders meet to discuss the crisis pending on the camp and how to alert Aeneas who has gone to seek Evander's help:

> ductores Teucrum primi, delecta iuuentus,
> consilium summis regni de rebus habebant,
> quid facerent quisue Aeneae iam nuntius esset.
> stant longis adnixi hastis et scuta tenentes
> castrorum et campi medio.

> The first leaders of the Trojans, chosen youth, were holding a council on the kingdom's pressing affairs, what they should do, and who should be a messenger to Aeneas. They stand, leaning on their long spears and holding the shields in the middle of the camp and the plain. (Virgil, *Aen.* 9.226–30)

---

[38] Barker (2009) 115–16.

[39] *Od.* 8.46–7 ὣς ἄρα φωνήσας ἡγήσατο, τοὶ δ᾽ ἅμ᾽ ἕποντο | σκηπτοῦχοι·. Cf. *Aen.* 5.74 *sequitur quos cetera pubes*.

[40] See Polybius 6.54.2 with Flower (1996) 128–58.

[41] See *Aen.* 4.136 (of Dido) with Austin (1964) 45 *ad Aen.* 2.40; Cicero, *Mur.* 69; Livy 4.14.6 and 6.14.3; Sallust, *Cat.* 14.1 *stipatorum cateruas* (of Catiline's followers). Fratantuono and Smith (2015) 182–3 *ad Aen.* 5.76 define the use of the word *caterua* as "ominous."

188   Epic Demagoguery

As Servius informs us ad loc., the phrase *consilium summis . . . habebant* in
v. 227 is taken from Lucilius' *Satires*, in which the council of the Gods
debates how to come to the rescue of mankind after the death of Lupus.
The word *regnum*, inserted into the Lucilian phrase, both disrupts the
Republican veneer of the model and gestures to the Homeric "council of
kings."[42] Virgil is going to some pains to establish the nondeliberative
nature of this night council. As scholars have recognized, the scene is
rooted in the two-night *boulai* of *Iliad* 10 (10.194–5 τοὶ δ' ἄμ' ἕποντο |
Ἀργείων βασιλῆες ὅσοι κεκλήατο βουλήν; 10.302 τοὺς ὅ γε συγκαλέσας
πυκινὴν ἀρτύνετο βουλήν): both feature an elder – Nestor and Hector
respectively – calling a gathering of the heroes to seek volunteers to act as
spies in the enemy's camp. However, Virgil plays on the standard equivo-
cation between *consilium* and *concilium* by suggesting deliberation (v. 228
qui facerent quis . . . nuntius esset), while simultaneously omitting the actual
discussion from the view of his readers and resorting instead to indirect
speech.

The Trojans are standing (v. 229 *stant*), holding their shields and
balancing their bodies on their spears. In doing so, they are following the
example of Hector, who addresses his people outside the Greek camp
leaning on his spear rather than on the *skeptron* (*Il.* 8.494), a pose that
was interpreted as putting on display his manliness.[43] Moreover, commentators point to Virgil's translation of two Homeric lines describing the
Achaeans and Trojans as leaning on their shields in *Il.* 3.134–5.[44] Notice,
however, that, in these lines, Iris is describing how the Trojans and
Achaeans tired from the battle are *seated*: "sitting down in silence, for the
war has stopped; leaning on their shields, their long spears are beside them"
(*Il.* 3.134–5 οἳ δὴ νῦν ἕαται σιγῇ, πόλεμος δὲ πέπαυται, | ἀσπίσι κεκλιμένοι,
παρὰ δ' ἔγχεα μακρὰ πέπηγεν). Servius comments on the innovation
when he says that "this is an extraordinary look for a *consilium*: for in a time
of uncertainty, they do not sit down but rather they stand" (*Servius Dan. ad
Aen.* 9.227 *mira facies consilii: in rebus dubiis non sedent, sed stant*). Servius is
here referring to the Homeric norm of sitting down during deliberation.[45]
Yet the standing pose of the Roman in public gatherings was also

---

[42] Cf. also *Aen.* 9.223 *regem* of Ascanius.
[43] See *Sch. T in Il.* 8.494 *ex.* and see further Schlunk (1974) 60–2 with Hardie (1994) 116 ad loc.
[44] Hardie (1994) 116 ad loc.
[45] That this was the norm is apparent among other things by the exception at *Il.* 18.246–8, where the
standing pose of the gathered Trojans is marked and interpreted as a symptom of their fear on
hearing of Achilles' return: ὀρθῶν δ' ἑσταότων ἀγορὴ γένετ', οὐδέ τις ἔτλη | ἕζεσθαι· πάντας γὰρ
ἔχε τρόμος, οὕνεκ' Ἀχιλλεὺς | ἐξεφάνη.

Rewriting the Homeric Assembly: concilia *in the* Aeneid   189

a cornerstone of ethnic self-definition.[46] In the passage of the *Pro Flacco* (15–17) discussed above, Cicero comments on the abhorrent behavior of the Greeks who make rash decisions while *sitting down* in theaters (16 *cum in theatro imperiti homines rerum omnium rudes ignarique consederant, tum bella inutilia suscipiebant*). By contrast, the Roman people in assembly stood.[47] Thus, in 154 BCE, Cornelius Scipio Nasica was able to make the case for the destruction of a recently erected stone theater by arguing that "the virility of a standing posture appropriate to the Roman race should be renowned even when the mind was relaxed" (Valerius Maximus 2.4.2 *ut scilicet remissioni animorum standi uirilitas propria Romanae gentis nota esset*). The standing pose of the Roman *pubes* in the night council leverages traditional anti-Hellenic discourse by reproducing a dichotomy between Greek inactive petulance and Roman self-restrained speech. Similarly, later in book 11, Turnus condemns of the futility of the Latin council in the face of the military attack of Aeneas with a reference to the sitting pose, which not only reinforces the opposition between word and deed but also exploits the Roman critique of rhetoric.[48]

Together with the council of the gods in *Aen.* 10, of which there are important echoes, the council of the Latins is the only extended formal *concilium* in the poem.[49] The council consists of four speeches: one (11.243–95) by Venulus, reporting on Diomedes' response to the Latins' request for aid against Aeneas; one by Latinus (11.302–35); one by Drances (11.336–75); and one by Turnus (11.376–444). The episode combines two important type-scenes from earlier in the poem: the embassy and the assembly. Book 11 opens with an embassy scene in which Drances, one of the *oratores* sent by Latinus to ask for a burial truce, responds to Aeneas with a hyperbolic eulogy of the Trojan leader (11.124–31).[50] After the burial of the dead, the ambassadors, headed by Venulus, are seen arriving back from Diomedes and Latinus summons a council of the elders in his palace. A brief description of the reaction of the crowd to Venulus' speech is followed by the three speeches of Latinus, Drances and Turnus. The council begins with the speech of Venulus, the *orator* sent by Latinus to Diomedes to request military aid. Diomedes' negative response, quoted in

---

[46] Taylor (1966) 28–33.

[47] See Servius *ad Buc.* 1.33.1 on Caesar's new building for the comitia in the Campus Martius as designed for *stans populus Romanus*.

[48] Note the emphatic *sedentes* at *Aen.* 11.460 in Turnus' words: *cogite concilium et pacem laudate sedentes;* | *illi armis in regna ruunt.*

[49] On the echoes of the council of the gods, see Fantham (1999) 274–5.

[50] See Hardie (2012) 146–7 on the ways in which Drances' speech recuperates the mode of *basilikos logos*, which is associated with the rhetorical aims of the *Aeneid* itself.

190   Epic Demagoguery

indirect speech by Venulus (11.243–95), is the catalyst for a rhetorical match between Drances, whom we have already seen as critical of the Rutulian king, and Turnus, who, rejecting Latinus' proposal to seek peace, volunteers instead to fight Aeneas in a duel, which eventually will bring the poem to a close in the following book. The council is disrupted abruptly by the news that Aeneas is approaching with his troops.

The assembly of the Italians blends Homeric and Roman rhetoric, creating a council scene that eschews the popular element of the Homeric *agorē*, while at the same time "homericizing" the Roman institution of the senatorial debate. Once again, Virgil elides the popular debate by using free indirect discourse to report the dissenting opinion of the Latins. Drances' insistence that Turnus alone be called to fight Aeneas (11.220–1 *ingrauat haec saeuus Drances solumque uocari | testatur, solum posci in certamina Turnum*) is presented as a report of a debate in the assembly (*sententia*), the content of which is in indirect speech: "in opposition, there was a widespread feeling with varied expression on Turnus' behalf" (11.222.3 *multa simul contra uariis sententia dictis | pro Turno*).[51] Here the *uaria dicta* are omitted from view, replaced instead by the triptych of speeches that follows Venulus' report.

As news of the latter's arrival spreads, we witness Latinus summoning the people and the elders to his palace for the gathering (*concilium*).[52]

> ergo concilium magnum primosque suorum
> imperio accitos alta intra limina cogit.   235
> olli conuenere fluuntque ad regia plenis
> tecta uiis. sedet in mediis et maximus aeuo
> et primus sceptris haud laeta fronte Latinus.

> So he summoned a great council and the leaders of his people by command and gathered them within his lofty threshold. They came together and streamed towards the royal palace through the crowded streets. In their midst sits Latinus, the oldest and most powerful, with no happy face. (Virgil, *Aen.* 11.234–8)

The language conjures up a hybrid of the *boulē*, the restricted council of the elders (see v. 234 *primos suorum*), and the *agorē*, the public assembly (see v. 234 *concilium*).[53] Turnus, however, later refers to the Latin council as the

---

[51] See Horsfall (2003) 162 ad loc. on *sententia* referring to "an opinion expressed in an assembly" (*OLD* 4).
[52] Cf. *Aen.* 11.304 *cogere concilium*; 460 *cogite concilium*; 469–70 *concilium . . . deserit.*
[53] This combination of *concilium* and *boulē* is perhaps inspired by *Il.* 9.9–12, where Agamemnon calls a general assembly through the heralds (*Il.* 9.10–11 κηρύκεσσι λιγυφθόγγοισι κελεύων | κλήδην εἰς

Rewriting the Homeric Assembly: concilia *in the* Aeneid   191

curia (11.380 *curia*; cf. 7.174), one of the Roman names for Senate.[54] This *concilium* takes places in the palace of the king (11.236–7 *ad regia plenis | tecta uiis*) and the Latin kings are said to be endowed with both the Homeric scepter and the Roman consular *fasces* (7.173–4 *hic sceptra accipere et primos attollere fascis | regibus omen erat*).[55] The setting of the *curia* in the royal palace would immediately have struck a jarring note for Roman readers given that the Senate, the main deliberating body of the Roman state, would not be meeting in a private home. Yet, as Servius reminds us (*ad Aen.* 11.235), back in book 7, Latinus' palace was described as a *templum* and as a site for meetings of the *curia* (7.174 *hoc illis curia templum*), an expression that clearly echoes the Roman requirement that the Senate should meet in *templa per augures constituta* (Gellius 14.7.7).[56] In turn, as Horsfall notes, this combination of palace and *templum* "can hardly have failed to suggest the juxtaposition of the *domus Augusti* and the temple of the Palatine Apollo," the latter of which was used by its founder, Augustus, for meetings of the Senate.[57]

Formally speaking, the debate between Turnus and Drances recalls late Republican typologies in which forensic, deliberative and epideictic modes are fused together. Both Servius and Tiberius Cl. Donatus are far more sensitive than modern critics to Turnus' rhetorical manipulation. Donatus notes an *occulta vituperatio* directed at Latinus, whose title *pater* is interpreted ironically.[58] Servius notes the use of *insinuatio*, a method for securing good will in the exordium through rhetorical dissimulation, in other words through a clever and refined speech (*callida et subtilis oratio*);[59] *Servius Dan. ad* 11.378 calls the speech a "rhetorical response" consisting of self-defense followed by exposition of Turnus' opinion on the war.[60] This rhetorical reading points to a productive generic contradiction: although we are theoretically witnessing a debate leading to a deliberation, Turnus' style of *refutatio* fits within a forensic setting, revealing the speech as

---

ἀγορὴν κικλήσκειν ἄνδρα ἕκαστον), while he personally summons the leaders (*Il.* 9.12 αὐτὸς δὲ μετὰ πρώτοισι πονεῖτο).
[54] And cf. the references to the audience as *ciues* ("citizens"): *Aen.* 11.243, 305, 459.
[55] See Livy 1.8.2; 2.1.7; Ovid, *Fast.* 1.79–82.
[56] Servius *ad Aen.* 11.235 *quaeritur cur ad priuatam domum conuocetur senatus.*
[57] Horsfall (2000) 150 *ad* 7.174; see Suetonius, *Aug.* 29.3; Servius *ad Aen.* 11.235 *idcirco etiam in Palatii atrio, quod augurato conditum est, apud maiores consulebatur senatus*; see also Rosivach (1980) 145–52.
[58] *Interpretationes Vergilianae* vol. 2, pp. 477.23–478.4.
[59] Servius *ad Aen.* 11.411 *insinuatione utitur, id est callido et subtili aditu ad persuadendum* and see *Rhet. Her.* 1.7.11.
[60] *Servius Dan. ad Aen.* 11.378 *sane rhetorice responsurus Turnus bene coepit a Drance. ante enim se defendit, tunc de bello sententiam dicit.*

192 Epic Demagoguery

a defense in court.[61] As Fantham notes, this slippage between deliberative and forensic in the speeches of Drances and Turnus does not evoke Homeric council scenes but rather looks forward to Roman Republican rhetoric, as for example Cicero's *De provinciis consularibus*, a deliberative speech delivered to the Senate on the topic of Caesar's reappointment in Gaul that contains embedded elements of praise for Caesar and invective directed at Piso and Gabinius.[62] In the uncanny way typical of Virgil's representation of the Latins both as enemies of Aeneas and as primitive ancestors of the Romans, the council scene of book 11 projects the impinging political reality of Rome onto Homeric epic.

The debate between Drances and Turnus echoes above all *Il.* 2, in which Thersites' challenge to king Agamemnon in the assembly is physically and rhetorically suppressed by Odysseus. The setting of the council of the Latins clearly evokes the *agorē* summoned by Agamemnon.[63] Latinus' speech (11.302–35) matches Agamemnon's deceptive testing of the troops (*Il.* 2.110–41), followed by the demagogic rhetoric of Drances and Thersites, which is in turn followed by a response and resumption of the hostilities. In his first introduction, Drances is described as "old, always loathed by the young Turnus for his hatred and accusations" (11.122–3 *Tum senior semperque odiis et crimine Drances | infensus iuueni Turno*). While the vocabulary of hatred (*odiis, infensus*) recalls Homer's presentation of Thersites "as the most hated" (*Il.* 2.220 ἔχθιστος), the reference to *crimen* conjures up the late Republican criminal trials through which personal vendetta were often transacted.[64]

After Latinus' speech, Drances is reintroduced with a fuller portrayal that updates the Homeric Thersites by way of Sallust's demagogues:

> tum Drances idem infensus, quem gloria Turni
> obliqua inuidia stimulisque agitabat amaris,
> largus opum et lingua melior, sed frigida bello
> dextera, consiliis habitus non futtilis auctor,
> seditione potens (genus huic materna superbum   340
> nobilitas dabat, incertum de patre ferebat),
> surgit et his onerat dictis atque aggerat iras.

> Then Drances as hostile as before, whom Turnus' glory drove with the bitter sting of covert envy, lavish of his wealth, and better with his tongue, but

---

[61] Fantham (1999) 266: "seen in judicial terms, Latinus becomes president of the court, the Latins the jury, and Turnus the accused."
[62] See Grillo (2015) 19–20.   [63] See Highet (1972) 210–1.   [64] Horsfall (2003) 117 *ad Aen.* 11.122.

> with a right hand feeble in war; held to be no worthless adviser in counsel, powerful in sedition – his mother's nobility granted him a proud descent, his father's origin he proclaimed unknown – he stands up and with these words he aggravates and builds up their anger. (Virgil, *Aen.* 11.336–42)

Drances' loquacity recalls the logorrhea of Thersites: the word *largus* (v. 338), which technically refers to Drances' wealth, reminds us of Thersites' words that are said to be "many and without order" (*Il.* 2.213 ἔπεα . . . ἄκοσμά τε πολλά τε).[65] But Virgil has otherwise deeply "*rhetoricized*" the Homeric Thersites. As Philip Hardie has noted, Drances is a fully rhetorical figure – his effective kindling of audience emotions (v. 342 *onerat . . . aggerat iras*) echoes the earlier appearance by *Fama* and her manipulation through speech (*Aen.* 4.197 *incenditque animum dictis atque aggerat iras*).[66] Moreover, Virgil has turned the confrontation into a much more balanced rhetorical antithesis between eloquence (v. 338 *lingua melior*) and arms (v. 338–9 *frigida bello dextera*). This contrast upends a cornerstone of the style of Homeric heroes understood in Richard Martin's helpful formulation as "a total notion: a proportion of word and deed."[67] Thersites violates the epic code not just politically, by attacking the leaders whom he is supposed to follow, but, above all, aesthetically with an ugly speech that matches his unpleasant physique.[68] Thus, when we first see Odysseus silencing the men from the *dēmos*, among whom Thersites is the last standing, he is upbraiding them as "worthless in both war and council" (*Il.* 2.202 οὔτε ποτ' ἐν πολέμῳ ἐναρίθμιος οὔτ' ἐνὶ βουλῇ). When he addresses Thersites, he calls him "undiscriminated in speech" (*Il.* 2.246 ἀκριτόμυθε) and tells him to restrain himself "even though you are a clear speaker" (λιγύς περ ἐὼν ἀγορητής).[69]

Although Drances has often been understood as embodying Virgil's antipathy for rhetoric, Virgil's reinvention of the Homeric demagogue is itself a deeply rhetorical operation in which the clear aesthetic and political hierarchy of *Il.* 2 pitting the shameful plebeian against the rightful aristocrat is transformed into a rhetorical *agōn* whose structure anticipates the final duel of *Aen.* 12. The contrast between word and deed around which the narrative is (re)organized has an important role in Roman political

---

[65] *Il.* 2.212–14 Θερσίτης δ' ἔτι μοῦνος ἀμετροεπὴς ἐκολῴα, | ὃς ἔπεα φρεσὶν ᾗσιν ἄκοσμά τε πολλά τε ᾔδη | μάψ, ἀτὰρ οὐ κατὰ κόσμον.

[66] Hardie (2012) 135. For the Incendiary capacity of demagogues, see Sallust, *Cat.* 38 *homines adulescentes summam potentiam nacti, quibus aetas animusque ferox erat, coepere senatum criminando plebem exagitare, dein largiundo atque pollicitando magis incendere, ita ipsi clari potentesque fieri.*

[67] Martin (1989) 111. [68] See Nagy (1979) 260 on Thersites as the representative of blame poetry.

[69] Kirk (1985) 142 ad loc. interprets the comment as "sarcastic."

194   Epic Demagoguery

thought of the late Republic. Sallust uses it to justify his own venture into historiography in the preface to the *Bellum Catilinae* (3.1–2). "Acting well in the interest of the state" (*bene facere rei publicae*) – a phrase employed by Cato – is initially contrasted with "speaking well" (*bene dicere*), but Sallust argues that the two activities are not so different: praise accrues both to those who perform actions and to those who write about the acts of others.[70] The blurring of this dichotomy is enhanced by Sallust's choice to call the performer the *auctor rerum*, a word that can also denote the author of a literary text.[71]

Sallust's unraveling of this dichotomy is polemical, but the Platonic distrust of eloquence divorced from wisdom clearly informs the portrayal of the enemies of the Republic, which Virgil is incorporating in his rewriting of Thersites. Drances' nobility on his mother's side (*Aen.* 11.340–1) distinguishes him from the "plebeian" Thersites and echoes instead the aristocratic roots of Catiline (*Cat.* 5.1 *nobili genere natus*), in whom eloquence is divorced from wisdom (5.4 *satis eloquentiae, sapientiae parum*).[72] The emphasis on *gloria* (*Aen.* 11.336) as a motivator fits the epic obsession with *kleos* but it is also a key aspect of Sallust's presentation of the moral demise of the Roman state.[73]

Similarly, when Drances is said to be *seditione potens*, the reference to the role of civic dissent recalls Sallust's account of late Republican history. Moreover, *seditio* connects Drances to the simile of the orator in the storm in *Aen.* 1.149, the only other occurrence of this word in the poem, given that the orator's speech quells a popular *seditio*.[74] The expression *largus opum* (v. 338), "generous in giving his wealth," while hinting at the out-of-control size of the Homeric Thersites, gestures toward the notion of bribery (*largitio*), which Sallust, among others, identifies as one of the primary causes of Roman decline.[75]

---

[70] Sallust, *Cat.* 3.1 *pulchrum est bene facere rei publicae, etiam bene dicere haud absurdum est; uel pace uel bello clarum fieri licet; et qui fecere et qui facta aliorum scripsere, multi laudantur.*

[71] *Cat.* 3.2 *ac mihi quidem, tametsi haudquaquam par gloria sequitur scriptorem et auctorem rerum, tamen in primis arduum uidetur res gestas scribere.* See further Feldherr (2013) 54–5.

[72] Cf. Cicero, *Cat.* 3.16 *Erat ei consilium ad facinus aptum, consilio autem neque lingua neque manus deerat.* For other examples of this topos see Sallust, *Iug.*44 *lingua quam manu promptior*; Livy 3.11.7 *ad ea munera data a dis et ipse addiderat multa belli decora facundiamque in foro, ut nemo, non lingua, non manu promptior in ciuitate haberetur.*

[73] For *gloria* in Sallust, see Earl (1961) 9–14.

[74] On *seditio* as the root cause for Roman decline, see *Rhet. Her.* 4.66 *nunc uestris seditionibus, o ciues, uexor* (prosopopoeia of Rome); Sallust, *Cat.* 51.32 *homines scelestos et factiosos, qui seditionibus rem publicam exagitauerant, merito necatos aiebant*; Horace, *Carm.* 3.6.13–14 *paene occupatam seditionibus | deleuit urbem Dacus et Aethiops* with Nisbet and Rudd (2004) 104 ad loc.

[75] See Sallust, *Cat.* 3.4.

Rewriting the Homeric Assembly: concilia *in the* Aeneid 195

This presentation of Drances' character by the narrator as a cowardly verbal manipulator (esp. v. 338 *largus opum et lingua melior*) is echoed later in the episode in Turnus' opening words (esp. v. 378 *larga quidem semper, Drance, tibi copia fandi*). Here, the narrator and Turnus seem to agree in using Drances' reliance on words as a sign of cowardice. Moreover, when the assembly is interrupted by the news that the army of Aeneas is close to the city, the narrator describes the breaking of the gathering thus:

> illi haec inter se dubiis de rebus agebant
> certantes: castra Aeneas aciemque mouebat.

> Arguing, they were debating about these uncertain matters among themselves: meanwhile, Aeneas moved his camp and battle line. (Virgil, *Aen.* 11.445–6)

The prominently placed participle, *certantes*, applies a word about physical confrontation to a verbal conflict, highlighting the ways in which the debate has been an inappropriate and unwise substitute for action.[76]

While it is tempting to read the council as setting up an opposition between Drances' empty rhetoric and Turnus' traditionally heroic propensity for action, in his supposedly anti-rhetorical tirade, Turnus uses a stock motif of Roman invective: the phrase *fugacibus pedibus* is used in the pseudo-Sallustian and pseudo-Ciceronian *Inuectiuae* (*in Sall.* 10 *pedes fugaces; in Cic.* 5 *pedes fugaces*) and is first attested in the late Augustan rhetor Rutilius (*Rhet. Lat. Min.* Halm p. 11).[77] Moreover, Virgil prevents us from discounting Drances' rhetorical performance first and foremost by constructing Turnus as a second Paris. The council of the Latin rewrites two *agorai* from the *Iliad* – the assembly of the Achaeans in book 2 and the Trojan councils of books 7 (7.345–80) and 18 (18.243–313).[78] Drances' speech, which echoes Antenor's advice to return Helen in the Trojan council in *Il.* 7.348–53, implicitly sets up Turnus as a Paris figure who refuses to surrender. A less flattering implication of this reading is that it is not simply the case that Turnus will not give up his wife-to-be (like Paris) but that (also like Paris) he is afraid to fight. Secondly, the contrast between word and deed set up in vv. 338–40 is implicitly undermined by the echoes of Polydamas' speech in *Il.* 18.254–83, advising the Trojans against camping

---

[76] Hardie (2004) 220 *ad Met.* 13.6.
[77] See Nisbet (1958) However, the accusation moved against the enemy caught fleeing is in itself Homeric (e.g. *Il.* 8.94 Diomedes to Odysseus) and returns later in book 11 in Ligus' words to Camilla (11.706–8 . . . *dimitte fugam et te comminus aequo mecum crede . . . iam nosces uentosa ferat cui gloria fraudem*). See Horsfall (2003) 225–6 *ad* 11.351.
[78] Knauer (1964) 283–93.

196   Epic Demagoguery

out in the open plain after Achilles rejoined the battle. The context recalls the Homeric narrator's portrayal of Polydamas as "Hector's companion, born in the same night; yet one excelled at words, the other with the spear" (18.248–9 Ἕκτορι δ' ἦεν ἑταῖρος, ἰῇ δ' ἐν νυκτὶ γένοντο, | ἀλλ' ὁ μὲν ἄρ μύθοισιν, ὁ δ' ἔγχεϊ πολλὸν ἐνίκα). The expression *consiliis habitus non futtilis auctor* in 11.349 has puzzled interpreters: is it an acknowledgment of Drances' verbal dexterity? Or a reference to his role as "valued *bouleutēs*"?[79] It makes sense to read the phrase as an acknowledgment of the fact that Drances' proposal of a duel with Aeneas will essentially be the resolution to the conflict and to the narrative in the next book. Yet the emphasis on *consilia* also echoes the Homeric narrator's acknowledgment that Hector's plan was bad planning (*Il.* 18.312 κακὰ μητιόωντι) while Polydamas' advice, disregarded by Hector and the Trojans, was the best counsel (*Il.* 18.313 Πουλυδάμαντι δ' ἄρ' οὔ τις ὃς ἐσθλὴν φράζετο βουλήν). Viewed through the lens of *Il.* 18, Turnus is acting like Hector in demagogically seeking the approval of the crowd by disowning the rhetorical medium.

The background of the Homeric narrator's judgment effectively prevents the reader from accepting the contrast between *muthos* and *enkhos*, between *lingua* and *dextera*, as a sustainable one in the context of the narrative. Moreover, when Turnus refers to Drances as *artificis scelus* (v. 407), we may be encouraged to identify Drances as a second Ulysses, if we remember that the phrase *artificis scelus* was used before of Ulysses' criminal plotting in *Aen.* 2.125.[80] At the same time, the phrase Turnus appropriates comes from Sinon's speech and the repetition may thus underscore Turnus' hypocrisy. In book 2, it is Sinon's artful speech that leads to the collapse of Troy: whose artful speech will it be this time?

Thus, in Virgil's construction of the council, the opposition between word and action reveals itself as nothing more than a rhetorical ploy as neither of the main speakers offers a trustworthy point of view. In harnessing a long-standing critique of the assembly, Virgil signals an ironic awareness of the distance between the fighting rhetoric of the *concilium* and the epic needs of the narrative through his sustained reworking of the assembly scene in *Il.* 2. The council is framed by two similes, one comparing the roaring reaction (*fremor*) of the crowd to Venulus' speech to a gushing torrent (11.296–301) and one comparing the noise of the assembly dismantling at the news of the impending attack of the Trojans (11.456–8) to the noise of birds and swans on the Po river. These two similes single out

[79] Horsfall (2003) 218 ad loc.
[80] *Aen.* 2.124–5 *et mihi iam multi crudele canebant* | *artificis scelus.*

Rewriting the Homeric Assembly: concilia *in the* Aeneid   197

two Homeric similes, one which describes the reaction of the crowd to Agamemnon's testing of the troops (*Il.* 2.142–9) and one belonging to a series of seven similes that concludes the council of the Greeks in *Il.* 2 and activates the transition to the Catalogue of the Ships (*Il.* 2.445–87).[81] As had already been remarked in antiquity, this is the longest series of similes in the *Iliad.*[82] Whereas, in Homer, the crowd's upheaval is compared to the waves of the sea or the movement of grains caused by heavy wind (*Il.* 2.142–9), Virgil chooses different water imagery, that of the sound of rushing water on a stream:

> uix ea legati, uariusque per ora cucurrit
> Ausonidum turbata fremor, ceu saxa morantur
> cum rapidos amnis, fit clauso gurgite murmur
> uicinaeque fremunt ripae crepitantibus undis.
> ut primum placati animi et trepida ora quierunt,   300
> praefatus diuos solio rex infit ab alto.

> The envoys had hardly spoken, when a mixed murmuring ran through the troubled mouths of the Ausonians, as when rocks delay swift rivers, there is a roar in the enclosed pool and the neighboring banks resound with the rumbling waves. As soon as spirits were calmed and anxious mouths fell quiet, the king having prayed beforehand to the gods began from his lofty throne. (Virgil, *Aen.* 11.296–301)

The simile picks up on the presentation of the crowd streaming into the palace as moving bodies of water earlier in the book (11.236 *fluunt*). Yet the comparison of the seditious crowd to stormy waters takes us back to two crucial scenes of political upheaval: the first simile of the poem describing the placated sea with a reference to the orator calming a crowd (1.148–53), in which the traffic of signification inverts the Iliadic comparison of political sedition to storm, and the simile comparing Latinus' attempt to stall the violence of the mob reacting to the death of Galaesus to an unmovable cliff resisting the rush of the sea (*Aen.* 7.586 *uelut pelago rupes immota resistit*).[83]

---

[81] See Elmer (2013) 100–4 for the ways in which these similes describe the loss and recovery of consensus in the episode of the testing of the troops.

[82] *Scholia abT in Il.* 2.455–6 *ex.*: νῦν μάλιστα ἡ δύναμις τοῦ ποιητοῦ, ὅτε καθ᾽ ἕκαστον πρᾶγμα διαφόρων εἰκόνων εὐπορεῖ (here the power of the poet is especially incredible when he gives to each thing a different simile).

[83] See Cowan (2015) and Feeney (2014) 219–20 on the connection between *Aen.* 1.148–53 and 7.585–90. The gathering mob (*Aen.* 7.582 *undique collecti coeunt*) reminds us of the connection between gathering and assembly: see on *Aen.* 5.43 *coetus* above. This etymology is in contrast with that deriving *agorē* from speaking (*agoreuein*): see Porphyry, *Homeric Questions*, Θ 2.5: "assembly meaning a gathering has been made, not from to speak *agoreuein*, but from to assemble *ageiresthai*."

198 Epic Demagoguery

The second simile, which concludes the council, picks up more explicitly one of the similes describing the gathering Greek troops at the conclusion of the assembly scene (*Il.* 2.459–66):

> ... hic undique clamor
> dissensu uario magnus se tollit in auras,   455
> haud secus atque alto in luco cum forte cateruae
> consedere auium, piscosoue amne Padusae
> dant sonitum rauci per stagna loquacia cycni.

> Now on all sides a great clamor rises to the skies amid manifold discord, no differently than when packs of birds by chance settle down in a toll grove, or the hoarse swans emit their sound by Padusa's fish-filled stream over the noisy marshes. (Virgil, *Aen.* 11.454–8)

By describing the birds as "sitting" (*consedere*) in "packs" (*cateruae*), the simile blurs the line between animal and human. While *caterua* had already been used of animal gatherings by Lucretius, it clearly marks an intrusion of the human element in the animal sphere. The trespass between the political dimension of the tenor (assembly of Greeks) and the natural setting of the vehicle (birds assembled) is also evident in the marked placement of *consedere* ("sitting"): the birds are congregating in a seated position just like the Latins.[84]

The simile involving these assembled birds self-consciously pits rhetorical modes of speech against poetic ones. While, in Homer, "races of birds, geese, cranes and long-necked swans are gathering by Cayster's streams on the fields of Asia," Virgil mentions only the swans of fish-filled Padusa, modern Padova, on the Po delta. The epithet "fish-filled" reproduces the Homeric *ikhthuoeis* but the reference to Virgil's native region of the Po Valley (cf. *G.* 2.199) highlights the connection between the swans and the craft of song. This biographical connection is all the more noteworthy given that the swan is often considered a symbol of poetry.[85] Indeed, this swan simile is intratextually related to a passage from the catalogue of the Italians in which Messapus and his troops singing their king are compared to the noise of swans on the Asian marshes (7.699–705), a comparison that was already understood by Servius as a veiled reference to the poet Ennius, who boasted his descent from Messapus.[86] The swans, which in the earlier

---

[84] By contrast to the Homeric original in which the birds, to which the noisy Greeks are compared, are "flying here and there": *Il.* 2.462 ἔνθα καὶ ἔνθα ποτῶνται.

[85] Cf. *Aen.* 7.699–700; 10.188–93 with Harrison (1997) 119–20 ad loc.

[86] Servius *ad Aen.* 7.691. See Hornsby (1970) 58–60, which analyzes the two similes in relation to the same Homeric model.

simile were described as emitting "tuneful melodies" (7.700–1 *canoros* |
dant ... modos), are here described as *rauci* "hoarse."[87] Servius tries to
rationalize the negativity of this description in one of his notes, where he
explains that Virgil uses *raucus* as a neutral term "as per the custom of his
native parlance according to which well singing swans are said to be
rauciores" (Servius *ad Aen.* 7.705 *secundum morem prouinciae suae locutum,
in qua bene canentes cycni rauciores uocantur*). Given that *raucus* elsewhere
in Virgil often refers either to the noise of the sea or to the din of metals, the
swans of this simile are clearly departing from their expected tune.[88] As if to
signal the tension between the poetic needs of the narrative and the rhetoric
of the council scene, the swans' problematic sound on the chatty swamps of
the Po leverages the critique of rhetoric as empty noise that has been
Turnus' main point.[89]

Armorum iudicium: Rhetoric, Epic and Belatedness

The "rhetoricizing" of the conflict between Drances and Turnus in the
council of the Latins is partially enacted through the superimposition of
the episode of the debate between Odysseus and Ajax over the arms of
Achilles and the structural device of the *agōn*, absent in Homer's narrative
of Thersites, but central to fifth-century BCE versions of the episode and to
the tragic adaptation of the story by Roman tragedians, and perhaps
present already in the epic cycle (*Aethiopis* and *Little Iliad*).[90] Already in
the earliest Greek sources, the episode casts the rupture between the epic
past and the present moment as a byproduct of rhetoric, both formally in
replacing the battlefield with the court as an agonistic venue and thematically in privileging the man of word, Odysseus, over the man of action,
Ajax. By staging a critical reassessment of key moments of the *Iliad*, the
Judgment of the Arms acts as a vehicle for a self-conscious exploration of
the making, interpreting and continuation of tradition. The result is that,
with his reliance on word at the exclusion of deed, the demagogue is both
in a relation of alterity to the epic tradition and simultaneously a figure for
the poet's verbal performance.

---

[87] Cf. also *Ecl.* 9.36, where the swans are described as *argutos olores*.
[88] E.g. *G.* 1.109–10 *raucum ... murmur; Aen.* 2.545 *rauco ... aere* and see Tartari Chersoni (1988). For
raucus applied to bad poets, see Cordus in Juvenal 1.2 with Mayor and Henderson (2007) 90 ad loc.
[89] See Mackie (1996) 38–41 for a comparable analysis of *Il.* 3.151–2 in which the chatting of the Trojan
elders is compared to the singing of cicadas.
[90] Pindar, *Nem.* 7.20–30 and 8.21–34; Aeschylus, *Hoplōn Krisis*; Antisthenes, *Logos of Ajax* and *Logos of
Odysseus*. On the background to Ovid's treatment of these sources, see Puccioni (1985) 147–8; Huyck
(1991) 10–53; Hardie (2012) 148–50.

Epic Demagoguery

It is hard not to notice that the contest for the arms of Achilles is quintessentially not just an interpretative exercise on key moments of the Trojan war; above all, as a debate over which hero is the best after Achilles, it functions as a reassessment of epic heroism. Since several sources contained an *agōn* between Odysseus and Ajax, rhetoric plays an essential structural role in this debate. Substantively, Odysseus' legacy as well as his performance was constructed heavily in these texts as dependent on his ability to persuade.[91] Whether a debate between the two heroes was staged in the epic cycle is uncertain.[92] By the fifth century, the rhetorical *agōn* between Odysseus and Ajax is part and parcel of the standard narrative. Aeschylus' "Judgment of the Arms" certainly had an element of direct confrontation between Odysseus and Ajax, who in a fragment praised the simplicity of his own truthful account.[93] In Pindar, the Judgment of the Arms is implicitly presented as a conflict between word and deed: in *Nem.* 8.24–5, in the context of narrating Ajax's defeat, Pindar remarks that "oblivion takes hold of a man lacking in tongue but with a valiant heart" (ἤ τιν' ἄγλωσσον μέν, ἦτορ δ' ἄλκιμον, λάθα κατέχει | ἐν λυγρῷ νείκει). However, such a contrast is explicitly laid out in the first attested full narrative of the episode, the set of paired speeches by Ajax and Odysseus written by the sophist Antisthenes at the end of the fifth century.[94] In making his plea to the judges, Ajax begins by deploring that the dispute over the arms is being settled through speeches since the matter was transacted through deed (*Logos of Ajax* 1 Caizzi καὶ ταῦτα διὰ λόγων; τὸ δὲ πρᾶγμα ἐγίγνετο ἔργῳ). He then asks them to "acknowledge that argument has no power in relation to action" (*Logos of Ajax* 7–8 Caizzi γνώσεσθε ὅτι οὐδεμίαν ἔχει λόγος πρὸς ἔργον ἰσχύν) and that, furthermore, "many and long speeches are spoken because of a dearth of deeds" (8 δι' ἀπορίαν ἔργων πολλοὶ καὶ μακροὶ λόγοι λέγονται).

In the context of the Judgment of the Arms, this rhetorical opposition between word and deed has obvious metapoetic implications.[95] On

---

[91] On the reception of Odysseus in rhetorical texts, see Worman (1999).   [92] Severyns (1928) 331.

[93] See *Hoplōn Krisis*; fr. 176 (Radt) where it is presumably Ajax who says that "the words of truth are simple" ἁπλᾶ γάρ ἐστι τῆς ἀληθείας ἔπη. See March (1991) 5–6.

[94] Stanford (1968) 90–117 is still valuable on the reception of Odysseus in these texts. See also Hesk (2000) 118–22 analyzing Antisthenes' intervention side by side with Plato's *Hippias Minor*, which offers a positive portrayal of Odysseus' cunning tricks (365b3–5).

[95] On the Ovidian Judgment of the Arms as metapoetic, see Miller (2015) 102, who reads the victory of Ulixes' *facundia* as a triumph of the Ovidian unconventional vision of epic over more traditional epic models; Pavlock (2009) 110–31 at 112 reads Ulixes as "an imaginative and deconstructive rhetorician analogous to the poet who thoroughly destabilizes the genre of epic in the *Metamorphoses*." For Papaioannou (2007) 205, Ulixes is also an image of the poet and "[his *facundia*] convincingly conveys the message that a great epic is above all an epic whose success

Armorum iudicium: Rhetoric, Epic and Belatedness

a simple level, Odysseus' verbal abilities mirror the poet's already in the *Odyssey*.[96] This slippage has been noticed in connection with Pindar's account of the dispute over the arms in *Nemean 7*, in which Homer's deceit is held responsible for the misjudgment of the Achaeans and mistreatment of Ajax:

ἐγὼ δὲ πλέον' ἔλπομαι
λόγον Ὀδυσσέος ἢ πάθαν
διὰ τὸν ἁδυεπῆ γενέσθ' Ὅμηρον·

ἐπεὶ ψεύδεσί οἱ ποτανᾷ <τε> μαχανᾷ
σεμνὸν ἔπεστί τι· σοφία
δὲ κλέπτει παράγοισα μύθοις.

I believe that the story of Odysseus has become greater than his suffering because of Homer and his sweet verses; for upon his lies and soaring art something holy rests, and his skill deceives leading astray with tales. (Pindar, *Nem.* 7.20–4)

The λόγος Ὀδυσσέος in v. 21 is notoriously ambiguous: it is naturally taken to refer to Homer's account of Odysseus' story but can also be taken to refer to Odysseus' own retelling of his story at Alcinous' court in *Od.* 9–12.[97] As Nancy Worman argues, "the merging of Homeric and Odyssean style here effects a link between the poet [Homer] and the politician [Odysseus], between the activities of the rhapsode and those of the rhetor."[98]

Moreover, the opposition between word and deed translates visually into a contrast between presence and absence and between autopsy and verbal retelling. In Antisthenes and Ovid, Ajax opens by decrying the judges' lack of direct witnessing of the events at hand (1.1), pitting his openly visible deeds against Odysseus' secret and covert acting.[99] Odysseus' predilection for covert action means that his *kleos* actively *relies* on his own verbal retelling as opposed to the audience's first-hand knowledge. The medium of the *agōn* is the message: activating the rhetorical prowess of Odysseus' character, the *agōn* highlights the overlap between

---

depends on its ability to be rewritten and reinterpreted." My analysis will focus on the role of Ulixes' rhetoric in the construction of the judgment qua metapoetic space.

[96] Goldhill (1991) 56–68, esp. 66 on *Od.* 21.405–9, in which the hero is explicitly compared to a poet.
[97] See Most (1985) 148–56.
[98] Worman (2002) 118. And see also *Sch. in Od.* 1.1 cited in ch. 1 on Odysseus' *polutropia* being a marker for Homer's.
[99] This theme is also highlighted in Accius' play *Iudicium Armorum*: see fr. 115 *uidi te, Ulixes . . . uidi.* For a similar point on the unreliability of *logos* in comparison to autopsy in a roughly contemporary sophistic text, see Gorgias, *Pal.* 34–5.

202 Epic Demagoguery

martial and rhetorical duel. Narrative retelling is presented at once as enacting a measure of distance from the epic past and as the very essence of the epic tradition. In these texts, Odysseus' reliance on rhetoric, which was a pivotal feature of his character in the *Odyssey*, becomes a trope for the post-Homeric tradition, its attempt to restage the epics and its belatedness in relation to the Homeric model.

In addition, from its first attestation, the story of the Judgment of the Arms stages a clash between the heroic individual and the public in which the role of reception and interpretation is highlighted as critical to the continuation of the epic tradition. In the *Odyssey*, Odysseus says that "Thetis set out the arms; the children of the Trojans and of Pallas Athena acted as judges" (11.546–7 ἔθηκε δὲ πότνια μήτηρ, | παῖδες δὲ Τρώων δίκασαν καὶ Παλλὰς Ἀθήνη). This emphasis on public judgment is also found in the *Little Iliad* (fr. 2 West) where the Greeks send men to the Trojan walls to overhear a conversation between two Trojan girls debating whether Ajax's carrying of Achilles' body should be considered a marker of heroism. In another version, cited by the scholia to the *Odyssey*, Agamemnon asks Trojan prisoners of war whether Odysseus or Ajax has done the most harm and awards the arms to Odysseus when the prisoners answer that he has inflicted the most pain.[100] In either version, the decision rests in the hands of those – women and prisoners – who are in the margins of the epic. In the narrative, women have the capacity to act as aesthetic judges: one of the girls is overheard decrying the lack of *kosmos* in the other's speech (*Little Iliad* f2 West οὐ κατὰ κόσμον ἔειπες) and denigrating Ajax's carrying of the body of Achilles away from the battlefield as a womanly task (*Little Iliad* f2 West καί κε γυνὴ φέροι ἄχθος). Pindar also constructs the contest as a clash between civic and heroic ethos as Ajax's defeat is presented as a triumph of the democratic secret ballot. For, in Pindar's words, "with secret votes the Danaans favored Odysseus, while Ajax stripped of the golden arms, wrestled with slaughter" (*Nem.* 8.27–8).[101]

This emphasis on communal responsibility for the award of the arms self-consciously perverts the epic logic of the individual duel. In so doing, it

---

[100] Sch. *HQV in Od.* 11.547. West (2013) 176 thinks that this may have been the version found in the *Aethiopis*. See also Accius fr. 118 Warmington *hem, uereor plus quam fas est captiuam hiscere*.

[101] For Sophocles' treatment in the *Ajax*, see the references to a judgment tainted by the Atreidai at *Aj.* 445–6, 1135 and 1243 with March (1993) 7–8. See also Pacuvius' play on the same theme, esp. 24 Ribbeck *de virtute is ego cernundi do potestatem omnibus*, probably from Agamemnon's speech, similarly emphasizing communal decision making. The visual evidence similarly juxtaposes the episode with other scenes of democratic behavior, insisting on the role of the episode in negotiating the shift from heroic to democratic ethics: see Pinney and Hamilton (1982).

operates a "democratization" of heroism, shifting attention away from individual accomplishment to the response of the community whether in the democratic medium of the assembly or as in the cycle in the interpretation of epic's "subalterns."[102] The response of the audience becomes dependent not solely on personal memory of martial display but on the effective verbal recreation of the past. As such, the judgment (*krisis/ iudicium*) of the arms dramatizes the dynamics of literary reception, activating the metaphor of literary criticism as judicial arbitration and constructing the Greeks as a mirror image of the poem's audience.[103]

In the council of the Latins, the character of Turnus is inflected through the figure of Ajax as constructed in the debate over the arms of Achilles.[104] It has been noted that Turnus' sarcasm is an echo of the proverbial *gelōs* of Ajax.[105] The dispute over the arms of Achilles was a pivotal episode in the epic cycle. According to Proclus' summaries, the *Aethiopis* ended with the episode (*Aethiopis*, Arg. 4 West), while the *Little Iliad* began with it (*Little Iliad*, Arg. 1 West) and went on to narrate Ajax's eventual madness and his suicide. When Turnus reassures Drances, the demagogue, that he will not lower himself to killing him – *Aen.* 11.408–9 *numquam animam talem dextra hac ... amittes* – we may detect a contrast with the fate of Thersites in the *Aethiopis*, in which Achilles kills the demagogue after the latter had accused him of being in love with Penthesilea (*Aethiopis*, Arg. 1 West Ἀχιλλεὺς Θερσίτην ἀναιρεῖ λοιδορηθεὶς πρὸς αὐτοῦ καὶ ὀνειδισθεὶς τὸν ἐπὶ τῇ Πενθεσιλείᾳ λεγόμενον ἔρωτα). In *Met.* 13, Ovid constructs a narrative of the episode that builds on the connection between the rhetoric of Ulixes and the belatedness of the tradition in which the epic exploits of the two heroes are no longer witnessed but simply rehearsed.[106] Ovid too structures the opposition between Ulixes and Ajax as one of word over deed in his recreation of the *armorum iudicium*, in which Ajax's unsuccessful plea to be accepted as the rightful heir to Achilles is followed by Ulixes' speech of self-defense and promotion.[107] Not only is the verbal duel presented as an alternative to a martial encounter but Ulixes actively predicates the superiority of the one over the other: "in our bodies the mind is more powerful than the hand; all our strength resides in it" (*Met.*

---

[102] See the important remarks on the democratization of heroic dissent in Sophocles, *Ajax* by Barker (2009) 281–324.
[103] Moretti (1997) and see Chapter 6. [104] Torres Murciano (2014)
[105] E.g. *Aen.* 11.389–91 (*an tibi Mauors | uentosa in lingua pedibusque fugacibus istis | semper erit?*) is an echo of the proverbial *gelōs* of Ajax (cf. Accius, *Armoroum Iudicium* fr. 115–117 Warmington).
[106] "Ulixes" is here used of the Ovidian recreation of the character of Odysseus.
[107] See Hardie (2007).

204 Epic Demagoguery

13.368–9 *nec non in corpore nostro | pectora sunt potiora manu; uigor omnis in illis*). The subversion of the ideal Homeric balance of word and deed is a striking element of continuity between all three epic demagogues – Thersites, Drances and Ulixes. Ovid alerts us to this connection when, in his opening gambit, his Ajax echoes the negative assessment of Drances' reliance on the tongue (*uerba/lingua*) as opposed to the hand (*manus/ dextera*) (*Met.* 13.9–10 *tutius est igitur fictis contendere uerbis | quam pugnare manu ~ Aen.* 11.338–9 *largus opum et lingua melior, sed frigida bello | dextera; Aen.* 380–1 *sed non replenda est curia uerbis | quae tuto tibi magna uolant*).

In line with previous accounts, the Ovidian narrator presents Ulixes' victory as a morally problematic triumph of eloquence over force.[108] When Ulixes concludes his speech, his victory is presented as one of *facundia*:

> mota manus procerum est, et quid facundia posset,
> re patuit, fortisque uiri tulit arma disertus.

> The hand of the elders was moved and by fact it became apparent how much power eloquence had, and the clever speaker took the weapons of the brave man. (Ovid, *Met.* 13.382–3)

The movement of the elders in v. 382 is at once a physical showing of hands and a reminder of Ulixes' masterful control over the emotions of his audience. Indeed, throughout his speech, Ulixes highlights the ways in which his eloquence, which he recognizes as a gift (*Met.* 13. 137 *meaque haec facundia*; cf. 13.127 *neque abest facundis gratia dictis*), was a key tool in his epic accomplishments: Ulixes quotes twice from his own past oratorical performances – his exhortatory speech to Achilles hiding in disguise quoted at vv. 168–9 and his address to the troops at 225–7 narrated in *Il.* 2. He also refers to several other verbal triumphs: from his speech persuading Agamemnon to sacrifice Iphigenia for the common good (v.188 *ingenium uerbis ad publica commoda uerti*), to his embassy to Troy (v.196 *mittor . . . audax orator*) to reclaim Helen.[109] Ovid's Ulixes is in fact keenly aware of his own role in the rhetorical tradition: as well as mentioning his function as an orator in that episode, he holds his eyes down (v. 125 *oculos paulum tellure moratos*) as Odysseus does in the passage in which the embassy is described by the Trojan elders (*Iliad* 3.216–24), and which is also quoted as a proto-rhetorical discussion of style by Cicero (*Brut.* 40) and Quintilian (11.3.158; 12.10.64). Moreover, Ulixes' ability to use tricks

---

[108] Tarrant (1995).
[109] Additionally, by insisting on his command of emotions, Ulixes self-consciously presents himself as a skilled orator: see esp. 13.228–9 (*in quae dolor ipse disertum | fecerat*) with Quintilian 6.2.26.

Armorum iudicium: *Rhetoric, Epic and Belatedness*   205

and deception (103–4 *quo tamen haec Ithaco, qui clam, qui semper inermis* | *rem gerit et furtis incautum decipit hostem?*) leverages the widespread use of this Homeric character as an exemplum for rhetorical *dissimulatio* in the rhetorical tradition.[110]

Yet Ulixes' *facundia* represents a polemical blend of rhetorical and poetic performance. As Barbara Pavlock has shown, Ulixes' radical retelling of key Iliadic episodes – most notably the Doloneia (238–52) and the *aristeia* of Diomedes (255–62) – is in many ways a mirror of the poet's restaging of the epic.[111] Indeed, while Ajax constructs the ability to lift the shield as a critical test of fitness (v. 116 *tarda futura tibi est gestamina tanta trahenti*), for Ulixes the ability to interpret its contents is the paramount consideration:

> . . . neque enim clipei caelamina nouit,
> Oceanum et terras cumque alto sidera caelo
> Pleiadasque Hyadasque inmunemque aequoris Arcton
> diuersosque urbes nitidumque Orionis ensem.
> postulat, ut capiat, quae non intellegit, arma!

> He does not even understand the reliefs on the shield – Oceanus, the lands and the stars with the deep sky, the Pleiades, the Hyades and the Bear that is untouched by the sea, the two cities and the shining sword of Orion. He asks to receive weapons which he does not comprehend. (Ovid, *Met.* 13.291–5)

In line with his general tendency to highlight the power of the word to subsume and replace physical action, Ulixes plays on the double meaning of *capere* (v. 295) as both understanding and conquest.[112] Ulixes' reliance on gestures of showing and pointing (v. 132–3 *lacrimantia tersit* | *lumina*; v. 264 *uestemque manu deduxit*; v. 381 *ostendit*) acknowledges the dramatic models from which the story of the judgment would have been known to Ovid.[113] Yet, as Sophia Papaioannou has argued, Ulixes' speech is in other ways self-consciously presented as text, as, for example, when he begs the Greeks to put an end to his toil (v. 373 *iam labor in fine est*) by adding a *titulus* (v. 372 *hunc titulum meritis pensandum reddite nostris*), a word that can denote both the prize of the arms and the title of a work.[114]

Moreover, the recurrent emphasis on paternity can also be interpreted as channeling issues of literary as well as genealogical succession. Both Ajax

---

[110] E.g. Quintilian 6.3.96; 10.1.29–30; Ps. Dionysius of Halicarnassus, *Ars Rhet.* 9.8 and see Worman (1999).

[111] Pavlock (2009) 115–20.

[112] Hopkinson (2000) 146 ad loc. Note, however, that since Bentley, some editors, including Richard Tarrant in his Oxford Classical Text, mark line 295 as an interpolation.

[113] Huyck (1991) 44–54 on the fragments of the Roman tragedians and D'Anna (1958).

[114] Papaioannou (2007) 203–5.

206 Epic Demagoguery

and Ulixes begin with the issue of lineage, the one claiming to be third in line from Jupiter via his grandfather Aeacus (21–33) and therefore Achilles' cousin, the other claiming the same lineage through his grandfather Arcesius as well as through his mother (140–7).[115] Ajax's emphasis on the nobility of his lineage (v. 23 *nobilitate potens essem*) picks up on Drances' whose power was said to be connected to the nobility on his mother's side while his father's lineage remained uncertain (*Aen.* 11.340–1 *seditione potens genus huic materna superbum | nobilitas dabat, incertum de patre ferebat*).[116] Given that the relationship between authors and their models is often constructed as one of paternity, the focus on genealogy throws attention to the parallel phenomenon of literary succession.[117] The intersection of paternity and imitation was explicitly raised by Ajax in Accius' tragedy:

> . . . mest aecum frui
> fraternis armis mihique adiudicarier,
> uel quod propinquus uel quod uirtute aemulus.

> It is fair that I enjoy my cousin's weapons and that they should be adjudged to me, whether because I am his relative or because I am his rival in virtue. (Accius, fr. 1036–7 Warmington)

Aemulatio and *propinquitas*, which frame the last line, are presented as mutually substitutable forms of legitimate succession. In Ovid, Ulixes uses wordplay to frame succession (v. 133 *quis . . . succedat Achilli*) as participation (v. 134 *per quem magnus Danais successit Achilles?*) or as entering the fray.[118] But Ulixes also operates under a metonymic view of heroism whereby he claims ownership for other heroes' deeds by presenting his words as responsible for the outcomes of their actions.[119] This is most notable in vv. 162–80, in which Ulixes argues that his speech to Achilles on Skyros – cited at vv. 168–9 – motivated the epic hero to join the war at Troy

---

[115] For the handling of the theme of genealogy in rhetorical contexts, see Quintilian 5.10.23–4. The theme was raised in Aeschylus, *Hoplōn Krisis* fr. 175 Radt in which Ajax accuses Odysseus of being Sisyphus' son.

[116] As Servius *ad Aen.* 11.341 notices, *incertum* ("unknown") glosses by contrast *nobilitas* (from *nosco*, to know), thus highlighting Drances' mixed pedigree as the hybrid offspring of the Homeric Thersites and of the Virgilian imagination.

[117] For the intersection of politics and literature in narratives of succession, see Hardie (1993) 88–119; Peirano (2013) 99–100.

[118] For these usages of *succedere* see *OLD* 4a "to move up into position": e.g. Virgil, *Aen.* 9.221–2 *illi succedunt seruantque uices*; Caesar, *BGall.* 3.4.3 *alii integris uiribus succedebant*; and *OLD* 5 "to become a successor."

[119] As Kirk Freudenburg points out to me, this equivalence is already implicit in Homer, *Il.* 3.222, where Odysseus' words are compared to a snow storm, an image elsewhere used to illustrate the onslaught of an army (e.g. *Il.* 12.277–90).

Armorum iudicium: *Rhetoric, Epic and Belatedness* 207

and that, therefore, Achilles' deeds are in fact his (v. 171 *opera illius mea sunt*). This metonymic view of heroism helps Ulixes collapse epic action and rhetorical performance, turning the speaker into a doer.

Ulixes' obsession with claiming responsibility for the deeds of others goes hand in hand with a recurrent emphasis on shared ownership of actions, words and ethical principles. Ajax refers to his shared lineage with Achilles (vv. 29–30 *series ... cum magno non est communis Achille*). Ulixes deploys shamelessly the vocabulary of community to stake a claim to his ownership of the deeds of others: he refers to his embassy to Troy as aimed at advancing the communal cause of Greece (v. 199 *quam mihi mandarat communis Graecia causam*); Ulixes highlights Diomedes' sharing of information with him as a mark of distinction (v. 239 *Tydides mecum communicat acta*); and refers to his hiding to prevent joining the war at Troy as a crime he shares with Achilles (vv. 303–4 *crimen cum tanto commune viro*). The tension between individual and communal ownership is also exploited when Ulixes criticizes Ajax for his tendentious retelling of the fight to save the Greek ships from burning in *Iliad* 15 (vv. 82–93). Ulixes criticizes Ajax for his claim that he alone saved the ships and argues instead that this was rather due to Patroclus' disguising himself as Achilles:

> sed ne communia solus
> occupet atque aliquem uobis quoque reddat honorem;
> reppulit Actorides sub imagine tutus Achillis
> Troas ab arsuris cum defensore carinis.

> Lest he should take sole credit for things shared by many and to give some recognition to you: it was the grandson of Actor safe under the guise of Achilles who drove back the Trojans from the ships when they were about to go up in flames together with their defender. (Ovid, *Met.* 13.271–4)

The vocabulary of *communitas/koinōnia* in these passages not only focuses on ethical questions about individual versus collective responsibility that are at the heart of the *Iliad* but also points to different kinds of verbal recasting – of rhetorical topoi (*loci communes/topoi koinoi*) as well as traditional narratives.[120] Here, we witness the productive intersection of the formal and substantive qualities of rhetorical discourse. Rhetoric is relevant in this text not simply on a formal level in structuring the

---

[120] For *loci communes*, see Cicero, *Inv. rhet.* 2.68, *Top.* 29; Quintilian 5.10.53. For *communia* as traditional material, see Horace, *Ars P.* 128 *difficile est proprie communia dicere* and Porphyrio, *In Hor. Artem Poet.* 128 ad loc. The interpretation of this phrase is famously vexed: for other possibilities, see White (1977) and Brink (1971) 432–40. See further Callimachus, *Epigr.* 28.4; Demetrius, *Eloc.* 113; Philodemus, *On Poems* 1, 195.8 Janko.

208 Epic Demagoguery

Judgment of the Arms as a verbal performance aimed at persuasion. It is also meaningfully evoked as offering a paradigm for reenactment.[121] Rhetorical exercises invite speakers to give a novel spin to traditional material through the use of *colores* (rhetorical slants), through *anaplerosis* (the filling up of gaps left open by the model) and *paraphrasis* (rewording of an original).[122] We might think back about Seneca the Elder's construction of Ovid as a rhetor in Chapter 2 and remember that it was the incapacity to "leave well enough alone" (*Controv.* 9.5.17 *nescit quod bene cessit relinquere*) that characterized both the *scholasticus* Montanus and the poet Ovid.

This reading comes to the fore in the final stages of the narrative when the flower into which Ajax is metamorphosed has its petals inscribed with the hero's name in the vocative case, *AIAI*, also the sound for lamentation:[123]

> littera communis mediis pueroque uiroque
> inscripta est foliis, haec nominis, illa querellae

> One inscription is in the middle of the petals, shared between the youth and the man: the latter being of his name, the former of a lament. (Ovid, *Met.* 13.397–8)

Ovid refers to this inscription as the common property (v. 395 *littera communis*) of Ajax and Hyacinthus, whose transformation into the same plant Ovid recounted in book 10.162–219 (esp. 215–16 *ipse suos gemitus foliis inscribit, et AIAI | flos habet inscriptum*). It is ironic that with his distrust of the word Ajax should be metamorphosed into a flower bearing a written sign. Yet the hero's transformation into shared writing is but the crowning moment in a series of gestures of (sometimes agonistic) appropriation, rewriting and recasting of traditional material, gestures that both dominate Ovid's approach to the literary tradition and are at the heart of rhetoric's obsession with reenactment.

Comparison between the two heroes (v. 6 *confertur*; v. 79 *contende*; v. 98 *conferat*; v. 338 *conferat*), reenactment and repetition (v. 4 *respexit*; v. 77 *redeamus*; 78 *redde*; 229 *reduxi*; 248 *reuerti*) are other key themes that self-consciously gesture toward Ovid's restaging of the mythical narrative. Ajax in particular invites reenactment: in vv. 77–8, the hero proposes to go back to the past and, playing on the ambiguity between *locus* as a physical place

---

[121] Connolly (2007a) 237–54.   [122] Peirano (2012) 16–19.
[123] On the Hellenistic background to this story, see Euphorion fr. 40 Powell; Theocritus, *Id.* 10.28; Servius *ad Buc.* 3.106 and see further Sophocles, *Aj.* 430–2. On the passage, see Papaioannou (2007) 163–4.

Armorum iudicium: *Rhetoric, Epic and Belatedness*   209

and *locus* as a passage in a book, he invites Ulixes to go back to the place/passage of *Il.* 11.434–88 (v. 77 *locum redeamus in illum*) in which he protects and rescues the wounded Ulixes. Furthermore, in his *peroratio*, Ajax urges the Greeks to cease from debate and reenact instead the battle for the arms of Achilles to see which of the two heroes would come out victorious:

> denique (quid uerbis opus est?) spectemur agendo!
> arma uiri fortis medios mittantur in hostes:
> inde iubete peti et referentem ornate relatis.

> Finally, what need is there for words? Observe us in action! Let the weapons of the great hero be thrust in the middle of the enemy lines: then order that they be sought back and honor he who recovers them back with that which has been recovered. (Ovid, *Met.* 13.120–2)

The slippage between word and action is prominently staged one last time in the invitation to be judged in action (*agendo*), the first word of Ajax's speech and one which was used earlier to refer to the conducting of a case (v. 5–6 *agimus . . . causam*).[124] Seneca the Elder tells us that, in this passage, Ovid took over (*transtulerit*) a *sententia* of his teacher Latro, who had used the phrase "let us send the arms among the enemy and let us go and recover them" (*Controv.* 2.2.8 *mittamus arma in hostes et petamus*).[125] Ovid once again uses wordplay to emphasize that replay of the past in the episode of the debate over the arms is at once a rhetorical effect and an act of poetic creation. Considering the widespread allegorical interpretation of the shield not only as a representation of the *kosmos* but as metonymy for the *Iliad*, the repetition of *re-* in v. 122 (*referentem . . . relatis*) points to the act of bringing the weapons back but also brings to mind the emphasis on retelling of the Iliadic tradition in the speech of Ulixes.[126] In this formulation, we see a productive overlap between the physical act of recovering the weapons and the verbal retelling of the story: bringing back the weapons is at once an act of physical mastery and of cultural appropriation through discourse.

As we have seen, the rhetoricity of the demagogue's discourse – his *facundia* – is denounced as foreign by the epic narrator and constructed in

---

[124] Hardie (2007) 392–3.

[125] Because of its rhetorical structure, the debate over the arms of Achilles was a popular theme in rhetorical exercises: e.g. *Rhet. Her.* 1.18, 2.28–30; Cicero, *Inv. rhet.* 1.11.3; 1.92.4–6; Quintilian 1.5.43; 5.10.41.

[126] v. 205 *longa referre mora est*; 255 *quid Lycii referam Sarpedonis*; v. 269 *arma tulisse refert*. On allegorical readings of the shield of Achilles see Hardie (1986) 336–75. Thus at *Met.* 12.620–1 the shield's ability to stir war (*ipse etiam, ut, cuius fuerit, cognoscere posses,* | *bella mouet clipeus, deque armis arma feruntur*) echoes the Virgilian narrator's epic voice (see esp. *Aen.* 7.45 *maius opus moueo*) and see also Ennius, *Ann.* 403; *Aen.* 6.820; 12.333; Horace, *Carm.* 4.1.2.

the scholarship as reflective of a process of hybridization and influence of one medium (the rhetorical) over the other (poetry). Yet such denunciation is fundamentally short-circuited by the overlap between Ulixes' skewed retelling and the narrator's plastic reworking of the literary tradition. The same concerns with finding a better expression for a well-expressed idea (Seneca the Elder, *Suas.* 2.20 *sensum bene dictum posse dici melius*) dominate both discussion of rhetorical variation and *colores* ("rhetorical slants") and theories of literary imitation.[127] In turning the Odyssean rhetor into a doublet for the poet, Ovid is self-consciously leveraging concerns with rhetoric both as successful repetition and as artifice to cast light onto the belatedness of his own poetic project. Far from operating an unexamined metamorphosis of the poet into a rhetor, the rhetorical *agōn* embedded in the epic leverages rhetorical discourse to insist on poetry's scope for innovation through retelling of the past. With his verbosity, the demagogue is a paradoxical figure who is simultaneously disowned as alien and coopted to justify the belatedness of tradition.

Turnus and Drances beyond Virgil

The reception of the Latin council in post-Virgilian epic provides a unique perspective on the "rhetoricity" of Turnus' and Drances' speeches.[128] The Virgilian scene naturally becomes a model for the representation of political debates in the epics of Lucan, Statius and Silius. Interestingly, while Drances informs the moral characterization of the demagogues, it is Turnus' uncompromising pro-war position that resonated with these writers as they built their portrayal of out-of-control rhetoricians.

It was Richard Bruère who first argued that the character of Lentulus in Lucan's *Pharsalia* brings together echoes of both Turnus and Drances.[129] In the debate after Pharsalus in book 8, Lentulus opposes Pompey's proposal to seek the help of the Parthians and instead proposes to go to Egypt (8.330–454). Lentulus' defiant stance in his response to Pompey (8.331–454) recalls Turnus' refusal to come to terms with the Trojans in the section of his speech addressed to Latinus. So, when Lentulus begins by asking Pompey why the defeat of Pharsalus has broken his courage, one is reminded of Turnus' opening:

---

[127] I discuss this point at length in Peirano (2013).   [128] La Penna (1976); Bruère (1971).
[129] Bruère (1971) 31.

Turnus and Drances beyond Virgil

> sicine Thessalicae mentem fregere ruinae?
> una dies mundi damnauit fata? secundum
> Emathiam lis tanta datur? iacet omne cruenti
> uolneris auxilium? solos tibi, Magne, reliquit
> Parthorum Fortuna pedes?

Has rout in Thessaly completely broken your spirit? Has one day sealed the fate of the world? Is such a great dispute to be decided according to Emathia? Is every remedy for our bloody wound of no avail? Has Fortune left you, Magnus, nothing but the Parthians' feet? (Lucan 8.331–5)

> multa dies uariique labor mutabilis aeui
> rettulit in melius, multos alterna reuisens
> lusit et in solido rursus Fortuna locauit.

Time, and the mutable toils of age with its changes improve much, again and again Fortune looks back on many, deceives them, then sets them up again on solid ground. (Virgil, *Aen.* 11.425–7)

Thanks to Macrobius (*Sat.* 6.2.16), we know that the Virgilian lines that Lentulus takes as the starting point for his harangue echo while at the same time subverting a line of Ennius' *Annales* on the mutability of Fortune in war (*Ann.* 258 *multa dies in bello conficit unus*).[130] While Lentulus is first introduced as an anti-Thersites, "superior to all on account of the goads of virtue and the nobility of his suffering" (Lucan 8.329–330 *quos Lentulus omnes | uirtutis stimulis et nobilitate dolendi | praecessit*), his demagogic appeal is underscored by the narrator's comment following his speech – "how much freedom of speech does desperate hope possess!" *quantum, spes ultima rerum, | libertatis habes*! (*Lucan* 8.454–5) – in which the freedom of speech (*libertas*) is seen as a cover for feelings of despair.[131]

Drances is also a central figure in the construction of the two demagogic figures in Silius Italicus' *Punica*.[132] In Carthage, it is Hanno whose *inuidia* of Hannibal (Silius 2.227 *ductorem infestans odiis gentilibus, Hanno*) reminds us of Drances' unmotivated hatred for Turnus (*Aen.* 11.123 *infensus iuueni Turno*, 336 *Drances . . . infensus*).[133] But, whereas Hanno substantially reproduces Drances "pacifist" rhetoric, his Roman equivalent, the consul Varro, has Drancean moral traits while all the while pursuing an aggressive pro-war policy that replicates Turnus' position. Particularly interesting in this regard is Varro's emphasis on *mora*: he opposes Fabius' delay tactic

---

[130] Elliott (2013) 130–1.
[131] Lucan 8.299 *uirtutis stimulis* (of Lentulus) – *Aen.* 11.337 *stimulisque agitabat amaris* (of Drances).
[132] Fucecchi (1999); Ariemma (2009).
[133] See also as his feigned fear of Hannibal's retaliation (Silius 2.280–1 – *Aen.* 11.348).

212 Epic Demagoguery

(*morae increpitare* 8.263; 8.279 *impellit moras*) and, in so doing, echoes
Turnus' anti-delay rhetoric, especially from book 12 (12.11 *nulla mora est in
Turno*). In his portrayal of Varro, Silius borrows from Virgil's synthesis of
Homeric and Sallustian demagogues to construct a character who seeks to
advance an epic agenda from the rostra:

> subnixus rapto plebei muneris ostro
> saeuit iam rostris Varro ingentique ruinae
> festinans aperire locum fata admouet urbi.   245
> atque illi sine luce genus surdumque parentum
> nomen, at immodice uibrabat in ore canoro
> lingua procax. hinc auctus opes largusque rapinae,
> infima dum uulgi fouet oblatratque senatum
> . . .
> sic debilis arte
> belligera Martemque rudis uersare nec ullo   260
> spectatus ferro, lingua sperabat adire
> ad dextrae decus atque e rostris bella ciebat.

Meanwhile Varro, relying on the purple that he had seized by gift of the
people, was already ranting on the Rostra, and, by his haste to prepare the
way of a mighty downfall, brought Rome near to destruction. His birth was
obscure; the name of his ancestors was never heard; but his impudent
tongue quivered beyond measure in a sing-song voice. Thus he got wealth
and was liberal with his plunder while courting the dregs of the people and
railing at the senate . . . also though a bad citizen, skillful to stir up trouble
and kindle hatred, he was helpless in the field, unpracticed in the conduct of
war, and not approved by any deed of valor; but he hoped to gain martial
glory by his tongue and sounded the war-cry from the rostra. (Silius 8.243–9,
259–62)

The emphasis on wealth (v. 248 *auctus opes largusque rapinae*) reproduces
and amplifies Drances' *largitia* (11.338 *largus opum*).[134] Yet Varro amplifies
the epic pretensions of Drances: whereas the latter is said to build up the
anger of the assembly (11.342 *aggerat iras*) even as he advocates an end to the
hostilities pitting an entire people against the other, Varro's eloquence is
"stirring war from the rostra" (v. 262 *e rostris bella ciebat*) and Varro himself
"rages" (v. 244 *saeuit*; cf. *Aen.* 11.220 *saeuus Drances*) and his tongue
"quivered" (v. 247 *uibrabat*) like an epic weapon or the flash of the
thunderbolt.[135] With his "sing-song voice" (v. 247 *ore canoro*), Varro

---

[134] In some ways, Silius has made Varro closer to Thersites than Drances: see, for example, Varro's low
birth (*surdumque parentum | nomen*) at vv. 245–6.
[135] For the phrase *bella ciere*, see Lucretius 2.42, 324; *Aen.* 1.541; 5.585; 6.828–9 *heu quantum inter se
bellum, si lumina uitae | attigerint, quantas acies stragemque ciebunt*; 9.766; 12.158; Livy 1.12.2 with

Turnus and Drances beyond Virgil   213

embodies the collapse of rhetorical and epic categories, as *canorus* is both a positive trait associated with peaceful oratory in Cicero and a quintessential quality of poetic song.[136]

With Lentulus and Varro, the figure of the demagogue has thus undergone a paradoxical shift: while, in Homer, Thersites is a figure who is quintessentially at odds with the epic mission and embraces instead the genre of blame, the Roman demagogues have become the spokespersons for an uncompromising epic vision in which the traditional balance between word and deed is destroyed and now replaced with an inflexibly destructive position. Paradoxically, the demagogue has become an über-epic character, whose rhetoric resembles the fury of epic, exasperating Cicero's characterization of the assembly as suited to the grand style. This shift is nowhere more visible than in Lucan's portrayal of Cicero (7.62–85) in the debate before Pharsalus in book 7 in which it is the orator's *facundia* that spurs an unwilling Pompey to action.[137]

> cunctorum uoces Romani maximus auctor
> Tullius eloquii, cuius sub iure togaque
> pacificas saeuus tremuit Catilina secures,
> pertulit iratus bellis, cum rostra forumque   65
> optaret passus tam longa silentia miles.
> addidit inualidae robur facundia causae.

The voice of the collective was Tullius, the greatest model of Roman eloquence, under whose sway of the law and civil authority Catiline trembled at the axes of peace. He was angry at war, since he longed for the rostra and the forum having endured silence for so long as a soldier. To a weak argument did his eloquence added strength. (Lucan 7.62–7)

In "adding strength to a weak argument" (v. 67), Cicero here epitomizes rhetoric's ability to "make the weaker argument the stronger" (Aristotle, *Rh.* 2.24.1402a23 τὸν ἥττω λόγον κρείττω ποιεῖν). The contrast between *robur* and the juxtaposed *facundia* points to Cicero's paradoxical transformation from the emblem of the power of civil society – the opening of his *De consulatu suo* famously constituted an exhortation for war to give way to the toga of the consul *"cedant arma togae"* – to a war-mongering, suitably angry (v. 65 *iratus*) epic hero, responsible for setting in motion the central

---

Horsfall (2013b) 565 *ad* 6.828 suggesting a possible Ennian origin; for *uibrare* used of epic weapons, see *Aen.* 9.769; 10.484; 11.606; 12.100 and of the thunderbolt *Aen.* 8.524.

[136] Cicero, *Brut.* 105 and 317 *canorum oratorem*; 268 and 303 *uox canora*; Propertius 2.34.84–5 *canorus . . . olor*; Virgil, *Aen.* 7.700–1 *canoros . . . modos.*

[137] Narducci (2003); Malcovati (1953). For the ways in which Silius' Varro echoes the bellicose rhetoric of Cicero and Lentulus, see Ariemma (2009) 252–4.

214 Epic Demagoguery

battle of the poem and of the entire civil wars. In this perverse universe, *facundia* is no longer *opposed* to epic deed; it has rather become the engine of epic in its most destructive and extreme form.[138]

The hybrid figure of the demagogue should be read as a critique of Cicero's claim that, while the soldier protects the state in time of war, the orator is the pillar of civil society. In a famous section of the *Pro Murena*, Cicero identifies the *artes* of the general (*imperator*) and of the good orator (*bonus orator*) as the most capable of conferring honor.

> duae sint artes igitur quae possint locare homines in amplissimo gradu dignitatis, una imperatoris, altera oratoris boni. ab hoc enim pacis ornamenta retinentur, ab illo belli pericula repelluntur ... etenim, ut ait ingeniosus poeta et auctor ualde bonus, "proeliis promulgatis pellitur e medio" non solum ista uestra uerbosa simulatio prudentiae sed etiam ipsa illa domina rerum, "sapientia; ui geritur res, spernitur orator" non solum odiosus in dicendo ac loquax uerum etiam "bonus; horridus miles amatur," uestrum uero studium totum iacet. "Non ex iure manum consertum, sed mage ferro" inquit "rem repetunt." quod si ita est, cedat, opinor, Sulpici, forum castris, otium militiae, stilus gladio, umbra soli; sit denique in ciuitate ea prima res propter quam ipsa est ciuitas omnium princeps.

> There are, therefore, two professions which can raise men to the highest place of distinction; one, that of a general, the other, that of a good orator. For by the latter, the ornaments of peace are retained; by the former, the dangers of war are repelled ... For as that talented poet and a very estimable author declares, "when battle is declared, from our midst is driven" not only your wordy pretense of knowledge, but even that mistress of things herself, "wisdom. The issue is decided by force. The orator is thrust aside", not only he who is tiresome in speaking, and garrulous, but even "the good one; the uncouth soldier is loved." Your profession is abandoned; "men seek their rights not by law, but by the sword," he says. And if that is the case, Sulpicius, then let the forum yield to the camp; peace yield to war, pen to the sword, and the shade to the sun. And may first place in our city be given to that on account of which the city itself occupies first place among all. (Cicero, *Mur.* 30)

A fragment from Ennius *Annales* book 8 (247–53 Skutsch) is brought in to illustrate the claim that war leaves no space for oratory. In the breakdown of civil society, force (*uis*) is contrasted with speech (*orator*), law (*iure*) to weapons (*ferrum*), the pen (*stilus*) to the sword (*gladius*), the shade to the sun. Anticipating his later celebration of the power of the consulship and recuperating an argument about the civilizing power of eloquence, Cicero

---

[138] On the theme of epic as *furor* in Lucan, see Hershkowitz (1998) 197–246.

Conclusion

insists that oratory is not just the pillar of the state but that which ensures its primacy and survival.

The epic demagogue takes us back to the Ciceronian claim about the civilizing force of rhetoric, with which the *Aeneid* engaged in its first simile, but only to subvert it. Far from being bastions of legality, the orator and the assembly not only engineer the collapse of the *res publica* but are also virtually indistinguishable from the violence that they were supposed to forestall. In contesting Cicero's identification of oratory and peace, the demagogue may well be seen as attacking the ideals of Republican *libertas*. But this political claim has deep repercussions on a poetic level: for, in relying on words as opposed to deeds, the demagogue is essentially a doublet for the poet and his incendiary ability to set war in motion dangerously close to the epic narrator's voice.

Conclusion

From Thersites to Drances, from the Ulixes of the Judgment of the Arms to Lucan's Cicero, the demagogue is a transgressive figure who fundamentally breaches the epic code whether by adopting the language of blame or by upsetting the epic balance between word and deed. We have seen how in constructing the demagogue as an epic transgressor, Virgil and Ovid mobilize a rich tradition of rhetorical, anti-rhetorical and anti-Hellenic discourse. In the case of Virgil, his recreation of the Homeric *agorē* involves a triangulated response to the Homeric assembly, its exegesis thereof and the Roman critique of Greek democratic practices. Drances' otherness is emphasized through sustained allusion to Sallustian narratives of Roman cultural decline and through symbolic imagery that pits the elegant voice of the epic swan against the raucous noise of the demagogue. In the case of Ovid, the character of Ulixes is built with an awareness of his role in the rhetorical tradition, more conspicuously as a model for the ideal orator and as exemplifying rhetoric's ability to conceal its artistry. Yet, while mobilizing this richly layered anti-rhetorical discourse, the critique of demagoguery ultimately *implicates* the epic voice – in the case of Virgil, by deconstructing the opposition between *lingua* and *dextera* through intertextually layering both demagogic and nondemagogic typologies of speech in the characters of Turnus and Drances and by suggesting an overlap between Drancean rhetoric and the voice of the epic narrator. The collapse of this distinction is observable in the reception of the scene in post-Virgilian epic in which it is Turnus, rather than Drances, who becomes a model for demagogic discourse. Ovid's layering of the figures of

Thersites, Drances and Ulixes in the judgment of the Arms offers another important perspective on the role of the demagogue in the epic tradition. Here, Ovid self-consciously latches onto the ways in which the rendering of the conflict between Ajax and Ulixes as rhetorical debate turned the episode into a reflection on the tralaticiousness and belatedness of post-Homeric poetry. By speaking rather than doing, by activating the audience's hearing rather than relying on their sight, by verbally reenacting rather than being in the moment, the heroes in the debate embody the condition of the post-Homeric epic voice caught between repetition, opposition, continuation and tendentious recasting of the Homeric material. In these Roman texts, the narrowing of the ideal gap between rhetoric's tendentious and perennially derivative voice and epic poetry's claim to truth is self-consciously and polemically used whether to highlight poetry's potential to find innovation in repetition or to embody the very collapse of discourse in the frenzy of Lucan's civil wars. Once again, this awareness of the capacity of the epic voice to become subsumed by the rhetorical is mutually shared between poets and rhetorical theorists. For just as the poets can be seen to respond to the appropriation of the Homeric text by rhetorical theorists – now accepting and even exasperating Odysseus' role as a rhetor, now contesting the notion of rhetoric as civilizing discourse – Cicero's characterization of the ideal orator as master and tamer of the crowd's violent emotions is itself constructed by appeal to epic models of conquest and grandeur. In the last analysis, one might approach this insistence on the "rhetoricity" of poetry not as a symptom of decline but as a powerful reflection on the role of emulation, repetition and belatedness in the making of literary traditions.

PART III

"Rhetoricizing" Poetry

CHAPTER 6

Non minus orator quam poeta: *Virgil the Orator in Late Antiquity*

Parts I and II of the book have explored respectively the role of poetry in the definition of rhetoric and the poets' response to and engagement with these definitions. While Quintilian and Seneca the Elder are keen to distance rhetoric and poetry as related but essentially different genres, their disavowal is clearly accompanied by a more ambiguous appeal to and appropriation of epic models to bolster the authority of the rhetorical medium. By late antiquity, however, this picture has clearly shifted: Virgil is now regarded, in Macrobius' formulation, as "no less an orator than a poet" (*Sat.* 5.1.1 *Virgilium non minus oratorem quam poetam habendum pronuntiabant*) and his masterpiece, the *Aeneid*, read as an oration in praise of Aeneas and his most illustrious descendant, the emperor Augustus.[1] The image of Virgil the orator has a clear precedent in Homeric reception. Cicero is our earliest attestation of the view that Homer's praise for the oratory of his characters is an expression of his own rhetorical skills, which are reflected not just in the artfully constructed speeches but in the narrative as a whole:[2]

> neque enim iam Troicis temporibus tantum laudis in dicendo Ulixi tribuisset Homerus et Nestori, quorum alterum uim habere uoluit, alterum suauitatem, nisi iam tum esset honos eloquentiae; neque ipse poeta hic tam [idem] ornatus in dicendo ac plane orator fuisset.

> And at the time of the Trojan war Homer would not have attributed such praise for speaking to Ulysses and Nestor – to the one he chose to assign force, to the other charm – unless even then there was a place of honor for eloquence. Nor would the same poet speaking in his own person [i.e. in narrative] have been so embellished when it came to speaking – put plain and simply an orator. (Cicero, *Brut.* 40)

---

[1] Cf. Servius, *Praef. in Aen. intentio Vergilii haec est, Homerum imitari et Augustum laudare a parentibus.* On the ethics of praise, see Kaster (2011a) and Starr (1992).

[2] See Radermacher (1951) 6–10; North (1952); Kennedy (1957) 23; and further Keith (2000) 8–35.

219

220 *Non minus orator quam poeta*

The detailed demonstration of Homer's mastery of rhetoric is focused in the scholia not just on speeches but also on character building, diction, *inuentio* and *dispositio*, mining both speeches and narrative for rhetorical exempla, a procedure found already in Aristotle's *Rhetoric*.[3] Ps. Plutarch's *Life and Poetry of Homer*, a text of uncertain date that contains the most extensive discussion of rhetoric in Homeric poetry to have survived from antiquity, insists that Homer is above all the father of deliberative oratory: "political discourse is a function of the craft of rhetoric, which Homer seems to have been the first to understand" (161, trans. Keaney and Lamberton).[4] The bulk of his painstaking analysis (169–70) focuses on the use of rhetorical technique in the embassy scene in *Il.* 9. In these readings, Homer is often presented as a teacher of rhetoric who illustrates aspects of his art through expert deployment of rhetorical figures and principles of arrangement. In the Ps. Plutarchean treatise, Homer is said to "demonstrate" the importance of arrangement, "to give" appropriateness to each character's speech, to represent the orators as employing different techniques, to demonstrate strategies for accusation and to be acquainted with antithesis and recapitulation.[5]

The deployment of poetry as exempla in rhetorical texts, which in the case of Virgil began as early as Quintilian, implicitly sets up the poet as, at the very minimum, a model for the orator, anticipating and paving the way for the systematic use of rhetorical techniques in nonpoetic texts.[6] Once no longer focused on the Homeric poems but applied to post-rhetorical texts, this rhetorical reading practice has the potential to cast the poet as a rhetor, purposefully deploying techniques of rhetoric in his text. Macrobius' approach is unique in bringing to fruition this tendency that is already lurking beneath the surface in the tradition that precedes him, approaching the whole work, and not just individual elements of speeches, as a rhetorically driven enterprise. This phenomenon is peculiar to the late antique reception of Virgil and consistently framed in the scholarship as a perverse misreading of Virgil's classic. This image of *Vergilius orator* is typically censored as an anachronistic projection of late antique readers' own hybrid version of rhetorical poetics on the pristine and pre- or hyporhetorical Virgilian original. Criticizing Norden's emphasis on rhetorical

---

[3] See Nünlist (2009) index rhetoric and esp. 218–21; Richardson (1980) 281; Lehnert (1896).
[4] According to Keaney and Lamberton (1996) 2, the work is "largely impossible to date" but "could well have been written in the time of Plutarch."
[5] On this characterization of the poet as a teacher, see Sluiter (1999).
[6] On the potential of exempla to be regarded as both exceptional and representative, see Barchiesi (2009a).

influence on Virgil in his commentary on *Aeneid 6*, Heinze comments, "the ancient critics were even worse [than Norden] in this respect; there is nothing more unsatisfactory and boring than, for example, Macrobius' discussion of Virgilian pathos from the standpoint of the rhetoric of the schools."[7] According to Gilbert Highet, in his influential study of Virgil's speeches, "no one is likely to make such a mistake today, anymore than to seek in the Homeric epics for arcane philosophical doctrines."[8] A deeper subtext about literary history runs through this scholarly narrative, one in which this contamination and hybridization of rhetoric and poetics, which is traced back to Ovid and the first century CE, is but a manifestation of a larger pattern of decline that reaches its pinnacle in late antique literary culture and eventually leads to the dark period of the Middle Ages.[9] Clearly what is at stake in this characterization of late antique rhetorical readings are important sets of assumptions about postclassical cultures as fundamentally "corrupt," about classical poetry as artless or natural language and about the role of rhetoric as a catalyst for decline.[10]

This chapter examines the characterization of Virgil as an orator and the implications of this late antique "rhetoricizing" of the Virgilian text for understanding postclassical constructions of authorship, authority and literary criticism. What kind of interrelationship between author, text and reader does this "rhetorical" mode of reading promote? What consequences does this conceptual move from author to orator have on the reading of the Virgilian classic? And, finally, how might this examination of rhetorical interpretative practices open up a productive space for reexamining our own attitudes to the rhetorical?

My analysis of late antique discussions of Virgilian oratory will center primarily on Macrobius' work and its presumed source – the fragmentary dialogue *Vergilius Orator an Poeta* attributed to Florus – while the commentaries by Servius and Tiberius Cl. Donatus will be brought in to illuminate aspects of the main case studies. Macrobius' text embodies what I will define as the two key ways in which Virgil's work is "rhetoricized" in late antiquity. On a micro level, the *Aeneid* is seen as exemplifying rhetorical theory in the areas of *pathos, elocutio, dispositio* and *inuentio*

---

[7] Heinze (1993) 346. Although in his monumental *Antike Kunstprosa* Norden had argued that Virgil was restrained in his usage of "das Rhetorische" (Norden [1898] 891), his subsequent edition of *Aen. 6* is replete with observations about Virgil's "indebtedness" to the rhetorical schools, a theory that Heinze, and others after him, were keen to refute.

[8] Highet (1972) 278.

[9] Comparetti (1967) 83: "la decadenza che in essa . . . si mostra sì avanzata, aveva già cominciato da un pezzo."

[10] On the intersection of the categories of postclassical, late and corrupt, see Formisano (2007).

with epic speeches being the primary target of rhetorical analysis. In this reading, largely modeled on rhetorical criticism of the Homeric poems, Virgil's role as a teacher of rhetoric is highlighted and the text is viewed as a repository of rhetorical principles that can be studied and redeployed by its readers. Yet this seemingly conventional use of the poet's text as the medium for rhetorical exempla is put to the service of an ambitious cultural mission geared at claiming the Greco-Roman system of rhetoric as a civilizing force. Thus the very rhetorical categories that Virgil's text is supposedly exemplifying are themselves constructed in Virgilian language, most notably in Macrobius' analysis of Virgil's deployment of the four styles (*Sat.* 5.1). Virgil not only illustrates elements of rhetoric but is actually seen as founding the language of nature that is used to describe style. This interconnection of rhetorical and poetic language serves to showcase rhetoric as a practice rooted in nature and as the engine of civilization.

Secondly, the "rhetoricizing" of Virgil's text is also operating on a macro level: in addition to the text being evoked as a repository of rhetorical exempla, Virgil, the author, is framed as an advocate defending Aeneas' case. Here, that is, the poet himself is viewed as a rhetor, whose objective is to persuade through his narrative at the macro level, influencing the emotions of his audience toward the different characters. This image of Virgil as an orator and advocate is also crucial to understanding the apologetic framework of Macrobius' discussion of Virgilian oratory, which is emphatically presented as a *defense* of the value of Virgilian poetry in the face of the attack of the dialogue's skeptical character (Evangelus). Just as Virgil himself is framed as an advocate defending Aeneas' case, so the speakers in Macrobius' dialogue are acting as defenders of Virgil's reputation and status.

"Micro-Rhetoricizing"

The tendency to "micro-rhetoricize" the Virgilian text, to mine, that is, the Virgilian poems for illustrations of different rhetorical principles, is well attested in grammatical and rhetorical sources and is clearly tied to the aim of establishing the Latin poet as the *Homerus Romanus*.[11] The most important loci for micro-rhetorical analysis in the Servian commentaries are comments on rhetorical techniques of *inuentio* and *dispositio*. Unsurprisingly, discussion of rhetoric in the *Aeneid* is focused on speeches

---

[11] See Pellizzari (2003) 26–7 and Farrell (2008).

"Micro-Rhetoricizing" 223

given by characters. For example, in Servius, the words *rhetoricus* ("rheto-rical") and *rhetorice* ("rhetorically") cluster around speeches. Servius Danielis (DS) contains an extended note that illustrates the theory of *narratio* with reference to Sinon's speech.[12] The speech of Ilioneus, Aeneas' ambassador to Dido in *Aen.* 1.522–58, receives extensive rhetorical commentary in DS, with special attention being paid to his strategies for soliciting the queen's *beneuolentia*.[13] Similarly, the main two scenes of debate in the poem – the council of the gods in book 10 and the council of the Latins in book 11 – engender comments on rhetorical strategy, ranging from issues of arrangement (Servius *ad Aen.* 10.38), to construc-tions of prologue (Servius *ad Aen.* 10.55), to stasis theory (Servius *ad Aen.* 10.74; 11.43; 343, 378). Rhetorical critics are particularly captivated by moments in the text that can be analyzed as *controuersiae*: so DS labels the debate between Anchises and Aeneas over whether the latter should leave the former behind as a rhetorical deliberation (*Servius Dan. ad Aen.* 2.657 *rhetorice per deliberationem tractatur an Aeneae relicto patre fugiendum sit*) and Anchises' speech as begging Aeneas to leave him behind as a "rhetorical *suasoria*" (*rhetorica suasio*), which Servius analyzes as insincere.[14] Indeed, a note by Servius on the opening of Venus' speech in *Aen.* 10 is often cited as evidence that the Virgilian epic was mined for passages to be used as platforms for *controuersiae* (Servius *ad Aen.* 10.18).[15] Two more speeches are described as *suasoriae*: Aeneas' speech to Evander in *Aen.* 8.127–51 is analyzed by DS for its masterful use of persona;[16] Venus' speech to Vulcan in the same book (8.374–86) is also called by DS a *rhetorica suasio* and praised for its arrangement, use of character and pathos.[17]

However, although, as we have seen, the Servian commentaries are replete with rhetorical analysis, Servius makes a fundamental distinc-tion between grammar and rhetoric. According to Quintilian, the job of the *grammaticus* includes not just highlighting tropes and figures but also teaching rhetorical organization among other things (Quintilian 1.8.16–17). As a *grammaticus*, in his commentary on

---

[12] *Serv, Dan. ad Aen.* 2.135 *sane in arte rhetorica omnem narrationem cum rei partibus dicunt conuenire debere, loco tempore materia causa persona . . . hic ad singula respondetur.*

[13] Servius *ad Aen.* 1.522 and *Serv, Dan. ad Aen.* 1.522. See further Servius *ad Aen.* 1.520, 526 and 1.539 and Tiberius Cl. Donatus ad loc with Pirovano (2006) 61–8.

[14] *Serv. Dan. ad Aen* 2.638 *sane rhetorica suasio est, deliberatur enim de ipsa re, utrum fugiendum sit.* On this term see Pirovano (2006) 166–71.

[15] See Pirovano (2004).

[16] *Serv. Dan. ad Aen* 8.127 *et est rhetorica persuasio: nam principium ex utriusque persona sumpsit.*

[17] *Serv. Dan. ad Aen* 8.374 *sane haec oratio rhetorica suasio est.*

224   *Non minus orator quam poeta*

Virgil, Servius is conscientious about pointing out examples of figurative devices such as metaphor, synecdoche and hyperbaton, which he describes as *metaplasmi*, that is, departures from the proper or natural meaning of a word.[18] Servius is self-conscious about the fact that such alterations to standard usage are especially found in poets: "it must be understood clearly that if this vice occurs in prose, it is called solecism; if it occurs in poetry, it is called a figure" (*Commentarius in Artem Donati* 447.2 Keil: *plane sciendum est quoniam, si in prosa oratione fiat hoc uitium, tunc soloecismus uocatur; in poemate schema dicitur*). In so doing, Servius rehearses the traditional characterization of tropes as "poetic" both on account of their widespread use in poetry and on account of the fact they were taught by grammarians by way of poetic *exempla*.[19] According to Servius, however, there is a fundamental difference between grammatical figures, where the deviation from ordinary usage affects words (*in sermone*), and rhetorical figures, where the deviation affects meaning (*in sensu*) and which are the province of the rhetorical teacher and the orator.[20] Although he does single out a number of oratorical *figurae*, consonant with his interest in the Latin language, his commentary is more interested in grammatical figures.[21] Indeed, in Macrobius, Servius is appointed to discuss "figurative usages [*figurata*] that were not taken over from earlier writers but were rather shaped by the poet himself or adopted with a poet's daring in a novel yet becoming way" (*Sat.* 6.6.1), but these examples are metaphorical extensions of ordinary meaning rather than figures of speech.[22] In light of this distinction, it is not difficult to understand why Tiberius Cl. Donatus, who was probably also writing in the fourth century, emphasized that the exposition of

---

[18] On *figurae* in Servius, see Kaster (1988) 174–6; Moore (1891a) 160–92; Moore (1891b). Servius does not seem overly interested in rigid schematic distinctions between tropes and figures (on which see Quintilian 9.1.5–7) and the term *metaplasm* encompasses both: see Servius *ad Aen.* 5.120 *ergo metaplasmus et figura media sunt, et discernuntur peritia et imperitia. Fiunt autem ad ornatum* with Kaster (1988) 173.

[19] Ps. Plutarch, *Life and Poetry of Homer* 15–71; Dionysius Thrax 1.1.5 defines the explanation of poetic tropes (ἐξήγησις κατὰ τοὺς ἐνυπάρχοντας ποιητικοὺς τρόπους) as one of the parts of grammar; Tryphon, *De Tropis* 191.18–22 Spengel.

[20] Servius, *Comm. in Don.* 448.1–7 *Plane sciendum est quoniam schema in sermone factum ad grammaticos pertinet, in sensu factum ad oratores. nam cum dico 'pars in frusta secant', quoniam in uerbis est quaestio, figura grammaticalis est; quando autem dicit Virgilius 'quid memorem infandas caedes', id est cum dicit se non dicturum facta Mezentii et nihilo minus dicit, quoniam in sensu res est, ad oratores pertinet haec figura.* For this traditional, if somewhat muddled distinction, see Quintilian 9.3.2 and Ps. Dionysius, *Ars Rhet.* 9 with Granatelli (1994).

[21] Servius *ad G.* 1.104 and *ad Aen.* 8.483 are the only named instances of *oratoriae figurae*.

[22] Marinone (1946) 26–7.

"Micro-Rhetoricizing" 225

Virgilian rhetoric should be left not to the grammarians but to orators.[23]

While the use of Virgil's text to illustrate different rhetorical principles is beyond question, what is at stake here is the presentation by our sources of the relationship between rhetorical precepts and Virgilian poetry. By remarking on issues of rhetorical strategy in the speeches of these various characters, Servius is framing the *Aeneid* as a source for rhetorical exempla and implicitly suggesting that Virgil has constructed these speeches with knowledge of rhetorical techniques. Such a conceit is actually explicit in Macrobius' *Saturnalia*, where Virgil is memorably defined as "no less an orator than a poet" (5.1.1) at the beginning of book 5.[24] The guests' acknowledgment of Virgil's rhetorical prowess at the beginning of book 5 is in response to Eusebius, who is elsewhere introduced as "a rhetorician distinguished by his Greek learning and eloquence" (*Sat.* 1.5.6 *Graia et doctrina et facundia clarum rhetorem*), and comes on the heels of an in-depth discussion of the poet's deployment of rhetorical techniques for representing emotions in the previous book, of which only a fragmentary section survives. Although the speaker of book 4 is not identified in the surviving sections, it is reasonable to assume that the task of elucidating Virgil's rhetoric of the emotions was given to Eusebius and that the section on the emotions in fact constituted the epilogue to book 4.[25] Virgil's rhetorical skills, however, were announced as a topic already in book 1 by the orator Symmachus, who was likely also a speaker in the sections of book 4 now lost and who promised to "make plain the rhetorical skill of Virgil's oeuvre – its most forceful conceits and expressions (*uiolentissima inuenta uel sensa rhetoricae*)" (*Sat.* 1.24.14).[26]

While Symmachus' portion of the discussion is now lost, Eusebius' contribution in book 4 well exemplifies the practice of "micro-rhetoricizing."[27] Eusebius surveys a number of areas that are key to pathos in the three core areas of diction (*elocutio*), argument (*inventio*) and arrangement (*dispositio*): demeanor (4.1 *habitus*), tone (4.2 *tenor*) and

---

[23] Tiberius Cl. Donatus, *Interpretationes Vergilianae*, vol. 1, pr.4.24–8 *si Maronis carmina competenter attenderis et eorum mentem congrue comprehenderis, inuenies in poetam rhetorem summum atque inde intelleges Vergilium non grammaticos, sed oratores praecipuos tradere debuisse.*

[24] On this passage, see Goldlust (2010) 372–99.

[25] Kaster (2011b) vol. 1, xxxi and vol. 2, 213 n. 35.

[26] On this passage and the image of Virgil in Macrobius in general, see Pelttari (2014) 25–43.

[27] Goldlust (2010) 362–71, Bestul (1975) and Vietti (1979) are essential discussions of book 4. For a comparable discussion of Virgilian pathos in Servius, see, e.g., *ad Aen.* 3.718 (in relation to the ending of book 2) and *ad Aen.* 4.1 (on book 4). See further Marinone (1946) 27–31 for a comparison of Macrobius and Servius on the topic of pathos.

especially pity and indignation, topics (*argumenta*), which include, for example, means (4.3–4.4), fortune (4.3.6) and age (4.3.16), and various figures of thought and diction (4.6) such as, for example, hyperbole (4.6.15) and exclamation (4.6.17). Juno's speech at *Aen.* 7.292–322 is discussed line by line and praised for the variety of its tone and figures (*Sat.* 4.2.9 *uides quam saepe orationem mutauerit ac frequentibus figuris uariauerit*). Predictably, Eusebius' discussion frequently evokes categories singled out by Quintilian's rhetorical handbook even as the Virgilian examples selected differ.[28]

In Macrobius, Virgil is represented as stirring pathos (*pathos mouere*) by way of various devices and compared to Cicero and Demosthenes in his ability to elicit an emotional response to the character's motivation and means (4.4.1–3; cf. 4.4.12 and 17).[29] Eusebius summarizes his point thus:

> et singula quidem enumerauimus, ex quibus apud rhetoras pathos nascitur, quibus ostendimus usum Maronem.
>
> I've now catalogued the individual sources of emotion, according to rhetorical doctrine, and I have shown how Maro uses them. (Macrobius, Sat. 4.4.19)

When the conversation resumes in book 5, all guests laud Virgil's knowledge of oratory, which Eusebius has expounded in book 4, and the young Avienus provocatively challenges the Greek rhetor to a comparison between Virgil and Cicero:

> post haec cum paulisper Eusebius quieuisset, omnes inter se consono murmure Vergilium non minus oratorem quam poetam habendum pronuntiabant, in quo et tanta orandi disciplina et tam diligens obseruatio rhetoricae artis ostenderetur. et Auienus: Dicas mihi, inquit, uolo, doctorum optime, si concedimus, sicuti necesse est, oratorem fuisse Vergilium, si quis nunc uelit orandi artem consequi, utrum magis ex Vergilio an ex Cicerone proficiat? Video quid agas, inquit Eusebius, quid intendas, quo me trahere coneris: eo scilicet, quo minime uolo, ad conparationem Maronis et Tullii. uerecunde enim interrogasti, uter eorum praestantior, quandoquidem necessario is plurimum conlaturus sit qui ipse plurimum praestat.
>
> After these remarks, when Eusebius had had a brief respite, all declared, with no murmur of dissent, that Virgil had to be considered no less an orator than a poet, seeing that he was shown to be so skilled in the ways of oratory and so

---

[28] Topics of overlap include: indignation and pity (*Sat.* 4.2 ~ Quintilian 6.2.20); argumenta (*Sat.* 4.3 ~ Quintilian 5.10); hyperbole (*Sat.* 4.6.15 ~ Quintilian 8.6.68–76); aposiopesis (*Sat.* 4.6.20 ~ Quintilian 9.2.54).

[29] For the text and translation of Macrobius' *Saturnalia*, I have used Kaster's Loeb edition.

"Micro-Rhetoricizing" 227

keen a student of rhetoric. And Avienus said: "Please tell me this, best of teachers: if we grant (as we must), that Virgil was an orator, would someone now aiming to become a skilled orator gain more from reading Virgil or Cicero?" "I see what you are up to," Eusebius said, "I see where you're headed and where you're trying to drag me – to a place I don't at all want to go, a comparison of Maro and Tully. You put circumspectly the question you really want answered – which of them is superior – since he will inevitably provide the greatest benefits who is himself the greatest."
(Macrobius, *Sat.* 5.1.1–3)

The guests' conclusion in *Sat.* 5.1 that Virgil "observed" rhetorical theory diligently – *tam diligens obseruatio rhetoricae artis* – renders explicit what is only implied by Eusebius' careful illustration of rhetorical categories by way of Virgilian exempla. In response to Avienus' provocation, Eusebius argues that, while Cicero was only versed in one style – the abundant and copious – it is Virgil who paradoxically comes closest to the Ciceronian ideal of full mastery of all styles of oratory. To illustrate the point, Eusebius brings in four passages that typify respectively the compressed style (*breue*) associated with Sallust, the abundant one (*copiose*) associated with Cicero, the dry style (*sicce*) tied to Fronto, the rich style (*pingue*) of Pliny the Younger and recently of Symmachus and a fifth passage, from book 1 of the *Georgics*, which exemplifies the judicious mixture of all four styles.[30]

This notion has a parallel in rhetorical criticism of Homeric texts. In line with the general tendency to view Homer as the father of all inventions, the three branches of oratory – deliberative, forensic and epideictic – were all traced back to the Homeric poems as was the theory of the three styles, commonly illustrated with reference to Homer's description of Menelaus, Nestor and Ulysses.[31] In Quintilian (12.10.64), for example, the theory of the three styles is illustrated with reference to a famous section of the *teikhoskopia* in *Il.* 3 in which Antenor recalls the embassy of Odysseus and Menelaus to Troy before the start of the war and describes the different styles of speaking of the Greek leaders: Menelaus represents the low style, Nestor the middle style, while Odysseus is the representative of the grand style (see Chapter 4, p. 140).

Eusebius' use of the Virgilian passage to illustrate the different styles is inspired by this tradition. His analysis, however, does more than simply

---

[30] On this passage, see Haverling (1990). This fourfold subdivision of style is a variation on the standard theory of the three styles: e.g. Demetrius, *Eloc.* 36 and see Innes (1985).

[31] On Homer as the inventor of the three genres, see Ps. Plutarch, *Life and Poetry of Homer* 161; *Schol. AbT in Il.* 2.283 *ex.*; *Schol. bT in Il.* 9.443 *ex.*; on the three styles theory and Homer, see Ps. Plutarch, *Life and Poetry of Homer* 172; Seneca, *Ep.* 40.2; Quintilian 12.10.64; and see further Pernot (2005) 3–6. Quintilian's passage is discussed at length in Chapter 4.

228 *Non minus orator quam poeta*

reduplicate rhetorical frames of analysis that had a long history in Homeric criticism. To begin with, in the Homeric tradition the three styles were associated with three different *speakers* and their characterization – Menelaus for the low style, Nestor for the middle style and Ulysses for the grand style. By contrast, just like Homer in the *Brutus* is said to showcase his oratory (*Brut.* 40 *ipse ... plane orator*), so, for Eusebius, Virgil exemplifies each style in his own *narrative*. First, Troy's destruction as summarized by Aeneas in a selection of passages from books 2 and 3 illustrates respectively the abundant and the concise styles. The brief style (*paucissimis uerbis*) is illustrated by the half-line description of the leveled Troy (*Aen.* 3.11 *et campos ubi Troia fuit* "and the plains where Troy was") with curious consequences: Virgil is cast as the destructive force that is being described in the narrative. Thus the poet is said to "have drained" (*hausit*) the city and to have "left not even ruin" (*non reliquit illi nec ruinam*) (Macrobius, *Sat.* 5.1.8). Next, with the emotional power of the grand style (*copiosissime*), the poet's force is compared in a crescendo to moving bodies of water (Macrobius, *Sat.* 5.1.10 *fons ... torrens ... mare*). The choice of passages from book 2 (2.324–7; 2.241–2; 2.361–3) is extremely pointed: Eusebius has zoomed in on two of Aeneas' interruptions to the storytelling that also attracted the attention of the Servian commentary for their appeal to the emotions.[32] All three passages contain excerptible examples of rhetorical devices such as *geminatio* (*Aen.* 2.325 *fuimus Troes, fuit Ilium*), tricola in crescendo, exclamation (*Aen.* 2.241 *o patria, o diuum domos Ilium ...*) and rhetorical questions (*Aen.* 2.361–2 *quis cladem ... quis funera fando | explicet*). More to the point, Aeneas' reflection on the ineffability of grief (*Aen.* 2.361–2 *quis ... possit lacrimas aequare dolorem*) echoes the opening of his speech at 2.3–8 (*infandum ... dolorem ... quis talia fando ... temperet a lacrimis*), as Tiberius Cl. Donatus notes in his rhetorical commentary.[33] It is significant that Eusebius has chosen a passage in which not only does Aeneas, as an embedded narrator, prominently recall the authorial voice of the poet but one in which the very topic at hand is the power of crafted speech to match and reproduce reality. In other words, by choosing a passage that, if read in isolation, would be well at home in a rhetorical manual, Eusebius is suggesting that Virgil is a rhetor in disguise.

Similarly, the passage illustrating the luxuriant style (Macrobius, *Sat.* 5.1.12 *quo cultu quam florida oratione*) is drawn from the narrator's

---

[32] *Serv. Dan. ad Aen.* 2.361 *et bene interrupta narratione exclamauit, ut affectum moueret.*
[33] Tiberius Cl. Donatus, *Interpretationes Vergilianae* vol.1, p. 196, 21–5.

"Micro-Rhetoricizing" 229

description of the outlandish warrior and priest of Cybele, Chloreus (*Aen.* 11.768–73; 11.777). Once again, the relation between example and the style it represents deserves consideration: the description of the warrior is not just an instantiation of the luxuriant style but actually taps into metaphorical vocabulary typically associated with decadence in rhetorical style. Thus the weapons shining (*fulgebat in armis*) in gold (*auro*), red (*ferrugine*) and purple (*ostro*) are all stock motifs in rhetorical sources. As we have seen in Chapter 3 (p. 124), Quintilian, for example, comments on the fact that the weapons of the orator should not be "be foul with neglect and rust; they should have the brilliance that strikes terror, the brilliance of steel that dazzles both mind and eye, not that of gold and silver, which is unwarlike and more dangerous to its possessor than to the foe" (10.1.27–30 *neque ego arma squalere situ ac robigine uelim, sed fulgorem in iis esse qui terreat qualis est ferri, quo mens simul uisusque praestringitur, non qualis auri argentique, inbellis et potius habenti periculosus*). In these examples, there is a noticeable instantiation of the phenomenon of trespass of theory and quotation well studied by Doreen Innes in that the quotation does not simply illustrate the theory but also contains technical vocabulary.[34] With this choice of passages, Eusebius does not simply illustrate the style but rather programmatically presents theory as a "natural" constituent of Virgilian poetry. Poetry is not an alien mode of discourse that illustrates rhetorical norms but rather the latter can be seen to be already there, albeit *in nuce*, in poetic texts.

It is with an awareness of this "rhetoricizing" strategy that one should approach the final passage illustrating the mingling of all four styles and "a kind of beautifully balanced mixture from their whole diverse range" (Macrobius, *Sat.* 5.1.13 *quoddam ex omni diuersitate pulcherimmum temperamentum*). The passage in question is the seemingly plain description of stubble-burning in *G.* 1.84–93, in which Virgil speculates whether the practice is beneficial because it fertilizes the soil, or because it sweats out the soil's flaws, or whether the heat opens up so as to allow the rain to nourish the soil or whether, to the contrary, it constricts it and protects it from the elements:[35]

> sed haec quidem inter se separata sunt. uis autem uidere, quemadmodum haec quattuor genera dicendi Vergilius ipse permisceat, et faciat unum quoddam ex omni diversitate pulcherrimum temperamentum?

---

[34] Innes (1994) and, on the trespass between theory and exempla, see further Goldhill (1994).

[35] On this curious passage, see Thomas (1988) 81 ad loc., who points out that through this description Virgil introduces the four key natural elements: hot, cold, dry and wet.

230 *Non minus orator quam poeta*

> saepe etiam steriles incendere profuit agros
> atque leuem stipulam crepitantibus urere flammis:
> siue inde occultas uires et pabula terrae
> pinguia concipiunt, siue illis omne per ignem
> excoquitur uitium atque exudat inutilis umor,
> seu plures calor ille uias et caeca relaxat
> spiramenta, nouas ueniat qua sucus in herbas,
> seu durat magis et uenas astringit hiantes,
> ne tenues pluuiae rapidiue potentia solis
> acrior aut Boreae penetrabile frigus adurat.

But the examples I've given are distinct in their styles: would you like to see how Virgil himself mingles the four styles and makes a kind of beautifully balanced mixture from their whole diverse range? [*G.* 1.84–93]
"Often, too, it has helped to burn infertile fields and scorch the light stubble with crackling

flames: whether because the lands take from that an invisible strength and rich sustenance, or because the fire bakes out all flaws and sweats out unhelpful dampness, or because the heat opens more paths and unseen passages, to let the juice reach new-grown grass, or rather because it toughens and constricts the gaping channels, lest the fine rains or the ravenous sun's power, when it's too fierce, or the North wind's piercing cold do damage" (Macrobius, *Sat.* 5.1.13)

On the surface, it is not immediately obvious why this rather technical passage on care of the soil should exemplify the perfect blend (*temperamentum*) of the four styles as Eusebius maintains. Yet the comments in the subsequent section clarify that the *Georgics* passage does not so much exemplify any one style or blend of styles but rather *describes* the physical effects of heat, fire, dryness and so on *associated with* such stylistic categories. Virgil's style, that is, mirrors now the brevity, now the dryness, now the fertile abundance of the natural phenomena he describes:

> ecce dicendi genus quod nusquam alibi deprehendes, in quo nec praeceps breuitas nec infrunita copia, nec ieiuna siccitas nec laetitia pinguis ... nam qualiter eloquentia Maronis ad omnium mores integra est, nunc breuis nunc copiosa nunc sicca nunc florida nunc simul omnia, interdum lenis aut torrens: sic terra ipsa hic laeta segetibus et pratis ibi siluis et rupibus hispida, his sicca harenis hic irrigua fontibus, pars uasto aperitur mari. ignoscite, nec nimium me uocetis, qui naturae rerum Vergilium conparaui. Intra ipsum enim mihi uisum est, si dicerem decem rhetorum qui apud Athenas Atticas floruerunt stilos inter se diuersos hunc unum permiscuisse.

> There you have a style you'll find nowhere else, with a brevity that is not abrupt, and abundance that is not mindless, a dryness that's not barren, a luxuriance that's not cloying ... Just as Maro's eloquence is a complete whole that responds to the characters of all people – now brief, now abundant, now dry, now colorful, now all at once, sometimes gentle, sometimes turbulent – so the earth itself has fertile fields and meadows in one place, shaggy woods and ragged crags in another, dry desert sands here, places soaked by springs there, and parts opened up to the desolate expanse of the sea. Forgive me, then, and don't say that I exaggerate in comparing Virgil to the natural world: for I thought it would fall short of his true measure, were I to say that he combined, all by himself, the divergent styles of the ten orators who flourished in the Athens of Attica. (Macrobius, *Sat.* 5.1.15, 19–20)

Eusebius' presentation of Virgil's rhetoric is founded on an allegorical interpretation of the poem:[36] not only is Maro's eloquence as rich and diverse as the natural phenomena he describes but the poet himself is here compared to nature. Macrobius' comparison between the poet, his text and the natural world that it describes should also be understood within the late antique tradition of allegorical readings of Virgil that we can parallel in Fulgentius' view that, in the *Aeneid*, Virgil has revealed the full development of human life (Fulgentius, *Exp. Verg.87 Helm pleniorem humanae uitae monstrassem statum*) or in Aelius Donatus' notion that Virgil's poetic career reflects the development of human civilization from pastoral life, to agriculture and war (Donatus, *Praef. in Buc. 57 Vergilium processurum ad alia carmina non aliunde coepisse nisi ab ea uita*).[37] Virgil's embracing of the natural world and the styles used to represent it culminates in the medieval *rota Vergilii*, a circular diagram in which the poet's life, works and styles are visualized in an encompassing wheel.[38] Yet, in comparing Virgil's language to nature itself (*natura rerum*), Macrobius also deploys a traditional comparison of "good rhetorical language with a good harvest," which has been analyzed by Catherine Connors as one of the mechanism used by the Romans to naturalize Greek rhetoric.[39] Macrobius is implicitly alluding to the traditional view of rhetoric as the main engine of human civilization responsible among

---

[36] MacCormack (1998) 87–8.
[37] The comparison between the poet, his poem and *natura*, however, ultimately goes back to Lucretius: see Hardie (1986) 173.
[38] Ziolkowski and Putnam (2008) 744–50.
[39] Connors (1997) 76; and see also Connolly (2007a) 104–17 on Cicero's construction of a naturalized Roman rhetoric and further Chapter 3 in this book on Quintilian's use of the *Georgics* to illustrate proper rhetorical training.

232   *Non minus orator quam poeta*

other things for the invention of agriculture (Cicero, *Inv. rhet.* 1.2; *De or.* 1.33). If the language of persuasion is understood as the ultimate expression of man's training of nature, Virgil's capacity to reflect the complexity of natural phenomena turns the poet into a latent rhetorician and the *Georgics* into an allegorical outline of rhetoric.

Macrobius' presentation of Virgil as a skilled orator, implementing precepts from the rhetorical handbooks, has typically encountered the resistance of modern scholars unwilling to accept that Virgil may have been "slave to the traditions and conventions of [his] own day" and rather inclined to analyze Macrobius' rhetorical categories as an alien and somewhat frigid set of conventions used to capture the natural, pre-rhetorical genius of Virgilian expression.[40] Yet the micro-rhetoricizing approach of Macrobius and his contemporaries deserves to be understood as a strategy of reading and framed in the context of the late antique reception of Virgil and the rhetoric of his text. For Macrobius' guests, the poet is not just the first rhetorician in disguise but represents the very image of human nature, embodying human history and evolution. This approach not only presents Virgil as a latent rhetorician but also constructs the poet and his text as foundational for rhetoric and for all aspects of human life and endeavors.[41]

Macro-Rhetoric

Macrobius' discussion of Virgil's deployment of the four styles makes rhetoric a feature not just of direct speech but of the entire narrative texture. Here, that is, the poet himself is viewed as a rhetor, whose objective is to persuade through his narrative at the macro level, influencing the emotions of his audience to gain their approval or condemnation of the characters. Such tendency to view the poem as an act of persuasion, which I have called "macro-rhetoricizing," is evident in Servius who, in the preface to his commentary, argues that Virgil's aim in writing the *Aeneid* was to imitate Homer and praise Augustus from his ancestors (Servius, *Praef. intentio Vergilii haec est, Homerum imitari et Augustum laudare a parentibus*; see n. 1 above).[42] Similarly, Tiberius Cl. Donatus reads the *Aeneid* as a long oration in support and praise of Aeneas, and the tradition of reading the poem as an extended encomium of its hero and his

---

[40] Clarke (1949) 16.   [41] See Cameron (2011) 608 on this approach to Virgil as the "pagan bible."
[42] Kallendorf (1989) but see already Aristotle, *Poetics* 1448b24–7 with Woodman (1988) 41–4. On Tiberius Cl. Donatus' presentation of the *Aeneid* as an "epic of praise," see Starr (1992). On Servius' defensive reading of the character of Aeneas, see Thomas (2001) 106–10.

Macro-Rhetoric

descendants extends to the modern period in the work of, for example, Maffeo Vegio.[43]

Given this tradition of reading the epic as a form of epideictic, it is no surprise that lament and invective, which are prime vehicles for praise and blame, are often analyzed rhetorically in the Servian commentaries.[44] In particular, the poet's own verbal performance is labeled as "rhetorical" when it seems to be in the epideictic mode: the passage about the *puer* in *Ecl.* 4 is read as a rhetorically driven *laudatio* (Servius *ad Ecl.* 4.18 *rhetorice digesta laudatio*) and, in a similar vein, Virgil is said to "praise the hope in the little boy in rhetorical fashion" (Servius *ad Aen.* 6.875 *rhetorice spem laudat in puero*), according to Cicero's recommendation for eulogizing young men.[45] Less frequently, other aspects of the narrative are analyzed as "rhetorical": the description of the strewn soldiers on the battlefield is praised for rhetorically arranging the bodies according to their rank (Servius *ad Aen.* 7.535 *et rhetorice uiles trudit in medium, nobiles uero primo et ultimo commemorat loco*), while in the proem to *G.* 4, Virgil is said to "promise great things in a rhetorical fashion so as to elevate a light subject matter and make his listener more intent" (Servius *ad G.* 4.1 *rhetorice dicturus de minoribus rebus magna promittit, ut et leuem materiam subleuet et attentum faciat auditorem*).

In this macro-rhetorical reading, the *Aeneid* is a long oration in praise of his main character and even material seemingly devoid of panegyrical intent can, on closer inspection, be seen to further the larger encomiastic aim of the work. Thus, according to Tiberius Cl. Donatus, "[the poem] certainly belongs to the epideictic genre, and this fact remains unnoticed and concealed because with his outstanding talent for the art of praise, while he goes through Aeneas' deeds, he himself is shown to have incorporated also incidental subject matters of other kinds, which nevertheless were not extraneous to the functions of praise. For these were brought in to aid the praise of Aeneas (*ut Aeneae laudationi proficerent*)" (*Interpretationes Vergilianae*, vol. 1, pr.2.9–10:).[46] In this mode of reading, the poet is seen as an advocate and the critic's task is that of highlighting strategies used to

---

[43] See Hardie (2016) 79–82.

[44] Lament of Euryalus' mother (Servius *ad Aen.* 9.479 *et est conquestio matris Euryali plena artis rhetoricae*); Numanus Remulus' invective against the Trojans (Servius *ad Aen.* 9.611 *uituperatio Troianorum in qua utitur argumentis quae in rhetoricis commemorat Cicero . . .*). On lament as a form of epideictic, see Burgess (1902) 111.

[45] Cf. Servius *ad Aen.* 6.847, where Virgil is said to use a rhetorical topos, and Servius *ad Aen.* 1.151, where Virgil is said to follow Cicero's "rhetorical definition" of the orator as a good man skilled as speaking in his portrayal of a politician calming an angry mob.

[46] On this passage, see Pirovano (2006) 39–42.

234   *Non minus orator quam poeta*

praise and defend Aeneas.[47] So, according to Servius, for example, Virgil's intention in book 2 is twofold: "to avoid that it should seem disgraceful either for Troy that it was conquered or for Aeneas that he fled" (Servius *ad Aen.* 2.13 *ne uel Troiae quod uicta est, uel Aeneae turpe uideatur esse quod fugit*).[48] Elsewhere, Servius highlights how Aeneas is implicitly defending himself from the accusation of being a coward or, worse still, a collaborator of the Greeks.[49] In book 4, it is Aeneas who acts once again as his own advocate when Dido begins accusing Aeneas "as if he were a defendant" (*Serv. Dan. ad Aen.* 4.305 *hic quasi reus Aeneas a Didone accusatur*), while Aeneas' speech can be analyzed as a *controuersia* in which Aeneas rejects the charge of ingratitude and justifies his own departure (Servius *ad Aen.* 4.333).[50] Indeed, the speeches between Dido and Aeneas at *Aen.* 4.279–415 have long been a *locus classicus* for discussions of Virgilian rhetoric and, unsurprisingly, they lent themselves to several rhetorical rewritings in late antiquity. In particular, two verse compositions from the *Codex Salmasianus* rewrite and supplement Dido's two speeches to Aeneas (4.305–30 and 365–87) as well as Ovid, *Her.* 7 – namely, the anonymous *Epistula Didonis ad Aeneam* (*Anthologia Latina* 71 Shackleton Bailey) and a Virgilian *thema, Nec Tibi, Diua parens* (*Anthologia Latina* 249 Shackleton Bailey), both of which recast Dido's invective at 4.365–87.[51] Also relevant is Ennodius' *Dictio* 28, a prose *ethopoiia* that rewrites the same speech constructing a counter defense of Dido, much like Tiberius Cl. Donatus, who, in his commentary, also provides his own paraphrastic rewriting of the queen's speech (*Interpretationes Vergilianae*, vol. 1, pp. 406–9 *ad Aen.* 4.362–84).[52] What these texts have in common is an interest in using Dido as a vehicle for voicing the criticism of Aeneas to which Virgil is supposed to be responding and thus implicitly turning the reading of the epic into a court room experience in which the reader is called to take the side of a character at the expense of another.

This image of Virgil as an orator and advocate is crucial to understanding the discussion of Virgilian oratory in Macrobius. Going back to Symmachus' speech in book 1, where the topic of Virgilian oratory was first introduced, it is important to notice that the ensuing conversation is

---

[47] See Clément-Tarantino (2011).   [48] For the history of this accusation, see Horsfall (1979).

[49] Servius *ad Aen.* 2.17; 2.201; 2.735; 12.15. For the theme in late antiquity, see Horsfall (2009) on Dictys.

[50] See Pirovano (2006) 158–67 and, for the medieval fortune of the Dido episode in rhetorical theory, see Woods (2009).

[51] On the *thema*, see McGill (2003) 106–13 and, on the *Epistula Didonis*, see Solimano (1988).

[52] See Pirovano (2010).

Macro-Rhetoric

emphatically presented as a *defense* of the value of Virgilian poetry in the face of the attack of the dialogue's skeptical character, Evangelus, who had criticized Virgil as a sloppy poet:

> cumque adhuc dicentem omnes exhorruissent, subtexuit Symmachus: Haec est quidem, Euangele, Maronis gloria, ut nullius laudibus crescat, nullius uituperatione minuatur: uerum ista quae proscindis defendere quilibet potest ex plebeia grammaticorum cohorte, ne Seruio nostro, qui priscos, ut mea fert opinio, praeceptores doctrina praestat, in excusandis talibus quaeratur iniuria: sed quaero, utrum, cum poetica tibi in tanto poeta displicuerit, nerui tamen oratorii, qui in eodem ualidissimi sunt, placere uideantur?

> When they all had shuddered with repugnance while he was still speaking, Symmachus followed up by saying: "Such is Maro's glory, Evangelus, that no man's praise makes it greater, and no man's attacks make it less. As for those points you pick at, anyone from the common run of grammarians could fend off your criticisms, not to insult our friend Servius, who I think more learned than the teachers of old, by having him make excuses for such things. But tell me: granted that you take no pleasure in the great poet's poetry, does his oratorical muscle, which he also has in abundance, seem to meet your standard? (Macrobius, *Sat.* 1.24.8)

Symmachus' argument that Maro's glory is such that "no one can add to it by praise or detract from it through disparagement" sets up the conversation that follows as a subspecies of epideictic. The speakers are thus imagined to "defend" (*defendere*) the poet against the accusations of Evangelus. It is once again Evangelus' accusation that Virgil did not know anything about Greek literature in book 5 that acts as a trigger and transition from the discussion of Virgil the orator to the disquisition on the poet's adaptation of Greek models (5.2.1).

Some have argued that the skeptical voice of Evangelus represents a Christian reaction against the Pagan heritage embodied by Virgil.[53] This opinion, however, has been vigorously refuted by Alan Cameron who instead sees Evangelus as a "reflection of Macrobius' first- and second-century sources, skillfully adapted to provide a foil for his own glorification of Vergil."[54] According to Cameron, Evangelus voices the concerns of the Virgilian critics of the early first century mentioned at Donatus' *Vita* 43–6 in response to whom Asconius Pedianus supposedly wrote his *contra obtrectatores*: writers such as

---

[53] Sic MacCormack (1998) 74, 86–7.
[54] Cameron (2011) 596 and see Kaster (2011b) vol. 1, xxxii–xxxiv and see further Olmos (2012).

236   *Non minus orator quam poeta*

Numitorius, author of the *Antibucolica,* and Perellius Faustus, who compiled a list of Virgil's thefts.[55]

While an easy dichotomy between pagan and Christian based on pro- or anti-Virgilian sentiments must surely be rejected, the apologetic framework of Macrobius' presentation of Virgil in the *Saturnalia* can be seen as a strategy for responding to the authorial figure of the poet/advocate rather than simply as a reflection of Macrobius' dependence on earlier sources or worse still as a counterattack by a pagan community of readers. Just as Virgil himself is framed as an advocate defending Aeneas' case, so the speakers in Macrobius' dialogue are acting as self-conscious defenders of Virgil's reputation and status. For Tiberius Cl. Donatus too, the critic's job involves defending the poet from the accusations of these critics.[56] Moreover, defense in general is a recurrent theme in the commentary: from Aeneas' failed defense of Troy, to Virgil's and other characters' defense of Aeneas' conduct, to the commentator's defending his adding to the existing scholarship on Virgil, literary reception is a judicial activity in which teacher and example, classroom and courtroom are intertwined.[57] In this "epideictic" form of literary criticism of Virgilian poetry, the participants in the dialogue are not only illuminating Virgil's rhetorical powers but actively putting into practice the very same rhetorical skills they admire in their Classical master. If, as Chin has argued, literary activity as constructed in the *Saturnalia* is always viewed as "the result of debts that must be discharged," the defense of Virgil allows the participants in the dialogue simultaneously to discharge the tie of obligation to their master that Chin identifies as central to the nexus of religious and literary piety in the *Saturnalia* and to re-perform the rhetorical moves of their model.[58]

Performance and the Rhetor: Florus' *Vergilius Orator an Poeta*

Performance then offers a useful lens through which to approach not just poetry as rhetorically constructed discourse but also the very relation between critic and text that this approach to poetry as oratory promotes. We have already seen how the epic voyage informs Quintilian's depiction

---

[55] See Courtney (2003) 284–6 and Görler (1987). For Macrobius' supposed dependence on these sources, see also Jocelyn (1964).

[56] *Interpretationes Vergilianae,* vol. 1, pr.5.26–7 *nec te perturbent inperitorum uel obtrectatorum Vergiliani carminis uoces inimicae.*

[57] Moretti (1997).

[58] Chin (2008) 56 and chap. 3 passim on the interconnection of grammar and piety in the *Saturnalia* and see further Kaster (1980).

Performance and the Rhetor: *Florus'* Vergilius Orator an Poeta   237

of his own project, while the epic figure of the general at war is appropriated to define the ideal orator. The blurring of the lines between poetic model and rhetorical instruction is even more evident in the fragmentary dialogue entitled *Vergilius Orator an Poeta*. The work was found in only one twelfth-century manuscript and only its narrative introduction survives. Whether the Publius Annius Florus to whom the work is attributed in the manuscript is the same as Florus the epitomator or is to be identified with Florus the poet, friend with Hadrian, remains unclear.[59] Based on the title, it is reasonable to assume that the work tackled the same topic as *Saturnalia* book 5 but only the narrative context to the dialogue is extant: in a temple in Tarraconensis (modern Tarragona) in northeastern Spain, a poet from Africa by the name of Florus meets a learned man (*litteris pereruditus*) from Baetica to whom he tells of his traveling in the Mediterranean and his own job as a school teacher. In accordance with the conventions of the genre, the dialogue opens with the character Florus narrating his encounter with the stranger:

> †capienti mihi in templo et saucium uigilia caput plurimarum arborum amoenitate, euriporum frigore, aeris libertate recreanti obuiam subito quidam fuere, quos ab urbis spectaculo Baeticam reuertentes sinister Africae uentus in hoc litus excusserat. quorum unus, uir, ut postea apparuit, litteris pereruditus, subito ad me conuenit et "salue," inquit "hospes: nisi molestum est, dic nomen tuum; nam nescio quid oculi mei admonent et quasi per nubilum recognosco".

> As I was [?] in a temple and reviving my head hurt by the lack of sleep with the beauty of the trees, the freshness of the waters and the freedom of the air, some people came upon me whom the inauspicious wind from Africa had cast upon this shore as they made their way back to Baetica from the spectacle of the city. Among these, a man and learned at that, as it became obvious later, at once approached me and said "Hello there, stranger, unless it's a problem for you, tell me your name: my eyes are telling me something, I'm not sure what, and I recognize you as if through a cloud. (Florus, *Vergilius Orator an Poeta* 1.1–3)

The two characters and the setting of the dialogue are constructed in strikingly Virgilian terms. The scene is a mix of several Virgilian passages: the encounter between a man diverted by the winds on his return home and the references to recognition through a cloud (*quasi per nubilum recognosco*) remind us of Aeneas' shipwreck and his meeting with Venus

---

[59] Verweij (2015); Baldwin (1988).

238 *Non minus orator quam poeta*

in *Aen.* 1 (1.412 *et multo nebulae circum dea fudit amictu*).[60] *Hospes* is of course a recurrent epithet for Aeneas.[61] It turns out that the narrator, Florus, who had won a prize in the Alban Games under Domitian, later left out spite when his prize was taken away and settled in Tarraconensis:[62]

> si fata Romam negant patriam, saltim hic manere contingat. quid, quod consuetudo res fortis est? et ecce iam familiaritate continua ciuitas nobis ipsa blanditur, quae, si quid credis mihi qui multa cognoui, omnium [rerum] quae ad quietem eliguntur gratissima est. populum uides, o hospes et amice, probum, frugi, quietum, tarde quidem, sed iudicio hospitalem. caelum peculiariter temperatum miscet uices, et notam ueris totus annus imitatur. terra fertilis campis et magis collibus – nam Italiae uites adfectat et comparat areas – serotino non erubescit autumno.

> If the fates deny me Rome as a fatherland, at least let it be my lot to stay here. What am I to say except that habit is a great force? And here you see this very city entices me on account of our long acquaintance, a city which, if you believe at all in me who have much experience, is the most pleasant of all things which are chosen for the sake of peace. You see its people, stranger and friend: they are honest, frugal, peaceful, hospitable slowly but with discretion. An especially temperate climate attenuates the changes and the whole year is patterned after the characteristics of spring. The land is fertile with fields and more with hills – for it strives after and rivals the vineyards of Italy and its threshing floors – and it does not blush with a Fall season that is late to arrive. (Florus, *Vergilius Orator an Poeta* 2.6–8)

Broadly speaking, Florus' self-imposed departure from Rome recalls both Moelibeus' forced exile and Aeneas' detour in Carthage. His praise of the temperate climate of Spain (7.1–8) conforms to rhetorical prescriptions for encomia of places and looks back at the *laudes Italiae* at *G.* 2.136–76, specifically in its mention of the perennial spring at 7 (*notam ueris totus annus imitatur*).[63] Florus' grief-stricken meanderings in his reaction to

---

[60] For the cloud as inhibiting recognition of gods, see Horace, *Carm.* 1.2.31 with Nisbet and Hubbard (1970) 29–30. Aeneas and Achates are also shrouded by a cloud to avoid being seen at Virgil, *Aen.* 1.516 *dissimulant et nube caua speculantur amicti.*

[61] See Virgil, *Aen.* 1.753; 4.10, 323; 8.123, 188, 364.

[62] Hardie (2002) 137 and 139 argues that Florus wrote for the games of 87 or 88 CE. The town is identifiable because of references to its foundation by Caesar and its temple of Jupiter Ammon at 8.3–9.5, see Jal (1967) 120.

[63] See *G.* 2.149 *hic uer adsiduum atque alienis mensibus aestas* with Thomas (1988) 184 ad loc. and, for the history of the motif, see Horace, *Carm.* 2.6.17 *uer ubi longum*; Ovid. *Met.* 1.107 *uer erat aeternum.* For the phrase *campis et collibus*, see also the description of agriculture at Lucretius 5.1372–3 *prata lacus riuos segetes uinetaque laeta | collibus et campis ut haberent.* For the tradition of encomia of places, see Servius *ad G.* 2.136.

Performance and the Rhetor: Florus' Vergilius Orator an Poeta 239

being stripped of his prize at the poetry contest also echo both the Virgilian Dido and her Greek model, Medea:[64]

> quod ad me pertinet, ex illo die, cuius [quo] tu mihi testis es, postquam ereptam manibus et capiti coronam meo uidi, tota mens, totus animus resiliit atque abhorruit ab illa ciuitate, adeoque sum percussus et consternatus illo dolore, ut patriae quoque meae oblitus <et> parentum carissimorum similis furenti huc et illuc uager per diuersa terrarum.

> As far I am concerned, from that day when (you are my witness) I saw the crown being ripped away from my hands and head, my whole mind and soul recoiled and abhorred from that city. I was so hurt and dismayed by that pain that forgetful even of my fatherland and of my beloved parents, like a mad person I wandered here and there all over different lands. (Florus, *Vergilius Orator an Poeta* 1.9)

In his incessant wanderings, Florus compares himself to Triptolemus, who was instructed by Demeter to spread her gifts all over the earth from a chariot drawn by winged serpents (2.4–5.3).[65] In his description of his exilic wanderings, he echoes Polynices in Seneca's *Phoenissae*.[66] His character, however, also displays some of Aeneas' traits. His wanderings take him to some of Aeneas' sights in the Mediterranean – Sicily, Crete and the Cyclades – though not in the same order. Others, such as the sources of the Nile (*ora Nili*) or the Alps (*Gallicas Alpes*) are more familiar from historiography. His personal characteristics include the *uerecundia* he displays when he is recognized by the stranger from Baetica (*quae cum me uideret uerecunde agnoscentem*).[67] Furthermore, in his response to the foreigner's questions about his traveling, Florus echoes Aeneas' connection between pain and memory at the beginning of *Aen.* 2: 8.4–5 "For this reason, stop opening back up the pain of my suffering by bringing me back to the memory of old times" *Quare desine me in memoriam priorem reducendo uulnus dolorum meorum rescindere.*[68]

We do not know exactly how the subject of Virgilian oratory was introduced and what the outcome of the discussion might have been. All

---

[64] See esp. *Vergilius Orator an Poeta* 1.9.7 *similis furenti huc et illuc uager per diuersa terrarum* – *Aen.* 4.68–9 *uritur infelix Dido totaque uagatur | urbe furens*; Catullus 63.3–4 *furenti | rabie uagus animi*; Seneca, *Ag.* 724 *cui nunc uagor uesana? cui bacchor furens?*

[65] The myth is featured in Ovid, *Met.* 5.642–56, see esp. 5.648–9 *iam super Europen sublimis et Asida terram | uectus erat iuuenis: Scythicas aduertitur oras* and Statius, *Silv.* 4.2.34–6.

[66] Florus, *Vergilius Orator an Poeta* 2.5.4 6 *quousque uagabimur? an semper hospites erimus?* – Seneca, *Phoen.* 586–7 *ut profugus errem semper? ut patria arcear | opemque gentis hospes externae sequar?*

[67] On the role of the Aeneadic *uerecundia* in the construction of the grammarian's persona, see Kaster (1980).

[68] See Virgil, *Aen.* 2.3 *infandum, regina, iubes renouare dolorem.*

240 *Non minus orator quam poeta*

we can tell is that, in response to the foreigner who praises Florus' strength of character in humbling himself to the level of becoming a school teacher, the author responds with a defense of the profession and the role of literature in forming young minds just before the text breaks up.

> bone Iuppiter, quam imperatorium, quam regium est sedere a suggestu praecipientem bonos mores et sacrarum studia litterarum, iam carmina praelegentem, quibus ora mentesque formantur, iam sententiis uariis sensus excitantem, iam exemplis ro <manae>

> Good God, how worthy of an emperor, how worthy of a king it is to sit on a raised platform, teaching good customs, the study of sacred letters, now doing a reading of the poetry with by which the voice and mind are shaped, now exciting the senses with different memorable phrases, now with *exempla of Roman* ... (Florus, *Vergilius Orator an Poeta* 3.8)

The technical reference to the elementary exercise of the *praelectio* – the reading aloud of poetry by the grammarian – is accompanied by references to *sententiae* and *exempla* that may hint at the study of historiographical texts.[69] We can only speculate that, given his background as a teacher, Florus may have been well positioned to mount an argument for treating Virgil both as a poet and as an orator. It should be noted, however, that the narrative structure of this work may have been closer to an autobiographical novel than to a Platonic dialogue: if the Baetic stranger took the opposite position to Florus, the dialogue probably departed somewhat from the more complex architecture involving several speakers and positions evident, for example, in Cicero's *De oratore*, whose opening it imitates.[70] It may even be speculated whether the author wished to construct the narrative as a first person account of events on the model of Aeneas' narrative of the fall of Troy and its aftermath (books 2 and 3 of the *Aeneid*). Be that as it may, the character of the teacher, modeled as it is in several respects on Aeneas, blurs the line between instruction and poetry constructing the interpretation of the *Aeneid* as a re-performance of its hero's journey.

---

[69] For the *praelectio*, see Quintilian 1.2.15 and 2.5.4. The expression *sacrae litterae* also describes the job of the *professor litterarum* in Quintilian 10.1.92 *nos tamen sacra litterarum colentes* and see Seneca, *De uita beata* 26.7 *suscipite uirtutem, credite iis qui illam diu secuti magnum quiddam ipsos et quod in dies maius appareat sequi clamant, et ipsam ut deos ac professores eius ut antistites colite et, quotiens mentio sacrarum litterarum interuenerit, fauete linguis*; Tacitus, *Dial.* 20.5 *ex Horatii et Vergilii et Lucani sacrario prolatus.*

[70] *Vergilius Orator an Poeta* 1.1 *capienti mihi ... recreanti ~ De Or.* 1.1 *cogitanti mihi saepe ... repetenti* and see Jal (1967) 106.

Conclusion

At the most basic level, Virgil's text is "micro-rhetoricized" when elements of the poem – be they topoi deployed by characters in direct speech or rhetorical figures – are read as exemplifying a given rhetorical principle. In this reading, the poet tends to be constructed as a trained orator in full control of the art of rhetoric or as a teacher using his poem to showcase different rhetorical precepts. Yet we have also seen that, in the discussion of Virgilian oratory in *Sat.* 5, the trespass of theory into the example by which it is supposedly illustrated implicitly presents the language of persuasion as a foundational component of the poet's text and as a practice rooted in nature. On the macro level, the poet himself is viewed as manipulating the emotions of his audience toward the characters, especially Aeneas whom Virgil is seen as defending. This epideictic approach to storytelling trickles into the practice of interpretation, which becomes itself a Virgilian performance in which the critic rehearses and expands on Virgil's defense of Aeneas. The apologetic frame of the discussion of Virgilian rhetoric is as relevant as its content: while the participants in the *Saturnalia* perform a defense of the poet, Florus is entrusted with a defense of his profession and the role of poetry in the formation of the young. What is more, in Florus' dialogue, the apologetic mission is entrusted to a character who in his exilic peregrinations re-performs some of the experiences of the Aeneadic hero. In the perspective of these readers, rhetoric is not a foreign discipline applied or transposed to poetry but one that is naturally rooted in the epic. In turn, the experience of reading, criticism and interpretation narrows the gap between reader and author, catalyzing the re-performance of the rhetorical act that, for these readers, lies at the heart of Virgil's poem.

This late antique construction of Virgil as an orator is typically read as an aberrant anachronism flying in the face of the theoretical and practical divide between poetry and rhetoric, as enshrined in the titles of Aristotle's two works on style – the *Rhetoric* and the *Poetics*. This book has sought to provide a counter narrative to this and other accounts of Roman literary history that posit the relationship between rhetoric and poetry as one of hybridization and inexorable conquest by one of the other. Central to this endeavor has been the effort to shed light on the role of discussions of the affinity and difference between rhetoric and poetry in narratives of stylistic, cultural and literary decline. All the way from the polemical evocation of poetry by Cicero, Seneca the Elder and Quintilian as a foil for the definition of appropriate, manly and civilized rhetorical speech, to the leveraging of the concept of rhetorical influence in the context of historical accounts of Roman literature, the relationship between poetry and rhetoric is repeatedly found to be central to narratives of literary decline. The argument advanced here is twofold. On the one hand, the divide between rhetoric and poetry as articulated by rhetorical sources is fraught from the very beginning with unresolved tensions. Performance, pleasure and display are elements both repeatedly evoked in critiques of rhetorical discourse and explicitly singled out as traits that distinguish poetic language from the more restrained deployment of adornment in rhetorical speech. Yet precisely because it is evoked in acts of polemical self-definition and self-defense, poetry in rhetorical sources is not an inert body subject to analysis but rather a rival to which rhetorical theorists such as Seneca the Elder and Quintilian have recourse to validate their medium by appeal to epic models – for example, in framing the work of the orator and the grand style – and which they can at times disavow as foreign to rhetoric. The argument advanced here is thus that the exemplary role of the poetic in rhetorical texts destabilizes the possibility of ever fully separating the poetic and the rhetorical and encourages instead the idea of approaching poets like Homer as foils, models for and even proto-versions of the orator.

On the other, the book has sought to move away from a "colonial" model whereby rhetoric's relationship to poetry is framed as one of influence of the foreign on the primitively poetic. Instead, Part II of the book has sought to revitalize the poets' response to and engagement with sources such as Cicero as an area of studies central to an understanding of the relationship between poetry and rhetoric. Roman poets – here exemplified by Virgil, Ovid, Lucan and Silius Italicus – selectively engage with and debunk the Ciceronian narrative about the civilizing power of rhetoric while seemingly reviving a claim for the primacy of poetic discourse when it comes to the deployment of the grand style. And yet rhetoric can also be coopted, though ambiguously so, not just as a model for style or composition but rather as a paradigm for framing the reliance of post-Virgilian poetry on repetition, recasting and creative retelling. For sure, Macrobius' construction of Virgil as "no less an orator than a poet" exemplifies the process whereby the Augustan classic, from its earliest reception employed to bolster the authority of the rhetorical medium in Seneca the Elder and Quintilian, became an almost inevitable foundational text for any and all areas of human endeavor. Yet this *Vergilius orator* is also a powerful and almost logical synthesis of centuries of critical debates about the differences and similarities between rhetorical and poetic discourse. The hybridity of this construct and the role it has served in narratives of Virgilian reception should serve as an invitation to reexamine both the productive entanglement of the categories and what is at stake in the effort to extricate them.

References

Adamietz, J. (1966) *M.F. Quintiliani Institutionis Oratoriae Liber III*. Munich.

Ahl, F. (1976) *Lucan: An Introduction*. Ithaca, NY.

(2010) "Quintilian and Lucan," in *Lucan's* Bellum Civile: *Between Epic Tradition and Aesthetic Innovation*, ed. N. Hömke and C. Reitz. New York, NY: 1–16.

Arena, V. (2012) *Libertas and the Practice of Politics in the Late Roman Republic*. Cambridge.

(2013) "The Orator and his audience: the rhetorical perspective in the art of deliberation," in *Community and Communication: Oratory and Politics in Republican Rome*, ed. C. Steel and H. van der Bloom. Oxford: 195–209.

Ariemma, E. M. (2009) "*Fons cuncti Varro mali*: the demagogue Varro in *Punica* 8–10," in *Brill's Companion to Silius Italicus*, ed. A. Augoustakis. Leiden: 241–76.

Asmis, E. (1992) "Neoptolemus and the classification of poetry," *CP* 87: 206–31.

(2005) "A new kind of model: Cicero's Roman constitution in *De Republica*," *AJP* 126: 377–416.

Assfahl, G. (1932) *Vergleich und Metapher bei Quintilian*. Stuttgart.

Auhagen, U. (2007) "Rhetoric and Ovid," in *A Companion to Roman Rhetoric*, ed. W. Dominik and J. Hall. Malden, MA: 413–24.

Austin, R. G. (1944) "Quintilian on painting and statuary," *CQ* 38: 17–26.

(1954) *Quintiliani Institutionis Oratoriae Liber XII*. Oxford.

(1964) *Aeneidos: Liber Secundus*. Oxford.

Ax, W. (2011) *Quintilians Grammatik (Inst. Orat. 1,4–8)*. Berlin.

Axelson, B. (1945) *Unpoetische Wörter: Ein Beitrag zur Kenntnis der Lateinischen Dichtersprache*. Lund.

Baldwin, B. (1988) "Four problems with Florus," *Latomus* 47: 134–42.

Barchiesi, A. (2009a) "Exemplarity: between practice and text," in *Latinitas Perennis, vol. 2:* Appropriation and Latin Literature, ed. Y. Maes, J. Papy and W. Verbaal. Leiden: 41–62.

(2009b) "*Senatus Consultum de Lycaone*: concili degli dèi e immaginazione politica nelle *Metamorfosi* di Ovidio," *MD* 61, *Callida Musa: Papers on Latin Literature in Honor of Elaine Fantham*: 117–45.

Barker, E. T. E. (2009) *Entering the Agon: Dissent and Authority in Homer, Historiography and Tragedy*. Oxford.

References

Barthes, R. (1988) *The Semiotic Challenge*. New York, NY.

Barwick, K. (1922) "Die Gliederung der rhetorischen Techne und die Horazische *Epistula ad Pisones*," *Hermes* 57: 1–62.

Bender, J. B. and Wellbery, D. E. (1990) *The Ends of Rhetoric: History, Theory, Practice*. Stanford, CA.

Bennett, B. (2007) "Spanish Declaimers in the Elder Seneca," *Advances in the History of Rhetoric* 10: 1–17.

Berger, A. (2002) *Encyclopedic Dictionary of Roman Law*. Union, NJ.

Bers, V. (1984) *Greek Poetic Syntax in the Classical Age*. New Haven, CT.

Berti, E. (2007) *Scholasticorum Studia: Seneca il Vecchio e la Cultura Retorica e Letteraria della Prima Età Imperiale*. Pisa.

Bestul, T. H. (1975) "The *Saturnalia* of Macrobius and the *Praecepta Artis Rhetoricae* of Julius Severianus," *CJ* 70: 10–16.

Billmayer, K. (1932) *Rhetorische Studien zu den Reden in Vergils Aeneis*. Würzburg.

Bloomer, W. M. (1997a) *Latinity and Literary Society at Rome*. Philadelphia, PA.

(1997b) "Schooling in persona: imagination and subordination in Roman education," *CA* 16: 57–78.

Bonner, S. F. (1949) *Roman Declamation in the Late Republic and Early Empire*. Berkeley, CA.

(1966) "Lucan and the declamation schools," *AJP* 87: 257–89.

(1977) *Education in Ancient Rome: From the Elder Cato to the Younger Pliny*. London.

Booth, W. (1983) *The Rhetoric of Fiction*, 2nd ed. Chicago, IL.

Bornecque, H. (1902) *Les Déclamations et les Déclamateurs d'après Sénèque Le Père*. Lille.

Botsford, G. W. (1909) *The Roman Assemblies from their Origin to the End of the Republic*. New York.

Bowersock, G. W. (1965) *Augustus and the Greek World*. Oxford.

Brink, C. O. (1963) *Horace on Poetry*. Cambridge.

(1971) *Horace on Poetry: The* Ars Poetica. Cambridge.

(1989) "Quintilian's *De Causis Corruptae Eloquentiae* and Tacitus' *Dialogus de Oratoribus*," *CQ* 39: 472–503.

Brogan, T. V. F. and Burris, S. (1993) "Poetic license," in *Princeton Encyclopedia of Poetry and Poetics*, ed. A. Preminger and T. V. F. Brogan. Princeton, NJ: 928.

Brooks, C. (1947) *The Well Wrought Urn: Studies in the Structure of Poetry*. San Diego, CA.

Bruère, R. T. (1971) "Some recollections of Virgil's Drances in later epic," *CP* 66: 30–4.

Burgess, T. C. (1902) *Epideictic Literature*. Chicago, IL.

Burke, K. (1950) *A Rhetoric of Motives*. New York, NY.

Cairns, F. (1989) *Virgil's Augustan Epic*. Cambridge.

(2007) *Generic Composition in Greek and Roman Poetry*, rev. ed. Edinburgh.

Calboli, G. (1987) "*Oratores*," in *Enciclopedia Virgiliana III*. Rome: 869–72.

(1995) "Quintilian and Horace," *Scholia* 4: 79–100.

(1998) "From Aristotelian *lexis* to *elocutio*," *Rhetorica* 16: 47–80.

246 *References*

Calboli Montefusco, L. (1986) *La Dottrina degli "Status" nella Retorica Greca e Romana*. Hildesheim and New York, NY.

Cameron, A. (2011) *The Last Pagans of Rome*. New York, NY.

Carey, C. (2013) "Rhetoric in the (other) Menander," in *Hellenistic Oratory*, ed. C. Kremmydas and K. Tempest. Oxford: 93–107.

Casali, S. (1997) "*Qvaerenti Plvra Legendvm*: on the necessity of 'reading more' in Ovid's exile poetry," *Ramus* 26: 80–112.

(2010) "The *Bellum Civile* as an anti-Aeneid," in *Brill's Companion to Lucan*, ed. P. Asso. Leiden: 81–110.

Chin, C. M. (2008) *Grammar and Christianity in the Late Roman World*. Philadelphia, PA.

Christes, J. (1979) *Sklaven und Freigelassene als Grammatiker und Philologen im Antiken Rom*. Wiesbaden.

Clarke, M. L. (1949) "Rhetorical influences in the Aeneid," *G&R* 18: 14–27.

Clément-Tarantino, S. (2011) "Éloge et Défense dans le commentaire de Servius à l'*Énéide*," in *Servius et sa Réception de l'Antiquité à la Renaissance*, ed. M. Bouquet and B. Méniel. Rennes: 101–20.

Cole, C. N. (1906) "Quintilian's quotations from the Latin Poets," *CR* 20: 47–51.

Cole, T. (1991) *The Origins of Rhetoric in Ancient Greece*. Baltimore, MD.

Coleman, R. G. G. (1999) "Poetic diction, poetic discourse and the poetic register," in *Aspects of the Language of Latin Poetry*, ed. J. N. Adams and R. Mayer. Oxford: 21–96.

Colson, F. H. (1924) *M. Fabii Quintiliani Institutionis Oratoriae Liber I*. Cambridge.

Comparetti, D. (1967) *Virgilio nel Medio Evo*. Florence.

Connolly, J. (2007a) *The State of Speech: Rhetoric and Political Thought in Ancient Rome*. Princeton, NJ.

(2007b) "Virile tongues: rhetoric and masculinity," *A Companion to Roman Rhetoric*, ed. W. Dominik and J. Hall. Malden, MA: 83–97.

Connors, C. (1997) "Field and forum: culture and agriculture in Roman rhetoric," in *Roman Eloquence: Rhetoric in Society and Literature*, ed. W. J. Dominik. New York, NY: 71–89.

(1998) *Petronius the Poet: Verse and Literary Tradition in the* Satyricon. New York, NY.

Courtney, E. (2001) *A Companion to Petronius*. Oxford.

(2003) *The Fragmentary Latin Poets*. Oxford.

Cousin, J. (1967) *Études sur Quintilien*. Amsterdam.

Cowan, R. (2015) "On the weak king according to Vergil: Aeolus, Latinus, and political allegoresis in the *Aeneid*," *Vergilius* 61: 97–124.

Culler, J. D. (1982) *On Deconstruction: Theory and Criticism after Structuralism*. Ithaca, NY.

Curtius, E. R. (1953) *European Literature and the Latin Middle Ages*. New York, NY.

D'Anna, G. (1958) "La tragedia latina arcaica nelle *Metamorfosi*," *Atti del Convegno Internazionale Ovidiano* 2: 217–34.

References

De Man, P. (1979) *Allegories of Reading: Figural Language in Rousseau, Nietzsche, Rilke, and Proust*. New Haven, CT.

(1984) *The Rhetoric of Romanticism*. New York, NY.

Decker, J. de (1913) *Juvenalis Declamans, Étude sur la Rhétorique Declamatoire dans les Satires de Juvénal*. Ghent.

Degl'Innocenti Pierini, R. (2003) "Ritratto di famiglia: Seneca e i suoi nella *Consolatio Ad Helviam*," in *Gli Annei: Una Famiglia nella Storia e nella Cultura di Roma Imperiale*, ed. I. Gualandri and G. Mazzoli. Como: 339–56.

Denniston, J. D. (1952) *Greek Prose Style*. Oxford.

Derrida, J. (1982) *Margins of Philosophy*, trans. A. Bass. Chicago, IL.

Di Gregorio, L. (1975) *Scholia Vetera in Hesiodi Theogoniam*. Milan.

Dinter, M. (2005) "Epic and epigram: minor heroes in Virgil's *Aeneid*," *CQ* 55: 153–69.

Dominik, W. J. (1994) *Speech and Rhetoric in Statius' Thebaid*. Hildesheim.

Douglas, A. E. (1956) "Cicero, Quintilian, and the canon of Ten Attic Orators," *Mnemosyne* 9: 30–40.

Dozier, C. (2012) "Poetry, politics, and pleasure in Quintilian," in *Aesthetic Value in Classical Antiquity*, ed. R. M. Rosen and I. Sluiter. Leiden: 345–62.

Duban, J. M. (1980) "Poets and kings in the *Theogony* invocation," *QUCC* 4: 7–21.

Dugan, J. (2005) *Making a New Man: Ciceronian Self-Fashioning in the Rhetorical Works*. Oxford.

Eagleton, T. (1983) *Literary Theory: An Introduction*. Minneapolis, MN and London.

Earl, D. C. (1961) *The Political Thought of Sallust*. Cambridge.

Edward, W. A. (1996) *Seneca the Elder: Suasoriae*. London and Newburyport, MA.

Edwards, C. (1993) *The Politics of Immorality in Ancient Rome*. Cambridge.

Elliott, J. (2009) "Ennius *Cunctator* and the history of a gerund in the Roman historiographical tradition," *CQ* 59: 532–42.

(2013) *Ennius and the Architecture of the* Annales. Cambridge.

Elmer, D. F. (2013) *The Poetics of Consent: Collective Decision Making and the Iliad*. Baltimore, MD.

Elsner, J. and Meyer, M. (2014) *Art and Rhetoric in Roman Culture*. Cambridge.

Enterline, L. (2012) *Shakespeare's Schoolroom: Rhetoric, Discipline, Emotion*. Philadelphia, PA.

Evans, H. B. (1976) "Ovid's apology for *Ex Ponto* 1–3," *Hermes* 104: 103–12.

Fairweather, J. (1981) *Seneca the Elder*. Cambridge.

Fantham, E. (1972) *Comparative Studies in Republican Latin Imagery*. Toronto, ON.

(1978) "Imitation and decline: rhetorical theory and practice in the first century after Christ," *CP* 73: 102–16.

(1985) "Caesar and the mutiny: Lucan's reshaping of the historical tradition in *De Bello Civili* 5. 237–373," *CP* 80: 119–31.

(1992) "Lucan's Medusa-excursus: its design and purpose," *MD* 29: 95–119.

(1995) "The concept of nature and human nature in Quintilian's psychology and theory of instruction," *Rhetorica* 13: 125–36.

(1996) *Roman Literary Culture: From Cicero to Apuleius*. Baltimore, MD.

(1997) "The contexts and occasions of Roman public rhetoric," in *Roman Eloquence: Rhetoric in Society and Literature*, ed. W. J. Dominik. London and New York, NY: 111–28.

(1999) "Fighting words: Turnus at bay in the Latin council (*Aen.* 11.234–466)," *AJP* 120: 259–80.

(2002) "Orator and/et Actor," in *Greek and Roman Actors: Aspects of an Ancient Profession*, ed. P. Easterling and E. Hall. Cambridge: 362–76.

(2010) "Caesar's voice and Caesarian voices," in *Lucan's Bellum ciuile: Between Epic Tradition and Aesthetic Innovation*, ed. N. Hömke and C. Reitz. Berlin and New York, NY: 53–70.

Farrell, J. (1997) "Towards a rhetoric of (Roman?) epic," in *Roman Eloquence: Rhetoric in Society and Literature*, ed. W. J. Dominik. London and New York, NY: 131–46.

(2002) "Greek lives and Roman careers in the classical *vita* tradition," in *European Literary Careers: The Author from Antiquity to the Renaissance*, ed. P. Cheney and F. de Armas. Toronto, ON: 24–46.

(2008) "Servius and the Homeric scholia," in *Servio: Stratificazioni Esegetiche e Modelli Culturali/Servius: Exegetical Stratifications and Cultural Models*, ed. S. Casali and F. Stok. Brussels: 112–31.

Feeney, D. (1983) "The taciturnity of Aeneas," *CQ* 33: 204–19.

(1995) "Criticism ancient and modern," in *Ethics and Rhetoric: Classical Essays for Donald Russell on his Seventy-fifth Birthday*, ed. D. Innes, H. Hine and C. Pelling. Oxford and New York, NY: 301–12.

(2014) "First similes in epic," *TAPA* 144: 189–228.

Feldherr, A. (2013) "Free spirits: Sallust and the citation of Catiline," *AJP* 134: 49–66.

Ferguson, M. W. (1983) *Trials of Desire: Renaissance Defenses of Poetry*. New Haven, CT.

Fish, S. E. (1980) *Is There a Text in This Class? The Authority of Interpretive Communities*. Cambridge, MA.

Fletcher, R. (2016) "Philosophy in the expanded field: Ciceronian dialogue in Pollio's letters from Spain (*Fam.* 10.31–33)," *Arethusa* 49, 549–73.

Flower, H. (1996) *Ancestor Masks and Aristocratic Power in Roman Culture*. Oxford.

Ford, A. (2002) *The Origins of Criticism: Literary Culture and Poetic Theory in Classical Greece*. Princeton, NJ.

Formisano, M. (2007) "Towards an aesthetic paradigm of late antiquity," *Antiquité Tardive* 15: 277–84.

Fox, M. (2007) "Rhetoric and literature at Rome," in *A Companion to Roman Rhetoric*, ed. W. J. Dominik and J. Hall. Malden, MA: 369–81.

Fränkel, H. (1945) *Ovid: A Poet between Two Worlds*. Berkeley, CA.

Fratantuono, L. and Smith, R. A. (2015) Aeneid *5: Text, Translation and Commentary*. Boston, MA and Leiden.

Freudenburg, K. (2013) "The afterlife of Varro in Horace's *Sermones*," in *Generic Interfaces in Latin Literature: Encounters, Interactions and Transformations*, ed. T. D. Papanghelis, S. J. Harrison and S. Frangoulidis. Berlin and Boston, MA: 297–336.

(2018) "Epic anger, and the state of the (Roman) soul in Virgil's first simile," in *Augustan Poetry: New Trends and Revaluations*, ed. P. Martins. São Paulo: 287–311.

Frye, N. (2000) *Anatomy of Criticism: Four Essays*, rev. ed. Princeton, NJ.

Fucecchi, M. (1999) "La vigilia di Canne nei *Punica* e un contributo allo studio dei rapporti fra Silio Italico e Lucano," in *Interpretare Lucano: Miscellanea di Studi*, ed. P. Esposito and L. Nicastri. Naples: 305–42.

Gaertner, J. F. (2005) *Epistulae Ex Ponto, Book I*. Oxford.

Galasso, L. (1995) *P. Ovidii Nasonis Epistularum Ex Ponto Liber II*. Florence.

Galinsky, K. (1996) *Augustan Culture: An Interpretive Introduction*. Princeton, NJ.

Gebhard, V. (1934) "Thersites," *RE* 5:2455–71.

Genette, G. (1982) *Figures of Literary Discourse*. New York, NY.

Gibson, R. K. (2003) Ovid: *Ars Amatoria*. Cambridge.

Gleason, M. W. (1995) *Making Men: Sophists and Self-Presentation in Ancient Rome*. Princeton, NJ.

Godzich, W. and Kittay, J. (1987) *The Emergence of Prose: An Essay in Prosaics*. Minneapolis, MN.

Goebel, G. H. (1981) "Rhetorical and poetical thinking in Lucan's harangues (7.250–382)," *TAPA* 111: 79–94.

Goldberg, S. M. (1999) "Appreciating Aper: the defence of modernity in Tacitus' *Dialogus de Oratoribus*," *CQ* 49: 224–37.

Goldhill, S. (1991) *The Poet's Voice: Essays on Poetics and Greek Literature*. Cambridge.

(1994) "The failure of exemplarity," in *Modern Critical Theory and Classical Literature*, ed. I. de Jong and J. P. Sullivan. Boston, MA and Leiden: 51–73.

(2002) *The Invention of Prose*. Oxford.

(2009) Review of R. Webb, *Ekphrasis, Imagination and Persuasion in Ancient Rhetorical Theory and Practice, Bryn Mawr Classical Review 2009.10.03* [online], http://bmcr.brynmawr.edu/2009/2009-10-03.html.

Goldlust, B. (2010) *Rhétorique et Poétique de Macrobe dans les* Saturnales. Turnhout.

Gómez-Pantoja, J. (1987) "Another rhetor from Calagurris," *Faventia* 9: 79–84.

Görler, W. (1987) "*Obtrectatores*," in *Enciclopedia Virgiliana III*. Rome: 807–13.

Graff, R. (2005) "Prose versus poetry in early Greek theories of style," *Rhetorica* 23: 303–35.

Granatelli, R. (1994) "Le definizioni di figura in Quintiliano *Inst.* ix.1.10–14 e il loro rapporto con la grammatica e le *controversiae figuratae*," *Rhetorica* 12: 383–425.

Grant, M. A. and Fiske, G. C. (1924) "Cicero's *Orator* and Horace's *Ars Poetica*," *HSCP* 35: 1–74.

Griffin, M. (1972) "The Elder Seneca and Spain," *JRS* 62: 1–19.

Grillo, L. (2015) *Cicero's* De Provinciis Consularibus Oratio. New York, NY.

Gruen, E. S. (1990) *Studies in Greek Culture and Roman Policy*. Leiden and New York, NY.

Gudeman, A. (1914) *P. Cornelii Taciti* Dialogus de Oratoribus, 2 vols. Leipzig and Berlin.

Gunderson, E. (2000) *Staging Masculinity: The Rhetoric of Performance in the Roman World*. Ann Arbor, MI.

  (2003) *Declamation, Paternity, and Roman Identity: Authority and the Rhetorical Self*. Cambridge.

  (2009) "The rhetoric of rhetorical theory," in *The Cambridge Companion to Ancient Rhetoric*, ed. E. Gunderson. Cambridge: 109–25.

Habinek, T. (1998) "Singing, speaking, making, writing: classical alternatives to literature and literary studies," *Stanford Humanities Review* 6: 65–75.

Halliwell, S. (1986) *Aristotle's* Poetics. London.

Hammer, D. (2002) *The* Iliad *as Politics: The Performance of Political Thought*. Norman, OK.

Hardie, A. (1983) *Statius and the* Silvae*: Poets, Patrons, and Epideixis in the Graeco-Roman World*. Liverpool.

  (2002) "Poetry and politics at the Games of Domitian," in *Flavian Rome: Culture, Image and Text*, ed. A. Boyle and W. Dominik. Leiden and Boston, MA: 125–47.

Hardie, P. (1986) *Virgil's* Aeneid*: Cosmos and Imperium*. Oxford.

  (1993) *The Epic Successors of Virgil: A Study in the Dynamics of a Tradition*. Cambridge.

  (1994) *Aeneid. Book IX*. Cambridge.

  (2004) *Ovidio:* Metamorfosi. *Volume VI: Libri XIII–XV*. Milan.

  (2007) "Warring words: Ovid's 'Contest for the Arms of Achilles' (Met. 13.1–398)," in *Contests and Rewards in the Homeric Epics (Proceedings of the 10th International Symposium on the Odyssey, Centre for Odyssean Studies)*, ed. M. Paizi-Apostopolou, A. Rengakos and C. Tsagalis. Ithaca, NY: 389–98.

  (2012) *Rumour and Renown: Representations of Fama in Western Literature*. Cambridge.

  (2016) *The Last Trojan Hero: A Cultural History of Virgil's* Aeneid. London and New York, NY.

Harrison, S. J. (1988) "Vergil on kingship: the first simile of the *Aeneid*," *Cambridge Classical Journal* 34, 55–9.

  (1997) *Vergil*, Aeneid *10*. Oxford.

  (2007) *Generic Enrichment in Vergil and Horace*. Oxford.

Haverling, G. (1990) "Symmachus and the *genus pingue et floridum* in Macr. *Sat.* 5.1.7," *Eranos* 88: 107–20.

Heath, M. (2003) "Pseudo-Dionysius *Art of Rhetoric* 8–11: figured speech, declamation, and criticism," *AJP* 124: 81–105.

Heinze, R. (1993) *Virgil's Epic Technique*. Berkeley, CA.

Helzle, M. (1994) "Indocilis Privata Loqui: the characterization of Lucan's Caesar," *Symbolae Osloenses* 69: 121–36.

  (1996) *Der Stil ist der Mensch: Redner und Reden im römischen Epos*. Stuttgart.

Henderson, J. (1998a) *Fighting for Rome: Poets and Caesars, History, and Civil War.* Cambridge.

(1998b) *A Roman Life: Rutilius Gallicus on Paper and in Stone.* Exeter.

Hendrickson, G. L. (1904) "The peripatetic mean of style and the three stylistic characters," *AJP* 25: 125–46.

(1905) "The origin and meaning of the ancient characters of style," *AJP* 26: 249–376.

Herrick, M. (1948) "The place of rhetoric in poetic theory," *Quarterly Journal of Speech* 34: 1–22.

Hershkowitz, D. (1998) *The Madness of Epic: Reading Insanity from Homer to Statius.* Oxford.

Hesk, J. (2000) *Deception and Democracy in Classical Athens.* Cambridge.

Higham, T. F. (1958) "Ovid and rhetoric," in *Ovidiana: recherches sur Ovide*, ed. N. Herescu. Paris: 32–48.

Highet, G. (1972) *The Speeches in Vergil's Aeneid.* Princeton, NJ.

Hine, H. (1987) "Aeneas and the arts (Vergil, *Aeneid* 6.847–50)," in *Homo Viator: Classical Essays for John Bramble*, ed. M. Whitby, P. Hardie and M. Whitby. Bristol: 173–83.

(2005) "Poetic influence on prose: the case of the younger Seneca," in *Aspects of the Language of Latin Prose*, ed. M. Lapidge and J. N. Adams. Oxford: 211–37.

Hölkeskamp, K.-J. (1997) "Agorai bei Homer," in *Volk und Verfassung im Vorhellenistischen Griechenland*, ed. W. Eder and K-J. Hölkeskamp. Stuttgart: 1–19.

(2004) *Senatus Populusque Romanus. Die politische Kultur der Republik: Dimensionen und Deutungen.* Stuttgart.

Hollis, A. S. (1970) *Ovid:* Metamorphoses, *Book 8.* Oxford.

Hopkinson, N. (2000) Metamorphoses. *Book XIII.* Cambridge.

Hornsby, R. A. (1970) *Patterns of Action in the* Aeneid: *An Interpretation of Vergil's Epic Similes.* Iowa City, IA.

Horsfall, N. (1979) "Some problems in the Aeneas legend," *CQ* 29: 372–90.

(1995) "Style, language and meter," in *A Companion to the Study of Virgil*, ed. N. Horsfall. *Mnemosyne Suppl.* 151. Leiden and New York, NY: 217–48.

(2000) *Virgil*, Aeneid *7: A Commentary.* Leiden and Boston, MA.

(2003) *Virgil*, Aeneid *11: A Commentary.* Leiden and Boston, MA.

(2008) *Virgil*, Aeneid *2: A Commentary.* Leiden and Boston, MA.

(2009) "Dictys's Ephemeris and the parody of scholarship," *Illinois Classical Studies*, 33–34: 41–63.

(2013a) "Poets and poetry in Virgil's underworld," *Vergilius* 59: 23–8.

(2013b) *Virgil*, Aeneid *6: A Commentary.* Berlin.

Howell, W. S. (1975) *Poetics, Rhetoric, and Logic: Studies in the Basic Disciplines of Criticism.* Ithaca, NY.

Hübner, U. (1972) "Hypallage in Lucans *Pharsalia*," *Hermes* 100: 577–600.

(1975) "Studien zur Pointentechnik in Lucans *Pharsalia*," *Hermes* 103: 200–11.

252 *References*

Huelsenbeck, B. (2011) "Seneca *Contr.* 2.2.8 and 2.2.1: the rhetor Arellius Fuscus and Latin literary history," *MD* 66: 175–94.

(2018) *Figures in the Shadows: Identities in Artistic Prose from the Anthology of the Elder Seneca.* Berlin.

Hunter, R. L. (2009) *Critical Moments in Classical Literature: Studies in the Ancient View of Literature and Its Uses.* Cambridge.

Hutchinson, G. O. (2008) *Talking Books: Readings in Hellenistic and Roman Books of Poetry.* Oxford.

(2009) "Read the instructions: didactic poetry and didactic prose," *CQ* 59: 196–211.

Huxley, H. (1952) "Storm and shipwreck in Roman literature," *G&R* 21: 117–24.

Huyck, J. (1991) "A commentary on Ovid's *Armorum Iudicium, Metamorphoses* 12.612–13.398." PhD dissertation, Harvard University.

Ingleheart, J. (2006) "Ovid, *Tristia* 1.2: high drama on the high seas," *G&R* 53: 73–91.

(2010) *A Commentary on Ovid,* Tristia, *Book 2.* Oxford.

Innes, D. (1985) "Theophrastus and the theory of style," in *Theophrastus of Eresus. On His Life and Work,* ed. W. Fortenbaugh. New Brunswick, NJ: 251–67.

(1988) "Cicero on tropes," *Rhetorica* 6: 307–25.

(1989) "Augustan critics," *The Cambridge History of Literary Criticism* 1: 245–73.

(1994) "Period and colon: theory and example in Demetrius and Longinus," in *Peripatetic Rhetoric after Aristotle,* ed. W. Fortenbaugh and D. Mirhady. New Brunswick, NJ: 36–53.

(2002) "Longinus and Caecilius: models of the sublime," *Mnemosyne* 55: 259–84.

(2011) "The *Panegyricus* and rhetorical theory," in *Pliny's Praise: The Panegyricus in the Roman World,* ed. P. Roche. Cambridge: 67–84.

Jacobson, H. (1974) *Ovid's Heroides.* Princeton, NJ.

Jakobson, R. (1960) "Linguistics and poetics," in *Style in Language,* ed. T. Sebeok. Cambridge, MA: 350–77.

Jal, P. (1967) *Florus: Oeuvres.* Paris.

Janko, R. (2000) *Philodemus: On Poems, Book One.* Oxford.

Janson, T. (1964) *Latin Prose Prefaces: Studies in Literary Conventions.* Stockholm.

Javitch, D. (1978) *Poetry and Courtliness in Renaissance England.* Princeton, NJ.

Jocelyn, H. (1964) "Ancient scholarship and Virgil's use of republican Latin poetry. I," *CQ* 14: 280–95.

Joly, D. (1979) "Rhétorique et poésie d'après l'*Institution Oratoire*," in *Colloque sur la Rhétorique: Calliope I,* ed. R. Chevallier. Paris: 101–13.

Jones, H. (2001) *Strabo, Geography,* 8 vols. Cambridge, MA.

Jonge, C. (2008) *Between Grammar and Rhetoric: Dionysius of Halicarnassus on Language, Linguistics and Literature.* Leiden.

Joseph, M. (1947) *Shakespeare's Use of the Arts of Language.* New York, NY.

Jullien, E. (1885) *Les Professeurs de Littérature dans L'Ancienne Rome et leur Enseignement depuis l'Origine jusqu'à la Mort d'Auguste.* Paris.

References

Kallendorf, C. (1989) *In Praise of Aeneas: Virgil and Epideictic Rhetoric in the Early Italian Renaissance*. Oxford.

Kant, E. (1911) *The Critique of Aesthetic Judgment*, trans. J. Creed Meredith. Oxford.

Kaster, R. (1980) "Macrobius and Servius: Verecundia and the grammarian's function," *HSCP* 84: 220–62.

(1988) *Guardians of Language: The Grammarian and Society in Late Antiquity*. Berkeley, CA.

(1995) *Suetonius*, De Grammaticis et Rhetoribus. Oxford.

(2011a) "Honor culture, praise, and Servius' *Aeneid*," *Reception and the Classics: An Interdisciplinary Approach to the Classical Tradition*, ed. W. Brockliss, A. Haimson Lushkov and K. Wasdin. Cambridge: 45–56.

(2011b) *Macrobius*, Saturnalia, 3 vols. Cambridge, MA.

Keaney, J. J. and Lamberton, R. (1996) *Essay on the Life and Poetry of Homer*. Atlanta, GA.

Keay, S. J. (1988) *Roman Spain*. Berkeley, CA and London.

Keith, A. M. (2000) *Engendering Rome: Women in Latin Epic*. Cambridge.

Kennedy, G. (1957) "The ancient dispute over rhetoric in Homer," *AJP* 78: 23–35.

(1972) *The Art of Rhetoric in the Roman World, 300 B.C.–A.D. 300*. Princeton, NJ.

(1978) "Encolpius and Agamemnon in Petronius," *AJP* 99: 171–8.

Kenney, E. J. (2002) "Ovid's language and style," in *Brill's Companion to Ovid*, ed. B. W. Boyd. Leiden: 27–89.

Kenney, E. J. and Clausen, W. V. (1982) *The Cambridge History of Classical Literature*, Vol. 2: *Latin Literature*. Cambridge.

Kerferd, G. B. (1981) *The Sophistic Movement*. Cambridge.

Kirby, J. T. (1997) "Aristotle on metaphor," *AJP* 118: 517–54.

Kirk, G. S. (1985) *The Iliad: A Commentary*, vol. 1: *Books 1–4*. Cambridge.

Knauer, G. (1964) *Die Aeneis und Homer; Studien zur poetischen Technik Vergils, mit Listen der Homerzitate in der* Aeneis. Göttingen.

Kroll, W. (1964) *M. Tulii Ciceronis* Orator. Zurich and Berlin.

La Penna, A. (1976) "Fra Tersite e Drance. note sulla fortuna di un personaggio virgiliano," in *Présence de Virgile*, ed. R. Chevalier. Paris: 347–65.

Laird, A. (1999) *Powers of Expression, Expressions of Power: Speech Presentation and Latin Literature*. Oxford.

Lanham, R. A. (1974) *Style: an Anti-Textbook*. New Haven, CT.

(1991) *A Handlist of Rhetorical Terms: A Guide for Students of English Literature*, 2nd ed. Berkeley, CA.

Lapidge, M. (1979) "Lucan's imagery of cosmic dissolution," *Hermes* 107: 344–70.

Lausberg, H. (1998) *Handbook of Literary Rhetoric: A Foundation for Literary Study*, trans. M. T. Bliss, A. Jansen and D. E. Orton and ed. D. E. Orton and R. Dean Anderson. Boston, MA and Leiden.

Leeman, A. D. (1963) Orationis Ratio: *The Stylistic Theories and Practice of the Roman Orators, Historians and Philosophers*. Amsterdam.

Lehnert, G. (1896) *De scholiis ad Homerum rhetoricis*. Leipzig.

References

Leigh, M. (1997) *Lucan: Spectacle and Engagement*. Oxford.
  (2004) "The *Pro Caelio* and comedy," *CP* 99: 300–35.
Levene, D. S. (2010) *Livy on the Hannibalic War*. Oxford.
Littlewood, R. J. (2011) *A Commentary on Silius Italicus' Punica 7*. Oxford.
Lowrie, M. (2009) *Writing, Performance, and Authority in Augustan Rome*. Oxford.
Luraghi, N. (2003) "Dionysios von Halikarnassos zwischen Griechen und Römern," in *Formen römischer Geschichtsschreibung von den Anfängen bis Livius*, ed. U. Eigler, U. Gotter, N. Luraghi and U. Walter. Darmstadt: 268–86.
Lyne, R. (2011) *Shakespeare, Rhetoric and Cognition*. Cambridge.
MacCormack, S. (1998) *The Shadows of Poetry: Vergil in the Mind of Augustine*. Berkeley, CA.
Mackie, H. S. (1996) *Talking Trojan: Speech and Community in the Iliad*. Lanham, MD.
Malcovati, E. (1953) "Lucano e Cicerone," *Athenaeum* 31: 288–97.
Mangoni, C. (1993) *Filodemo: Il quinto libro della* Poetica. Naples.
Manolaraki, E. (2008) "Political and rhetorical seascapes in Pliny's *Panegyricus*," *CP* 103: 374–94.
March, J. R. (1993) "Sophocles' *Ajax*: the death and burial of a hero," *BICS* 38, 1–36.
Marincola, J. (1997) *Authority and Tradition in Ancient Historiography*. Cambridge.
Marinone, N. (1946) *Elio Donato, Macrobio e Servio Commentatori di Vergilio*. Vercelli.
Martin, R. (1984) "Hesiod, Odysseus, and the instruction of princes," *TAPA* 114: 29–48.
  (1989) *The Language of Heroes: Speech and Performance in the* Iliad. Ithaca, NY.
Martindale, C. (1976) "Paradox, hyperbole and literary novelty in Lucan's *De Bello Civili*," *BICS* 23: 45–54.
Masters, J. (1992) *Poetry and Civil War in Lucan's* Bellum Civile. Cambridge.
Mastrorosa, I. (2000) "Similitudini, metafore e lessico militari nella trattatistica retorica latina: Cicerone e Quintiliano," in *Lingue tecniche del greco e del latino III*, ed. S. Sconocchia and L. Toneatto. Bologna: 277–310.
Matthews, M. (2008) *Caesar and the Storm: A Commentary on Lucan,* De Bello Civili, *Book 5, Lines 476–721*. Oxford.
May, J. M. and Wisse, J. (2001) *Cicero:* On the Ideal Orator. New York, NY and Oxford.
Mayer, R. (2001) *Tacitus:* Dialogus de Oratoribus. Cambridge.
Mayor, J. E. B. and Henderson, J. (2007) *Mayor's Juvenal Thirteen Satires*. Bristol.
McGill, S. (2003) "Other Aeneids: rewriting three passages of the *Aeneid* in the *Codex Salmasianus*," *Vergilius* 49: 84–113.
  (2013) *Plagiarism in Latin Literature*. Cambridge.
McNelis, C. (2007) "Grammarians and rhetoricians," in *A Companion to Roman Rhetoric*, ed. W. J. Dominik and J. Hall. Malden, MA: 285–96.
Meijering, R. (1987) *Literary and Rhetorical Theories in Greek Scholia*. Groningen.

References

Milanese, G. (1985) "Ilioneo," in *Enciclopedia Virgiliana II*, Rome: 913–14.

Millar, F. (1998) *The Crowd in Rome in the Late Republic*. Ann Arbor, MI.

Miller, R. (2015) "The Roman Odysseus." PhD dissertation, Harvard University.

Mirmont, H. de (1910) "Les Déclamateurs Espagnols au temps d'Auguste et de Tibère," *Bulletin Hispanique* 12, 1–22.

Montanari, F., Blank, D. L. and Dyck, A. R. (1988) *I Frammenti dei Grammatici Agathokles, Hellanikos, Ptolemaios Epithetes. In Appendice i Grammatici Theophilos, Anaxagoras, Xenon*. Berlin and New York, NY.

Moore, J. L. (1891a) "Servius on the tropes and figures of Vergil," *AJP* 12: 157–92.

(1891b) "Servius on the tropes and figures of Vergil: second paper," *AJP* 12: 267–92.

Morales, H. (1996) "The torturer's apprentice: Parrhasius and the limits of art," in *Art and Text in Roman Culture*, ed. J. Elsner. Cambridge: 182–209.

Moretti, G. (1997) "The poet in court. Judiciary model in literary criticism: the case of Tiberius Claudius Donatus," in *Studi di Retorica oggi in Italia*, ed. A. Pennacini. Rome: 59–71.

Morford, M. P. O. (1967a) *The Poet Lucan: Studies in Rhetorical Epic*. Oxford.

(1967b) "The purpose of Lucan's ninth book," *Latomus* 26: 123–9.

Morstein-Marx, R. (2004) *Mass Oratory and Political Power in the Late Roman Republic*. Cambridge.

Morton Braund, S. (1998) "Praise and protreptic in early imperial panegyric: Cicero, Seneca and Pliny," in *The Propaganda of Power: The Role of Panegyric in Late Antiquity*, ed. M. Whitby. Leiden: 53–76.

(2004) "*Libertas* or *Licentia?* Freedom and criticism in Roman satire," in *Free Speech in Classical Antiquity*, ed. R. M. Rosen and I. Sluiter. Leiden: 409–27.

Morwood, J. (1998) "Virgil's pious man and Menenius Agrippa: a note on *Aeneid* 1. 148–53," *G&R* 45: 195–8.

Most, G. W. (1985) *The Measures of Praise: Structure and Function in Pindar's Second* Pythian *and Seventh* Nemean Odes. Göttingen.

(2006) *Hesiod: Theogony, Works and Days and Testimonia*. Cambridge, MA.

Mouritsen, H. (2001) *Plebs and Politics in the Late Roman Republic*. Cambridge.

(2017) *Politics in the Roman Republic*. Cambridge.

Mynors, R. A. B. (1990) *Georgics*. Oxford.

Nagy, G. (1979) *The Best of the Achaeans: Concepts of the Hero in Archaic Greek Poetry*. Baltimore, MD.

(1990) *Pindar's Homer: The Lyric Possession of an Epic Past*. Baltimore, MD.

Narducci, E. (2003) "Cicerone nella *Pharsalia* di Lucano," in *Aspetti della Fortuna di Cicerone nella Cultura Latina*, ed. E. Narducci. Florence: 78–91.

(2007) "Rhetoric and epic: Vergil's *Aeneid* and Lucan's *Bellum Civile*," in *A Companion to Roman Rhetoric*, ed. W. J. Dominik and J. Hall. Malden, MA: 382–95.

Neuhauser, W. (1958) *Patronus und Orator: eine Geschichte der Begriffe von ihren Anfängen bis in die augusteische Zeit*. Innsbruck.

Nisbet, R. G. (1958) "The *Invectiva in Ciceronem* and *Epistula Secunda* of Pseudo-Sallust," *JRS* 48: 30–2.

References

Nisbet, R. G. M. and Hubbard, M. (1970) *A Commentary on Horace, Odes, Book 1.* Oxford.

(1978) *A Commentary on Horace, Odes, Book 2.* Oxford.

Nisbet, R. G. M. and Rudd, N. (2004) *A Commentary on Horace, Odes 3.* Oxford.

Norden, E. (1898) *Die antike Kunstprosa vom VI. Jahrhundert v. Chr. bis in die Zeit der Renaissance.* Leipzig.

(1905) "Die Composition und Litteraturgattung der Horazischen *Epistula Ad Pisones,*" *Hermes* 40: 481–528.

(1957) *Aeneis Buch VI.* Stuttgart.

Norlin, G. (2000) *Isocrates,* 3 vols. Cambridge, MA.

Norris, C. (1988) *Paul De Man, Deconstruction and the Critique of Aesthetic Ideology.* New York.

North, H. (1952) "The use of poetry in the training of the ancient orator," *Traditio* 8: 1–33.

Nünlist, R. (2009) *The Ancient Critic at Work: Terms and Concepts of Literary Criticism in Greek Scholia.* Cambridge.

Odgers, M. M. (1933) "Quintilian's use of earlier literature," *CP* 28: 182–8.

Olmos, P. (2012) "Euge, Graeculi Nostri! Greek scholars among Latin connoisseurs in Macrobius' *Saturnalia,*" in *Greek Science in the Long Run: Essays on the Greek Scientific Tradition (4th C. BCE–17th C. CE),* ed. P. Olmos. Newcastle-upon-Tyne: 96–126.

Ong, W. J. (1942) "The province of rhetoric and poetic," *The Modern Schoolman* 19: 24–7.

O'Sullivan, N. (1992) *Alcidamas, Aristophanes and the Beginnings of Greek Stylistic Theory.* Stuttgart.

Papaioannou, S. (2007) *Redesigning Achilles: "Recycling" the Epic Cycle in the "Little Iliad": (Ovid, Metamorphoses 12.1–13.622).* Berlin and New York, NY.

Paschalis, M. (1997) *Virgil's Aeneid: Semantic Relations and Proper Names.* Oxford.

Pavlock, B. (2009) *The Image of the Poet in Ovid's Metamorphoses.* Madison, WI.

Peirano, I. (2012) *The Rhetoric of the Roman Fake: Latin Pseudepigrapha in Context.* Cambridge.

(2013) "*Non subripiendi causa sed palam mutuandi*: intertextuality and literary deviancy between law, rhetoric, and literature in roman imperial culture," *AJP* 134: 83–100.

Pellizzari, A. (2003) *Servio. Storia, Cultura e Istituzioni nell'Opera di un Grammatico Tardoantico.* Florence.

Pelttari, A. (2014) *The Space that Remains: Reading Latin Poetry in Late Antiquity.* Ithaca, NY.

Pernot, L. (1993) *La Rhètorique de l'Èloge dans le Monde Grèco-Romain.* Paris.

(2005) *Rhetoric in Antiquity.* Washington, DC.

Peterson, W. (1981) *Quintiliani Institutionis Oratoriae Liber X.* Chicago, IL.

Pinney, G. F. and Hamilton, R. (1982) "Secret Ballot," *American Journal of Archeology* 86: 581–4.

Pirovano, L. (2004) "Tiziano, Calvo ei *Themata* Virgiliani (Servio *ad Aen.* 10.18)," in *Il Dilettoso Monte: Raccolta di Saggi di Filologia e Tradizione Classica,* ed. M. Gioseffi. Milan: 139–66.

References

(2006) *Le* Interpretationes Vergilianae *di Tiberio Claudio Donato: problemi di retorica*. Rome.

(2010) "La *Dictio* 28 di Ennodio. Un'etopea parafrastica," in *Uso, riuso e abuso dei testi classici*, ed. M. Gioseffi. Milan: 15–52.

Plett, H. F. (2004) *Rhetoric and Renaissance Culture*. Berlin and New York, NY.

Pontani, F. (2007) *Scholia Graeca in Odysseam*. Rome.

Porter, J. (2016) *The Sublime in Antiquity*. Cambridge.

Pöschl, V. (1962) *The Art of Vergil: Image and Symbol in the* Aeneid. Ann Arbor, MI.

Puccioni, G. (1985) *Saggi Virgiliani*. Bologna.

Putnam, M. (1992) "Umbro, Nireus and love's threnody," *Vergilius* 38: 12–23.

Quint, D. (2011) "Virgil's double cross: chiasmus and the *Aeneid*," *AJP* 132: 273–300.

Raaflaub, K. (2004) "Aristocracy and freedom of speech in the Greco-Roman world," in *Free Speech in Classical Antiquity*, ed. I Sluiter and R. Rosen. Boston, MA and Leiden: 41–61.

Radermacher, L. (1951) *Artium Scriptores; Reste der voraristotelischen Rhetorik*, Österreichische Akademie der Wissenschaften Philosophisch-Historische Klasse Sitzungsberichte, 227 vol. 3 Abhandlungen. Vienna.

Rawson, E. (1985) *Intellectual Life in the Late Roman Republic*. London.

Rebhorn, W. A. (1995) *The Emperor of Men's Minds: Literature and the Renaissance Discourse of Rhetoric*. Ithaca, NY.

Reinhardt, T. (2006) "Propertius and rhetoric," in *Brills' Companion to Propertius*, ed. H.-C. Günther. Leiden: 199–216.

(2013) "The *Ars Poetica*," in *Brill's Companion to Horace*, ed. H.-C. Günther. Leiden: 499–526.

Reinhardt, T. and Winterbottom, M. (2006) *Institutio Oratoria: Book 2*. Oxford.

Ribbeck, O. (1897) *Scaenicae Romanorum Poesis Fragmenta*, Vol. 1. Leipzig.

Richards, I. A. (2004) *Practical Criticism: A Study of Literary Judgment*, rev. ed. New Brunswick, NJ.

Richards, J. (2008) *Rhetoric*. London and New York, NY.

Richardson, N. J. (1980) "Literary criticism in the exegetical scholia to the *Iliad*: a sketch," *CQ* 30: 265–87.

Richlin, A. (1997) "Gender and rhetoric: producing manhood in the schools," in *Roman Eloquence: Rhetoric in Society and Literature*, ed. W. J. Dominik. New York, NY: 90–110.

Rochette, B. (1997) *Le Latin dans le Monde Grec: Recherches sur la Diffusion de la Langue et des Lettres Latines dans les Provinces Hellénophones de l'Empire Romain*. Brussels.

Romilly, J. d. (1975) *Magic and Rhetoric in Ancient Greece*. Cambridge, MA.

Rosivach, V. J. (1980) "Latinus' genealogy and the palace of Picus (*Aeneid* 7. 45–9, 170–91)," *CQ* 30: 140–52.

Rossi, A. (2004) "Parallel lives: Hannibal and Scipio in Livy's third Decade," *TAPA* 134: 359–81.

Rowe, G. O. (1997) "Style," in *Handbook of Classical Rhetoric in the Hellenistic Period 330 BC–AD*, ed. S. Porter. Leiden and New York, NY: 124–50.

258 *References*

Russell, D. A. (1967) "Rhetoric and criticism," *G&R* 14, 130–44.
(1979) "*De Imitatione*," in *Creative Imitation and Latin Literature*, ed. D. A. West and A. J. Woodman. Cambridge: 1–16.
(1979) "Rhetors at the Wedding," *PCPS* 25: 104–17.
(1981) *Criticism in Antiquity*. London.
(1983) *Greek Declamation*. Cambridge.
(1998) "The panegyrists and their teachers," in *The Propaganda of Power: The Role of Panegyric in Late Antiquity*, ed. M. Whitby. Leiden: 17–52.
(2001a) "Figured speeches: Dionysius *Art of Rhetoric* VIII–IX," in *The Orator in Theory and Action in Greece and Rome*, ed. C. W. Wooten. Leiden: 156–68.
(2001b) *Quintilian, The Orator's Education*, 5 vols. Cambridge, MA.
Russell, D. A. and Wilson, N. G. (1981) *Menander Rhetor*. Oxford.
Russell, D. A. and Winterbottom, M. (ed.) (1972) *Ancient Literary Criticism: The Principal Texts in New Translations*. Oxford.
Rutherford, I. (1992) "Inverting the canon: Hermogenes on literature," *HSCP* 94: 355–78.
(1998) *Canons of Style in the Antonine Age: Idea-Theory in Its Literary Context*. Oxford.
Rutledge, S. H. (2001) *Imperial Inquisitions: Prosecutors and Informants from Tiberius to Domitian*. London and New York, NY.
Rutz, W. (1970) "Lucan und die Rhetorik," in *Lucain*, ed. M. Durry. Geneva: 235–65.
Sandys, J. E. (1979) *M. Tulli Ciceronis ad M. Brutum Orator: A Revised Text*. New York, NY.
Sansone, D. (2012) *Greek Drama and the Invention of Rhetoric*. Malden, MA.
Scaliger, G. C. (1905) *Select Translations from Scaliger's Poetics*, trans. F. M. Padelford. New York.
Schenkeveld, D. M. (1991) "Figures and tropes: a border-case between grammar and rhetoric," in *Rhetorik zwischen den Wissenschaften: Geschichte, System, Praxis als Probleme des "Historischen Wörterbuchs der Rhetorik,"* ed. G. Ueding. Tübingen: 149–60.
Schiappa, E. (1999) *The Beginnings of Rhetorical Theory in Classical Greece*. New Haven, CT.
Schiesaro, A. (2002) "Ovid and the professional discourses of scholarship, religion, rhetoric," in *The Cambridge Companion to Ovid*, ed. P. Hardie. Cambridge: 62–75.
Schlunk, R. (1974) *The Homeric Scholia and the Aeneid: A Study of the Influence of Ancient Homeric Literary Criticism on Vergil*. Ann Arbor, MI.
Schneider, B. (1983) "Die Stellung des zehnten Buches im Gesamtplan der *Institutio Oratoria* des Quintilian," *Wiener Studien* 17: 109–25.
Schofield, M. (1986) "*Euboulia* in the Iliad," *CQ* 36: 6–31.
Sciarrino, E. (2011) *Cato the Censor and the Beginnings of Latin Prose: From Poetic Translation to Elite Transcription*. Columbus, OH.
Seel, O. (1977) *Quintilian oder Die Kunst des Redens und Schweigens*. Stuttgart.
Segal, C. (1987) "Writer as hero: the heroic ethos in Longinus, *On the Sublime*," in *Stemmata: Mélanges de Philologie, d'Histoire et d'Archéologie Grecques offerts à*

References

Jules Labarbe, ed. J. Servais, T. Hackens, B. Servais-Soyez and J. Labarbe. Liège: 207–29.

Severyns, A. (1928) *Le Cycle Épique dans l'École d'Aristarque*. Liège.

Seymour, T. D. (1914) *Life in the Homeric Age*. New York, NY.

Shackleton Bailey, D. R. (1965) *Cicero's Letters to Atticus*. Cambridge.

(2003) *Statius*, Siluae. Cambridge, MA.

Silk, M. S. (1974) *Interaction in Poetic Imagery: With Special Reference to Early Greek Poetry*. London and New York, NY.

(2003) "Metaphor and metonymy: Aristotle, Jakobson, Ricoeur, and others," in *Metaphor, Analogy and the Classical Tradition: Ancient Thought and Modern Revisions*, ed. G. R. Boys-Stones. Oxford: 115–47.

Skutsch, O. (1985) *The Annals of Q. Ennius*. Oxford.

Sluiter, I. (1999) "Commentaries and the didactic tradition," in *Commentaries: Kommentare*, ed. G. W. Most. Göttingen: 173–205.

Solimano, G. (1988) Epistula Didonis ad Aeneam: *Introduzione, Testo, Traduzione e Commento*. Genoa.

Solmsen, F. (1932) "Drei Rekonstruktionen zur antiken Rhetorik und Poetik," *Hermes* 67: 133–54.

(1941) "The Aristotelian tradition in ancient rhetoric," *AJP* 62: 35–50.

(1954) "The gift of speech in Homer and Hesiod," *TAPA* 85: 1–15.

Spence, S. (1988) *Rhetorics of Reason and Desire: Vergil, Augustine, and the Troubadours*. Ithaca, NY.

Spengel, L. (1856) *Rhetores Graeci*, Vol. 3. Leipzig.

Spina, L. (1984) "Tersite a Roma," *Vichiana* 13: 350–63.

Stanford, W. B. (1968) *The Ulysses Theme: A Study in the Adaptability of a Traditional Hero*. Ann Arbor, MI.

Starr, R. J. (1992) "An epic of praise: Tiberius Claudius Donatus and Vergil's *Aeneid*," *CA* 11, 159–74.

Stem, R. (2005) "The first eloquent Stoic: Cicero on Cato the Younger," *CJ* 101, 37–49.

Stoddard, K. (2003) "The programmatic message of the kings and singers passage: Hesiod, *Theogony* 80–103," *TAPA* 133: 1–16.

Stover, T. (2012) *Epic and Empire in Vespasianic Rome: A New Reading of Valerius Flaccus' Argonautica*. Oxford.

Summers, W. C. (1910) *Select Letters of Seneca*. London.

Sussman, L. A. (1977) "Arellius Fuscus and the unity of the Elder Seneca's *Suasoriae*," *Rheinisches Museum für Philologie* 120: 303–23.

(1978) *The Elder Seneca*. Leiden.

Syme, R. (1969) "Pliny the Procurator," *HSCP* 73: 201–36.

(1978) *History in Ovid*. Oxford.

(1982) "The marriage of Rubellius Blandus," *AJP* 103: 62–85.

(1986) *The Augustan Aristocracy*. Oxford.

Taoka, Y. (2011) "Quintilian, Seneca, *imitatio*: re-reading *Institutio Oratoria* 10.1.125–31," *Arethusa* 44: 123–37.

Tarrant, R. (1976) *Agamemnon*. Cambridge.

260 *References*

(1995) "Ovid and the failure of rhetoric," in *Ethics and Rhetoric: Classical Essays for Donald Russell on His Seventy-Fifth Birthday*, ed. D. Innes, H. M. Hine and C. B. R. Pelling. Oxford: 63–74.

(2002) "Chaos in Ovid's *Metamorphoses* and its Neronian influence," *Arethusa* 35: 349–60.

Tartari Chersoni, M. (1988) "*raucus*," in *Enciclopedia Virgiliana IV*. Rome: 406.

Tateo, F. (1960) *Retorica e Poetica fra Medioevo e Rinascimento*. Bari.

Taylor, L. R. (1966) *Roman Voting Assemblies from the Hannibalic War to the Dictatorship of Caesar*. Ann Arbor, MI.

Thomas, R. F. (1982) *Lands and Peoples in Roman Poetry: The Ethnographical Tradition*. Cambridge.

(1988) *Virgil:* Georgics *1–2*. Cambridge.

(2001) *Virgil and the Augustan Reception*. Cambridge and New York, NY.

Thompson, L. and Bruere, R. T. (1968) "Lucan's use of Virgilian reminiscence," *CP* 63: 1–21.

(1970) "The Virgilian background of Lucan's Fourth Book," *CP* 65: 152–72.

Todorov, T. (1982) *Theories of the Symbol*. Ithaca, NY.

Too, Y. L. (1995) *The Rhetoric of Identity in Isocrates: Text, Power, Pedagogy*. Cambridge.

Torres-Murciano, A. R. (2014) "Mauors in Lingua. Hombres de Acción y hombres de Palabras en la épica romana," *Cuadernos de Filología Clásica. Estudios Latinos* 34: 195–223.

Torzi, I. (2000) Ratio et Usus: *Dibattiti Antichi sulla Dottrina delle Figure*. Milan.

Treggiari, S. (1969) *Roman Freedmen during the Late Republic*. Oxford.

Van den Berg, C. (2014) *The World of Tacitus'* Dialogus de Oratoribus: *Aesthetics and Empire in Ancient Rome*. Cambridge.

Van Der Blom, H. (2011) "Pompey in the *Contio*," *CQ* 61: 553–73.

Van Hook, L. (1905) *The Metaphorical Terminology of Greek Rhetoric and Literary Criticism*. Chicago, IL.

Varwig, F. R. (1976) *Der rhetorische Naturbegriff bei Quintilian: Studien zu einem Argumentationstopos in der rhetorischen Bildung der Antike*. Heidelberg.

Verweij, M. (2015) "Florus and his 'Vergilius orator an poeta': the Brussels manuscript revisited", WS 128, 83–105.

Vickers, B. (1968) *The Artistry of Shakespeare's Prose*. London.

(ed.) (1982) *Rhetoric Revalued: Papers from the International Society for the History of Rhetoric*. Binghamton, NY.

(1983) "Epideictic and epic in the Renaissance," *New Literary History* 14: 497–537.

(1988a) *In Defence of Rhetoric*. Oxford.

(1988b) "Rhetoric and poetics," in *The Cambridge History of Renaissance Philosophy*, ed. C. B. Schmitt, Q. Skinner and E. Kessler. Cambridge: 715–45.

Vietti, M. (1979) "Pathos virgiliano e retorica in Macrobio," *Atti della Accademia delle Scienze di Torino. Classe di Scienze Morali, Storiche e Filologiche* 113: 219–43.

Walker, J. (2000) *Rhetoric and Poetics in Antiquity*. Oxford and New York, NY.

Wallace-Hadrill, A. (1998) "To be Roman go Greek: thoughts on Hellenization at Rome," *Bulletin of the Institute of Classical Studies. Supplement* 71: 79–91.

Ward, J. O. (1995) "Quintilian and the rhetorical revolution of the Middle Ages," *Rhetorica* 13: 231–84.

Wardy, R. (1996) *The Birth of Rhetoric: Gorgias, Plato, and their Successors.* London and New York, NY.

Warmington, E. H. (1982) *Remains of Old Latin: Livius Andronicus, Naevius, Pacuvius and Accius.* Cambridge, MA.

Weaire, G. (2005) "Dionysius of Halicarnassus' professional situation and the *De Thucydide*," *Phoenix* 59: 246–66.

Webb, R. (1997) "Poetry and rhetoric," in *Handbook of Classical Rhetoric in the Hellenistic Period*, ed. S. Porter. Boston: 339–69.

Weinberg, B. (1961) *A History of Literary Criticism in the Italian Renaissance.* Chicago.

Wellbery, D. E. (2000) "The transformation of rhetoric: Romanticism," in *Cambridge History of Literary Criticism, vol. 5: Romanticism*, ed. M. Brown. Cambridge: 185–202.

West, M. L. (1965) "Tryphon *De Tropis*," *CQ* 15: 230–48.

(1966) *Theogony.* Oxford.

(2003) *Greek Epic Fragments from the Seventh to the Fifth Centuries BC.* Cambridge, MA.

(2013) *The Epic Cycle: A Commentary on the Lost Troy Epics.* Oxford.

Wheeler, S. (2002) "Lucan's reception of Ovid's *Metamorphoses*," *Arethusa* 35: 361–80.

White, P. (1977) "Horace *A.P.* 128–30: the intent of the wording," *CQ* 27: 191–201.

(2010) *Cicero in Letters: Epistolary Relations of the Late Republic.* New York, NY.

Whitmarsh, T. (2001) *Greek Literature and the Roman Empire: The Politics of Imitation.* Oxford.

Whittington, L. (2016) *Renaissance Suppliants: Poetry, Antiquity, Reconciliation.* Oxford.

Wick, C. (2004) *M. Annaeus Lucanus, Bellum Civile, Liber IX.* Munich.

Williams, G. W. (1980) *Figures of Thought in Roman Poetry.* New Haven, CT.

Winterbottom, M. (1964) "Quintilian and the *Vir Bonus*," *JRS* 54: 90–7.

(1974) *The Elder Seneca, Declamations*, 2 vols. Cambridge, MA.

(1979) "Review of Lewis A. Sussman: The Elder Seneca," *CR* 29: 231–2.

(1982) "Schoolroom and courtroom," in *Rhetoric Revalued: Papers from the International Society for the History of Rhetoric*, ed. B. Vickers. Binghamton, NY: 59–70.

(1983) "Quintilian and declamation," in *Hommages à Jean Cousin: Rencontres avec l' Antiquité Classique*, Paris: 225–35.

Wiseman, T. P. (1979) *Clio's Cosmetics: Three Studies in Greco-Roman Literature.* Leicester.

Woodman, A. J. (1988) *Rhetoric in Classical Historiography: Four Studies.* London.

Woods, M. (2009) "The classroom as courtroom: Cicero's attributes of persons and the interpretation of classical literary characters in the Renaissance,"

Ciceroniana: Atti del XIII Colloquium Tullianum, Milano 27–29 marzo 2008. Rome: 203–15.

Woolf, G. (2011) *Tales of the Barbarians: Ethnography and Empire in the Roman West.* Malden, MA.

Wooten,C. (1987) *Hermogenes,* On Types of Style. Chapel Hill, NC.

Worman, N. (1999) "Odysseus Panourgos: the liar's style in oratory and tragedy," *Helios* 26: 35–68.

(2002). *The Cast of Character: Style in Greek Literature.* Austin, TX.

Yeats, W. B. (1918) *Per Amica Silentia Lunae.* London.

Zaffagno, E. (1988) *"fulgor/fulgeo/fulmen,"* in *Enciclopedia Virgiliana II.* Rome: 605–6.

Zetzel, J. (1999) *Cicero:* On the Commonwealth *and* On the laws. Cambridge.

Ziolkowski, J. M. and Putnam, M. C. J. (2008) *The Virgilian Tradition: The First Fifteen Hundred Years.* New Haven, CT.

Zundel, E. (1981) *Lehrstil und rhetorischer Stil in Quintilians Institutio Oratoria.* Frankfurt Main.

Index Locorum

GREEK

Aeschylus
  Hoplōn Krisis
    fr. 175 Radt, 206n
    fr. 176 Radt, 200n

Alcidamas
  On the Sophists
    10–11, 32

Antisthenes
  Logos of Ajax (Caizzi)
    1, 200
    1.1, 201
    7.8, 200
    8, 200

Apollonius Rhodius
  Argonautica
    4.1237–49, 170n
    4.1264–71, 170n

Appian
  Hannibalike
    18, 144n

Aristophanes
  Acharnians
    530–31, 151
  Frogs
    909–10, 154n
    961–62, 154n
    1029–36, 24
    1032, 24n

Aristotle
  Nicomachean Ethics
    1113a, 178
  Poetics
    1415b1–11, 93n

    1415a36-b5, 92n
    1448b24–27, 34n, 232n
    1457b1-13, 37
    1457b16-33, 98n
    1459a5-8, 37
    1459a9-13, 98
    1460b11-13, 91n
  Politics
    1285a, 178
  Rhetoric
    1.1.1355b10–11, 5
    1.3, 33n
    1.9.1367b35-1368a7, 34n
    2.24.1402a23, 213
    3.1.1404a20–21, 19n
    3.1.1404a24–34, 35
    3.1.1404a34f., 98n
    3.2.1404b31–3, 98
    3.2.1404b34, 98
    3.2.1405b10-11, 98
    3.3.1406b, 98
    3.8.1408b21–22, 93
    3.8.1408b28–31, 93
    3.10.1411a, 98
    3.11.1412a, 98n
    3.12, 33n

Callimachus
  Epigrammata
    28.4, 207n

Critias
  B25.1–4 (Diels-Kranz), 26n

Demetrius
  De elocutione
    36, 227n
    37, 153n, 153
    59–67, 38n
    78, 99n

263

Index Locorum

Demetrius (cont.)
78–90, 38n
83–84, 100n
113, 207n
116, 93n
181, 41n

Democritus
B5.8.1 (Diels-Kranz),
26n

Dio Cassius
41.27–35, 162n
42.13, 169n
55.4, 83n
56.27, 83n
58.18, 62n

Dio Chrysostomus
Orationes
18, 102n

Dionysius of Halicarnassus
De compositione verborum
24, 107n
25, 93n
25.8–10, 41n
De Demosthene
1, 140n
5, 33n
20, 33n

Dionysius Thrax
Techne Grammatike
1.1.5, 37n, 224n

Ps.Dionysius
Ars Rhetorica
9, 39n, 224n
9.8, 205n
10.17, 64n

Euphorion
fr. 40 (Powell), 208n

Euripides
Hecuba
816, 182n

Gorgias
Helena
8–14, 30, 154n
9–14, 30
Palamedes
34–35, 201n

Hermogenes of Tarsus
On Types of Style
1.6.28–30, 151
1.6.40–46,
152n
2.10.231–80, 59n
2.10.231–3, 34
2.10.266–72, 34n
2.10.297–9, 34
2.10.330–2, 34n

Herodotus
Histories
7.16, 146n

Ps.Herodotus
Vita Homeri
25, 141n

Hesiod
Theogony
83–84, 149
84–92, 148

Homer
Iliad
1.57, 186
1.225, 139
1.247–49, 142
1.248, 142
1.249, 140
1.258, 176
1.365ff., 138
1.490–91, 176
2.87–91, 170
2.92–93, 186n
2.110–24, 192
2.142–49, 197
2.144–49, 146,
149
2.196–97, 178
2.202, 193
2.212, 175
2.212–14, 193n
2.213, 193
2.220, 192
2.246, 193
2.272, 37
2.391, 178
2.445–87, 197
2.459–66, 198
2.485ff, 115
2.547, 178
3.134–35, 188
3.151–52, 199n

3.182, 139
3.214, 175
3.215, 140
3.216–24, 204
3.221, 130
3.222, 152, 175,
  206n
3.223, 140
7.345–80, 195
8.94, 195n
8.494, 188
9.9–12, 190n
9.10–11, 190–191n
9.12, 191n
9.53–54, 176
9.442–43, 139, 141
9.443, 175
10.194–95, 188
10.302, 188
11.83, 125n
12.277–90, 206n
11.434–88, 208
14.484–90, 184n
15.82–93, 207
18.243–313, 195
18.246–48, 188n
18.248–49, 196
18.254–83, 195
18.312, 196
18.313, 196
18.498, 139
21.195–97, 107
Odyssey
  1.2.4–5, 40
  4.72, 125n
  8.12, 187
  8.46–47, 187n
  8.167–77, 149
  8.173, 140, 149n
  10.4–7, 151
  11.368, 141n
  11.546–47, 202
  15.624ff., 151
  21.405–9, 141n,
    201n

Homerica (from West, *Greek
  Epic Fragments*)
  Aethiopis
    Argumentum 1, 203
    Argumentum 4,
      203
  Little Iliad
    Argumentum 1
    fr. 2, 202

Libanius
  Declamationes
    3, 140n
    4, 140n

Isocrates
  Antidosis
    46–47, 30–1
    192, 32
    209–214, 27n
  Contra sophistas
    15, 33
  Evagoras
    5, 34n
    8–10, 31
    9–10, 37n
    9–11, 32
  To Nicocles
    12–14, 27n
    42–49, 31n
  Panathenaicus
    2, 31n

Longinus
  On the Sublime
    9.3, 33n
    12, 100
    13.3–4, 41–42n
    15.2, 42
    16–29, 38n
    32, 100n
    36.4, 166n

Menander Rhetor
  On Epideictic
    430.12–28, 29
    434.11, 29

Philodemus
  On Poems
    1, 200 (Janko), 41n
    1, 195.8 (Janko), 207n
    5 col. 14.5–11 (Mangoni), 25n

Phoebamon
  De figuris
    130.1, 38

Pindar
  Nemeans
    7.20–24, 201
    7.20–30, 199n
    8.21–34, 199n
    8.24–25, 200
    8.27–28, 202

266   *Index Locorum*

Plato
Gorgias
501e, 32
502c12, 180
502d, 32
502e, 32
Hippias Minor
365b3–5, 200n
Laws
1.649a9, 179n
7.801ff., 34n
7.817c, 32n
Phaedrus
257a, 42n
Protagoras
316d, 27
325, 34n
Respublica
3.413d, 154n
10.602d, 154n
10.607, 34n

Plutarch
Cat. Minor
44, 146n
56, 169n
Cicero
4, 49n
Theseus
25, 178
Timoleon
13, 53n

Ps.Plutarch
*Life and Poetry of
Homer*
15–17, 37n
15–71, 224n
161, 139, 220,
227n
168, 179n
169–70, 139,
220
170, 175n
172, 140n,
227n
176, 178
177, 178
178, 178
182, 178, 179
182–83, 178

Polybius
6.54.2, 187n
11.29.10–11, 146n

Porphyry
Homeric questions
θ 2.5, 197n

Scholia
Schol. Hes. Theog
91b, 149
93, 150
Scholia in Hom. Il.
Schol. A in Il.
9.33a, 179n
Schol. Ab in Il.
1.249, 142
Schol. AbT in Il.
2.283, 227n
2.455–56, 197n
Schol. b in Il.
3.222a1, 152
Schol. bT in Il.
1.366, 138
2.336–59, 179n
9.443, 140, 175n,
227n
12.215a, 179n
16.273–74, 179n
17.248–55, 179n
19.167, 179n
Schol. T in Il.
8.494, 188n
Scholia in Hom. Od.
1.1, 201n
1.1.12–16, 141–2
Scholia HQV in Od.
11.547, 202n

Sophocles
Ajax
430–32, 208n
445–46, 202n
1135, 202n
1243, 202n

Strabo
1.2.6, 40–1, 107
3.4.3, 77n
17.20, 170n

Theocritus
Idylls
10.28,
208n

Theon
Progymnasmata
13, 102n

Index Locorum

Tryphon
De Tropis (Spengel)
191.12, 39n
191.18–22, 37–8, 224n

Xenophon
Memorabilia
4.3.11, 27n
Oeconomicus
4.21, 119

LATIN
Accius
fr. 115 (Warmington), 201n
fr. 115–17 (Warmington), 203n
fr. 118 (Warmington), 202n
fr. 1036–37 (Warmington), 206
fr. 115–17 (Warmington), 203n

Anonymous, *Rhetorica
ad Herennium*
1.1, 102
1.7.11, 191n
1.18, 50n, 209n
1.18–25, 50n
1.19, 50n
1.20, 50n
1.23, 50n
2.28–30, 209n
3.1, 50n
3.10–15, 33n
3.20, 60
4, 103n
4.1, 88n, 88
4.2, 88
4.7, 88
4.11–16, 140n
4.42, 38n
4.56.69, 102n
4.66, 194n

Anthologia Latina (Shackleton
Bailey)
71, 234
249, 234

Cato
Orationes
130.3 (Malcovati), 184n
Origines
22, 184n

Catullus
Carmina
63.3–4, 239n

64.42–46, 125
95, 114
95.1–2, 114n

Cicero
Ad familiares
9.15.3, 167n
9.16.7, 54n
9.18.1, 53
10.31–33, 78n
16.21, 76n
16.21.5, 52n
Ad Quintum fratrem
3.3.4, 52n
Brutus
8, 58n
37, 55n
40, 28n, 89n, 137n, 140n, 204, 219,
228
45, 147
50, 137n
54, 147,
56, 147
57, 142
69, 38
70, 131
71, 131n
105, 213n
118, 159n
121, 21n
139, 123
180, 75n
201, 152
203, 152
205–7, 144n
225, 68n
239, 159
251–55, 159n
254–55, 49n
268, 213n
284–91, 131
285, 55n
303, 213n
310, 51n
317, 213n
De amicitia
1, 66n
De consolatu suo
65, 213
De inventione
1.2, 27, 147
1.11.3, 209n
1.92.4–6, 209n
2.68, 207n
2.177–78, 33n

268   *Index Locorum*

Cicero (cont.)
De natura deorum
1.79, 69n
10.1.88, 69n
10.1.98, 69n
10.1.130, 69n
De officiis
1.3, 55n
De oratore
1.1, 240n
1.30–35, 147
1.31, 153n
1.33, 27n
1.62–63, 17n
1.70, 43, 44, 67n, 92
1.73, 20n, 53
1.81, 21n
1.251, 60n
2.43–47, 33n
2.88, 117
2.187, 183
2.189–96, 23n
2.187, 183
2.193–94, 108n
2.194, 21n
2.292–303, 123
2.315, 185n
2.295, 55n
2.333, 181
2.334, 181
2.337–38, 153n, 153, 182
2.341, 34
3, 97
3.41–49, 33n
3.69, 153–4
3.94–95, 51
3.106, 22n
3.109, 50n
3.153, 91n
3.156, 100, 151
3.157, 100, 151
3.164, 100
3.165, 100
3.166–70, 38
3.166–72, 138
3.178, 120
3.178–81, 120
3.179, 120
3.179–80, 120
3.181, 120
3.182–86, 93n, 94
3.184, 68n, 93, 94
3.155, 100
3.202–7, 38

De republica
1.41, 181
1.44, 181
1.47, 181
1.65, 147–8
6 fr. 3, 148n
De senectute
17, 167n
59, 119
Epistulae ad Atticum
2.7.4, 167n
9.4.2, 52
9.14.12.2, 54
14.20.4, 54
14.22.1, 54
In Catilinam
3.16, 194n
Orationes Philippicae
2.42, 53
2.67, 130
Orator ad M. Brutum
25.4, 50
29, 151
37–38, 33n
37–40, 33n
37–42, 33n
46, 50n
47, 53
65–67, 59n
66, 19
67, 41n, 93n
67–69, 33
68, 67n
69, 152
69–99, 130
69–112, 140n, 153
75, 114n
81, 100n
91–92, 55n
92, 21n
96, 33n
97, 130n
109, 153n
135–39, 38
136, 100
145, 74n
230, 63n
Paradoxa Stoicorum
1–3, 159n
Partitiones oratoriae
72, 33n
Pro Cluentio
138, 146n
Pro Flacco
15–17, 189

16, 180
57, 180
Pro Ligario, 97
Pro Milone
9, 123
11, 123
81, 130
Pro Murena
36, 100
44, 60n
69, 187n
Pro Plancio
83, 53
Pro Sexto Roscio Amerino
82, 60n
Topica
29, 207n
Tusculanae disputationes
1.7.13, 52
1.64, 108n
3.27, 53n
In Verrem
2.4.148, 60
2.4.149, 60n

Ps.Cicero
Invectiva in Sallustium
5, 195

Corpus Inscriptionum Latinarum
(1863-) (*CIL*)
X.901, 64n

Columella
1.*Praef.30*, 17n
3.13.4, 120n
3.15.1, 120n

Curtius Rufus
3.10, 125n

Digest
10.1, 43n

Ennius
Annales (Skutsch),
202, 184n, 184
247–53, 214
248–51, 142n
258, 211
268–86, 143–4
304, 232.2, 144
374, 144n
403, 209n
486, 97

508, 166n
593 (inc.), 184

Ennodius
Dicta
28, 234
Festus
Glossaria Latina (Lindsay)
33.26, 186n
182.30–46, 185n
199.30–33, 185n

Gellius
Noctes Atticae
1.2.4, 142n
1.21.5, 17n
6.14.1, 153n
6.14.7, 130n, 140n
12.4, 142n
13.16.3, 179n
14.7.7, 191
15.11.1–2, 52n

Horace
Ars Poetica
9–10, 67n
26, 22n
28, 151
41, 17n
101-3n, 24
128, 207n
311, 115n
359, 115n, 115
388, 114
392, 24n
393–401, 24
402, 115n
408–11, 166n
Carmina
1.2.31, 238n
1.10.1, 184n
1.12.5–12, 25n
2.1.19, 125n
2.6.17, 238n
2.15.4–8, 119
3.6.13–14, 194n
3.9.23, 163n
3.11.1–3, 25n
4.1, 84n
4.1.2, 209n
4.15.3–4., 114n
Epistulae
1.19.21–22, 115
2.1.211–13,
155

270 Index Locorum

Horace (cont.)
Satires
  1.1, 115
  1.2.26–27, 75n
  1.4, 115
  1.4.45–62, 93n
  1.5.6, 225
  1.10, 115
  1.10.22, 76
  1.24.14, 225
  2.1.2–3, 21n
  2.5.40, 99
  2.6.78, 64n

Isidore
Etymologiae
  6.16.12, 186n
  8.7.1–2, 24n

Julius Caesar
Bellum Gallicum
  3.4.3, 206n

Justinus
Epitome
  9.13.11, 125n

Juvenal
Satires
  1.2, 199n
  12.18–24, 150

Livy
Ab urbe condita
  1.8.2, 191n
  1.12.2, 212n
  2.1.7, 191n
  2.33, 147n
  2.50.2, 129n
  2.64.5, 129n
  3.11.7, 194n
  3.55, 147n
  4.14.6, 187n
  6.14.3, 187n
  7.217–18, 155n
  7.235–36, 155n
  9.17.1, 129n
  9.17.16, 125
  9.40.4, 125–6
  10.24, 144n
  21.32.7, 129n
  21.5.11, 129n
  22.14, 155n
  22.14.15, 156n

22.16, 122
22.16.5, 156
22.28.8, 125n
24.48.12, 129n
27.18.8, 129n
28.27.9, 146n
31.1.5, 114n
32.4.6, 129n
32.33.11, 129n
36.17.10, 129n
Periochae
  112, 169n

Lucan
  1.148–49, 163
  1.183–85, 160
  1.204–12, 160
  1.209–10, 161
  1.228–30, 161
  1.361, 169n
  1.498–504, 167
  2.596–97, 159n
  2.680–736, 161
  3.298–762, 161
  3.362–66, 163n
  4.23, 161
  4.48–49, 161–2
  4.77–78, 161n
  4.104–5, 161n
  4.337–401, 162
  5.4.581–824, 162
  5.237–373, 160, 169
  5.255, 162
  5.261–95, 162
  5.262–95, 169n
  5.280, 169n
  5.304, 165
  5.316–17, 162n
  5.316–18, 167
  5.319–64, 162
  5.322–23, 163
  5.325, 169n
  5.336–39, 163
  5.364, 163
  5.369, 169n
  5.372–73, 163n
  5.373, 164
  5.374–402, 162
  5.374–677, 160
  5.400, 162
  5.403–61, 162
  5.407, 163
  5.412, 163, 164
  5.442, 163
  5.455, 163

Index Locorum

5.480, 163
5.484–85, 170
5.504–653, 162
5.515–21, 164
5.516, 164
5.517, 164n
5.523, 164n
5.523–25, 164n
5.535–38, 165
5.538–39, 165
5.539, 164n
5.540, 168
5.540–56, 168
5.544–45, 168n
5.546–47, 168n
5.551–52, 168n
5.553–54, 168n
5.571, 162
5.577, 163n
5.577–93, 163n
5.578, 163
5.579–80, 165n
5.583, 165
5.592, 162
5.577–93, 162
5.620–24, 166n
5.645–46, 166
5.653–71, 162, 163n
5.654–71, 167
5.668–71, 167
5.671, 163n
5.672–77, 167
5.673–74, 167
5.703–21, 162
7.62–63, 17n
7.62–67, 213
7.67, 213
7.62–85, 213
7.123–25, 159n
7.214–16, 125n
7.342–82, 159
7.381, 159
7.382, 159
7.383, 159
8.298–99, 211
8.299, 211n
8.327–28, 159n
8.330–454, 210
8.331–35, 11.134, 208, 211
8.331–454, 210
8.454.55, 211
9.188, 144n
9.215–93, 160
9.222–23, 169n

9.227–51, 169n
9.256–84, 169
9.272, 169n
9.281–82, 169n
9.283–93, 169
9.288, 170
9.293, 169n
9.294–949, 160
9.300–302, 170
9.303–67, 170
9.379–406, 171
9.385, 171n
9.402–3, 171–2
9.406–7, 171
9.446–49, 171
9.494–95, 171
9.499, 171
9.511–86, 170
9.604–937, 170
9.742, 171
10.472, 185n

Lucretius
De natura rerum
1.936–38, 116
2.42, 212n
2.324, 212n
5.1372–73, 238n

Macrobius
Saturnalia
1.5.6, 225
1.24.8, 235
2.2.13, 76n
3.4.12, 60n
4.2, 226n
4.2.9, 226
4.4.1–3, 226
4.4.12, 226
4.4.17, 226
4.4.19, 226
4.6.15, 226n
4.6.20, 226n
5.1, 222, 226–7
5.1.1, 219, 225
5.1.1–3, 226–7
5.1.8, 228
5.1.10, 228
5.1.12, 228
5.1.13, 229, 230–1
5.1.15, 231
5.1.19–20, 231
5.2.1, 211, 235
6.2.20, 226n

Index Locorum

Manilius
  1.887, 166n
  2.8, 28n, 89n

Martial
  7.74.1, 184n
  8.72.5–6, 84

Nepos
  Atticus
    6, 146n

Ovid
  Amores
    1.1.18, 22n
    1.2, 61
    1.2.11–12, 61
    1.8.20, 17n
    1.15.13–14, 111
    3.9.25, 107n
    3.12.41, 92n
  Ars amatoria
    1.461–62, 17n
    3.257, 166n
    3.295, 69n
  Fasti
    1.21–24, 20n
    1.79–82, 191n
    3.495, 69n
    3.593, 166n
    6.760, 166n
  Heroides
    7, 234
  Metamorphoses
    1.107, 238n
    1.243–312, 166n
    1.262ff., 150
    1.291–92, 161n
    5.638, 166n
    5.642–56, 239n
    5.648–49, 239n
    8.626, 165n
    8.630, 164n
    8.641, 164n
    8.699, 164n
    8.877–888, 68n
    10.162–219, 208
    10.215, 208
    11.492–94, 166n
    11.503–4, 166n
    12.620–21, 209n
    13.4, 208
    13.5–6, 209
    13.6, 195n, 208
    13.9, 204

13.21–33, 206
13.23, 206
13.29–30, 207
13.77, 208
13.77–78, 209
13.78, 208
13.79, 208
13.98, 208
13.103–4, 205
13.116, 205
13.120–22, 209
13.121–22, 61
13.122, 209
13.125, 204
13.128, 204
13.132–33, 205
13.133, 206
13.134, 206
13.137, 204
13.140–47, 206
13.162–80, 206
13.168–69, 204, 206
13.171, 207
13.188, 204
13.196, 185n, 204
13.199, 207
13.205, 209n
13.225–27, 204
13.228–29, 204n
13.229, 208
13.232–33, 179n
13.238–52, 205
13.239, 207
13.248, 208
13.255–62, 205
13.264, 205
13.269n, 209n
13.271–74, 207
13.291–95, 205
13.295, 205
13.303–4, 207
13.338, 208
13.339, 155n
13.368–69, 203–4
13.372, 205
13.373, 205
13.381, 205
13.382, 204
13.382–83, 204
13.395, 238
13.397–98, 208
Epistulae ex Ponto
  1.2, 23
  1.2, 113–18, 23
  1.2.67–68, 22

Index Locorum

1.2.113–18, 23
1.5, 22
1.6.7, 20n, 21
1.7, 22
1.9, 22
2.1, 22
2.1.1, 20
2.2.49, 21n
2.2.49–56, 23
2.3, 22n, 22
2.5, 20, 75n
2.5.65–70, 108n
2.8, 22
2.9.47–48, 21
2.29, 21n
3.2, 22
3.5.15, 22n
3.6, 22
4.11, 62n
Remedia amoris, 166n
Tristia
1.2.32, 166n
1.9.45, 21
1.9.45–46, 17n
1.11.21–22, 166n
4.1.43, 21n
4.4.1–10, 23
4.9.49, 22n
4.10, 68
4.10.17–18, 17n
4.10.23–26, 68n
5.6.12, 166n

Pacuvius
24 (Ribbeck), 202n
177 (Ribbeck), 182
411–16 (Ribbeck), 100

Petronius
Satyrica
2, 56–7
3, 57, 58n

Plautus
Poenulus
599, 144n
Stichus
290, 184n

Pliny the Elder
Naturalis historia
5.26, 170n
10.21.6, 76
17.78, 120n
33.152, 64n

34.47, 19n
35.119, 64n

Pliny the Younger
Epistulae
1.20, 130n
1.20.19, 22–23, 175
2.14.10, 66n
2.5.6, 64n
4.11, 75
4.11.1, 75n
4.30.1, 19n

Pomponius Mela, 170n

Porphyryo
In Hor. Artem Poet.
128, 207n

Propertius
2.34.84–85, 213n
3.3.4, 22n
3.22.41, 17n

Publius Annius Florus
Vergilius orator an poeta
1.1–3, 237
1.9, 239
1.9.7, 238n
1.19, 125n
2.4–5.3, 239
2.5.4–6, 239n
2.6–8, 238
3.8, 240
7, 238
8.3–9.5, 238n
8.4–5, 239

Quintilian
Epistula ad Tryphonem, 113–14
191.12, 39n
3.191–206, 38n
Institutio oratoria
1–1.pr.3, 114
1.pr.6, 103n
1.pr.21–25, 102n
1.2.15, 240n
1.2.26, 117
1.3.5, 117n, 117
1.3.12, 117
1.3.13, 117
1.4.2, 89
1.4.3, 106n
1.4.5, 117
1.5.2, 115n

Index Locorum

Quintilian (cont.)
1.5.43, 209n
1.5.52–53, 91
1.6.2, 92n
1.8.14, 92n
1.10.9, 25n
1.8.11, 33n, 59n
1.8.15–17, 223
1.10.9.7, 155n
2.4.3, 67n, 92n
2.4.8, 117n
2.4.10–12, 117–18
2.4.11, 117n, 117
2.4.19, 92
2.4.41–42, 55
2.4.42, 51n
2.5.4, 240n
2.5.8, 185n
2.5.15, 121n
2.638, 223n
2.10.10–13, 58–9
2.10.11, 33n
2.12.6.6, 155n
2.13.3, 121n, 129
2.13.8–12, 40
2.14.5, 126n
2.17.4, 166n
2.17.19–20, 122n
2.17.24, 166n
2.19, 166n
2.34.66, 111
2.226–370, 117
3.1.4, 117
3.1.18, 76n
3.4.6, 33n
3.4.12–14, 33n
3.7.6, 33
3.8.51, 60n
3.8.62–63, 33n
4.1.58, 67n, 91
4.2.2, 123n
5.10, 226n
5.10.23–24, 206n
5.10.41, 209n
5.10.53, 207n
5.14.33–35, 123
5.14.35, 123
6.1.11, 185n
6.2, 108
6.2.7, 108
6.2.20, 226n
6.2.21–22, 109
6.2.25–26, 23n
6.2.26, 204n
6.3, 108

6.3.96, 205n
6.129, 108
7.10.10, 122
7.10.13, 122
8.pr.15, 123
8.2.15, 100
8.3.2, 124
8.3.4, 41
8.3.5, 33n, 124
8.3.6, 118
8.3.6–7, 120
8.3.7–9, 119
8.3.11, 33, 59
8.3.35, 39
8.3.60, 115
8.3.72–78, 100
8.3.73, 59
8.3.76, 59n
8.3.78–79, 100
8.3.79, 97
8.3.80, 100
8.4, 100
8.5, 111
8pr.5, 96
8.5.25–31, 111
8.5.27, 68n
8.5.35, 29n
8.6.1, 39
8.6.6, 98
8.6.7, 120
8.6.11–12, 97
8.6.17, 33n, 59n, 92n
8.6.18, 121
8.6.19, 39
8.6.34, 98
8.6.35, 98
8.6.68–76, 226n
8.6.69, 39
9, 39, 40
9.1, 39n
9.1.1, 39
9.1.4, 39
9.1.5–7, 224n
9.1.11, 39–40
9.2, 100
9.2.1, 39
9.2.42–43, 80n
9.2.54, 226n
9.2.78, 129n
9.2.91, 63n, 80n
9.2.95, 80n
9.2.102, 76n
9.3, 39, 100
9.3.1–27, 101
9.3.2, 224n

Index Locorum

9.3.2–27, 91n
9.3.28–57, 101
9.3.44, 101
9.3.58–65, 101
9.3.66–68, 101
9.3.74, 101
9.3.89, 76n
9.4.56, 93–4
9.4.60, 94–5
9.4.72–111, 94
9.4.102, 94
10.1, 63
10.1.1, 105
10.1.20–26, 106
10.1.20–36, 109
10.1.22, 112
10.1.24, 115n
10.1.25, 115
10.1.27–30, 106, 108, 229–30
10.1.28, 59, 92n, 106
10.1.29, 129
10.1.29–30, 205n
10.1.31, 92n, 106
10.1.31–34, 106
10.1.35, 106
10.1.35–36, 106
10.1.37–39, 103–5
10.1.46, 88, 107
10.1.55, 108n
10.1.56, 115n
10.1.59, 105, 106
10.1.65, 115
10.1.67, 106
10.1.69, 108n
10.1.73–75, 109
10.1.76, 21n, 106
10.1.76–80, 109
10.1.80, 55n
10.1.81, 41n
10.1.81–82, 109
10.1.85, 109
10.1.85–131, 50n
10.1.86, 110
10.1.87, 110
10.1.88, 110
10.1.90, 111, 158
10.1.91, 105, 111
10.1.92, 240n
10.1.93, 115
10.1.94, 113
10.1.93, 110
10.1.98, 111
10.1.99–100, 110
10.1.100, 110
10.1.101, 110

10.1.105, 49n, 110
10.1.108–9, 111
10.1.114, 122n
10.1.116–17, 82
10.1.129, 112
10.1.129–30, 111
10.1.122, 112
10.2, 112
10.2.21–22, 107–8
10.2.14–26, 112
10.3–7, 105
10.5.17–18, 63n
10.5.19, 66n
11.1.36, 159n
11.3.57, 59n
11.3.158, 204
11.3.60.5, 155n
12.pr.2, 114n
12.pr.2–3, 127
12.1.1, 127
12.1.35, 127
12.1–9, 126, 128
12.2.3, 151n
12.3.11, 129n
12.4, 127
12.4.2, 130n
12.5, 126
12.5.1, 128
12.6, 126
12.7, 126
12.8, 126
12.9, 126
12.9.2–4, 129
12.9.21, 128
12.10.10–15, 126
12.10.16–26, 126
12.10.27–39, 126
12.10.42, 121n
12.10.58–72, 126
12.10.61, 130, 151
12.10.63, 130
12.10.64, 140, 205, 227n, 227
12.11, 126
12.11.4, 114n, 131, 166n
12.11.5, 131
12.11.6, 54n
12.11.26–27, 131

Rutilius
(*Rhetores Latini Minores*, Halm)
p. 11, 195

Sallust
Bellum Catilinae
3.1, 194n

276   Index Locorum

Sallust (cont.)
  3.1–2, 194
  3.2, 194n
  3.4, 194n
  5.1, 194
  5.4, 194
  14.1, 187n
  38, 193n
  51.32, 194n
  54, 159n
  Bellum Iugurthinum
  44, 194n
  78.2–4, 170n
  103.3, 144n
  108.1, 185n

Ps.Sallust Invectiva in Ciceronem
  10, 195

Seneca the Elder
  Controuersiae
  1.*Praef*.1, 47, 49, 77
  1.*Praef*.5, 77
  1.*Praef*.6–7, 47
  1.*Praef*.11, 54
  1.*Praef*.12, 49
  1.*Praef*.13, 62
  1.*Praef*.21, 63
  1.*Praef*.22, 62, 77n
  1.1.20, 75n
  1.1.22, 65n, 68
  1.7.18, 75
  1.2.22, 84n
  2, 46
  2.*Praef*.1, 78
  2.*Praef*.3–4, 79
  2.*Praef*.5, 51n, 74
  2.2, 66
  2.2.8, 61, 209
  2.2.8–12, 46
  2.2.12, 66–7
  2.3.6, 80n
  2.4.8, 65
  2.4.12, 65, 84n
  2.7, 62
  3.*Praef*., 52n
  3.*Praef*.5, 82
  3.*Praef*.7, 78
  3.*Praef*.8, 82
  3.*Praef*.12–14, 81
  3.*Praef*.15–17, 82
  3.*Praef*.8, 80n
  3.7.1, 68n
  4.*Praef*.2, 50, 84
  4.*Praef*.3, 78

4.*Praef*.4, 85
4.*Praef*.7, 65n, 85
4.*Praef*.9, 85
7.*Praef*.1, 21
7.*Praef*.4, 66, 69n
7.*Praef*.6, 80n
7.*Praef*.8, 83n
7.1, 73
7.1.27, 47, 72–3
7.4.3, 75n
7.5.12, 66n, 84
7.7.19, 72
8.*Praef*.18, 22n
9.*Praef*.1, 80n
9.*Praef*.2–5, 83
9.*Praef*.3, 63n
9.*Praef*.5, 68n
9.1.13–14, 70n
9.2.23, 65, 69
9.2.42, 80
9.3.13, 83n
9.5.15, 84
9.5.17, 46, 68, 208
9.6.11–12, 68n
9.6.16, 64
10.*Praef*.1, 77
10*Praef*.1, 47
10.*Praef*.2, 80n
10.*Praef*.3, 21, 78n
10.*Praef*.4, 50, 65n,
  78
10.*Praef*.8, 82n
10.*Praef*.11, 70
10.*Praef*.13, 62
10.*Praef*.15, 65
10.*Praef*.16, 62n
10.1.28–30, 124–5
10.4.20, 70
10.4.21, 70, 72
10.5, 71
10.5.20, 70, 71
10.5.21, 71
10.5.28, 71n
10.6.1, 71
Fragmenta 1, 80n
Suasoriae
  1.6.3, 155n
  2, 72
  2.19, 210
  2.19–20, 69–70
  2.21, 75
  3, 72, 73
  3 .4, 71
  3.4–5, 47
  3.5, 72

Index Locorum

3.6–7, 55n
4.4–5, 47
4.5, 64, 67n
7.12, 68n
7.13, 83
7.14, 75
9.1.13, 64

Seneca the Younger
Ad Helviam
4–5, 78n
Agamemnon
507, 166n
724, 239n
De ira
4.23, 178
9.4, 171n
De vita beata
26.7, 240n
Epistulae
40.2, 227n
85.30–37, 166n
104.32–33, 171n
104.33, 169n
114, 112
114.11, 69n
114.14, 59
Phoenissae
586–87, 239n
Quaestiones naturales
2.44.1, 92n

Servius
Comm. in artem Donati (Keil),
447.2, 224
448.1–7, 224n
ad Aen.
Praefatio, 35,
219n, 232
1.148, 146n
1.149, 146n, 148n
1.151, 233n
1.265, 138n
1.520, 184, 223n
1.522, 223n
1.526, 223n
1.539, 223n
2.13, 234
2.17, 234n
2.201, 234n
2.657, 138n, 223
2.735, 234n
3.616, 138n
3.718, 225n
4, 101n

4.1, 225n
4.333, 234
5.43, 186n
5.120, 224n
6.847, 233n
6.875, 138n, 233
7.535, 138n, 233
7.691, 198n
7.705, 199
8.483, 224n
9.479, 209n
10.38, 223
10.55, 223
10.74, 223
11.235, 191n
11.243, 138n
11.341, 206n
11.343, 138n, 223
11.378, 138n, 223
Serv. Dan. ad Aen.
1.522, 223n
2.135, 223n
2.361, 228n
2.638, 223n
4.305, 234
8.374, 223n
9.227, 188
11.378, 191n
Servius *ad Buc.*
1.33.1, 189n
3.106, 208n
4.18, 233
Servius *ad Georg.*
1.104, 224n
2.136, 238n
4.1, 138, 233

Silius Italicus
Punica
1.506, 157n
2.276–77, 211
2.272, 185n
2.280–81, 211n
3.227–28, 157n
4.296, 157n
5.94, 144n
5.114, 144n
5.538, 157n
7.1–19, 156n
7.91–92, 156n
7.97, 157n
7.217, 155
7.234, 156n
7.241–44, 156
7.248–49, 156n

278   *Index Locorum*

Silius Italicus (cont.)
  7.253, 157
  7.253–59,
    156–7
  7.254, 156n
  7.257, 157
  7.258, 157
  7.282–366,
    156n
  8.243–49, 212
  8.259–62, 212
  8.410–11, 17n
  9.283, 157n
  9.313, 157n
  9.516, 157n
  11.91, 157n
  12.11, 157n
  12.334, 157n
  15.131, 157n
  16.604–44, 157
  16.644, 157
  16.670, 157
  17.47–58, 158
  17.59, 158
  17.218–91, 158
  17.260–67,
    158n
  17.627, 158

Statius
 Silvae
  1.4, 17
  1.4.22–37, 18
  2.7.30ff., 62n
  4.2.34–36, 239n
 Thebais
  1.3, 21
  1.339–82, 247.3
  3.29, 166n
  8.409–11, 170n

Suetonius
 Divus Augustus
  29.3, 191n
  89, 76n
 De grammaticis et rhetoribus
  1.1–2, 29
  2, 144
  3, 144n
  22, 83n
  25, 159
  25.1, 52n
  25.3, 54n, 54
  26, 51

  26.2, 52
  28.1, 76
  30.3, 76
  fr. 2, 76
  fr. 3, 76
  fr. 4, 76
 Divus Iulius
  75.5, 76n
  69–70, 162n
 Tiberius
  73.2, 78n

Suetonius-Donatus, *Vita Vergilii*
  43–46, 235

Tacitus
 Agricola
  33, 125n
 Annales
  1.13, 85n
  1.68.4, 125n
  1.72, 83n
  3.57, 85n
  3.331, 84n
  3.66, 75n
  4.21, 83n
  4.34, 17n
  4.42, 84
  4.61, 85n, 85
  6.3, 62n
  6.27, 74
  13.37, 185n
  14.53, 78n
 Dialogus
  2.1, 66n
  4.4, 108n
  5.5–7, 123
  10.4–5, 16–17, 108n
  15.1, 55n
  18.5, 68n
  19, 82
  20.4, 21n, 66n
  20.5, 59, 238n
  20.8, 59n
  26.1, 62n
  26.5, 82n
  30.8, 20n
  31, 41n
  37.2–3, 159
  40, 147

Terence
 Heautontimorumenos
  11, 184n

Index Locorum

Hecyra
  9, 184n

Tiberius Cl. Donatus
  Interpretationes Vergilianae
    vol. 1, pr.2.9–10, 233
    vol. 1, pr.4.24–28, 225n
    vol. 1, pr.5.26–27, 236n
    vol. 1, p. 196, 21–25, 228n
    vol. 1, p. 406–9, 234
    vol. 2, p. 477.23–478.4,
      191n

Valerius Flaccus
  Argonautica
    1.578ff., 150

Valerius Maximus
  1.6ext.3, 17n
  2.4.2, 189
  9.12ext.7, 17n

Varro
  De lingua Latina
    6.43, 186n
    6.76, 123n
    7.41, 184
  Menippean Satires, 52
    257, 52n
  Rustica
    1.7.2, 120n
    1.23.4, 120n

Vegetius
  De re militari
    2.14, 125n

Velleius Paterculus
  2.29.3–4, 159

Virgil
  Aeneid
    1.90, 161n
    1.92–101, 163n, 167
    1.109, 100
    1.127, 156n, 185
    1.135, 156n
    1.138, 146
    1.141, 146
    1.142, 147n, 185
    1.142–56, 145–6
    1.148, 148
    1.148–53, 19/11
    1.148–53, 128, 197

1.148–56, 136
1.149, 194
1.151–53, 128
1.152, 149
1.153, 148, 154
1.197, 155
1.209, 155
1.412, 238
1.516, 238n
1.519, 184
1.520–60, 183
1.521, 185
1.525, 184
1.535–38, 184n
1.541, 212n
1.753, 238n
2.3, 239n
2.3–8, 228–9
2.135
2.38, 129n
2.40, 187n
2.55, 129n
2.88, 186n
2.125, 196n, 196
2.241, 228
2.325, 228
2.361–62, 228
2.545, 199n
2.657
2.307–8, 97
2.311–12, 96
2.324–27, 228
2.361–62, 228
2.553, 72
3.11, 228
3.197, 127
3.321–22, 109
3.679, 186n
4.10, 238n
4.41, 170n
4.68, 239n
4.136, 187n
4.143–44, 96
4.279–415, 234
4.305–30, 234
4.323, 238n
4.365–87, 234
4.379–80, 72
4.564, 168n
5.17–18, 165–166n
5.26–31, 163n
5.43, 197n
5.43–44, 186
5.74, 187n

280   *Index Locorum*

Virgil (cont.)
  5.75, 186n, 186
  5.76, 187n, 187
  5.192, 170n
  5.585, 212n
  6.1, 97
  6.16, 99
  6.60, 170n
  6.462, 124n
  6.820, 209n
  6.828, 213n
  6.828–29, 212n
  6.847–50, 49
  6.889, 171
  7.45, 209n
  7.153, 185n
  7.173–74, 191
  7.174, 191n, 191
  7.212–48, 183
  7.213–15, 184n
  7.292–322, 226
  7.440, 125n
  7.582, 197n
  7.585–90, 197n
  7.586, 197
  7.699–700, 198n
  7.699–705, 198
  7.700–701, 199, 213n
  7.808, 39
  8.123, 238n
  8.127, 223n
  8.127–51, 223
  8.188, 238n
  8.364, 238n
  8.374–86, 223
  8.505, 185n
  8.359–60, 164n
  8.524, 213n
  8.676–77, 166n
  8.728, 97, 151
  9.221–22, 206n
  9.223, 188n
  9.226–30, 187
  9.228, 188
  9.229, 188
  9.373–74, 126
  9.376, 156n
  9.476, 109
  9.611, 233n
  9.766, 212n
  9.769, 213n
  10.2, 186n
  10.188–93, 198n
  10.484, 213n
  10.782, 109

  11.40, 109
  11.43, 223
  11.60–61, 187
  11.89, 109
  11.100, 183, 185n
  11.100–121, 183
  11.122, 192n
  11.122–23, 192
  11.123, 211
  11.124–31, 189
  11.220, 212
  11.220–21, 190
  11.222.3, 190
  11.227, 183n
  11.234, 186n, 190
  11.234–38, 190
  11.235, 191
  11.236, 197
  11.236–37, 191
  11.239, 183n
  11.243, 191n
  11.243–95, 189, 190
  11.296, 183n
  11.296–301, 196, 197
  11.302–5, 189
  11.304, 186n, 190n
  11.305, 191n
  11.331, 183n, 185n
  11.336, 194, 211
  11.336–42, 192–3
  11.336–75, 189
  11.337, 211n
  11.338, 193, 194, 195, 212
  11.338–39, 193, 204
  11.338–40, 195
  11.340–41, 194, 206
  11.342, 193, 212
  11.348, 211n
  11.349, 196
  11.768–73, 229
  11.376–444, 189
  11.777, 50n
  11.378, 195
  11.380, 191
  11.380–81, 204
  11.383, 17n
  11.389–91, 203n
  11.407, 196
  11.408–9, 203
  11.411, 191n
  11.425–27, 211
  11.445–46, 195
  11.454–58, 198
  11.459, 191n
  11.460, 186n, 189n, 190n

Index Locorum

11.469, 186n
11.469–70, 190n
11.546–48, 196
11.606, 213n
11.706–8, 195n
11.749, 125n
12.15, 234n
12.100, 213n
12.158, 212n
12.333, 209n

Eclogues
4, 138
9.36, 199n

Georgics
1.72, 125n
1.84–93, 230–1
1.109–10, 199n
1.351–464, 168
1.357–59, 168n
1.360–64, 168n
1.427–29, 168n
1.441–44, 168n

1.456–57, 168
1.463–68, 168
1.495, 125
2, 117–18
2.41, 114n
2.136–76, 238
2.149, 238n
2.156, 129n
2.199, 198
2.268, 117n
2.272, 117
2.279–83, 120n
2.362–70, 117n, 118
2.462, 198n
3.79–84, 100
4, 138
4.59, 99
4.64, 170n, 170
4.69–70, 170
4.71, 170
4.510, 155
7.754–55, 155

General Index

Achilles, 138, 140, 199–209
  See also Homer: *Iliad*
adornment (*kosmos/ornatus*)
  poetry as, 35–45
  prose as, imitating poetry, 41. See also *kosmos*;
    ornatus
Aelius Lucius Stilo, 142, 144
Aemilius Scaurus, Mamercus, 62, 68, 78n, 84
Aeschylus, 200
agōn, 193, 199, 200, 201, 210–15
  See also boulē
agorē, 177–83, 179n, 186–99, 215
agriculture, 119–20
  Quintilian on, 117–18, 120
  and rhetoric, 118–20, 232
Ajax, 199–209
  See also Judgment of the Arms; words vs. deeds
    dichotomy
Albucius Silus, Gaius, 62, 66
Alfius Flavus, 68
allegory, 231
Amphion, 24
amplification, 100
Antisthenes, 141, 200
Aratus, 108
Arellius Fuscus, 46–7, 48, 61–73, 77, 78
  See also Porcius Latro
Aristotle
  on poetry and rhetoric, 34, 35–7, 43, 93
ars, 93
  of navigation, 166
  Quintilian's main focus, 126n, 126
ars/natura opposition
  in criticism of literary genres, etc., 93, 94,
    111, 166
artifex, 126n, 126, 127–8, 129
Asianism, 64n
Asinius Pollio, Gaius, 62–3, 65, 75, 84–5
assemblies
  Greek compared with Roman,
    177–83, 186

confuse politics with theater, 180–1
  Homeric, 183–99
  Roman, 181, 182–3, 187, 210
  compared with Greek, 129, 177–83, 187,
    188–9
  See also concilium

binary opposition, 43, 86
blame, language of, 213, 215
boulē, 177n, 178, 188, 190n, 190

Cairns, Francis, 15
Cassius Salanus, 19–20
Cassius Seuerus, 48, 78, 80, 81–3
  See also declamation; Seneca
caterua, 198
Cato
  journies of, 170, 171–2
  oratorical skills, 159–60, 169–70
Cestius Pius, Lucius, 47, 68, 70, 72–3, 75, 82, 83
Cicero, 27, 100, 105, 127, 131, 152–3
  compares poetry to rhetoric, 19, 94
  declamations of, 49, 51, 52–3
  De Consolatu Suo, 213–14
  De Oratore, 20–1, 122–3
  De Provinciis Consularibus, 192
  Quintilian cites, 41, 108–9, 111
    as model for, 103n, 105, 131–2
  and oratory, 49, 96, 216, 227
  Philippics of, 53
  See also oratory; rhetoric
Classics (academic field), 13–14
collectivity, 207
comedy, 110
comitia, 180
concilium, 183–99, 186n, 190n,
consilium, 186, 188
contio, 179, 180, 181, 182, 183, 186, 187
controuersia, 67, 223
  See also rhetoric
Cornelius Lentulus, Publius, 211

282

General Index

Cornelius Scipio Aemelianus Africanus, Publicus, 181
Cornelius Scipio Nasica Corculum, Publius, 189
criticism (negative), 32–3

debate, 59, 223
  between Ajax and Odysseus, 191, 199–209 (*see also under* words vs. deeds dichotomy)
  between Turnus and Drances, 191, 192
declamare, 60
declamation, 53, 55–6, 60, 65
  acquires negative connotations, 52–3, 56, 71
  Cicero instructs schoolboys in (Suetonius, Seneca), 54–5
  and Republic's death/decline (Cicero, Seneca), 49, 54, 55, 85
  Seneca defends traditional Roman, 59, 71, 85–6
  teaching of, 56, 65, 66
  See also orator; oratory; rhetoric
deconstruction, 13
demagogue
  discourse of, 177, 209–10, 213–14
  relies on words, not deeds, 199, 215–16 (*see also* words vs. deeds dichotomy)
  Virgil and Ovid on, 215
dēmēgoria, 180, 183
Demetrius of Phaleron, 55
democracy, 178–9, 181, 202. *See also* freedom of speech
Demosthenes, 93, 105, 109, 111
Dido, 234
  See also under Virgil
discourse, all forms, 34–5, 41
  collapse of, 216
  indirect, in Virgil, 188, 190
discourse, poetic, 13. *See also* poetry
discourse, rhetorical, 25, 49–50, 122
  See also rhetoric
display, 33–4. See also *ostentatio*
dispositio, 102, 122, 128, 220, 221, 222, 228
Drances, 194, 195, 206, 210–15. *See also under* Judgment of the Arms

education, Roman
  geared toward public speaking from elementary, 29
  poetry essential to, 29, 87. See also *grammaticus* (teacher of grammar); *scholasticus* (school teacher)
elegy, 110
elocutio, 88–9, 95–103, 123, 221, 222, 225. *See also* style
eloquence, 10–11, 55
  Homer as starting point for, 28–9, 107

eloquentia, 16, 17–18, 19, 108
  Cicero on, 19, 27
embassy, 183–4, 189–90, 220
encomia, 32, 34
Ennius, 110, 142–4
epic
  importance of assembly scenes in, 175–6
  and rhetoric, 128, 135–6, 145, 157, 173, 183, 199–209, 200–1n
  demagogue disturbs bounds between, 174
  epideictic, 233
  Quintilian uses to portray orator/oratory, 128
  See also oratory; poetry; rhetoric
epideictic (*genus demonstrativum*)
  criticized as poetic/entertaining, 32–4
  and poetry, 28–35
  See also poetry; rhetoric
etymology, 39, 60
eulogy, 32
exempla
  in poetry and prose (Quintilian), 96, 97, 101, 130, 220
  Homeric simile as, in grand style, 130
  Virgil as rhetorical (Servius), 225
  See also rhetoric; Virgil

Fabius Maximus Cunctator, Quintus, 155–7
Fabius Maximus, Paullus, 22, 84n
facundia, 17–18, 214
facundus, 144n, 144, 184n
figures (*figurae*)
  likened to bodily postures (Quintilian), 39, 40
  of speech, 39, 101, 224
  of thought, 39, 100
Florus, Publius Annius, 237–9, 240, 241
freedom of speech, 176, 179. *See also* democracy
Frye, Northrup, 11, 45
Furius Bibaculus, 99

Germanicus Iulius Caesar, 19–20
Goldhill, Simon, 15–16
Gorgias
  Aristotle on style of (*Rhet.*), 35
  Encomion of Helen, 29–30, 35
grammarians/grammar, 19, 29, 37n, 37–8
grammaticus (teacher of grammar), 89–90, 106
  duties of (Quintilian), 89–90, 95, 223
  Servius as, 223–4
  See also grammarians; grammar

Haterius, Quintus, 85
Helen of Troy, 29–30
Hermogenes of Tarsus, 34–5
Herodotus, 109
heroism, 127, 202–3, 206–7

284 *General Index*

Hesiod, 148–9
history
  importance to oratory (Quintilian), 106
  and rhetoric, 14–15
  See also oratory; rhetoric
Homer, 29, 177
  debates in, reimagined, 137 (*see also* Judgment
      of the Arms)
    Lucan, *Bellum Civile*, 137
    Ovid, *Metamorphoses*, 137
    Silius, *Punica*, 137
  inventor of rhetorical genres, 15, 28–9, 220,
      227, 242
    exemplifies deliberative, 139, 174–5
    teacher of, 137–8, 220
  oratorical praises as self-praise (Cicero),
      219, 228
  place on Quintilian's reading list, 109–10, 111
  portrays orators and poet/singers, 34–5
  rhetorical writers on, 28–9
  as source of many genres, 21, 88–9, 106–7
  as supreme poet, 18
  See also epic; poetry; poets; Virgil
Homerus Romanus. See Virgil
Horace, 24, 25–6, 28, 115–16, 119
Hybreas, 64
hyperbole, 37, 39

iambus, 98n. *See also* meter
Ilioneus, 184, 223
imitation, literary, 112
  Seneca the Elder on, 70, 71–2
  See also Arellius Fuscus; plagiarism
inventio (rhetorical technique), 102, 122, 128, 220,
      222–32
Isocrates, 30–1, 37n

Jakobson, Roman, 45n
"Judgment of the Arms" *(armorum iudicium)*
  Ovid on, 203, 206, 209–10
  See also words vs. deeds dichotomy
Julius Caesar, 160–1, 162, 163, 164–5, 166–7, 168–9
Junius Gallio, 62n,
Juvenal, 150–5

Kant, Immanuel, 10
kosmos, 37, 202, 209–10. *See also* adornment;
      ornatus

Lanham, R. A., 45n
licentia, 33, 43, 44, 63, 67, 68
licentia poetarum ("poetic license"), 63, 89–95
  negative denotations of, 44, 63, 92
    Seneca on, 67, 68
literature, Latin, 10, 12

logoi politikoi, 30–1
logos, 26, 30n, 30
  See also rhetoric
Lucan, *Bellum Civile*, 158–9
Lucilius, 115, 116, 188
Lucius Plotius Gallus, 51, 52

Macrobius 234, 236. *See also under* Virgil
Maecenas, 142
Menander, 108, 109
Menander Rhetor, 15, 28–9, 32n
Menenius Agrippa, 26
metaphors, 42, 96, 99, 123–6
  Aristotle on, 13, 37, 98
  of orator, 128–9, 151–2
  Quintilian on, 97, 99, 114–15, 121
    agricultural, 117, 118–20
    Cicero compared to on use of, 99–100, 120
metaplasmus, 91, 224
meter
  compared to rhythm, 93, 94
  as constraint on poets, 92, 106
  differentiates between poetry and prose, 30,
      92–3
  See also poetry
metonymy, 96, 209
Mill, J. S., 10–11
motus, 39, 40, 161
mouere, 25, 41
mulcere, 146, 148, 154
Muses, 31, 155

navigation, 166–7, 184. *See also* storm; stormy sea
Neptune, 136, 146, 155–8, 163–4
Nestor, 142
  See also under style (*elocutio*)
New Criticism, 11–12
nitor, 21n, 21,
Norden, Eduard, 10

Odysseus, 149, 175, 199–210, 215. *See also*
      Judgment of the Arms; words vs. deeds
      dichotomy
Ong, Walter, 11–12
oratio, 27, 46, 67, 68, 94, 95, 184. *See also* oratory;
      rhetoric
orator, 44, 53, 82, 101–16, 121–6, 127–8, 129, 136–7,
      142, 144, 145–50, 154, 156n, 159–60,
      184–5, 185n, 189, 214, 215
  See also oratory; poetry; rhetoric
oratory, 214
  calms unruly crowds (Cicero, Virgil, et al.),
      147–8
  compared to poetry, 127, 129, 131–2 (*see also*
      poetry)

General Index

285

Quintilian's view evolves in *Institutio Oratoria*, 131–2
decline in
  due to declamation, 56–8
  due to injection of poetic devices, 96, 241
  due to rhetoric, 186 (*see also* rhetoric)
  due to rise of demagogues, 176, 177
deliberative/forensic compared with epideictic, 34
difference with poetry dissipated by declamation, 60
and epic heroism, 175–6
as halfway between *natura* and *ars*
as heroic and "manly" compared to poetry, 126
history of Roman (Quintilian 9), 100–1
ineffective in "stormy" settings invoking epic, 136–7
  in Caesar, 136
  in Cato, 136
  in Lucan, *Bellum Civile*, 136
metaphors within (Quintilian), 121n
  draw from epic and historiography, 128–9
pathos most important emotion in (Quintilian), 108–9
perverted by declamation, 58, 86
poetry essential to discussion of, 88
Virgil excels Cicero at (Eusebius), 227
Virgil's opinion on Roman as enigmatic, 49
See also declamation; epideictic; rhetoric; Virgil
ornamentum, 123
ornatus (adornment; Gr. *kosmos*), 37, 38, 41–2, 44, 118–19, 120–1
composed of tropes and figures, 37–42, 95–101
excessive, 59, 228–9
presence in poetry and rhetoric, 45, 90
See also adornment; *kosmos*
Orpheus, 24
ostentatio, 28, 59. *See also* display
Ovid
  Ex ponto, 20–4
  and rhetoric, 9, 19–24, 221
    training in, 46, 61 (*see also* Arellius Fuscus; Porcius Latro)
  Seneca on, 66, 67–8, 78–9

panegyric, 34
  See also epideictic (*genus demonstrativum*)
parrhesia, 179n
pathos
  Macrobius on, 226
  Quintilian on, 108–9
Persius, 115
persuasion, 147–8, 207–8

Aeneid as act of (Macrobius), 232, 241 (*see also* Virgil: *Aeneid*)
See also oratory; rhetoric
Petronius, *Satyricon*, 151
philosopher
  compared to orator (Cicero), 154
philosophy, 13
  Quintilian on, 106, 112
Phoenix, 139–40, 141
plagiarism, of Greek models, 70–1
  See also imitation, literary; Seneca the Elder
Plato, 31–2, 109, 154
pleasure (*voluptas*), 33–4, 59
Pliny the Younger, 75, 174–5
poetic license, 44. See also *licentia poetarum*
poetry
  as adornment, 35–45 (*see also* adornment)
  as barometer of rhetorical excess, 86–7
  becomes "unmarked" form of discourse, 30
  blends utility and pleasure (Horace), 25
    popular in Renaissance, 25
  blends with rhetoric, 9–10, 16–28, 242 (Cicero), 243
    Francis Cairns on, 15
    Ovid and, 19–24, 46–7, 61–74, 86 (*see also* Ovid)
    as source for facility in, 106–9
  compared to oratory, 92, 129, 131–2, 242
    relationship fluid in Imperial period, 137
  comprises all verse genres, 17
  and declamation, 56–60, 96, 111–12
  as deviant from norms of language (Quintilian), 91–2, 96
  didactic
    (Lucretius, Virgil, et al.), 116–17
    agricultural metaphors illustrate (Quintilian), 117
    intersects with ornate didactic prose (Quintilian), 120
  as epideictic, 28–35
  essential to Roman education, 29
  as excessive *ars*, 94
  as font of style, exempla, for oratory, 88–9, 90–1
  foreignness of (Aristotle), 37
    compared with "appropriate" rhetoric, 44–5, 96 (*see also* rhetoric)
  Horace on, 5
  influence of rhetoric on, 9
    Romanticism on, 12, 14
  as "natural/artless language," 10–11
  older Roman mostly useless to orator (Quintilian), 110
  as persuasion, 5, 22–4
  pre-Ovidian as pre-rhetorical, 9

General Index

poetry (cont.)
primacy of, for epideictics, 32
rhetoric as more natural medium than, 89, 94
"rhetoricity" of, 216
Roman
and rhetorical theory, 13
swan as symbol of, 198 (*see also under* similes)
and training of orator (Quintilian 10), 101–16
(*see also* orators; oratory)
as victim of rhetoric, 16, 28
See also epic; oratory; poets; rhetoric; Virgil:
Aeneid
poets
as "kin" to orators, 43–4
compared with orators, 44–5, 89
analogy between (Cicero), 44
debate nature of rhetoric (Cicero), 18–19
and orators, receive inspiration from Muses,
149–50
as original civilizers of humanity
(Horace), 24–5
as original persuaders, 24
and rhetorical theory, 29–30, 216
as rhetors, 220
Virgil as, 220–1
role of fuses with orator's, 26
Odysseus as prime example, 141–2
as slaves to meter, 44, 92, 94
See also Homer; Virgil
polutropia, Odysseus's, 141, 201n
Pompey, 159
Porcius Latro, 46, 52, 62–3, 69
as *exemplum* for poets, 69, 70, 71
Ovid (and Virgil) and, 61–74, 86
pairs antithetically with Fuscus *passim*, 61–2,
63–5, 77
prefers private or small-group declaiming, 65
praelectio, 29, 90, 240n
prose, 37, 98, 116–19. *See also* oratory; rhetoric
Protagoras, 26
Puttenham, George, 5, 25–6

Quintilian, 41, 120
De causis corruptae eloquentiae, 112
on declamation, 55, 58–9
as educator, 102, 103
Institutio Oratoria, 88–132
preface to, 105, 126–7
reading list in book 10, 109–13
structure of, 101–3, 104–32, 126n,
departs from handbook mode, 102–3n,
102–3
on *ornatus,* 119, 120
on Roman literary genres inferior to
Greek, 110

readers/reading, 14, 105
Renaissance, 25–6
rhetoric
Aristotle's definition of, 5
binary oppositions in, 43
blends with poetry, 9, 15, 16–28, 210, 241
(*see also* poetry; poets)
"colonized" poetry, 172
compared with poetry, 16, 19 (Cicero),
20 (Ovid), 36–7 (Aristotle),
43 (Cicero), 172–3 (Virgil),
173 (Lucan), 132 (Quintilian)
as condition of existence, 12
defined, 4–5
education/training in, 14, 46, 52, 56, 61, 88
(*see also* Ovid; Quintilian)
evokes epic forces but can't control them,
171 (*see also* Caesar; Cato; storm)
and grand style/epic, 153, 154, 241 (*see also* style:
grand)
influence on poetry, 4, 9–16–19 (Ovid), 228–9
Ovid as "linchpin" of in early Empire, 46–8,
61–74
and Judgment of the Arms, 199–209, 209n
as language of the *polis* (Aristotle), 37
vs. poetry, 37
Lucan undermines Caesar's, 164–7
"macro-rhetoricizing," 221–2, 232–6, 240, 241
"micro-rhetoricizing," 222, 241
negative associations with, 10
opposed to truth (Virgil), 186
Ovid studied, 61 (*see also* Ovid)
poetry as origin of, 25–6, 107
used in instruction of, 29
Ps.Plutarch on Homer's, 220
"soothing" as manipulation/sorcery, 154–5,
158, 185, 233n
subsumes poetry, 172
Rhetorica ad Herennium, 38, 88, 102
rhetorical theory, 4, 5, 29–30, 34, 40–5, 145, 221–2
See also rhetoric
rhetorice, 138, 223
rhetoricus, 223
rhythm, 93–4
Richards, I. A., 11
Romantics, on poetry, 10, 12, 14
Rubellius Blandus, 74
Russell, Donald, 13, 15
Rutilius Gallicus, Gaius, 17–18

satire, 110, 113, 115–16
Scaliger, Joseph Justus, 25
scholasticus (schoolteacher), 65–6, 79, 81
seditio, 148, 163, 194n, 194
Seneca the Elder, 46–8, 54, 208

General Index

287

ambivalence toward declamation, 48, 80, 86
as best authority on Ovid and rhetoric, 46,
    61–74
biographical details of, 77–8, 79, 80
Controuersiae, 78
on declaimers, 62, 75–6, 83, 86–7
on Judgment of the Arms, 209
See also Arellius Fuscus; declamation; Porcius
    Latro
Seneca the Younger, 59, 78, 111, 112, 178–9
sententiae, 111
Servilius Geminus, 142–4
Servius, 224
on rhetorical theory, 5
Sidney, Sir Philip (*Defence of Poesy*), 26
similes, 59, 96
of animals, 161, 169–70
Homeric, in *Aeneid*, 196–9
in Virgil and oratory, 97, 100, 128, 146–8, 194
solecism, 91, 224
sophists, 26, 32–3
speaking, 101–16
    See also oratory; rhetoric; speech(es)
speech(es), 186, 229
Caesar's, 163, 164–7
    See also oratory; rhetoric
storm, 150–5, 158, 163–4, 165–6
abundant in Lucan, *Bellum Civile*, 158, 162
as generic beginning of Roman epic, 150–1
as metaphor/simile for popular unrest
    (Homer, Virgil, Plutarch), 19 Strabo,
    40–1, 107, 146, 147
style, 35–45, 60, 88–9, 95–101
theory of the three, 140–1, 227
grand (*genus grande*), 41–2, 130, 150–5, 171,
    172, 242
    Odysseus embodies (Quintilian), 130, 141
middle (*genus medium*) 152–3, 185
    Nestor associated with, 130, 140
and "oratory in the storm" trope, 136, 151–5
plain (*genus tenue*)
    Menelaus associated with, 130, 140
and poetic genres, 152–3
See also *elocutio*; rhetoric
suasoria, 50, 52, 67, 223
See also *controuersia*
Suetonius, 50, 76, 144
on Cicero's bilingual declamation, 51, 54
on ridiculing of Latin rhetoric
    teachers, 52
syllogism, 30
synecdoche, 39
Syrtes, 170

Theophrastus, 37, 93
theoxeny, 165
Thersites, 175, 176, 178, 192–3, 194
Thucydides, 109
Tiberius Cl. Donatus, 35, 223n, 224–5, 232,
    233, 234
Todorov, Zvetan, 42
Trojans, 179. *See also* democracy
tropes, 37–42, 95–101, 138, 224
defined, 38, 224n
as deviation from prosaic denotation, 39–40,
    45, 94
Quintilian on, 39–40, 91, 96, 97
Turnus, 195, 196, 210–15, 238
    See also demagogue; Drances

Ulixes. *See* Odysseus
utility, and beauty, 119–20

Valerius Messalla Corvinus, 52
Vegio, Maffeo, 233
Virgil
Aeneid, 177, 192, 232, 233
    Neptune simile compared to orator's
        calming of crowds, 128, 136
    as praise of Aeneas and Augustus, 35, 219,
        232, 233
    Quintilian draws on for military imagery,
        121, 123–6
as defender of Aeneas, 222, 233–4, 239, 241
as destructive force, 228
emulated and cited, 47, 72, 101, 232
    by Quintilian, 108, 109–10, 132
as foundation of all things and endeavors,
    231, 242
Georgics, 117–18, 231–2
Macrobius et al. defend poetry of, 222, 227, 235
as *orator* (post-Ovidian), 221–43
as teacher of rhetoric, 222, 228–9, 241
uoluptas, 28, 33
Votienus Montanus, 46, 48, 65–6, 68, 75,
    80, 83–4

weather, 168
words vs. deeds dichotomy, 137, 175–6, 177, 189,
    193, 195–6, 213
and debate between Ajax and Odysseus, 194,
    199, 200, 201–2, 203–4, 206–7, 209, 216
Pindar on, 200–1
    See also Ajax; Judgment of the Arms; Odysseus
Worman, Nancy, 201

Yeats, William Butler, 11n